YESTERDAY, ONCE MORE

LIAN SAMTE

Copyright © 2023 by Lian Samte

All rights reserved.

This book or any portion thereof may not be reproduced or used in any manner whatsoever without the express written permission of the respective writer of the respective content except for the use of brief quotations in a book review.

The writer of the respective work holds sole responsibility for the originality of the content and The Write Order is not responsible in any way whatsoever.

Printed in India

ISBN: 978-93-5776-587-9

First Printing, 2023

The Write Order

A division of Nasadiya Technologies Private Ltd.

Koramangala, Bangalore

Karnataka-560029

THE WRITE ORDER PUBLICATIONS.

www.thewriteorder.com

Typesetting - Aishwarya Wanjari

Book Cover designed - Vaishnavi Prodatturi

Publishing Consultant - Aishwarya Wanjari

To

My Father

A man who believed
And followed his heart
Back he held nothing
From vice to virtue
A man born poor
And died poor
A life fulfilled
Yet he lived

Contents

Approbation 1 1
Approbation 2 2
Preface 4

Section-I
Non-Fiction

The Night Rover 9
Learning Trades 18
Remembering a Fallen Comrade 36
One Day At A Time 52
The Drawers Affair 65
Somebody Touched Me 72
The Lame Beggarman 80
The Day God Saved Us 87
The Annual Day Of Kolkata Zomi Christian Fellowship 89
Sihzoupok And A Few Cookbook Tales 102
Liquid Tobacco 119
Some Cold Facts Of Life 127
Bitter-Sweet Tales 135
Winning A Friend 141
Beating The National Fever (Almost) 143
The Curse Of Petrapole 149
In Lockdown Phase-I 160
Sick Tales 166
In High Spirits 189
The Marriage Feast 195
A Team Of Baichungs 200
An Excellent Wife 204
Grandpa And His Stories 207
The Final Farewell 212

Section-Ii
Fiction

Into The Firing Line 233
Perfect Strangers 254
Friends, That's All 272
A Little Runaway 288
Her Secret 332
The Unsigned Letter 347

APPROBATION 1

I've always loved reading memoirs, particularly ones written by someone closer to home because it feels like I am reading my own story.

I've known U Lian (Lian Samte) from his first memoir titled *'The Good Old Days'*. I loved the book so much that I gifted a copy to a friend in Brisbane, Australia. I met him and his lovely family in May 2021 and learned about his new book *'Yesterday Once More'*.

Perhaps, the only written record of our indigenous culinary tradition is the story of *Sihzou* (Eurya) in Chapter 10. The distinctive indigenous *Tuibuk* (Liquid Tobacco) in Chapter 11 is also a rare topic in our literature. I am grateful to the author for engagingly bringing these topics to the limelight. The book offers many more selected accounts of intimate personal stories which I believe will find some connection with you in some way or the other.

The Fiction section of the book constitute a remarkable expansion of literary work within the Zomi-Paite community. In particular, the author's choice of the universal English medium is highly laudable as it provides access to non-native speakers worldwide. I believe that the value of this incredible book will grow with time.

In conclusion, this book is living proof of what an ordinary man with an extraordinary purpose can achieve in life.

—**David Neihguk**
Lexington, KY, USA

APPROBATION 2

The author, Mr. Lian Samte, is a man who wears many hats with immense ease. Writer, poet, painter, orator, film enthusiast, carpenter, plumber, handyman, you name it, he has it. I met him for the first time when my career in the corporate world took me to Kolkata. It was his storytelling skills, his knack for initiating a stimulating conversation on any topic at the mere drop of a hat that first got my attention. After a few meetings at the Kolkata Zomi Christian Fellowship's Sunday Worship Services, I became a friend who often drops by for tea, or dinners on Sundays with the sole aim of engaging in invigorating discussions on wide-ranging topics—from aliens to the Egyptian Civilization to the future of our hometown Lamka and of the Zomi people in general.

His storytelling skill goes beyond just spoken words; in fact, his writings in his native Paite Zomi language as well as English are rather 'unputdownable' and have the ability to create in the reader that urge to finish reading all at one go.

Unlike *'The Good Old Days,'* which is his first book, based mostly on his childhood experiences, *'Yesterday Once More'* has a non-fiction and fiction sections wherein his unique writing skills and storytelling are on full display. In this book, he skilfully transforms relatively obscure and everyday happenings, something as mundane as one's bowel movements or his first scooter ride into rather immersive and, more often than not, surprisingly captivating pieces of literature.

I love the way he seamlessly weaves his real-life stories with rather interesting anecdotes and gems tucked away in quiet corners, be it the workings of the *buk*—the Zo *hookah*—or how to prepare *sihzoupok*—the Zo delicacy, or the steps involved in preparing lye from wood ash—an essential ingredient in many Zo cuisines.

The six short fictions in the book, all narrating varied tales of love, and of life, with their own fair shares of twists and turns are a rather interesting read. Written at different intervals, and with no apparent connection between any two, the detailed descriptions in these stories nevertheless make one wonder how many of them are based on real-life instances and how many on pure fantasy.

In this book, the author claims that he 'keeps wired companies.' Considering the number of addas I've had with the author in the past which, in most cases, are thought-provoking and made me introspect on many occasions, I indeed feel fortunate to be one of those 'wired' souls.

—**Nangmuansang Lethil**
Bungmual, Lamka

PREFACE

My first attempt in writing a book-length prose in the English language was *'The Good Old Days',* released in September 2013. Truthfully, I'd never expected such a warm reception for it. Thank you all for reading me. This is my second attempt. Clearly a spinoff from the first. It is strongly inspired by the assuring interest shown the first book by readers and well-wishers. Please indulge me if I therefore keep taking its name every here and again in this volume. It heavily owes its origin to it.

The present book contains two sections. Captioned: Non-fiction and Fiction.

As the name suggests, stories in the first section are vignettes of my reminiscences. Most of them were written well back in the days. Some not so long ago though. Needless to say, they are true stories that happened to me. I had tried to avoid taking names where the scenes and characters come across as a little less likable. Should one slip through despite the care taken, it must be in inadvertence. I meant no malice at all.

Normally, stories that excite are high-octane thrillers and romances that rend the heart. Or biographies of great and illustrious people. This book is none of these. But I hold a simple belief. Every man, be he mighty or low, has a story to tell. I being the latter, if anything. Yet, I hope the very ordinariness of my tales would bring a curve to your lips and spring you a surprise in unexpected corners. In the Bollywood blockbuster movie called *Chennai Express,* the protagonist, Shah Rukh Khan, in his typical speech mannerism, roared at the antagonist: "Don't underestimate the power of the common man!" I subscribe to that attitude. The result is what you are holding in your hands right now.

The second unit of the book, need I repeat, contains fictions. They are short stories on which I had tried my hands years ago. Most of them had found their way into various publications in their edited, roughhewn, or sketchy versions. I am collating them here in a common volume. To my convenient alibi, I've lost many of the original manuscripts to the fire of Kuki-Zomi ethnic conflict of 1997-98. So, I took the liberty to redact and re-flesh them here to be more presentable. I have indicated the publications for the pieces I could still keep tab. Pencil sketches are from the North East Sun fortnightly where most of the stories had made their debuts. Other illustrations are from my personal preserves or simply harvested from free domains everywhere.

Admittedly, there's nothing special or amazing in the stories I tell. Nothing unique has ever happened to me that merited reminiscing as such. Rather, they are mundane affairs occurring to each and every one of us on a day-to-day basis. I simply chose to treasure them like a cache of jewels while others may chuck them as worthless trinkets. It takes guts to throw your life open to the general public. This is a cruel world. Even the friendliest elements can eat you up in minutes. Many great men refused to pen their memoirs exactly for that. But I am not a big shot. And there are no skeletons tumbling out of my cupboard. Rather, it is this very commonplaceness that allows me to spin my yarns without trepidation. They are reminders that I am leading a normal life. It's the normal things that amuse me more than the once-in-a-lifetime events to which I could not easily relate. It's the normal things that build me up and show me the simple joys of life. Some may not agree. But that's all that matters to me.

Let me take this opportunity to thank the few people who had direct hand in this venture. Thank you VZ Siam, Admin, Zogam Tourism, for the permission to use those photos for illustration: the old woman smoking *tuibuk* and the rows of cauldrons simmering with *sihzoupok*. I am indebted to Mr. David Neihguk, a research scholar presently stationed at Lexington, KY, USA, for pinching his time to share a note of approbation amidst his tight schedule. Pal, that's a mighty shot in the arm. No words for the undeserved approbation thrown in by Mr. Nangmuansang Lethil, a venturous proprietor in local outsourcing business from our own community. A friend since long.

—**The Author**

SECTION-I
NON-FICTION

"We write to taste life twice, in the moment and in retrospect."
 -Anais Nin

Chapter 1

THE NIGHT ROVER

Was it 1984 or 1985? I could not remember exactly any more. Perhaps, it was 1986? I am really not sure. But it was certainly thereabouts. I might've lost the date but the memory, if not as fresh, is still very much alive. Forget about the facts and figures. All I know is that I was very young. Barely crossing the ten-year mark. Or, to put in relative terms, just about scraping teens. The incident is still etched fine on the dusty layers of my mental hard disk, recoverable in hazy bits and pieces. Here, I am trying to piece them together in a coherent whole. All my childhood memories, nearly all literally, are closely connected with the picturesque village of Thanlon. This tale too has a spin on it. Here we go. On a trip to yesterday, once more.

There is one uncle of ours whom I was very fond. His name is Pauzamawi. We, children, address him as *'Pu Mawi'*. That is, 'Uncle Mawi', in anglicised version. It is our tradition to take the last syllable of the given name as a means of address. He was of course not a resident of Thanlon village. For what he came, I did not know or did not remember. But it's no brainer to presume that he had come to run an important errand or to keep an appointment of great consequence to him.

One fine day during his sojourn, Pu Mawi took me to Dialkhai village. Dialkhai is the second village to the south of Thanlon. For a grown man, it is just a few hours walk on foot. And foot was the primary and almost only means of transport in those days. Cabs or coaches had never been known in this part of the world. They neither are till today, I think. There was not a single motor-cycle at Thanlon or Dialkhai at that time. Or not that I know of. There may be few bicycles though.

There would be occasional state bus service to Thanlon from the District Headquarters Lamka. The bus service was called MSRTC (Manipur State Road Transport Corporation). Or you may come across a rare opportunity of a carrier truck on its way to the hinterlands to collect local agro-produce to haul back to Lamka, the commercial hub. But you have to be very lucky to catch one of these between inter-village journeys. By the way, a few motor scooters could be seen when I revisited thirty years after we left it.

So fond of my uncle was I that I had no mind asking why or for what he took me with him that day. I simply tagged along, excited as a child could be. Visiting another place always had a prospect of thrill and adventure to a village boy.

Actually, Dialkhai village is not unfamiliar to me. One of my father's younger sisters whom we called Ni Phanu—*ni* being the vernacular of auntie—was living there. Her husband was Hauzagin Samte. We call him Gang Gin. Here, *'gang'* is the anglicisation of uncle. For a non-indigenous reader, this may be quite confusing. We call uncles on our mother's side *'Pu'* whereas uncles married to our paternal aunts are called *'Gang'*. Indeed, our tribal dialect proves to be more prolific in this aspect than the English language.

This uncle and aunt of ours had a son and a daughter. Nephew and niece to us. Their names are Thangsonmung and Niangngaihlian.

There is yet a second younger sister of my father living at Thanlon village. We call her Aunt Chiinnu. Aunt Chiinu's family and ours were residing in close quarters in the southern edge of the village in the early part of the eighties. However, at the time of our unfolding story, we had moved to the hub of the village, the bazaar area, while Aunt Chiinnu and family shifted down to Hmar Veng.

Hmar Veng is an enclave set up in 1983 or thereabouts by Pu Rochunga Pudaite, specially for members of the Hmar community settling in Thanlon village. It is situated on a sloping knoll below the village proper about five hundred metres to the east. Just to mention, Pudaite was one of the first among the tribals of Manipur South District to have studied theology in a foreign country.

As for my Auntie's family, it was comprised of the parents and their three children: A son named Chonthang (May his soul rest in peace!), and two daughters, Kimboi and Chongboi. Another set of nephew and nieces to us.

Owing to the cruel vicissitudes of life, Aunt Phanu left way too early for her eternal abode, leaving her husband and children to fend for themselves. Closer home, for reasons never known to us, Aunt Chiinu got abandoned by her husband, Thangngir, right before the birth of their youngest child. Perhaps it was that misfortune that drew us kids very close. Especially the boys as we are roughly of the same age. I being the eldest of the lot, just to indicate.

Whenever we had free time, which was more often than not, we—my two nephews, my brother Ven, and I—would traverse up and down between Thanlon and Dialkhai villages, sleeping over and parting at our own sweet will. So, when Uncle Mawi proposed to take me there, I was naturally thrilled and overexcited.

We started off after breakfast. That must be about seven in the morning. Perhaps, we were not in a hurry. There were no cars or trucks to hitch or hire. So, we walked.

I did not remember the actual act of trudging to Dialkhai village. And upon arrival, I did not know in whose house we were put up for respite. But I very well remember whiling away in that very house, looking out at the wild mountains just across the hamlet. Waiting. Waiting for what or whom I did not know.

After quite a long time, Uncle Mawi asked me to stay put where I was and to not go anywhere. I was doing exactly that for hours already. Commanding me so, he made himself scarce tailing somebody who had come to collect him, thus leaving me to be with myself. Where is he going? I did not know. I dared not ask.

I just sat there wilting. Yearning to return back home. Uncle Mawi never reappeared. The sun was moving fast to the western sky. It would soon be dusk.

I was very afraid that Uncle Mawi would decide to stay overnight. There was a reason why I wanted to get back home that day itself by any means. My mother was running a small teashop at that time: *'Vungnou Nu Hotel'*, meaning Vungnou's Mother's Tea Stall. Vungnou being my elder sister and my parents' eldest. My father had gone to Lamka to bring essential groceries for the stall. And he was arriving that night. That means sweetmeats and eatables for us kids. And if we are lucky, we could get new shirts and a pair of trousers even. And some gifts too. I was itching to leave my post.

I dared not ask where Uncle Mawi has gone or where he was taken. The concept of abduction did not exist in my mind in those days. If not, I would have raised an alarm and caused quite a stir. I did not know whom to ask, actually. I was too shy and timid. And scared. Although I was quite familiar with the way to our auntie's house, a few hundred metres in fact, I was but a stranger who knew nobody else. I kept my quiet without complaining. Yet, my eyes could not leave the jagged mountains where the sun had started westing, splitting up in soft orange rays.

I gazed towards Thanlon village longingly, tears beginning to brim in the eyes. I was too ashamed to show an unmanly emotion like crying. I secretly wiped myself away with the sleeves of my shirt. Nobody came to ask how I was doing. I felt nobody cared for me.

I was beginning to get very upset inwardly. Imagination started playing tricks on my ears. I thought I heard the sound of Thanlon bus rumbling into the village from the northern end. Actually, the bus seldom arrived in time. The whole village would be already in bed when a loud foghorn would rattle the night sky to announce its arrival. That's the standard procedure.

I was a patient waiter. Even if I was not, I was left with no choice. I had not budged an inch since Uncle Mawi had taken off. That patience has carried well into my adulthood and stood me in good stead. I might have made a mention of it somewhere in this anthology. But nothing lasts forever. My patience began to wear off as the sun started sinking behind the hills.

Evening was on its way. Daylight would soon be gone. And with it, all my hopes of getting home and welcoming my father from his city trip. Uncle Mawi's face was still not to be seen.

Without a word, I suddenly got up and decided to make my way. In fact, I had made up my mind hours ago. I was leaving for home with or without Uncle Mawi. I stole out and never turned back. By the time I reached the outskirts of the village, it was already dark.

The Dialkhai precipice was looming sinisterly upon the left. On my right was sheer drop. In the dark, you feel sometimes you see better if you walk with your eyes closed. There was no moon. I guess there were stars although I never bothered to look up. I didn't need directions. Sometimes, the stars would shine through the rent of clouds. Then I could make out a faint trace of the asphalt that is Tipaimukh Road. In my mind's eye I could see a trail meandering down and up the Kangsat foothills. In damper sections, dewdrops would have already moistened the bitumen in a darkish hue. Such stretches would be virtually invisible.

There was nothing to fear. But for a little boy of eleven or twelve, the darkness itself spells terror. Before I reached Vaipheimual village, which is a minor hamlet midway between Dialkhai and Thanlon, I began to whimper and weep softly. I trudged on.

When I approached this halfway village, I could espy in a distance streaks of light from a kerosene lamp stealing through the gaps of the bamboo crosshatch of the cornermost hut. Writing this story after all these years, a certain aphorism struck my mind. It is said that even a far-away fire is enough to warm you when you are really cold. That was what I exactly felt at the time. But it was not much a relief. The longer way was still ahead.

Cooing like a dove and soaking up the ends of my shirt with tears, I tramped past Vaipheimual village. I wanted to rest my exhausted limbs for a while. But I was too scared. My heart was thumping tremulously all the while.

At times the clouds would part and allow starlight to filter through. The highway becomes easier to make out. Then I would sprint as fast as I could. But such stretches were few and far between. So, I had to tread carefully lest I misstep and take a tumble down the slope. My progress was slower than I would have liked to.

Before long, I was trotting downhill along the stream between Vaipheimual and Thanlon. This stream is called *Gamgi Lui*, meaning, the boundary river. Its other name is *Tongkampa Lui*, meaning Tongkam's Father's Stream or to shorten, Tongkampa's Stream. Who was Tongkam, and who was his father, I had not the faintest idea? It rings of a Gangte or Vaiphei appellation. That suggests that he must have been a prominent villager of Vaipheimual. Perhaps a warrior or a very eminent chief.

As I walked on the moss-covered culvert across the stream, I couldn't help but steal a glance over the left shoulder. It was blackness and nothing. Only noises. The streamlet was gurgling much louder than when we crossed it during the day. And I thought I heard somebody moan agonisingly under the thickets. A chilling recollection hit me instantly.

Days ago, a non-native trader, probably a Marwari or a Bihari, had died in Thanlon. He was cremated here, at this very spot, where the groans now emanate. I was probably imagining things. But it was as real as it gets at the time. In small villages like Thanlon, we, little children, were truly scared of deaths. Whenever somebody passed away, or if we heard the death knell tolling from the churchyard, we would take refuge in our beds, hiding under the covers and shaking ourselves to sleep. We were even more petrified with non-Christian deaths as it is the custom of the mainlanders and valley Manipuris to burn their dead. We were extremely terrified by the thought of being consumed by fire. And for what stupidity in the world, I hazily remember observing a cremation ritual, most probably the one I am describing. I reeked of the stench of death for a long time.

I sprinted.

My sobs began to grow louder. But there was nobody to hear me. I felt really abandoned and forlorn. I walked as fast as my tiny legs could carry me. The roadbuilders' settlement, or the *'Pioneer Camp'* as we call it, was a mere stone's throw now. Yet, I could hear not a rustle of a sound. Not even a sigh. Not a soul seemed to stir that night. I saw no ray of light as I did in the hamlet I just passed. Even a bad snore would have been music to the ears. But the night was as still as a muted tape. It was like passing through Necropolis.

I pushed on, weeping distressfully.

Many years later, somebody told me the stretch where I heard moaning noises used to teem with spectres. And it was haunted even in the daytime, especially in the dead of noon, they said. It was rumoured that hunters and wayfarers often encountered an old hag standing in the middle of the road disgorging her own entrails and coiling them round her neck, dripping with blood and gore. I don't know if the stories were true. But I was lucky to have not known them at the time.

Looking back today, I believe the road-layers, in their makeshift barracks, would think they've heard a ghost snivelling down the highway. No wonder they dared not raise their heads even to listen. How the hackles must have stood on the backs of their necks! I smirk in amusement as I write this line.

Those were long before the days of mobile phones. Steve Jobs might be busy launching his first Apple Macintosh in Cupertino. But there was not a single telephone in the entire vicinity of Thanlon. Well, the police might have had their wireless transmitters. But they were off limits to the civilian public. I wonder, on hindsight, if my Uncle Mawi had worried about me at all. He might have just smiled away in his good nature, presuming I had gone back home on my own. That was true, of course. But how a mere child made his way by himself, that too deep in the dark, seemed to have never occurred to his mind. No search party came. No alarms. No missing child registered. No distress calls. Nothing. Everything was normal. Sometimes, suffering the torture of normal is most painful and unbearable.

I could not remember how I managed to make it home. All my senses must have been dulled by fear. All the creeps seemed to have vanished from me. Or perhaps I was too scared to even talk about it.

When I reached home, my father had already arrived. He'd brought us a big carton of crispy S-shaped breads. We lovingly call them 'cookies'. Imagine two fern heads joined in the middle, the spiral-tips facing away from each other. You get the picture. Our Hindi teacher at Convention English School, Sir Thangkhanpau, had a playway of putting the figure into action. He would curve one hand over his forehead like an ostrich and the other behind his bum while lifting one leg backwards bent at the knee. And he would call out, *'Asigumbah'*. The word makes no sense in our tribal lingo. But in Meeteilon (language of the valley Manipuris), it simply means, 'Just like this!'

What else had my father brought home that day I did not remember. What I do remember is that I was overjoyed to be back and have my father back. All my fears melted away in the warmth of his embrace.

Today, in retrospection, I wonder whether my parents had not worried about me at all? Why had they not asked me anything when I reached home alone? Why had they not enquired about my Uncle Mawi? Or why had they not queried with whom I came back? Was everything really normal? I was but still a child. Was it usual for a child to walk home from several kilometres away? That too through jungles and forests where there could have been rogue beasts or hypnotising pythons coiling in the middle of the road, warming themselves on the dissipating heat of the metalled road. Let alone sighing ghosts and menacing hags.

I never knew when Uncle Mawi came back. Many years later, I learnt that he had bagged a teacher's job at Dialkhai village. Most probably we were there to ink the final contract. And he too never asked me, till today, where I had gone or how I had fared that day. Or that night, if you must.

In the summer of 2019, that is, thirty years later since we left the village, I took my family along with two siblings-in-law—Nenem and Mangboi Langel—and a good friend and former student, Tunzasiam Vualnam, on a revisit tour. We split our put-up at Aunt Chinnu's residence and at the quarters of Rev. M. Zalian Guite, Divisional Superintendent of Evangelical Baptist Convention Church, Thanlon.

I took them on a hike to the border river, Tongkampa's Stream. The riverbed had really grown dense and wild, making it very difficult to negotiate. As we were enjoying ourselves among the slippery rocks and bubbling waters, the weather grew unfriendly and threatened to open up. So, we decided to make an exit by the thick flanks in the hope to emerge on the culvert bridge or at least nearby.

Flash floods are a dangerous thing, especially down narrow streamlets between hills. They are natural water channels. We hacked out a path on the steep flank and clambered away from the water course. Raindrops began to patter. In a short while, we surfaced on the main road, a few metres from the culvert. That was the portion I had cried my way home years ago. I did not tell my companions anything. And certainly not the haunting ghouls.

About a year after the tour, over a dinner conversation, I happened to make a reference to the sprites that roamed the place. My wife suddenly got very upset with me. "You should have told us before," she said, giving me a naughty punch on the abs.

"You would've not come had I," I said nonchalantly.

Pat came the reply: "Certainly not!"

Leave these ghostly tales behind. Let me jog you down another memory lane.

Dialkhai holds another embarrassing memory of mine.

It must be in the mid or latter part of the eighties. We had gone there perhaps to participate in a certain church conference. Or were we just passing through on our way to somewhere I could not remember. We were a number of boys and girls. In my nebulous recollection, I could somehow hark back that our troupe leaders took us for a swim in a stream nearby.

I took a dive. My underwear parted ways with me somehow eloping with the water current. I sat under the freezing pool for a long time to keep my nakedness from plain view. The hills could be very cold even in daytime. And there was no way of staying in the water forever. So, I scampered like a thieving squirrel to the banks where my clothes lay a small pile. It was not much a scene. What if I did not have a shred of clothing on me? A little naked boy would not have attracted much attention whatsoever. But that doesn't mitigate the embarrassment one bit. It's good that I could not reminisce the incident properly anymore.

A more or less similar situation played out again some years later.

This time, it was at Tallian village. Tallian is to the north of Thanlon, exactly in the opposite direction to Dialkhai village. Situated in a low contour line, it also has exactly opposite climate. I could recollect this occasion a little clearer than the previous incident.

Lalthlamuon Pulamte, who later became an extended brother-in-law to me, took us there to participate in a United Pentecostal Church conference. Being budding young boys, we did not much care about attending the worship services. We preferred going to the nearby stream called Tuipi River and play mischief with the girls coming for a dip.

As the girls started splashing around in the rippling pools, we would swim up on them stealthily like prowling crocodiles. Then we would yank away the cloths wrapped around their armpits. That was the only cover they had on them. What a hell of a ruckus they raised! Protests of an angry mother-hen whose eggs were plucked from her nest is nowhere near comparable. That would send the boys laughing and hooting in lustful euphoria.

By my saying 'we' every now and again, the reader must not be misled that I was the mischief monger. I could not swim then. I still can't swim today. But being party with the pranksters and being the narrator of our tale, I should share responsibility and not avoid naming myself.

One more instance on the same trip yet.

It was a fine sunny day. Tallian is hot and humid. On that occasion, Thlamuon took me to a certain part of the village where the locals were occupying themselves with a certain activity in a pond. They were not swimming. It was a fishpond. They were throwing out the waters in order to catch the fishes in it. It was extremely muddy.

While the grownups were busy throwing out water, the boys were taking liberties before their beloved pool goes dry. We were complete strangers and not on familiar terms with anybody. But that doesn't prevent us from taking off our shirts and shorts and join the lads in the spur of the moment.

How did my friend, Thlamuon, manage I did not know. But I did not want to put on a wet underwear later. So, before taking the plunge, I stripped all the way down leaving the front-tail wagging free in the air. Silky sandy hairs had begun to appear on my pubes. So, it was a little awkward. Slowly, I slipped into the water before anybody took notice of the soft downy fur.

And being unable to swim, I simply grabbed the mud banks and threw my legs around in a bicycle kick, making huge splashes in the ruddy waters. I enjoyed myself a lot that way. The kids were screaming with glee in the middle of the sinking pond.

All this while, the water level was going down and getting thicker with slush. Before long, we had to give up our pleasurable escapade. The men were shooing us now. The boys clambered off the embankments and got themselves dressed in a trice. Then they stood around the mud-rim to watch the men beginning to catch the fishes with their bare hands.

I was not as quick to get out. I was lost in the ecstasy of the swimming experience. When I got out eventually, all eyes shifted from the fishermen to the starkness of my slimy skin.

If one could literally burn with embarrassment, I would certainly go up in flames that day.

Chapter 2

LEARNING TRADES

They say there's a first time for everything. And a first time for anything is as exciting as can be. Every dog has its day. I too had several of mine. A chance once presented in 1990. I did not let it go.

I was a tea-and-snack server in a certain hotel along Tedim Road, Zenhang Lamka. That's a fancier way of saying I was a hotel boy. I am not ashamed to be one. But I certainly am not proud of it. I do not remember by what name went the hotel. Perhaps, it doesn't have one at all. Let that be that.

Now, across the street there was an automobile workshop. Though not bosom-type friends, I was well acquainted with some of the handymen there. I would bring them tea and flat-cakes when they placed their orders at high noon. The workshop did fixing and repairing of all kinds of vehicles. Two and three wheelers seemed to be their speciality though. Besides, they did tyre works like patching, rethreading and all that stuff. Our shops were adjacent to one another. Well within earshot, to be precise.

One certain morning, our manager called out to us, the hotel boys and the workers in general, if we were ready for the day. I cried back: *"Hum tayyar hain!"* At that juncture, one of the workshop's handymen named Lelen happened to pass by. He overheard my words and got quite amused. Perhaps he was hearing the word 'tayyar' for the first time.

"We're the ones working on tyres," he remarked. "But you're the one taking the name for yourself!" He would mischievously tease me later, calling me *Tayyar! Tayyar!*

Hotel attendants were not the most respected section of the society in those days. My Hindi was as scratchy as it is today. With all intentions, what I had meant to say was we were 'up and ready'. I really don't know if that was the actual meaning or not. Anyways, that was what I thought the words meant. And I never felt the need to explain myself. I think I had carried myself across enough. And this Lelen spoke the language quite well himself. It was only his fun-loving-self playing naughty with me.

Now that doesn't mean we were not on cordial terms. We might not fraternise much. Yet not infrequently would we share gibes and light moments across the street. Agreed, we would spike our swipes and digs with personal snide and shady innuendoes. However, we were not foolish enough to lock horns over harmless banters. Probably for my joke-loving nature, the owner of the workshop took an apparent liking for me. One day, as I was serving them their usual high tea, he took me aside and said: "Do you want to drive an autorickshaw?"

I never dreamed I would lay my hands on an automobile. I was ecstatic. "Of course!" I shot back instantly, pouncing on the opportunity like a tiger prowling for the moment.

The following Sunday, early morning, he called me up, meaning to take me for a long drive.

He gave a few sharp tugs at the dynamo-stick. That's how auto engines started in those days. No battery-operated press studs. Then, he drove himself for some distance, all the while instructing me to keep my eyes on his hands and manoeuvres: How he controlled the handlebars. How and when to press the side-buttons and switches. How he worked around the electronics and how all those stuffs functioned.

A little distance later, he pulled up and let me take the helm. Putting into practice what my sharp eyes had observed, I revved up the engine and tested the brakes and the throttle. I twisted the clutch upwards. A command barked from behind me. I let it go.

The auto screamed and lurched like an unridden colt. We literally zoomed down Tiddim Road, hurtling towards the gas station at Hmar Veng in a breakneck speed. Lucky the thoroughfare was empty being a Sunday and early morning. The owner yelled at my back: "Slow down, slow down!"

The more I tried to slow down the harder I twirled the accelerator. One of the rear wheels went up in the air. The instructor immediately shifted his place to weigh it down. The other side lifted. He swung over to counterbalance it. All the while shrieking: "STOP! STOP!"

Not before we were about negotiating the gentle upgradient at Tuibuang Forest Gate, the engine spluttered and died on its own. Before I realised what was happening, the trainer grabbed me by the collar, yanked me out of the driver's cabin, shoved me into the backseat, and drove us back home himself. He never let me come near his three-wheeler again.

That was my first driving experience. It was exciting all right but in no way agreeable. And I lost a friend for my raw incompetence.

It was not about thirteen years later that I could lay my hands on another motor vehicle. I was still aching to learn driving. But being unable to afford one, the yearning remained a pipedream. To my good fortune I should say, an opportunity yet presented again.

A good friend, Mr. Ginkhopau Tonsing, had newly started a cable service called Angel's Vision. Under his banner, we had decided to make one local feature film. In those days, and I doubt till today, there were no organised film industry or moviemaking guilds in our place. And there were no special privileges, benefits or pecking order in the production team or among the crew personnel. There were no odd-jobbers to despatch around either. So, regardless of being the director and producer, I had to fulfil my own needs and requirements as any other of the crew would.

One fine day, we were shooting on location. An urgent need arose to collect some materials from my home which was about half a kilometre away. And I had to run my own errand. I was having no means of personal transport. For whatever reasons, I do not remember, but I had not taken my bicycle with me that day. I was in a quandary.

As luck would have it, a certain guy in the production team, or was he one of the artistes, happened to bring along his Bajaj scooter. Seeing the task cut out for me, he unhesitatingly offered his means of transport so that my momentary absence would not throw the day's schedule haywire or inconvenience the entire unit. Obviously, this magnanimous guy did not know my skill-level of driving. Had he, he would have never stepped forward with the good turn. Needless to say, I had never driven a motorbike before. The opportunity had simply not presented itself. And you could hardly call my first driving lesson a roaring success. But the temptation was so strong that I chose to keep the secret to myself.

There was no time for the luxury of a test drive. I asked the owner for a quick run of the basics. Then it was all up to me.

I fired up the engine all right. Pretending to be not unfamiliar, I revved it up as though to prepare the internals for the impending ride. In a short while, I pushed the motorbike off its stand and hoisted my butt to the saddle. I half-dangled on the seat because my legs could hardly reach the ground. Literally, I was on the tip of my toes. I cursed my short stature not for the first time. Then, cracking into gear, I let it go.

The auto jumped like an untrained donkey. It spurted for a brief moment. And died.

Yanking it back to its double-stand, I tried to resuscitate it by giving furious kicks on the kick-starter. Sometimes, it would cough promisingly. At that, I would quickly push it off the stand only to snatch it back to position. I had to go through this process until the sulking engine appeared to give up on me entirely.

Not before I broke into a heavy sweat, Bajaj allowed itself to be coaxed into a mild splutter. Then into a healthy purr. He was agreeing to hit the road again. Phew!

Now, in my incompetence, I was going too fast. Too fast even for my liking. I was yet to connect with the accelerator and learn how much fuel to gush into the firing chambers. Before getting familiar with the squeal, I had travelled quite a distance already. Not in minutes though, I began to get the grips and somehow smoothed down into a proper ride. From there it was nothing but an easy cruise up a narrow by-lane.

In truth, riding in our hometown is never a pleasant experience. Within a few hundred metres, the lane gave way to another lane that had seen much better days. Gravel and dirt took over the once metalled road. Dents and puddles scattered across its length and breadth. My butts and the seat parted ways on many occasions as I bumped and bounced around, skirting pits and pocks.

Up in a distance, I saw a bevy of girls leisurely ambling near to the middle of the road. That was nothing unordinary. In fact, that was the general habit of the townsfolk. I mean, walking in the middle of the road. Now, I wanted to sound these beauties off to the roadside so that I do not brush them or run them over. They say learners have the obnoxious tendency of somehow driving into where they least intended. So, being immoderate with the honker is nothing to be ashamed of unless you are in a no-horn zone. There are no no-horn zones in Lamka.

But sadly, my thumb could not quite get to the button in its natural position. A small man with a set of small limbs. I had to loosen my grip on the handle a bit to extend its reach. I had not yet acquired the necessary dexterity. So, this slight movement on the left hand offset a domino effect to the right hand. This in turn forced an involuntary twist on the accelerator. Bajaj roared in anger and dashed like a roan on whose flanks the cowboy had sunk his spurs.

I overshot the girls, teetering with a trail of soot and noisy rumble. The girls guffawed at my back. Were they laughing at my bumbling skill? Were they hollering at me for rashness? Or were they impressed with my speed flick? Before I could process the thoughts completely, a little uphill appeared. The need to sound the horn remained no more. I kind of regained control. But it was already too late. In the sudden rush, I had forgotten to switch into proper gear and put a steady pressure. Hardly overcoming the mound, my dear engine got into its fretting elements again, stuttering, and giving up the ghost in plain sight of the girls.

Awkward!

Perspiration covered me from head to toe in embarrassment.

I pulled the wayward Bajaj to a stand and pretended to attend to its mechanical components. But there was nothing I could do. Admittedly, I did not know how to open the side-cover even. And even if I did, I did not know what to tinker with or how to put it back. I kicked the starter with all my might, grunting and sweating all over the face. Nothing happened. I cursed the goddamned engine for putting me in such a humiliating spot. Bajaj seemed to have a mind of its own. Nothing like a beginner's luck for me. I secretly prayed to God to make it come back to life before the girls caught me up. Emergency prayers are seldom answered.

The girls did really catch up and walked me past with audible sniggers.

A minute or two later, the engine sputtered back to life somehow. Emergency prayers are answered after all. But I did not try to press the buzzer any more. And, of course, I drove a little slower to make sure I did not overtake the paragons of beauty and putter out yet again.

They say, for a person who knows how to pedal a bicycle, driving an auto engine is not a big issue. I drove it twice but to only prove the dictum wrong. The concept was nothing but a groundless myth. They certainly are not the same. Driving an engine vehicle needs a lot more concentration, coordination and confidence than riding an engine-less bicycle.

It was in the mid-1980s that I learnt to ride the bicycle. It was a Humber that belonged to a friend of mine. The first time I rode it, I hit the village pharmacist between the crack from behind. The second time, I could manoeuvre it with ease. And ever since, it took me no effort although I could never do the hands-free.

Being a younger generation certainly had its advantage. I didn't have to go through all the hassles and troubles my father had to. It was quite late in life that my father had the opportunity to try his hands on it. And he got all his trousers and shirt badly soiled and torn in the process. Yet he could not master the art. He never drove a bicycle nor an engine vehicle all his life.

To add, but overconfidence is not good for driving. It begets recklessness. In fact, majority of road accidents are caused not by lack of driving skill but by overconfidence and over-expertness.

One fine day, I was riding my Hero bicycle down to Rengkai Muollhum to pay my sister and my little nieces a visit. The path approaching their house was a dirt road cutting down a hillock on top of which lives a family that reared a number of cows. On rainy seasons, this dirt road would overflow with muck and manure from the cowsheds, rendering the trail very unfriendly to the nose and challenging to negotiate. Owing to this fact, my sister's brother-in-law named it 'The Road to Paradise'. If you know the difficulties prescribed for the road to heaven, this would not be an inconceivable analogy.

That fine day though, I was in luck. The track was covered only in dry cow-dung dust.

At the foot of the hillock is a brooklet which doubles up as a drainage. It could become quite a river in its spate. But now, the bed was as dry as hay. Spanning across the canal were two wrought iron T-rails laid flat-side up, side by side. An improvised pass.

I was riding leisurely down the knoll when I saw two lasses coming up from the other side of the canal. They were about reaching the banister-less pass. Suddenly, the urge to impress them struck my mind. The intention was to showcase a balancing feat on the groove of the T-rails to make the girls coo and whoo in admiration. I stepped hard on the pedal, building up velocity. In a matter of seconds, I was tearing down the cow-dung trail to pull off a magnum opera.

The rails were hardly eight inches wide each. And a raised edge of about an inch ran down the middle where the T-rails conjoined. It was not my first time riding over this makeshift overpass. But I had never tried a stunt before. Now, with two dainty dames sashaying up from the other side, the challenge was too tempting to not accept.

I was flying down, about to hit the metal work. But in one loose moment of distraction, perhaps I was gauging how much attention I could grab from the girls' eyes, I happened to hit right into the middle of the tracks where the raised edge came up. Much against what I had set out for, I rather plunged right into the ditch, my bicycle tumbling down on top of me. In my bid to admire the beauty of the girls and the excitement in their eyes, I had missed the groove and hit the edge instead.

The girls simply had a boisterous laugh between them and never came to my rescue. I could only pick myself up, dust and soldier out of the gutter without any helping hands. There was no major injury on my body though. Few scrapes and scratches on the elbows and the knees. It was my extreme luck that the canal was not a ravine. Had it been so, our story would have had an entirely different ending.

Frankly speaking, far from winning the hearts of the lissome lasses, I instead earned myself a boo and a hoo. Would any of the lovely duo happen to read this piece, I must still say it was not them who distracted me but my high-octane self-assuredness that landed me in that mortifying mess.

I repeat. Overconfidence is not good for driving.

Now, it came to such a pass that one friend of mine happened to owe me a few thousand bucks on loan. Even after the lapse of tenure and repeated reminders, he still could not square the account. So, he offered me to keep his motorcycle until he could redeem it later. He was stalling for time. And I did not insist on cash remittance. On the one hand, a desire to own a motor engine of sorts was still itching at the back of my mind. On the other, I would only be showing understanding which was the best I could do for a friend at that given moment.

The only problem was that I had never ridden a real motorcycle. My two driving experiences were back-to-back flops. And there was no time to learn it now either. My debtor had simply handed me the keys without much words. Surely, he was not at all enthusiastic to part with a property he obviously treasured. But I was rather pushy on my part because I was in need of making up the credit. I couldn't help but accept the offer.

So, I mounted the Yamaha Rx100 and inserted the key into the keyhole. I almost missed the keyhole. My hand shook. I felt a slight tremble in the pit of my stomach. I was not riding alone. My wife was with me with our one-week-old daughter on her back. We were visiting the hospital for the babe's routine check-up and dropping by our borrower on our way home. Now, they're here to ride pillion.

As demure and decorous as any woman, my wife hopped on sideways behind me, cradling the child to her bosom. That small addition of weight caused a sort of imbalance already as my toes could barely scrape the ground, let alone steady the bike. My friend, not being happy with losing an asset, did not even step out to give me the rudimentary instructions or lend a hand to my wife.

Motorcycles are not an uncommon sight in town. And I had been observant for a good number of years now. Besides, whenever I took a bus ride, I would invariably opt for the front seat and never let go my eyes from the activities involved in driving. Like shifting the gears, pressing the brakes, coordinating the clutch and all those related technicalities. I would even follow the helps around to observe them replace the tyres should we run into a flat or any other snag along the way. I knew the skills I gleaned thus would come in handy in good time, sooner or later. As for now, I thought I could manage with what I frequently saw with people starting up the bike and driving it around.

I kicked the Rx alive. Easy-peasy. I tested the brakes and the clutch. Another easy-peasy. Then, telling my wife to grab me fast by the waistline, I let the pressure go.

We're on the road.

For fear of letting the motor die, (remember my scooter experience?) I drove in constant shift which must be either the first gear or the second. It was loud. The engine complained with squeals and resounding pops and splutters. In a matter of seconds, we hit Tipaimukh Road and headed up north towards the suburbs of Chiengkonpang and Phailian. It was a much better ride than my previous two adventures. I began to feel assured and satisfied with myself. From the moment we rolled out, I had secretly decided to take the longer route to extend the practising exercise. 'Secretly' because had I let my intention known to my dearie, she would definitely not have approved of it. But don't you dare think I am a henpecked husband!

Slowly yet surely, I began to enjoy the experience and feel the thrill of the ride. I think I began to understand why young boys and girls are crazy for motorbike rides.

Inside a quarter of an hour, we came to the outskirt townlet of Phailian. My wife's paternal auntie lives there with her family. I pulled up and took my small family to drop by. That was not the primary objective. But their homestead having conveniently fallen along the way, it won't be unbecoming of us to at least give them a call. The main purpose being of course to give the Rx a badly needed time to cool. It was screaming all the way, protesting against my poor driving skills.

Sometime later, we reached home safe and sound.

I never told my wife that that was my first ever proper driving experience. That was my little secret. However, more than ten years later, I happened to let the cat out of the bag in a post dinner chat. My wife still turned livid: "Why didn't you tell me?" she demanded.

"You would've never taken the ride had I told you," I said.

"Of course not!"

She swore she would never sit on a bike driven by me again. But that was a vow she could not keep. She did ride with me a hundred times and more. For, my first time was well past then and I am quite a seasoned driver already. Hah!

Like any normal child, I should say, it was a habit of mine too to keenly observe whatever draws my interest.

In the late seventies and early eighties, Catholic fathers would occasionally bring film projectors with them when they come visiting our school. In the evenings of such visits, the whole village would come together to the school ground to enjoy a free movie. Some of the films I could hazily recollect are Cecil B. DeMille's 'The Ten Commandments', George Lucas's 'Star Wars', and The Bible, etc.

While everybody would fight for a vantage viewing point, I would persist for a place close to the cinema-projector itself. And when the audience fixed its stare on the silver screen, mine would turn the other way and get glued to the awe-inspiring electronic contraption from which sprang rays of moving images. The rotating spools that feed and receive the reels, the constant whirring noise, the brilliant light emanating from the lens, everything about the mechanism gripped me with endless fascination.

Later, I would clobber some waste planks together to fabricate a box to serve as projector. Then, I unrigged the glasses off my father's spectacles for the optics. I received a good thrashing for that. As for the light source, I would make use of the kerosene wick-lamp which worked somehow but a little too dim. After few experimentations, I learnt how to replace the sooty lamp with a 100-watt bulb drawing power from the local electricity supply.

In those days, there used to be a classic slide-viewer toy that uses positive films. Ripping the slides off their paper-cassettes, I'd put them to my homemade projector to produce slideshows. Friends would come to enjoy the pictures as well as to marvel at my creation. I would charge them a couple of marbles as entry fee. That way, I made enough marbles to clinch partnerships with friends who had initially refused to team with me due to my poor gift on the pitch.

Years later, in high school to be precise, another mechanical device captured my interest. It was the typewriter. Back in the days, I often saw typists in the sub-divisional office of our old village going clackety-clack all day long. I'd never imagined I would handle the machine myself. I did not know what purpose they would serve me. How would a child know he would be needing one to write all his stories and articles later in life?

Now, here at Churachandpur Higher Secondary School, the head clerk, Sir Tunpau Tonsing (May his soul rest in peace!), was enthralling me with his fingers on the wonderful apparatus. It was a treat to the eyes watching him work his magic on the tabs. Sheets of foolscap paper flying off the carrier-head in quick succession. He was a wizard indeed. He struck the chord of my fantasy. I was immediately hooked.

It was a prevalent practice in government schools (at least in ours) in those days that teachers would not care to go to their classes. On occasions, we could even catch them engaged in a game of ludo in the staff-room, minding their own business. So, we would be given more free-classes than we asked for. On such events, I would rush up the corridor to watch Sir Pau peck at the keys with amazing speed. From outside the office window, I would take mental notes of his finger positions and tab locations. Then, when I got back home after school, I would sketch the layout on a cardboard and pretend to type, picturing the real device in my mind.

A few weeks later, I felt I could practically handle the machine on my own. So, I went to Sir Pau to ask if he would allow me to do a certain notice for our school unit's Siamsinpawlpi, the Paite Students Association. I was the Secretary. Sir Pau was indeed a very kind and amiable person. He took down the typewriter from the steel locker and carried it to the table for me. Then, without any caution, he would simply let me take over. Just like that.

Gingerly, I fed a few semi see-through foolscap sheets into the carriage, blue carbon papers going in between every sheet. Then, lovingly, I would run my fingers on the keytops for a while, gently feeling their smooth, glossy surfaces. Soaking up the sense of satisfaction. Then, taking deep breaths and closing my eyes, I would visualise the pattern I drew a hundred times on a hard board and hit out endlessly for weeks.

Slowly, I made my first depression. The spring was stiffer than I imagined. I returned the carrier and tried again. Not in minutes, I could work the keys without the need to see where my fingers were travelling. Emulating a proper clerk's pose, I planted my sight on the handwritten memo and started banging out the typefaces without keeping an eye on the moving head. I've just learned typing!

From then on, whenever I had free periods, I would hurry over to the office and ask Sir Pau if he needed any extra hand. He did agree to take me on on several occasions for which I am forever grateful. In all earnestness, it was this very aptitude that landed me my first job as clerk-cum-office assistant at Jubilee Model School in

Jonai, Assam. It also became the foundation for my computer knowledge in the years to come.

Speaking of computers, I am reminded of how one came into my possession. When I was entrusted with the charge of computers in our section at Armed Forces Headquarters, New Delhi, in the fall of 2000, I had a hunch that this technological marvel would shortly take over the typewriter. Even after I walked out of the job, I still felt the need to own one. I did not know how or where to obtain it. And I certainly had no wherewithal for its purchase.

To my good fortune though, I happened to land a teacher's job at Rayburn High School. There, practical computer classes had been recently introduced. Rayburn High, as far as my knowledge is concerned, is the first institution to bring computer education to our hometown. As it were, the craze was yet to catch on. So, I firmly believed there must be a set to spare.

With the most unlikely hope, I went to the Principal, Sir Khen Tombing, and presumptuously requested him to let me have one on loan. He did not agree at first. But I was persistent. After weeks of ambitious pursuit, I eventually persuaded him to spare me one. I was on cloud nine. This was the configuration of my first personal computer, if I remember it correctly. The internal storage was 20GB HDD and the random access memory module was 256MB. I didn't have an idea of processors at the time. So, I do not remember such technical specifications anymore. But there was a floppy disk drive in which you insert a 1.44MB floppy diskette to read or write data on. However, this storage device was soon phased out with the advent of the glitzy Compact Discs and DVDs. My first upgrade was to add an optical drive or as we commonly call it, the CD-Drive. It soon became the craze of the day.

Having no prior knowledge of computers, I would frequently run into one problem or another. On such occasions, U Hrangthanmang would always come to my rescue.

One evening, friends and neighbours gathered in our house to watch a movie on my new proud PC. The movie kicked off all right. But every now and again it would go off and something like a jumble of pipes would start crawling across the blackened screen. Every time that happened, I had to shake or move the mouse to bring the movie back.

My First Personal Computer, 2001

One of the movie-watchers that day was Pu Paul Tonsing. He was an immediate neighbour who later became an extended in-law to me. He had left his task and rushed up to witness the highly sung and fanciful wonder-gadget. But with the screen going black every few minutes, he grew restive in no time.

"Computer!" he sighed in exasperation. "What a waste!" He mumbled as he walked across the door to take his leave. "At least with the TV you don't have to jiggle that piece of electronic every time and again."

The very next day, I took it down to U Hrangthanmang at Mualveng, Upper Lamka, and complained about the issue. I did not know what he did to it. As though with a touch of a magic wand, the blank screen never came back again. But I could not convince Pu Paul to come over and have a movie time with me on the computer again.

It was not years before I learnt how to toggle the 'screensaver' on or off at will. The rest, as they say, is history.

Having given you a peek at my first encounter with the PC, I think I should take you back to the time I conquered the MS Word. I was not an era ago. Just the year before. 2000.

I need not repeat that I was a clerk at the Armed Forces Headquarters in New Delhi. Computers had started appearing in offices at that time. I was not familiar with it yet. But it was thrust into my hands all the same. I did see a few PC sets in close quarters on several occasions from the desktop publishing centres in our hometown back in the latter part of the 1990s. Watching isn't learning though. Yet, I must immodestly claim that I was quite proficient in typing, having extensively used the Remington and the Godrej when I was working as Clerk cum Office Assistant at Jubilee Model School in 1995-96 at Jonai, Assam. Probably, I was entrusted the computer on the strength of that skill set.

I am not a man to throw in the towel easily. I took the challenge well in my stride. Firstly, I asked a colleague how to take a printout. His name was Ajay. I couldn't recollect his last name. Was it Sharma? Probably. He was an Assistant Grade officer.

In those days, the dot-matrix printers were huge and noisy. Special papers perforated along the sides had to be fed into the roller-heads. This enabled printing on long continuous pages. With the permission of the section officer, I pulled up all the help-files and printed them out. The office was filled with a rapid clacketing noise all day long. Yes, all day because a dot-matrix didn't print as fast as today's instant laserjet printers. And certainly not as quiet.

The prints ran into a good number of pages. I took them home to apply head and mind for days and nights. I would also take piecemeal projects to the office for practical exercises. By the end of the month, I think I was fit enough to face any Word-job thrown at me. I had acquired working knowledge of Microsoft Word.

Before long, the Brigadier, the head of our office, wanted me to take on PowerPoint. One Srinivas, a South Indian guy, if my memory serves me right, who handled his presentations, was due for transfer. So, he wanted me to take his charge once he was gone. I candidly admitted my lack of knowledge. To that he readily snapped that he had already instructed my section officer to find me an institute for a crash course. On the office's expense, I presume. For my salary, being a rookie, was obviously not fat enough to foot the extra bill. But I did not ask.

"That may hamper my office attendance, Sir," I stated out of pretended modesty. I was bubbling with excitement inwardly.

"You'll attend your classes in the morning," he replied. "And come to office in the afternoon. I'll see to that arrangement, too."

"I have already applied for a post-summer leave, Sir," I said again, almost out of turn.

"Never mind," said the Brigadier. "Come back soon."

I never came back.

I did not realise what I missed until I got myself into this Excel soup, seven years later when I joined my current job. I never thought spreadsheets would be part of anything I had to do. Like it or not, now I had to find a way to mind the gap in my computer knowledge. Everybody in the section I turned to let me down with the same pretext: "I don't know computer."

So, I took a step back as in the old days. The difference, however, being that I now owned a PC of my own and needed no print-outs. How I acquired my first PC is another story altogether. You may come across it elsewhere in the book. Possessing a personal home computer certainly quickened the learning pace. I picked up the basics with a few nights' labour. I did struggle with the technicalities but managed to string the rudiments together in no time. Moreover, I could take relevant files home to squeeze my mind on. It was not a custom of mine to carry office work home even when I was employed under private enterprises. But now, I was at a disadvantage. So, I made myself a concession although not to be continued as a habit.

In a couple of weeks, I felt confident enough to carry the job laden on my frail shoulders.

Enough of these bucolic escapades. Let me now move to a more metropolitan setting.

When a number of tribespeople come together in any given city, we tend to form some kind of socio-religious gatherings which we call 'Fellowship'. This is part to carry on our cultural and traditional values and practices and part to maintain our religious commitments in our home away from home. However, if I dare be so candid, attending Sunday masses or any other religious observances would be more a socialising event than a spiritual quest. You go to the fellowship/church to meet up with friends and acquaintances, to connect in a strange land where nostalgia and homesickness are rife. And to mingle in general. It is sort of a weekend hangout for our small communities.

In those days, it was only through mails and posts that you communicate. So, it was a must to go to church or join social events organised by the community. In fact, those were the time and place bearers and receivers meet up and deliver. It was not only paper correspondences. We would also receive parcels and packages including, among other things, indigenous foods which could never be procured in the cities. Some of our food items, with their distinct odours and aromas, would become the cause of bitter altercations and misunderstandings with local neighbours, especially in the national capital.

I used to insist on joining worship services without fail. Besides being a socialising event, it was a psychological necessity, much less a spiritual quest. I would often assert that a time would come when you won't be able to attend masses even if you're dying for it. Strictly speaking, I am not a religious person. But there are no other places in our society where you receive social messages and moral instructions as wholesome and nourishing than from the ministers. So, I felt the resolute need and compulsion for attending masses. The principle stuck even when I came to Kolkata for a job.

In cities, our places of worship are hardly located within walking distances. For a family with two tiny tots, crowded city buses were not an easy option. If the congestion is not enough, the excessive heat would step in to kill us. It is even worse for people prone to motion sickness. I don't know whether this susceptibility is hereditary or not. My mother and her siblings are known to be very averse to travelling in moving transportations.

In 2004, I was accompanying my maternal uncle to Dimapur to see him off to join his regained service with Sashastra Seema Bal, a unit of Central Armed Police Force of India. He got extremely sick in the bus. Even before we reached Kohima, he would piteously sob like a child, swearing every now and then to abandon the job and turn back. Perhaps inheriting this trait, I too am very poor in taking motion fatigue. As a matter of fact, I have taken after the poorer sides of my parents. My mother is fair yet very short. My father was about six feet tall but swarthy. I am short and dark.

To add to the woe, I perfectly took after the weaker attributes of my mother such as motion sickness. For small distances, I could do with a shooting headache. But on longer ones, I would throw up everything inside, down to the bile, until I would be near dead. I could not forget one particular journey between Guwahati and Imphal when I even lost consciousness after endlessly retching all along the way.

Probably absorbing this undesirable characteristic from me, my wife and children too find it very hard to sit in buses and cars. I remember one late evening in 2008. We were returning home from a certain church programme at Raghunathpur off VIP Road, Baguiati. There were no taxis to book at that time of night, which was not uncommon in those days. It was before the era of Ubers and Olas. So, we had to take a late-night bus that was packed to the brim. Despite being late in the night, the heat had not yet dissipated. This is Kolkata.

And the traffic was still horrible. We were literally crawling in a snail's pace. The stop-and-start progression and the incessantly droning engine soon churned up everything insides us. We had hardly reached Ultadanga Crossing which was infamous for its traffic snarls when we eventually came to a standstill. It took almost an hour to cover even a few hundred metres.

In the melee, our children, utterly soaked in sweat, would throw up endlessly and whimper in their half-sleep. We, their parents, had our fair share of sickness. But we had to fight back the urges for the sake of the toddlers. That was like bottling up carbonated drink after giving it a vigorous shake. We attended the babies while ourselves suffering nasty nausea and aching heads. So bad was our bus-sickness that day that a complete rest for the next couple of days could not entirely dispel the motion lag.

We did have a motorbike at that time. But to fit four members of a family on a bike and drive for a distance was not always practicable, especially at late nights. We did take the two-wheeler on a number of occasions previously. But due to increased rampancy of road accidents, a family bike-ride was not always advisable. So, we had tried to avoid it as far as practicable. In those days, the traffic sergeants would not much mind if you don't put on helmets. Even after knowing that it was a double risk, the inconvenience and discomfort would often dissuade us to wear one.

Let alone bus rides, our ordeals with the yellow taxis almost always ended in unpleasant spats. As I already related, my children would predictably get motion sick and vomit inside the cabs. Not eager to clean our puke, the drivers would yell and rant at us, threatening to push us out and dump us wherever we are. We used to have hard times reasoning that it was just a natural weakness to throw up. And the perpetrators are children after all. Nothing intentional. Then, we would be forced to wash and scrub the rubber mats before we would be allowed to take our seats and move again.

Not before enduring these humiliating happenstances for years, I at last felt I must do something about it. I was resenting deep inside to see myself so helpless in front of my kids and my better half. However, in spite of my resoluteness, there was nothing I could do. Either we give up socialising and attending masses or get ourselves a private means of transport in which to fit the children that are growing up faster than you could imagine. And of course travel in your own pace. Gandhiji got very angry when he was thrown out of a train in South Africa. He came home and drove out the entire White racial chauvinists called the British from the soil of India. My anger achieved nothing of that sort. It was only an impotent rage. An implosion.

I was a complete fool to think we should not—or could not—give up Sunday services or communal celebrations. Actually, I was afraid that doing so would cut us off from our society. With that as the primary reason, and of course not ignoring the comforts, I put up a proposal to my wife to go for at least a secondhand car. We took more than a year turning the idea over inside our heads.

In the meantime, as luck would have it, a used-car outlet called Kolkata Car Bazaar happened to setup shop just adjacent to our office. One afternoon, as I was exiting the office gate, a strong urge instigated me to set foot into the shop and make enquiries. Mr. Sumit Shaw, the proprietor, was extremely unctuous and persuasive.

I ended up settling for a secondhand Honda City sedan. I shall not recount how the proprietor short-changed me and never handed over the original smartcard. The vehicle would refuse to start when the engine heated up. A dozen servicings at Pinnacle Honda, an authorised service centre off E.M. Bypass, failed to solve the problem. But they ripped me off almost one and a half lakh rupees for the futile sessions. Years later, Kalim Automobiles got it fixed for me when I booked them through the Go Mechanic app. Whatever be the case, buying a car appears to be the poorest decision I've ever made.

I had to bargain a lot to clinch the deal. I've never purchased a four-wheeler before. It's not an exaggeration to declare that my knowledge of cars is next to zero. But, as I said, the proprietor was so glib and convincing that I thought I had a good bargain for two hundred thousand rupees. I quickly applied for a long-term loan from our employees' cooperative society. It was not before a year or so that I realised a perfect-condition secondhand of the same make and model could be bought at the same price without negotiating. The Bible has rightly said that a fool could not pay enough for his own folly. Let that suffice for that again.

Now, I've never driven a car in my life. I've not even run my hands on the steering wheel yet. But I absolutely could not afford a driving school. I was just believing that possessing one would enable me to drive it eventually.

It was a Saturday night when I took a friend named Sopei to bring the car home. Sopei is a nice and feisty fellow who loves cracking jokes. He was working as a driver with World Vision at the time, if I am not mistaken. He'd readily agreed to accompany me to the car shop. He made all the necessary inspection and took us to a test drive. With his approval, I made the final payment. And we drove home.

Being night already, I dared not try my hands on it. Early next morning, I tooled it out from the garage and drove around the campus for a couple of times by myself. At noon, I went through the process again to make sure I could really handle it. About three O' clock in the afternoon, I herded my family into the 'new' used-car and drove them to Moulali, near Sealdah railway station. We attended the evening service travelling in our own four-wheeler.

That was how I came to acquire the skill of driving a car!

Chapter 3

REMEMBERING A FALLEN COMRADE

Nights used to be spoilt by gunshots. Maddening crowds would break loose and rush to where the shots came. Gunfire and anarchic eruptions are good blood boilers. Especially, for the hills people obsessed with parochial tribal commitments and sensational communalisms.

But that was history: A history that rocked the Kukis and the Zomis in the second half of the 1990s; A history that blots their faces forever. A history, they thought, better left behind and, if possible, forgotten.

Gang-type gunfights and factional fallouts did create occasional aftershakes. At the height of the conflict these tremors must have readily flamed into communal passions. But the humble hill-man seemed to have learnt his lesson well. He is not as keen to reawaken the internecine ghost that haunted him for nearly a quarter of a decade. Not for now, at least. The storm had kind of blown over. Ruffled feathers, to a large extent, had been smoothed. Life had begun to drag on to normalcy. Slowly. But drag it did.

Now, cut to the middle of the next decade.

Early evening, August 20, 2006. Hebron Veng, New Lamka.

Sunday.

Nothing worth mentioning with the progressing twilight. The dusk was not unlike any other dusks. About slipping into night. Young and immature-dark. The moon had not yet risen. Or had it gone into hiding rather? Or was it a no-moon night? Before long, the sky turned into an inky black. Blank and sheer pitch.

The stage seemed set for the stars. But not one twinkler climbed the heavenly podium. They rather looked apprehensive or unwilling to don their glorious nocturnal robes. Wasn't the sky dark enough? Wasn't the setup perfect, as any star could have asked for? Why, then, did they still seem to shy?

Wait! There they are!

There's one; here's another. And there's yet another. Faint but glimmering none the less. Those were the few proud ones that showed up. But that was only to redeem their stellar pride. Far too few to create the unified gleam of a luminary host. In the larger congregation's absence, the spectacle was but pathetic. The heavenly dots seemed truly anxious. Had they foresensed something awful? Had they smelled a fishy horizon? An impending doom? Huff! What did a cluster of multi-spiked flickering objects high above the sky know about the future? Down with stupid superstitions! Down with the stars and their gazers and the heaven-readers and their entire ilk!

Down on earth, the air was relatively laid back. The mood at Hebron Veng and downtown Lamka, in general, was easy and relaxed. The only uneasiness being the weather. For a night in the hills, it was inordinately muggy. Humidity was hanging in the air like a shroud of heated vapour. The offensive heat seemed intent on sweating out some unspeakable vice running in the bloodstream of the townsfolks.

Not that the town nor its folks gave a hoot to the corrupting vile. They lolled around unwinding the day's stress, savouring the belated monsoon breeze that swept down from the surrounding ranges of Teisiang and Saikot mountains. In the meantime, moisture and darkness were building up in a bid to reach a saturation point.

Well! Let the clime and emptiness of the sky be. The world was at rest. All was right and nothing's wrong. It was a lazy night. It was a peaceful night. It also makes a perfect night to pay one's in-laws a visit.

So, I took my family down to my in-laws at College Veng. No particular purpose. Just to wait out the heat and laze till the night cools to bedtime temperature. My family, at that time, was a small and happy family: my daughter and my better half. My son was due four months later to make us an even happier family: *'Hum Do, Humare Do'!* As the official theme of Indian Family Planning goes.

There, at our in-laws', lightings were kept to the minimum. There was no power supply on that infernal evening. Luck is not a lady I met as often as I'd love to. There was no likelihood of our running into her tonight either. Had it not been for the Burmese-imported China-made-inverter, we would've been ruing and cursing the perennial load-shedding imposed upon the town since time immemorial. Thanks to the cheap Chinese dump electronics! Myanmar has come to the rescue of this part of India as far back as one's memory could recall.

For now, we joined up our in-laws enjoying a certain Meetei movie. I followed the play from the histrionics and mannerisms of the screen-characters. For, my *Meetei-lon* (language of the plains proper) was extremely limited. Restricted, in fact, to the elementary *'chak chabra'* and *'karino'*. (Have you had your food? What is it?) Admittedly, I've had a number of lurid moments in the mid-eighties at Imphal thanks to my Vitamin-L deficiency. L stands for language, linguistic, or any related word you may conjugate out of it. If I recount those moments of discomfitures, I must do so later elsewhere. They are off topic for now.

Meanwhile, the clock was looping in its own sweet circle of time. Not only was it a Sunday, it was a tranquil yet stifling day. By no means conducive to a hectic exertion. Yes, there wasn't any particular cause to hurry.

Vesper masses were going on all across the town. Indeed, one could easily see innumerable spires dotting the landscape of this small township. Presently, hymns in collective harmony with accompaniments of traditional drums pounding in leisurely tempo curled up to God like trails of frankincense. In passing, all these churches and local sects are founded on the same piece of rock called the Bible. No wonder they're constantly at loggerheads to outdo one another in claiming their respective churches and dogmas the rightest and the solely chosen. Could there be any place more religiously colourful than this! In plain contrast though, no townsman cared a dime to make piety his true portrayal to the wider world.

At the moment, the streets were deserted and empty. Barring a few lovebirds coquetting down Awnsuak Road or along the main boulevard called Tiddim Road, there weren't many souls to stray into the Devil's pen. Everybody seemed to have taken to the fastness of the temples.

Few more minutes fleeted. The hymns and drumbeats quietened. The wind slowed down to a gentle pause. Leaves halted rustling. A delicate satin of hush fell over the town as if paying reverence to the minister rising on the pulpit to sermonize his parishioners. Not long before, he would be hogging the limelight, charging at the congregation, almost fanatically, as though they are composed of the most sinful souls. Figuratively, he was a bull in a moral china shop.

For the early starters though, the stillness that momentarily pervaded would denote the close of ceremony. The clock had readied to strike seven. For an eastern time-zone, seven is quite a night already. The evening has matured. And it was time to make the hour known.

But!

Rat-a-tat, bang! Rat-a-tat, bang!

What the hell's going on? Ear-splitting rattles overtaking the clock before it could ring the proclamations.

Rat-a-tat, bang! Rat-a-tat, bang!
Spurts of gunfire. Deafeningly close range.
Public commotion ensued.

Not one of us had the wisdom of putting into practice the lesson learnt hardly a decade ago. Instead, we stared at one another as dumbstruck as the house-mouse scampering across the floor and getting himself caught in a Chinese-made sticky trap. In truth, the stun in our eyes got our mobility locked into place. Not milliseconds later, my daughter's uncle found his voice and blurted out: "Duck! Duck!"

Noise erupted across the lanes. Doors slammed. Windows clattered. A street scene of some western movie flashed across golden memory. Clint Eastwood or Terence Hill and Bud Spencer, or John Wayne—or whosoever it was—drew guns against the baddies who came abang-bangin' in the Wild, Wild West.

Then another voice, probably a lady's, cried: "Hit the ground! Hit the ground!"

Not many years ago, in the late 90s to be precise, even a five-year old knew to hit the ground at the slightest crack of the gun. But that was then. Now, peace had come back. And with it the vanity of the Zomis. No one wanted to be the first to fall face down. That's a disgrace: a sign of weakness. Lack of machismo. Mark of a coward. Which a Zomi definitely is not. To some, as much as to me, it may sound abject stupidity? But a belief is a belief. And the pride at stake is too high. Heed, *no Zomi ever cows in fear of a measly copper projectile!*

As for now, bullets sang happily in the air. They must not be from far. But it wasn't easy to tell a shot. Especially in a still night like this. Sometimes the reverberations sounded louder than the shot itself. But those we heard at the moment were certainly not echoes. They're coming directly from the muzzles with no chance of distortion: *Rat-a-tat-bang! Rat-a-tat-bang!*

A few rounds more.

Then, a gut-wrenching jangle began to fill the air in relay. The alarm bells were going off. Apparently stemming from the epicentre. Rapid tolls began to peal everywhere. Getting closer with each ripple, the distress call eventually reached the townhall at Hebron Veng.

An alarm bell, for a tribesman, is a call of the highest order. A call beyond the call of duty. Needless to say, answering an SOS of that urgency and gravity is to offer one's service in a voluntary manner. Every man comes prepared to render even a supreme sacrifice should the occasion demand. That's the tribal spirit: that's the altruism this alpine stock of Mongoloids lived by for centuries. True to the nature of the call, excited throngs began to rumble across New Lamka. Every man who calls himself a name poured out into the streets. Disoriented but determined. They did not know where to head. Everybody was asking everybody for directions. Besides, not unlike the beginning days of the Kuki-Zomi ethnic conflict, the people were unarmed and uninformed.

As if to heighten the bewilderment and rush of public adrenaline, the strident maydays kept calling ever more impatiently. Alarm bells were reverberating all across town. People who poured forth empty handed combed the grounds for wooden stumps or rotting logs or fist-sized-boulders. Or at least a piece of rusted metal thrown about by careless workers of a certain construction nearby. Everyone groped in the dark for whatever could make them a weapon.

Suddenly, somebody cried: "To Vengnuam EBC Church! To Vengnuam EBC Church!"

As if led by an invisible general, the mob started off to the east like a mighty onrush of floe. Cries and yells began to turn the peace that lorded over the skies a few hours ago into a blasphemous mockery. Thanks to the wonders of information technology! Inside a minute, droves of warriors began to rumble down from the two satellite townlets to the west, to name, Bungmual and Pearsonmun, to stand by their afflicted sister, New Lamka.

The moon had still not risen, or had gone into permanent hiding. Had visibility been more favourable, this band of brothers raging down the hillsides must have looked like the barbaric hordes of Attila, the Hun, raving furiously to earn their lord the soubriquet *The Scourge of God!*

Rising from my half-supine position, I decided to have a closer look into the din. Before I delved into adventure, I turned to my wife, whose young heart was shuddering in fear. "Don't you worry," I said as though I was a soldier leaving for the battlefield. "Whatever befalls befalls for the will of God and for the good of the Zomis." So saying and waving her and my daughter off as though that was our last moment, I then blended into the pulsating surge of the multitude. Sounds like a besotted youth uttering his parting words on being called up to roam the untamed jungles of Guite Kual as a revolutionary, eh? At that time, I think, I sounded so. And wanted to. To sound as fanatic and patriotic and as passionate as a true lover!

Looking back, today, I feel there was nothing patriotic in my immersion in that sea of infuriated humanoids. It had nothing to do with my love of Zomi or Zogam. It had nothing significant in terms of philanthropy despite my staunch believe in it. I was merely chipping in as a human being, playing my ordinary human part. Perhaps, I was just overzealous in my Zomism. Perhaps, my imagination, although as barren as the sky that night, was at work. Yes, I once was in a state of foolish delusion—dreaming up Utopian castles for my beloved Zogam. In reality, I was just reacting naturally as any individual would in the given situation.

A small bunch of neighbours had gathered around my in-law's residence. I joined them up before they proceeded to the centre of gravity.

Taking a by-lane and moving east, we, in no time, ran into a crowd hurrying down College Street. At the junction where Church Road meets T. Chinkhothang Street, the crowd cascaded into a pool of eddying furore. Before long, a sort of self-styled leaders made the most of the opportunity and took charge to discuss the next course of action.

By now, the chain of events had uncoiled and made the rounds like wildfire.

A group of unidentified miscreants had opened fire around Vengnuam EBC Church. Some believed it was a freak firing spree. Some said it was an exchange of fire between cadres of two rival outfits.

Truth, whatever the case, was a couple of churchgoers got mowed down in the crossfire.

This piece of rumour did not improve the crowd's patience that's presently running out fast. Voices rose to ever increasing decibels. A hungry lion growls for blood and flesh.

College Street that leads to the main theatre was jampacked. Everybody was milling into the tiny spaces between the ever-swelling multitude, gnashing and cursing and yelling incitements to rebellion. A rebellion against what, who or what cause—nobody cares. But a rebellion none the less!

A Zomi blood shall flow not in vain!

The mob swore in general, rolling fists and shaking them furiously at nobody in particular. At the same time, using whatever that comes in hand as tools, they pulled up a corroded underground drainage pipe and placed it in the middle of the road to hold down any vehicle that should come that way. However, this improvisation did not humour Mr. S. Vungzasiam, the erstwhile president of the Young Paite Association, New Lamka Block.

The President, with a pack of his councillors in tow, was scuttling every here and there coordinating and moderating the outpour. It was in one of his whirlwind tours that he came across these waylaying agitators. For a moment, there seemed to be an exchange of opinions between the President and the restive crowd. The roadblock, obviously, was the issue. Predictably, as almost always in a Zomi community, a leader's voice was given the upper hand. The mob acquiesced. The rusty pipe was rolled away.

Then, the dadgum swarm of heads, like a migrating colony of bees, moved on.

A human ocean had already formed in the vicinity of the Church, swirling in a cyclone of sentiments. An emotional crowd is a dangerous thing. It is like a bundle of dynamite-sticks with a fuse-cord way too short. Presently, the tension was intensifying with every passing second, climbing up the crowd's throat like a rising lump. The crowd was dry tinder waiting for a spark. The cauldron was simmering, ready to boil over at the slightest hint of provocation.

I, too, had a stub of bamboo in my hand. Where, when or how had I got hold of it I had no idea. Probably, I've picked it up somewhere along the way. Now, with all the confidence in the world and a sea of hotheads for support, I rushed headlong into the convergence point.

However, before I made much headway, there came a sound of a truck approaching the crowd from the eastern end. Maybe a furlong away. I thought the government forces had come to take stock of the situation. The throng suddenly got unsettled and started to spill over, disallowing me to make any further forward movement.

At an arm's length ahead, the road took a gentle turn. And on the left of the bend was a huge hoarding with a Bible verse painted on it. Today, nowhere is the Board to be seen, let alone preach. But then the sky-blue board was sermonizing at the frenzied horde milling around its feet, intent on some collective crime. As for me, being without a prospect of making way forward, I decided to seek refuge beneath the wings of the billboard.

Hmn, I thought. *Let's see what's coming out of this.*

Not before seconds, the truck ran into the crowd. Whether it was held up by the multitude I didn't know. The truck did stop but the engine kept running in low purr, prepared to sprint at any moment. A low nervous hum was beginning to rumble from the depths of the earth. Perhaps, a sort of negotiation was going on between the frontmen and those in the vehicle.

Momentarily, the truck seemed to bring the spark the mob had been begging for. Everybody suddenly became irritable. Tempers flew. That's a surefire formula of pandemonium-building.

While waiting on the talks, I tapped into the resources of my MIB (Mental Intelligence Bureau). *That's very unlike of the army,* I mused. *When had the police or the army started arriving so soon at a crime-scene or conflict spot?*

In fact, no security force in Lamka had ever acted so promptly. They were normally the last to make it, if they ever made it, that is. And, if they do at all, they would make sure their arrival was impressively noticed. They would run amok to finish the business left unfinished by the troublemakers. They would bash up anybody they could lay their hands on; grab an innocent guy or two and pump plenty of bullets into their heads point-blank, and, the following day, have the morning papers sing praises to their job well done. Perhaps, they did this to save their face. Or they are simply programmed that way. We shall never know unless, of course, the Fauji Bhais would tell us themselves! *Amar Jyoti Jawans! Friends of the Hills!*

This is Lamka. The land God has left a long time ago. The land where no felony springs a surprise too big. The land where nothing is too brutal, nothing too cold. Nothing too insensitive; nothing too weird. Here, everything is anticipated. Everything accepted. But nothing is understood.

Still in my mental CSI (for the uninitiated, the acronym stands for Crime Scene Investigation):

Now, there is no entry point from where the armoured van originated. It was a cul-de-sac. The road had ended a couple of metres east to the site of the incident. Beyond that, a brief stretch of dirt-road takes over and opens out into a wide belt of paddies.

Could the van be responsible for whisking the miscreants away? Had it been hiding there in the wet fields all this while? Are the gunmen in combat fatigue in the vehicle real government soldiers? Is the mayhem created by them hand-in-glove with a certain group of insurgents?

Nothing is impossible; especially in a trouble-torn state like Manipur in general, and Lamka in particular. Teaming up with one militant faction or another is not an uncommon practice by the security forces out here. Such a collaboration is rather a matter of honour for the rebels under contract. But for the army, it's nothing but a shrewd strategy to obtain easy fodder for the bullets. The very fact that the army presented itself in so spontaneous a manner deserved suspicion. My mind ran riot, probing every nook and cranny of possibilities. The more I deliberated, the more my doubts validated.

I patted myself on the back for being able to form these theories. I thought I should take up a career in a private detective firm. Only problem is, I had no answers to my own questions. And the theories I threw up were rather general and self-evident. And not so intricate as I made them to be. On second thoughts, I think, I better forget being a private detective.

Suddenly, a fricking roar woke me up from my investigative reverie. The mob had swung into action. Apparently, it was thinking on the same lines as I did. Blows began to rain on the bulletproof truck: on the hood and the flanks, and on the back. The windshield and the fenders were not spared either.

Wham! Bam! Slam!

Hails of fire in the days of the Egyptian chastisement came to mind. A quick Bible General Knowledge. Whether it is an appropriate analogy or not I do not know. I don't care. Just one habit of living in a devout town, I guess.

In response, gunshots rang out: Live rounds but blank fires.

The mob refused to let up. It's been waiting for this for too long. The motor, no more eager to stay on the receiving end, revved up furiously. Then, without warning, gunned forward, cutting the crowd in midriff.

I was still leaning on the wooden posts of the didactic signboard when the military truck came hurtling ahead, losing control, swaying dangerously from side to side. At the same time, a gunner on top of the van, probably in dark olive, masked and protected by a metallic shielding, was spraying free ammo to clear the way. This time, they were not meant for the heavens. They were spat on us.

The headlights of the van shone upon us like a thousand suns from the pits of hell. Just for a fleeting moment. But that's ample time for the gun-blaster to take pot shots on us like sitting ducks. That triggered a passing recollection of one particular night during the Kuki-Zomi standoff.

Teams were formed from all healthy men—from teens to middle aged—to patrol the fringes of the town day in and day out. Our company of six raw recruits was also issued two single-barrel guns and a belt of cartridges each.

We took position at the southwestern corner, behind the EOC Central Church at Hill Town. We made three shifts in twos. Commander Goulianthang slotted Mungboi and me for the second period—1 to 4am. When we manned the post, the night had already stridden across the small hours.

It was the darkest hour of the night. The world was asleep, if not dead. Even the foxes from the shorn hilltops had given up howling and curled up in their holes. The just-retired pair of sentries and the pair next in line were snoring their heads off more in inebriation and excessive consumption of roasted beef than tiredness. My partner chuckled at the somnolent drunks. I instantly got infected. But, before our smiles could reassume their natural curves, our attention got sharply drawn to the Eucalyptus grove on the far bank of Chiengkon River.

Beyond was the infamous Gangte Veng where a certain offshoot of Kuki militants holed up. It was said that a good number of Zomis kidnapped by them were spirited away there and put out of their misery.

Our ears caught dry leaves and twigs snap under scurrying footsteps. Shadows flitted in the reddish arc of our low-watt floodlight that swept the thickets. Although our job was to see to such intrusions, the very act of the same was unexpected. We narrowed our eyes trying to make out the mugging figures. But before our impaired visions could focus properly, familiar bursts suddenly rent the predawn sky.

The shadows were spewing fire at us with their sophisticated AK-47s. We responded with our age-old blunderbusses. Our quickest efforts to reload were no match to their automatic ejectors. So, we took more cover behind the bulwark of the trench than return bullet for bullet.

Our comrades stirred not an inch until we roused them for a switch at four. And, as an icing to the cake, they didn't believe what we had to say!

Blazes of machine gun still rang in the air. The gunner atop the van was obviously no sniper. But that's the only consolation we had. Whatever ego left in us played traitor, betraying us at the moment we needed it most. There was no more pride in us to keep us from hitting the ground—face up or face down. Every sane person dived on the dirt for cover. We are literally biting dust!

Without pre-plan, I hit an open gutter. Lucky me! It was hay-dry, no sopping sewage. Almost knee-deep. Half of my body disappeared from view in the bat of an eye. A shower of projectiles danced all over the ground, kicking up dusts in dull aching thuds. I don't remember if a gunshot was louder on location than in a distance. And what a blustering way to meet Milady Luck! But when is Missy Luck unwelcomed or unadored anyways?

The gunfire ceased as suddenly as it started.

The van zipped past. I picked myself up and dusted my trousers. But the calm was most short-lived. Before I could pat myself down and regain proper composure, shots began rapping again. This time, they came from a different source.

Tailing the armoured truck was a *Maruti Omni*. The army-van had only been a *Road Opening Party*. Inside the Omni were men armed to the teeth, in getups fit for formal warfare. Presently, they were giving the ROP a hand in spattering indiscriminate death.

All this live action played out in fast forward mode. The vehicles vanished like a retreating lightning. We were momentarily plunged into the depths of darkness again. Up ahead, I could hear gasps and murmurings. Somebody was hurt. However, the casualty seemed a minor one. He was taken away without much ado.

Later, when the crowd dispersed, I went over to my in-laws to turn in the two-celled Eveready torchlight I borrowed. And to enquire how they fared in the mêlée. From the fencing-gate I could see a flurry of movements inside the house. I rushed in. There, I saw my sisters-in-law and several other ladies carrying a plastic basin around in the kitchen. My mind immediately prepared for the worst-case-scenario.

Some long time ago, I saw in *Discovery Channel* a guy shot in a sports dressing room from nowhere. After rigorous detective work, it was discovered that it was a stray shot from a shooting facility nearby, though quite a range away. The bullet had ricocheted several times off hard surfaces until it found the back of this hapless man's head.

Had a certain in-law of mine taken a stray bullet? I walked across the small front yard with a heavy heart. They were attending a certain guy from whose right ear was leaking blood. It was not a case of fatality though. I heaved a huge sigh of relief. Then and there I learnt that the injured person was an acquaintance of mine. He was Mr. Mangnou, proprietor of *Ozone Art Studio*, a professional painter and stone engraver. A bullet had grazed his ear, leaving a snick somewhere on the lobe. He told me that it was I who was snorting dust behind him as the slugs were skipping around. Instantly, I realized it was him whose heels I could have grabbed as Jacob did his hairy brother Esau's. But in the dimness, no one knows who was who. For that matter, who crawls closer to Sheol.

Anyway, thank God he was not another roll the eventful night had to call. Before long, the artist was taken away to a doctor by some ladies led by my mother-in-law.

There was yet another case of injury. The mob carried him to a male doctor living nearby. If local hearsay were true, the doctor in question was a gynaecologist. But I think his medical acumen would do more than enough for the job in hand.

Back to the yarn:

I swam against the turbulent wave of the throng to get a first-hand observation of the goings-on. I have never known humans could be packed in such a tight bundle. Eventually, I managed to elbow my way into the campus of Vengnuam EBC Church. But not without paying a price: one of my shirt-buttons had escaped to La La Land, the land of sheer liberty!

In the churchyard, a small area was cleared out around which a ring of onlookers had formed. And in the encircled space were cots manufactured by pulling church-pews together. As far as I could see, there were three youths lying on the makeshifts.

Congealing spots of blood spoiled their attires that must have been quite decent a moment ago. One of them, lying on the stomach, was able to move his head. I could see his eyelashes flutter. He was wounded. On his left was the second man. He was lying on his back as if giving up the cause he had been fighting for all his life. He was evidently dolled up for the vesper service. His shirt was still tucked inside the trousers. And the creases drawn by the electric iron were still visible. Now, he had the front of his shirt, down to the third or fourth button, ripped open. A bony breast, rendered bonier by the departure of the soul, showed through the gap. A bosom frail and pale. But a bosom never the less. Strong enough to hold a heart that beat for his fellow Zomis. He made no movement whatsoever.

A coloured tie, half undone, hung limply by the side of his shirt, slightly quivering in the gentle zephyr. There were dark stains that looked darker under the low-wattage lightbulb hanging outside the porch of the Church. This second man had his head turned from me as if feeling guilty to face me for giving up so easily.

Just then, a certain elder, a YPA *Val Upa*, raised himself to the cot that doubled up as a dais. He hemmed and hawed like a bullfrog with bad bronchitis. Then, having got the public's ear, he made his voice heard above the droning Church generator.

"It is sad, but it's true," he pronounced. "Our friend Mr. S. Thawngkhanlian Ngaihte is no more...!"

Giant forks of thunderbolts clapped somewhere beyond the dark horizons. The multitude was dumbstruck. Every soul present lost his power of speech. Only raspy breaths that were more snorts and sniffles like a cold gust of wind susurrating in the bamboo grove. It took some time for the bolt to sink.

Then, there was a weak hustle. Then, there were murmurs. Then, asides; then, encouragements. Then, as suddenly as the silence fell, a thunderous roar broke out in a boom: Revenge! Revenge!

The initial shock and the following outcry drowned the remaining speech of the elder.

I could hardly see the third man because he was partly obscured from my view by the reignited crowd. Besides, the announcement had turned my heart into lead. And my emotional strength could bear the weight no further. In the heat of resentment, the assembly might have forgotten to shed a tear for its fallen comrade. But to me, it was a loss too huge to miss even for a moment.

I rushed off to nowhere until I located a spot free from eye-shots. There, in the privacy of the niche, I gave my tears freedom they had never known before. I did, however, have a hard time letting a cry not escape from my lips and showing symptoms of femininity. I promised myself to never disclose this secret breakdown. But my tears fell like leaves in the gathering autumn. The sight of a fallen comrade is too much for my forbearance!

A comrade! A very close comrade!

Mr. Ngaihte and I were the first elected executives of *Siamsinpawlpi,* New Lamka Unit, when it was brought into existence on 24 October 2004. He was the President, and I the Secretary. The *Pawlpi* was implementing its long due decision to institute units at the village level. New Lamka being the largest unit of Lamka Block, the seat of the General Headquarters.

That apart, we had a very special bonding. On many points our views—politically and socially—would coincide. His advice and opinions were sincere and worth taking to heart. He would generously share ideas and aspirations he nursed for his fellow Zomis. He had this habit of saying: *I will do my part. Let the world say what.*

He knew his views and ideologies were appreciated by as many people as that did not. But he was not a man to be so easily deterred. I still remember one jewel of advice he gave me. Rather, it was a discourse. For lack of a one-liner, let me boil it down to a summarization. To complicate my handicap, the fine grains of his words had started stealing between the fingers of my memory. I should have given more time diarizing.

I am a chicken-hearted man, easily discouraged, especially if criticized for what I have to write. I used to resent readers for not being appreciative enough of the efforts we'd spared as writers. To that he gave me this gem, with his tiny girlie giggle—

"The Zomis are not ready for serious reading," he said. I don't know what he meant by 'serious reading'. Anyway, he went on: "As a matter of fact, the entire tribal community of our district is not ready. Write to entertain if you are after appreciation. But if you wish to shape a nation, prepare our people for greatness and greater achievements, then, you must write what is right. Poke the truth. Nothing under the sun is beyond question. Let your conscience speak and follow your heart.

"Nobody likes the truth." He continued. "But the apostles died for it. Every great soul died for it. Even Jesus died for it. Do you think Jesus meant only the spiritual aspect when he says, 'Love your neighbours'? Truth is truth—spiritual or temporal. It is universal.

"If one in a thousand understands the truth, the world would be a better place. Similarly, if one in a thousand Zomi understands the truth our writers write, Zogam would have already been a reality. If one in a thousand Zomi understands what you write, then you are already an accomplished writer. Don't worry. Just write in your part. That's the challenge. Let the world say what!"

High flying philosophies, indeed.

Mr. Ngaihte was not a man to dispense advice he did not take. In fact, he took his own pills seriously. There was a mission to which he was committed before he slumbered: To dig up all the past literature that were politically and socially enlightening to the Zomis and reproduce them in the *Voice of New Lamka*, the local weekly he was editor to, till his final departure; and to give the new generation writers a boost by liberal publicity.

"I am a poor man. I could not get their stories published in a remunerative way," he used to say. "But at least I could take advantage of my editorship and give them the thrust they needed in their writing career."

With Mr. Ngaihte bowing out, I've lost a friend, a listener, a counsellor, a mentor. Whether the Zomis count it a loss I don't know. He was a courageous man who wavered not even when the odds favoured him not. A firm upholder of the principles he believed in. An advocate of abundant sharing of ideas for the common good. A man straightforward yet soft-spoken, mild yet firm in his judgment. And above all, affable.

On a personal plane, it was his attempt to reproduce some articles of mine, especially those laced with socio-political idiosyncrasies. In spite of my misgivings and lack of drive, he managed to talk me into giving up a story or two. For instance, he republished a certain story of mine that has the erstwhile run-up to state assembly elections as a point of reference. In consequence, I was aggressively disparaged from all cardinal points. In fact, the article was so old it elicited no response when it was first published in the *Lamka Post* on the eve of the previous polling about five years ago taken from that time.

Do these disapprovals or rather responses indicate our growing awareness in our socio-political condition today? Are we beginning to take more interest in our political and social wellbeing? Is my article taking effect in its second avatar? Did Mr. Ngaihte really foresee the coming of these socio-political curiosities? What must have he seen when he contemplated to disinter all those old stories?

At that time, I was filled with illusions, wasting time on an armature of a story called *Zogam: A Possibility*. Like any author, I would lay down my basic structure to trace my own course of progression. Obviously, such a roughhewn outline never made to the final cut. To tell the truth, the story itself never took off.

For the subtle skill of Ngaihte's persuasion, I happened to let him sneak a peek into this condensed preliminary. It appeared that I was putting down the very words in his mind. He would cluck his tongue and flash me that tiny, enigmatic smile of his. But he seldom nodded. And, you know, he had this peculiar mannerism of squinting both eyes simultaneously when he was sceptical or pleased. His lips would shut tight and slightly curve at the right corner. Actually, at such times he would look more like an old man trying to make out with his weakening eyesight. He passed me one of that look at the moment. Was he sceptical? Was he pleased? That's a puzzle he left me to work out alone. Later, he persisted to have a copy of the draft.

As everybody knows, a draft is nothing but an outline, a writer's lodestone, bristling with signposts, pointers and markers. A treasure map that makes no sense to the reader. Obviously, I refused. He stood his ground. I stood mine. Not till the peace-dove splayed its reconciliatory olive branch. Mr. Ngaihte was not a man to be contented with a downer. Without being pushy or causing any bitterness, he pressed on till he let me part with the prelude. The diplomat in him!

"You're making me look like a real writer," I joked.

"And you're acting like one," pat came a wisecrack almost before I could complete myself.

He never ran short of a repartee, at least as far as between us is concerned. His spirit of game was boisterous. His purposes were noble. It was my poor wordsmithy that dissuaded me from sharing my dream-story that's still in a conceptual phase. And perhaps will forever be!

A week later the preface made to the *Weekly's* editorial.

Indulge me to dwell a tad longer in a story that followed our outline episode.

As if to bear out Mr. Ngaihte's foresight, a year or thereabout later, a good friend of mine got appointed editor of a prestigious youth organization's Silver Jubilee Souvenir publication. He called on me one day to seek permission for reproduction of the article. He said he had come across the feature in a certain issue of the *Voice of New Lamka* some time back and so liked it that he preserved a cut-out. There was nobody who ever admitted to have liked anything I wrote. The human in me immediately buckled to the flattery. Did this friend of mine know he would be made editor of a publication one day? Or was it Mr. Ngaihte's prescience at work?

Days passed. I got disillusioned. The wind got blown off my sails. And my fancy project broke down. I tried to pick up the threads again later. But I got too practical in life. Absurdities like Zomi/Zogam could enchant me no more. I lost steam. The half-worked story got mummified in layers of dust and cobwebs within the binary coffins of a computer hard disk.

I never believed Zomis read with their hearts. It took a fallen comrade to teach me that some do! Had he still breathed the crispy air the Zomis breathe; Had he still drunk the icy waters the Zomis drink; Had he still walked the fragrant soil the Zomis walk today, he would surely nag me on to dot the last period in the book I once lost my heart to. Our heart! Our book!

Oh, comrade! Have you not fallen too soon? Was it true that whom God loves die young? Oh, death, the leveller! Have you not stung the wrong man at the wrong time? Alas! Alas!

Before I make myself go at it again and put my manliness to shame, let me drop the curtain by calling up a verse from the evergreen *Eagles'* number, *Hotel California*—

You can check out any time you like,

But you can never leave...

Adios, comrade! U Lian, fare thee well!

Chapter 4

ONE DAY AT A TIME

I am never known to be an early riser. I usually wake up at eight. Sometimes even later. I've got my legs pulled a lot for that. I loved sitting up late nights. Not to make up for the late-riser tag. Just habit. Being a night owl suits me better, I think. The nursery rhyme early-to-bed-and-early-to-rise-makes-a-man-healthy-wealthy-and-wise doesn't necessarily apply to me. As for me, when I wish to put down words on paper, late nights open my mind better than dozy mornings.

On a normal day, once up, I would begin my day with a visit to the loo. First things first. I am glad Sardar Vallabhbhai Patel, the iron man of India, shared the habit with me. He was said to have always spent his first waking hours in the toilet. So used to the custom that a slight miss would make my bowels sulk and remain unmoved for the whole day. Down with constipation!

Well, such a come down on a trivial issue like a non-cooperative gut may sound too harsh. But getting confined entire mornings in an Indian-type commode with a sullen bowel is justification enough, I guess. My father had put up on the restroom wall a handwritten slogan: "Give thanks to the Lord for your proper movement!" At the time, it sounded ridiculous. Even repulsive. But once the rebellious bowels take you over, you'd start realizing its real significance.

The frustrating restroom exercise done, I would pick up my blossoming toothbrush and walk over to the wash basin to admire me staring back from the mirror above the sink. Frankly speaking, there isn't much to adore in me or my looks despite my inward handsomeness. Especially now, with a glistening coat of sweat on the face and body-grease accumulated over the night. Unfortunate fact is that there's nothing I could do or add to my inborn appearance that's too far from good. Yet, that very fact always teaches me the first lesson of the day: Be glad with what God has for you!

In fact, it was a torture to watch the far-from-pleasant sight every morning and stick bristles into the orifice and furiously work up lather until thick gooey overflows the lips. That, in no way, is an improvement upon the grotesque vision. Okay, enough to this self-glorification, I mean, self-gorification. Let's turn to the other members of my family and see how they fared.

First, the larger part of me. My better half.

It's no brainer to guess that she would be up well before I do. Whether she took her first leak first, that I of course do not know. It's hard to tell because I never heard from her that typical brook-like gurgle women doing the thing makes. My wife, since I've known her, has conscientiously made it a point to make the least possible noise when answering nature's call.

In spite of such fuss over the pee, she loved pooping at the oddest of moments: Sometimes in the dead of night, sometimes dead at noon, sometimes at bedtime, and occasionally at mealtimes. This haphazard cleansing ritual would make many a lively topic for our marital debates. I would call it improper. She would conveniently brush it away as nature. No big deal, anyway.

However, I do know what she would do as she gets off the bed.

She would dive right into the kitchen and rattle among the pots and pans. Without much ado, she would locate the teapot and get the milk boiling in a trice. Turning the gas off, she would then rush to the other room where my daughter and her cousin-sister, Linda, shared their bed.

I hate to add this: But I must be remiss if I say my wife is the most soft-spoken person in the world. However, one should not jump to conclusions and make her a shrew. It's merely that her voice is innately high-pitched and she's not given to sweettalk—a quality I rather liked about her. She doesn't sugarcoat her words. She speaks straight from the heart.

In the early days of our dating, I too was of the impression that she was born with a blown fuse. Not that I am free from having trying times today figuring out if she's pleased or incensed. For, be it a fit of fury or frenzied jubilation, she would sound all the same. Regardless, to me, that's what makes her one in a thousand. Special. Unique. For that I heartily sing along with Jim Reeves:

But most of all I love you,

'Coz you are you...!

Enough of this wife-bashing! Where were we? Oh, yes! She was waking up our daughter.

Our dear baby, Kimkim, is not a soul to stir before a hundred shakes. A heavy sleeper that she was and still is! As a toddler, she would just recline on the settee, bottom planted on the floor, and slumber away as though she's snoozing on the comforts of a feathery bed. There's one easy way to rouse her though. Especially if she was half asleep which is much against the popular belief that a person half-asleep is hard to wake.

She was an obsessive thumb-sucker. And she twirled her locks. Except in deep sleep, she would constantly suckle on her thumb, rolling her tresses with the other forefinger at the same time. Pull the plugs and you get her up even without asking. She may offer a weak resistance and try to thrust the thumb back in. Hold it fast. She'll whine a little. But in no time, she'll get that it's time to give up her sleep and of course her thumb with it.

A while later, she would stagger into the study, still in a sleepy daze, only to flop down on the narrow coir-strip cut off from an old mattress and laid out on the floor for sitting or lying. Her big-finger finding her mouth again. Before she relapsed into another slumber, mother would disgorge her books from her schoolbag as she sat her up straight. Not in seconds, they would start engaging in a spelling spree or a scribbling fury. Concerned mother all the while hollering by her side:

"Learn, learn."

"Say like this. Do like that."

"Write like this,"....and all that jazz.

Mothers!

It is indeed hard to school your own children. Your reserve of patience runs out even before you start making use of it. A hand goes up on its own volition and down comes a crash before you realize. It would not be long before you hear a slap here, a pinch there, a knock here—blows delivered on the frailty personification called Kimkim, our dear daughter. I know all this ferocity comes not from hate and certainly not meant to harm. The hand seems to have a mind of its own but the heart grieves even before the strikes landed. Parents' love is indeed unfathomable and mysterious that even the slightest mistake evokes instant corrective action. Spare the rod and spoil the child, says the Bible.

In a short while, Kim's voice would begin to quaver like an opera singer, her eyes drowned in a pool of tears. In her fright for the next wallop, all she had learnt would fly away altogether. The harder she read the more she seemed to unlearn. And this, in turn, would infuriate mummy all the more.

Now, this hue and cry would snap me up from my morning reverie about taking an interesting turn. I would try to shut it out to catch a few more winks to get the dream going again. But the more I tried the more the morning noise percolated. To hell with education, I thought, not really meaning it.

The yesteryears seemed more promising than today, at least for the kids. In those days, there's no need to worry till they grow strong enough to take up their parents' trade which was nothing but a slash-and-burn cultivation. Today, in contrast, even a five-year old has to carry an oversized overweight schoolbag and bark at the print without making any sense out of it. Moreover, she must learn to write although her hands are yet too weak to hold a pencil, let alone develop a proper motor coordination. On top of that, we expect them to excel in their studies when everything to them is nothing but pure Greek.

Predictably, a hand goes up again and comes down in a dull thud. Daughter fended. But her puny hands were too poor a defence against the pile of flesh that bears down upon her. That does it all. Welling tears now began to rush in a mighty wave of a tsunami.

"Crying won't help you learn," yelled mother, outraged at the unleashing of tear-gate.

A palm rose again.

"No more, Mummy," pleaded daughter. "Please!"

"Why don't you put your head to it before I had to hit you?" mother herself would be in the brink of tears.

It's not that mother doesn't know the blows would be too much for her frail sweetie. It's only that her child not learning her lessons is too much for her to take. The thought of her children being ill-educated and lagging behind is what drives her mad.

I wiggled out of bed, abandoning the prospect of a fancier twist in the dream. They say morning dreams come truer than ordinary night dreams. But can I help? I'll try again next morning.

Now, as is my custom, I would step into the restroom where I would toil like a cartman lugging his pushcart up hill. There, in the confines of the privy, I would huff and puff and pant and push and shove. If you ever saw a new mother labouring, I think you get the picture of my plight.

Frequently alternating my weight on the knees didn't help. With plenty of time in hand, I would take my time cursing the eastern style commode. But would perching uncomfortably on a western pot ease me better? As far as I know, no. Because I never got used to the elongated commode! I hope to learn it one day.

In the meantime, the goings on in the study would soften my emotion to pulp. My precious daughter, I said to myself in silence, I hope you'll grow up one day and understand. The strikes that fall on your tender back fall as hard on our hearts. With every smack on your cheek, we are driving a spike into our own souls. Parents indeed discipline their children out of sheer love. And it takes me my own children to learn this lesson.

I sniffled hard. A little too hard, in fact. A powerful odour, pleasing in no way, shot up the veins upon the forehead. The point where the eyes and the nose meet felt a burning sensation. Indian toilets, even domestic ones, are not the best of places for such sharp nasal intake of air. Tears flowed with the sting of stench. The pulpy emotion instantly flitted away like scattered butterflies. I left the restroom in a huff.

Before dropping into the shower, I'd steal a peep into the bedroom to see our son, Dikdik, sprawled in the *Vitruvian-Man* style, still savouring his morning zees. Just a year more, I thought to myself. The knocks and whacks of learning are in store for you, young man. Just a year more. God!

Admittedly though, on most mornings even my son would overtake me in rising. Then, he, too, would be made to bury his head in his books although his studies were yet to be taken seriously. Not a nursery kid.

Now, facing the looking glass, I would take my sweet time admiring myself chewing on the blooming toothbrush. Meanwhile, the wall-clock would crawl to half past eight before mother would dismiss the study time.

What followed was most beautiful.

"Yay!" Kim would scream in glee, angelic beams of joy flashing across her little face as though nothing had happened and no blows delivered. Such innocence! The sea of pain in which she was drowned few minutes ago ebbed away in her childly exuberance. She put all the pinches and punches behind and began capering around with her little kid brother. Before long, they would be cackling like a pair of contented geese, screeching at the top of their tiny lungs. It seemed they wanted to make the most of the little time they still had before *naasta* and get dolled up for school. A jolly-molly time they had, indeed!

Not long before, laughter and gaiety would fill the house again like a sweet frankincense. The atmosphere lifted. Peace and harmony reigned supreme once more. Paradise regained, literally. And a house became a home again. Forsooth, children's voices are the sweetest music in the world!

Come breakfast time.

Mother had already had their cups of milk cooled to the right temperature with love. Then, she would scoop handsome measures of *Complan* into the cups and tip *Kellog's Cornflakes* or *Choco Duet* into their bowls of warm milk before feeding them with ever-solicitous hands of a mother. A picture of hairless fledglings twittering, opening their beaks as wide as they could as Mummy Birdie dips a worm each into every mouth, comes to mind. Mother's frayed nerves had instantaneously smoothed too.

Now she would be a mother as coddling as a mother could be. In no time, mother and children started playing in a jingling merriment. The day is on track again.

I rounded up my self-admiration as the kids got themselves done. No more time to lose, I would pull myself up in a cheap, local-made pair of shorts. But where are the goggles? These black glasses had their way of escaping my sight every day at this exact time. "Where've they gone?" I cried to no one in particular but meaning the obvious.

Mother would produce them in a flash as if by magic. Mothers do surely know every nook and cranny of the house. With glasses in place, we trotted down the flights of steps, kids holding both sides of my hands.

Sometimes, my niece, Linda, would leave for college before us. If so, mother would apply padlock to the door before coming after us. In addition to the kids' bags slung over her shoulders, she would have her hands occupied with oversized polythene-bags of garbage to be disposed at the community bin by the exit gate of the campus. In the meanwhile, I would be having the bike spurt to life and keep it running to warm the engine.

Dik would take his place, clambering on the gas tank and Kim would straddle to ride pillion. Behind them, mummy would expertly hop on to whatever little space left at the rear. Then, she hummed something like huh which is a signal for me to step onto gear and get going. I acted accordingly.

And off we go to school, purring on our *Bajaj Platina*.

There is one thing that gives me endless joy. Neither Dik nor Kim had ever hesitated going to school. Never did they throw tantrums. Rather, they loved their school. Or at least they seemed so. If they ever cried after us since their first day, I must have missed recollecting them!

There was one naughty incident involving Dik in the nursery though. One day, their teachers sent him home with the plastic holder of his identity card completely puffed up. His mother checked and found that the name label had been ripped into bits and pieces. It seemed he was quite stressed at something or somebody. That was the only thing my son ever broke or tore in tantrum till today.

To add a few lines more, my son had a speech difficulty. When he was just a toddler, learning to speak, we took him to Science City for a family outing. When it was time for breaking lunch, we ordered the famous *moghlai parantha* and ice-cream from the canteen. He would refuse to have either of them. He slavered with a clear saliva which suddenly raised our concern. His mother examined his mouth. And lo, erupting all over the soft membrane were white spots and pustules. No wonder he hesitated to take a bite of the crispy *moghlai*.

The ailment took some time to heal. But the damage was already done. It was right at the moment he was actively learning to speak. Since then, his words would drool and become unclear. This makes him reluctant to speak. Especially if you ask him to come again and again. He would rather shy away and refuse to open up. That seemed to have affected his psyche and sociability a lot. Not that he became irascible or rebellious. Rather, that makes him draw into his personal cave. He became an introvert. We had to try very hard to bring him out and make him utter words again. That's the only justification I had for his impatience and loss of temper in the school that day.

I had digressed.

Their school, at that time, was a Montessori playschool named *Empower*. It was at a stone's throw from our quarters complex. As such, fifteen minutes was quite sufficient for a trip to and from it. Apparently so, we would be home again without any loss of time.

Back home—

The instant we set foot into the house, I would rid myself of my attire, all the while cursing the morning heat with the best invectives I could make up. But don't presume I was doing the Archimedes-eureka-moment-act in front of my wife. I'll not demean myself with such an obscene behaviour. I was simply removing my shirt, leaving the upper torso naked but protecting the pride zone with a Manipuri *gamsa* wrapped around the waist. Such an act is contrarily called *'putting on uniform'* in our small-family parlance.

We've come to the frying plains from the chilly hills. So, adapting to the searing heat is no mean feat. We prayed for a skin as versatile as that of a chameleon's. But such prayers, being against nature, had no ready answers. Rather, we had to boost up our endurance power and find ways to cope with it. *Putting the uniform* is one basic defence mechanism.

As for the male folks, we would simply shed our covers when indoors at the flimsiest pretext unless you could afford a fixed air-conditioner or a *Thanda Thanda Cool Cool* talc. Unfortunately, though, this is not exactly suitable for the female folks. That, I think, is one disadvantage of being the fairer sex. They're not without a befitting dress code though. As if to override the demure code, the bolder ones would do with the scantiest of fabric on their framework. Hemlines would go up proportionately with the rise of the mercury. The V on the neckline would drop droolingly low. They're simply making way for freer air circulation.

Unfortunately, amorous mainland lechers would (mis)take this as a signal for readiness to mate. They would misconstrue that once these ladies get high on *Skimpy Derringdo*, they would far out-dare their male counterparts. They take our lasses would have no compunction in defying outdoor decorum. Apparently so, with their revealing apparels, our ladies, unbeknownst to them, often leave a long trail of unwanted admirers behind them.

To the mainland Romeos, they're paragons of beauties. Vanilla cream on top of a chocolate biscuit. *Princesses of Desire* adrift from *Fantasyland* into the world of *Fantasizeland.* Their thighs are pure tenderness, succulent shoots of *aloe vera*; their sweet cleavages plunged to captivate their horny eyeballs. Before long, much against their intention, they would steal a million hearts of drooling street-side gawkers. As rats are to the Pied Piper, mainland Romeos are to the chinky lasses. They have a huge eyeball-following wherever they go.

Enough of this didactic oration.

Presently, my wife whom I call 'Darl', short for Darling, would flick on the idiot box. Soap operas on Star Plus, to be precise. For a moment, she would disappear into the kitchen and reappear with our morning tea and snacks. Despite my initial lack of enthusiasm, I began to enjoy some serials like *Sasural Genda Phool, Tere Liye and Saath Nibhana Sathiya*. This last one we just called *Gopi Bahu* after the docile lady protagonist.

Perhaps, overexposure has won me over. I even developed a preference for the opus Tere Liye because it was set in Kolkata, the city I am living. The others I watched from the corners of my eyes while skimming the Kolkata edition of the *Times of India*. If no particular headline catches my eyes, then I would just weave through the subheads and spare the soaps more attention.

We sipped the tea while my Darl would enlighten me on the acts and scenes I missed out or failed to follow. You won't believe, she could even talk about the past and the future of the plays. Sometimes we engaged in animated disagreements about the drama or something completely different. I couldn't stop wondering how our womenfolk make out the Hindi dialogues so well without speaking a smattering themselves. One beauty of these soaps is that they leave a lot of room for speculation. Our inconclusive arguments would oftentimes spin out of control and end up in heated verbal contests! We would level our best efforts as though we are representing our respective species and losing would spell everlasting doom upon our kinds. But that's one joy of married romance, I guess. To tell the truth, I had cultivated the taste of soap operas to accommodate my wife's love for them.

Now, let truth be told: we shared a common guilty pleasure. We're heavy consumers of sweetened betel nuts that come by the trade name *Sweety Supari*. The same was familiar to us back home as Goldie. Why I choose to have this betel nut concoction with my wife is another story altogether.

In a short while, the operas would wind up one after another. They're mostly half-hour air-times. There is one kind of soap I cannot bring myself to like though: The Korean soaps. They are far too lengthy—running into hours and hours and even more. I do watch a couple of them however. I like *Four Sisters*. I also heard of *The Green Rose, Stairway to Heaven*, etc. But I didn't have the pleasure of boring myself with them.

Now, my Darl would do the teacups while I hit the bathroom yet again. It's that hot. This time, I would take a full-blown shower to re-emerge as fresh as the majestic Monarch Butterfly breaking out of its pupal chrysalis. Sliding into a pair of crisply ironed trousers, I again came to face the looking glass. This time, sizing up a much better-looking me. A generous mist of Brute under the armpits and the chest with an ample scoop of after-shower gel to slick up my ever-dry hair. Then, I would fling a formal *kameez* on top of my blubbery profile and tuck it between the faux leather belt and the paunch that's beginning to assume ungainly proportions.

Tucking the shirt is a rather recent habit of mine. I seldom practiced it in my younger days, unless put under compulsion by a formal situation or something like that. "Tuck your shirt in, you idiot!" My Darl would call after me in the early days of our wedlock. But I used to dismiss her so brusquely that she soon gave up reminding me altogether.

Putting on smart shoes is also not a custom of mine. Rubber flipflops do just fine for me. You won't miss me lazily dragging a pair of well-worn slippers on most occasions. But, of course, not on Sundays or special events when we had to make attendance in formal attires.

Anyway, in a jiffy, I would be done for office!

Now, with a black office-bag slung across the left shoulder down to the right hip, and a wallet in the shirt pocket, I started down the stairs again. My Darl would see me off to the door till I sunk out of view into the stairwell. Traditionally, we have no bye-byes, no ta-tas. No hugs and kisses. No come-back-soons. Just, "Fine, then". The same is with getting back home. Westerners would sorely miss these sweet-nothings should they take our ladies in marriage. And our ladies would have trying times learning to fawn their husbands so. Just my imagination. In reality, not a few of our women have entered into union with them. So, they might not be total strangers to the French kiss and bear hugs after all.

I would reach my office inside a minute. Being in the rank of the smallest fries, my office life bears no much import. It is humdrum at best. Apart from the clamour and wranglings of the local employees, or employees who speak the local language; a boss berating a subordinate; a direct recruit inducted without a scrap of training; or a senior officer denigrating a promotee-clerk, et al, there's nothing to provoke the reader's interest here.

One habit of these city folks confounds me no end though. Why should they always shout like they're all deaf? Are they really hard of hearing? Or, is that their normal way of communication? Are we to blame it on sound pollution? I leave that for you to take the shot.

By two in the afternoon, I would be back to the quarters for lunch. Our regular diet principally consisted of pulses and potatoes. I don't much like the vegetables out here. They are too sweetish and reek of fertilizers. My Darl would sometimes be still on her soaps. But mind you, there are no chores unattended because of her TV-time. I wonder how she fits everything so efficiently into her domestic workload. A friend of mine once told me that everybody is allotted equal time: 24 hours. "He who manages well," he said, "has time for everything." My darling is a living testament of this tenet.

Engorging yourself with my Darl's preparations is a feast in itself. Slurping that yellowy lentil curry with a mouthful of boiled rice that cannot stick together. That's nothing less than chicken-fry with your dearest beloved dining beside you! Before long, your hands run over a contented belly. Then I would laze happily on our triple-XL ULamlal-sized wooden chairs. Actually, the chairs themselves had been given us by him. The kids would either join us at the table or have their siestas. In no time, the heat and the food would sing me lullabies. Then, I would curl up like a fox in a foxhole and slip into a power nap.

About an hour later, I would be back in the office.

As already said, office stories are more or less similar for all office goers. I, therefore, need not dwell at length here to save time and space. Save for instances that broke the monotony once in a while, every day comes and goes at its own pace. Perhaps, that is why work-life is called 'routine'.

The thick walls of our office building and the Venetian blinds make marking outside time nearly impossible. Yet the biological clock does not miss. You simply know when the sun sinks to rest. Then, everybody would flutter away like birds homing for their nests.

Again, nights are as uneventful as days. Children would dance and prance and create havoc with their toys and dolls. Parents stay glued to the idiot-box, if not argue on a certain triviality. Or you're anticipating the masked Jason to axe his hapless victim to death when suddenly the channel jumped from *HBO to Cartoon Network*. What the heck! How did this technological glitch develop all of a sudden?

One pastime every family indulges in, I guess, is fighting for that piece of electronic called Remote Control. Parents and children are veritable rivals at it. As for the ongoing situation, one of the kids had laid a hand on the RC, and of course not without a hue and cry, the channel would be forced to jump back from where it had skipped over. This tug-of-war for the possession of the priceless trophy would end only with dinnertime—at least for the time being. If not Sunday, the fare would be the same dal, aloo curry!

Nine O' clock: *The Battle of Remote Control* resumes.

Stations zap from *World Movies to Pogo, Nickelodeon to Sony Pix, to Zee Cinema to Star Gold, to Tom and Jerry to Mr. Bean, the animated series*....so forth and so on. The battle raged on until mother would intervene, of course, with a tacit leaning towards the grownups. Not without a huff and a puff, the tiny contenders would be browbeaten to give in at last.

Now, soulful Hindi songs would start belting out from Sony's *Indian Idol*. My Darl would raise the volume as high as the neighbourhood would permit. Away with our own advisories for the kids to keep the decibels within decent limits. In days when *Idols* didn't compete, the children would be herded to their books until they read themselves to sleep. I need not retell the travails of their study routine.

By eleven or close to midnight, I would be given my quiet time.

Then, I would start going through a book or an article. Or I may start writing one on stupid subjects like the one you're reading right now.

Shortly later, I would take a brief shower before I hit the bed to finally call it a night.

I am an insomniac. My eyelids may pretend to die for one another. But hit the bed and they would start suing like a couple intent on going their respective ways. In the melee, sleep would quietly slip away through the windows. Then, I would be forced to walk down the halls of memory and lost myself in the lane of fantasy. I don't believe in counting sheep. That's European and doesn't apply to me. Rather, I'd sore my eyes reassessing the day that had just passed. Not to probe the wrongs I might have committed or the things that have gone awry. Yet, no attempt of mine to get sleep back would be crowned with success. So, the next natural thing that happens when you allow your mind to run riot on a sleepless night is to conjure up pictures of the terrible Second Coming of Christ or wallow in self-pity. Then, you would pray your heart out until you scare yourself to sleep.

But for me, all these things are redundant. I had tried them all. None of them worked anymore. Miss Somnolence seemed to have left me for good. She has flown to the farthest corners of the earth where my miserable pleas could never reach her ears. I would often play a trick to cajole her. I would feign sleep, hoping the goddess would steal a peep to see if I had actually fallen off without her help. I was fooling nobody but my own self. All my efforts went in vain. Eventually, I would decide to give up trying altogether.

Perhaps, my helplessness won her sympathy. Or has she fallen for the ruse after all? Lady Sleep began to drift in slowly through the casements with a whiff of cool air. From the mountaintops of my beloved Zogam? My mind raced, nearly scaring Wary Sleep off again. Stupid me! It's the sea breeze from the Bay of Bengal. Far, far away from my homeland. No more time to ruminate. The eyelids began to make peace. I am the winner now. But, by then, the night would have already marched into the wee hours of dawn. Twilight would already threaten to drive away the stars. Somehow, I must induce myself to sleep. Otherwise, anon, I shall be jolted out of a prospective morning dream again!

Wait! Wait! Before I finally draw the curtain, I still have one last reflection to make.

Hum! What a blessed day that was! The day that had just ended. A day of peace and merriment! A day of love and joy! What more could I ask? Now that the deep night had passed, I commit me and my family to our guardian angel. And a little prayer on the lips to be woken up to a sparkling new dawn. Yes, to a new page of life. To turn the wheel of yet another blessed karma! And that's all that matters in life.

One day at a time.

*

Suddenly, there was a blinding flash of light.

In the dazzle, I saw a lady with the most exceeding beauty. A beauty even the mind is not capable of conjuring up. She was in a lustrous gown of gossamer, billowing around her feet in whorls of gentle waves. Turning to me, her rosy lips slowly curved into a persuasive smile. Then, slowly, in a slow motion, her mouth opened. And called out in a strident voice: *Kimkim! Wake up!*

Lo, there goes my morning dream again!

Chapter 5

THE DRAWERS AFFAIR

It so lately happened that drawers of our office bureaux develop a sudden fondness for locking themselves up on their own accord. The first case of such 'drawer sulks' occurred to Miss Dolly Baral, our Deputy Office Superintendent. After several failed attempts, she turned to me for help. I gave it a try and found them engaged indeed somewhere at the back, inside the covering metal case. I knocked around for some time. First with gentle slaps, then jerks, then soon with almost violent rips. They didn't budge an inch.

Having no lock to hold fast, I could remove the topmost tray with no difficulty. Then, slithering my hand into the dark interiors of the box, I probed for a clasp or whatsoever the sliders are latched on to. I felt a steel rod which could be moved up and down. Gotcha! I patted myself on the back with a smirk of self-congratulation.

I pushed the hook down hoping to pop the trays out as if by magic. Nothing happened. I pulled. Nothing either. I pushed and pulled impulsively. The catch seemed to have perfectly fallen into place. And my coercions seemed to make the fasteners all the more defiant. The Miss D.O.S. would have definitely laughed at me had she seen my concealed helplessness.

Then, I slammed the tin side-panels hard as if to scare it to throw up its metal captives. I wasn't taking recourse to the proverbial wisdom of our legendary ancestors. Admittedly, many of such wise tales are nothing but pieces of fables. The sagacious anecdote to which I am referring here goes that a tortoise never let go once it bit your fingers until the thunder rumbles. Now, in all unlikeliness, freak accidents do really happen. A tortoise once really snapped on the fingers of a friend our ours. The wisdom I've just alluded to was so prevalent at the time that we, in spite of being minors, immediately knew what to do.

Looking around, we found a rusted oil tin which we drummed furiously above the critter's head. Fortunately, the tortoises that caused such mishaps weren't big enough to chew off our fingers. But it was unfortunate at the same time that our weather simulations did not work as our great sires had us believe. Such failures, however, did not shake our belief in our long-standing traditions and in the sagacity of our forefathers.

The steel locker held firm, resisting my massive efforts to deliver freedom to its oppressed metallic subjects. I was quite at a loss by now. Perhaps, it's time I admit it's a mechanic's job. After all, it is an automatic locking system presently hell bent on teaching the Miss a lesson to not mishandle it in the future. Should I manage to disengage the salvers without any equipment or special expertise—by sheer physical force as I was applying at the mo—wouldn't the very idea and purpose of a 'safety lock' be compromised? Would it be any less crime than picking somebody's private safe? And would the manufacturers be humoured by my 'forced entry' to render their guarantee of 'fool-proof security' an overstatement?

I scratched my head as everybody does when beaten or baffled. I felt like giving up and suggest a proper handler summoned instantly. But something in my heart, what Gandhiji would obsessively call 'inner voice', told me that I had come real close to uncovering the secrets of its working principle. Inwardly, inasmuch as the bureau was hell bent on holding on, I was hell bent on giving it another try.

My other instinct—everyone's got a pair each, don't we—however, reproached me to not meddle with public property, especially if things go technical or mechanical and you are not employed or paid to work it. If an auto-lock system has tripped, let it trip. It is doing what it's meant to do. It should stay put that way as proof of breach.

I hold both intuitions valid. The former being an inquisitive attitude of a contemporary scientific-tempered mind whereas the latter a sane man's approach to not-trouble-trouble-until-trouble-troubles-you. I've learned a lesson on the latter intuition the practical way.

It was one fine day in the office. Perhaps October or November 2007. I was a wet rookie in the service. That day, I heard a constant rattling noise coming from the computer cabinet nearby. It was a light unremitting clatter. But it was enough to interfere with the peace of the workroom. It was not a boomer but no less adding to the hum of the near-century-old blades of the overhead fans slicing the air with grating whooshes. My do-gooder nature instinctively jumped into action, prompting me to inspect the annoying PC case.

I was soon fiddling with the cabinet with a coin-driver, I mean, with a coin as a screwdriver. Trying to unscrew the flank panel. Evidently, there were no screwdrivers lying around in an office where jobs are more ministerial and clerical in nature. In no time, I detected that one of the side cooling fans had its fastening nuts loose. It might've been dislodged by the constant tremor of the whirring tiny fan-vanes.

I was nearly done with the screws when a certain Inspector, Debojit Kar by name, interjected: "Are you authorized to service that?"

"What if I am not?" I shot back immediately, somewhat peeved for his doubting my ability. "What use is your computer-knowledge if you cannot attend to such minor problems?"

"I don't mean that," he replied, taking no note of my sarcasm. I was almost happy that he sounded chastised. He continued: "What if the matter's worse than you thought? And you instead damage the machine further? Or if it later develops a snag and all blame is laid on you? You cannot produce a contract paper for servicing that PC. Can you? Are you ready to own up responsibility?"

A running tirade I did not expect.

Mr. Kar's voice was not a friendly type. It is high pitched and has a somewhat girly tinge. But his words that I initially considered contemptuous turned out to be clarified caution. It wasn't before a year that I came to see the red alert. I consequently developed respect for this gentleman although big pride stood in the way from making me admit it. I am not ready to take any responsibility on the event of further breakdown. Neither am I a qualified hardware geek. Not only was I not authorized, my service in that particular situation was not solicited, not wanted, and not required.

It suddenly dawned upon me that my do-gooder disposition could land me in a hotter soup. Better stick to my assigned job— nothing more, nothing less. Bitter truth is that, in Government fraternity, by and large, the altruistic notion of 'walking the extra mile' is not appreciated nor invited. Besides, in this particular circumstance, I did not possess the requisite expertise to 'walk' the 'extra mile'. Thanks to Mr. Kar's timely intervention. I was redeemed from being a butt of charges for my voluntary philanthropic service.

Back to the crux of the problem.

Miss Baral was still waiting by my side. My mental detour had not helped me extricate the drawers in any way. A tiny pair of hopeful eyes was bearing down on me, almost begging. She was visibly anxious that her files or whatever stuck inside had to be forced out somehow and damaged in the process. I cannot disappoint her. More so, I cannot disappoint me. Especially after having learnt where the obstacle lies. Fact is, only the solution eluded me.

Once again, I gingerly snaked my hands into the black inlands of the mysterious tin-box, groping for something I did not know but believed and expected to be there. Somewhere. Here...there...I fumbled around for a moment. And lo, there it was! An iron clasp. Obstinately clutching on to the left corner of the slider.

I pressed the clasp. It didn't move. I pressed it harder. Still nothing. How on earth could you open a door on which it is clearly stencilled PULL? I circled my index finger around the grab and applied a gentle lift. Bingo!

The salver sprang out like an animal freed from the bottom of a dry well. Using the same technique, I effortlessly set the lowest dish also free. Freer still was the relief breathing down my neck! Miss Baral flashed me an unrestrained smile. Probably her widest.

Now, even tables seemed to have their own peculiar way of spreading news. Not long before, one set of drawers after another began to throw the gauntlet down my face. They seemed to taunt me if I could beat them at their own mysterious game. So, they began to shut themselves tight until I should be compulsorily sent for. In fact, more than a couple of times had I to scuttle between the Establishment and the Accounts sections to fight for the 'Liberty of Drawers'. I think I had become a freedom fighter of sorts.

In no time, I became an expert in unlocking drawers!

Actually, that's an attribute credited to me by my mainland colleagues. They were simply amazed at the ease with which I wheedled the metal trays out after they'd spent all their wits in vain. That's what they said. Not my words. Once they recognized my skill, they would never bother to give it a try but send for me straight away. However, there's one imperfection in my so-called expertise. If you knock in the drawers back too hard, the auto-locks will trip and we would have to start probing the dark interiors all over again. This secret still evaded my proficiency. So, the only way to avoid the problem in future, as I advised or rather warned my friends, was: "Don't push in too hard!"

Naturally, everybody was curious to know how hard is "too hard". Within seconds, all the drawers would end up stuck and bolted again. Not before a few more demonstrations would they understand how hard is too hard. It was not until June 11, 2009 that a mechanic had to be brought in at last. For lack of finality in my execution, the drawers I freed would be unfreed all over again by one push a little too hard every time.

A Mr. Chittaranjan Mondal, T.A., dealing assistant of the G. L. Section, had me sent for. And without hesitation I performed my *jaadu,* as they called it, again. Mr. Mondal's drawers were the last I tackled before that fateful day in June. Being the last encounter is not what makes Mondal's desk stand out though. Rather it was the secret discovery I made in working out the elusive auto-lock system. I had not told anybody about it. That's my trade secret. Moreover, mainland *babus* (and everyone in general, I guess) are too unconcerned to ask what they considered not their business. I might have told them how to handle the situation had they bothered to ask from the beginning itself.

On the 11th instant, under the unbearably hot and humid noon of Kolkata summer, Miss Baral's drawers refused to turn out yet again. She was sweating more in irritation than from the heat. As a minor detail, I should mention that the central air conditioning system of our office had underperformed for some time now. That was a delight to me though. I could not stand the sharp odour of the coolant and the constant low temperature. I am with a lingering old asthma and joint pains. But the system could not stop toiling away for the others. It has to offer relief from the onrush of heat waves that were merciless and coming in unnatural frequency that year. And I could not simply complain about that. It would be too selfish.

As for the task at hand, had I not had that little secret up my sleeve, I would not have stopped wondering why all the drawers developed that sudden inclination to shut themselves up over and over again since the recent past.

At the moment, I was engaged with a certain work and couldn't spare time. Actually, that's a pretext to put off my supervisor from bidding me do her work at an easy beck and call. Moreover, I did not want to be labelled as the handyman of the office. So, I suggested she call a mechanic from anywhere she cares. She is the local and she must know, I said with a not so refined tone. She did as told but not without a grudge.

A gangly mechanic appeared as quick as a genie. Throwing his tool-bag open on the marble-floor, he launched into work in right earnest, making the same noises I had made before. He pushed, he pulled, he slapped. I had made use of all those antics to no fruition. In vain did the mechanic re-employ them presently. Moments later, he was as baffled as I was. Yet there was one basic difference between he and I. He gave up after a few tries with a readymade excuse. I neither gave up nor offered an excuse until I figured the matter out.

"Pay me Rs. 160/- in advance," he demanded. "The thing cannot be set right without the use of proper tools." He said something like the box had to be dismantled and the locks removed and reconstructed or replaced.

Miss Baral gestured at me to the Mechanic. "He could do it easily without charging a penny," she challenged. The Mechanic obviously did not believe her. So, the Miss asked me to demonstrate my expertise!

I had regretted a bit refusing her earlier because she was my superior. Moreover, I had lately tried to be an obedient subordinate, even a bootlicker if need be because of circumstances beyond my control. [If you are patient enough to read through till 'the bitter pills' series that follow later, you'll understand]. So, I momentarily freed myself from the work at hand and went over to the scene immediately.

Then, reaching into the black box, I surreptitiously lifted the invisible hook. Lo and behold, out rushed the drawers to celebrate their regained independence!

Now, the Mechanic's eyes blazed in apparent displeasure. He spoke not for he was evidently at a loss for words. His brows knitted between his eyes in a tight wavy formation. In an unspoken defiance, he argued that the security device would trip again when the sliders would be reinserted. I allowed myself a contented smile. A characteristic reaction of human arrogance when you get something right and others don't. Had he known that I had beaten the lockmakers in their own game a couple of days ago, he would've scampered away like a beaten jackal, tail between legs.

I deftly refitted the drawers, sliding them in and out, even banging them noisily into the bays as if to say, 'No matter how hard you push, it won't lock again'.

Now, I must tell you the trick.

The drawers were built in such a way that there are sliders with sidewise furrows at the bottom of each tray. There are also wafer-thin metal sticks attached to the inward sides of the slots. When the trays are put in place the flat receivers perfectly dovetailed into the cloven sliders.

The ingenuity of the mechanism is that even if you missed those narrow grooves, the trays will still glide in alright. But on meeting the end of the receptacle, they'll hit the hook that will happily catch hold of the drawer and lock it into place. It is devised in such a way that the auto-lock system would instantly set-off on account of such ill fittings. In fact, this improper reinsertion sends off a signal that an unauthorized attempt has been made. It is this smart contraption that had me bewildered for a long time.

Now, back to the plight of the Mechanic.

He was literally speechless, gaping at me in disbelief. Then, forgoing his demand of advance payment, he turned to take his leave. I think it will take him some time to darken our office door again. "I better give him [meaning 'me'] the money," Miss Baral cried after him as he was seeing himself out. Then, turning to me, she said, "Why don't you start a servicing centre yourself and charge money for it?"

"That's a good idea!" I exclaimed.

It was as ridiculous as it was brilliant. Yet it was most impractical for my station at the time. Apparently, one cannot be an office-goer and a manager of drawer-workshop at the same time. The Bible says a man cannot serve two masters. My Superior can't really mean her words.

A smile cut across her face, as they say, from ear to ear That's a fee enough, I thought to myself. A fee she paid with a rare smile which made her almost beautiful.

Chapter 6

SOMEBODY TOUCHED ME

It was already morning when I was woken up by a stinging pain on the small of my back. But it was way too early to get up. It was a Sunday. I wanted to have a little more sleep. I had not slept well the night before. I was engaged in a vicious *Battle of the Net:* A nightlong guerrilla warfare under the cover of darkness.

I was evidently the loser: I lost sleep. I left the battlefield in the morning, eyes wildly bloodshot with complications of a bleary vision and a thrumming headache. Seeing me so vanquished, my wife got clearly upset. She grabbed the most advanced weapon invented till date for the purpose and set herself on the path of revenge: To kill them all and come back alone!

Not in minutes, she was back with a triumphant grin, bringing home the mortal enemy—*the Mosquito*—shocked out of his senses. The electric racquet had absolutely stood up to its name. I let the coldblooded, relentless foe, Monsieur Mosquito, have it all: I squished him between my fingers, crushing him completely—bones, body and soul. So hard did I squash him that even his Maker won't recognise him when he walked up the gates of mosquito-heaven, let alone grant him entry into the golden ramparts of eternity.

Since the wee hours of this morning, my back had refused to respond to my will. A searing pain had shot up as I twisted to turn on my side. This happened for quite some time now with varying degrees of intensity. I tried to raise my torso. But it proved to be too heavy. I slumped back on the mattress.

Then, wriggling my way bit by bit, I pushed myself up to a sitting position. Even then, I could only sit with an acute crook for a few seconds only. I picked up the pillow and tried to lean on the wall. But the back won't allow that either. It shocked me wide awake with a sharp sting. Not before a number of attempts could I bring myself prone again to find a pose that's a little more comfortable. By that time, sleep had already flown off the window and dared not peek in again. I squirmed every now and then with suppressed agony. I feared my better half, who was peacefully asleep by my side, would be stirred unnecessarily. When I could strike a pose that least hurt, my mind would run riot cursing two days and my entire life in general.

A couple of months ago, we were having our dinner on the biggest dining table we could afford—the living room floor. We had given up the table to follow the newly introduced national soccer competition called the *Indian Super League* and a Hindi soap opera *Kulfi Kumar Bajewala*. They were beamed exactly to coincide with our dinnertime. And what does that have to do with my backache?

I was sitting on the speckled floor, reclining on the front of the settee, when a numbing sensation invaded the whole bummy estate. My bottoms had gone to sleep. Dinnerplate in the right hand, I rotated my torso to prop myself up on the sofa. A soft crack about six inches above the waist, audible only to me due to direct bone conduction, stopped me right on track.

It was not outright painful. But it left me half twisted. I had to pause for a full few seconds before I could force a complete turn to bring myself up on the sofa. Hardly had I settled down then the pain started to set in. I nearly dropped the plate. But I thought it wasn't a big deal. A momentary prick that would pass. I was wrong. The pain did not go away for a long time. Only consolation is that it didn't hurt so much as to count it an impairment. That was till the tenth of October 2018.

On that fateful morning, I was on my way to office at Custom House along the Hooghly River. I was riding my little *Maestro Edge*. Traffic was not that heavy on the *Maa Flyover* until it began to take a slight dip at the ramp over Park Circus railway station. Here, the flow began to clog up a bit. Two-wheelers generally string along the left edge to gain advantage, especially in times of heavy traffic. Perhaps, Hero named my scooterette with this very circumstance in mind.

Like all bikes before and after me, I too threaded along the gap between the cars and the concrete wall to the left. Suddenly, the car in front of me swerved, practically cutting off my passage. Although not on speed, I still had to squeeze the brakes flat to the handlebar to reduce myself to a halt. My scooty was yet to taste servicing since I bought it a year and a half ago. I am a lazy man. And I knew that the brakes had not given their best performance since the last couple of months. The bike behind me was even worse. And the rider clearly had no connect with his vehicle as I do. He lost control. He came right at me, giving a nasty kiss to my scooty's arse.

A dull ache jabbed up my back. I could hardly turn to see what hit me. But a series of *Crime Patrol* on Sony TV which was a craze with me and my wife at the time influenced so much so that I struggled around to take down the registration of the offending bike:

WB20A D5252.

With no toppling and tumbling and no tangible external injuries, the accident could not be termed as a serious one. Probably it might be categorized as a mild mishap. The rider profusely apologized showing me the bottom of his shoe that bore heavy scrape marks. "Sorry, my brakes didn't do their job enough," he jabbered inside his helmet.

I glared at him with burning displeasure. But there was nothing more I could do. Jumping down and picking up a fight, slowing down the traffic, and creating a ruckus would have no point at all. Moreover, I had the disadvantage of not being a local. Immodestly, I also presumed I had better sense and refinement. Besides, wasting time on a scuffle would only make me late for office. There was nothing to prove the accident except a shooting pain that's still travelling up and down the spinal column like tiny electric shocks. Government believes in bloodspills and dead bodies, not in pains and agonies invisible to the naked eye. My alibi effectively cancelled out on the spot.

To stretch a short story long, let me add: *Maa Flyover* has recently become quite dangerous for bikers due to kite-flying in its close vicinity. Kite-flyers normally use alloy-coated strings. I could often see boys flying kites in the afternoons on unguarded terraces that literally abutted the flyover. A few bikers had been caught in their necks or faces, causing them grievous injuries.

A gory picture that came on the *Times of India* in a certain morning issue featured the exact location where I once saw these local boys with their kites. In fact, when I was revising this story a year after I originally wrote it, the Times of India reported that a certain man had died caught by the *manja* strings on the flyover.

That apart, on your way to office or back, you could often pass by a breakdown car or bike getting stranded and holding up traffic for long moments. And on several occasions, you may come across splashes of glass fragments left as reminders to a mishap a little while ago. The other morning, I happened to pass by a helmet lying haphazardly on the road. Its visor and front-part were utterly crushed. I could only wonder what would happen to the rider who had faced such a powerful blow. I rode past with a chilly thought. The same could happen to anybody. Me being no exception. The scary thought nearly spoiled the mood for the day.

Enough of this digression.

As for now, the pain on the ass, I mean, on the back, has subsided to some extent. But it never fully passed. Thus began my existence with a vestige of lingering backache. The most difficult situation being allowing my spine to assume its natural curvature when it hits. I was beginning to get used to the condition until my neighbour usurped my parking space for the umpteenth time. He's had a selfish way of taking space for two. In his absence, I always had to push his bike aside to allow mine to park. The other day, I had to do the same again.

Prone to ill luck, I wrong-twisted my back in the act and dropped the bike to the ground. The smell of gasoline immediately pervaded the air. With a huge effort, I took the two-wheeler by its horns, lifted it off-ground and finally pushed it out of the way. By then the damage had already been done. I had to limp up the staircase, pulling myself up by the metal banister, to the third floor where our apartment was. By the time I hit the doorbell, I was shivering with pain.

Answering the door, my wife helped me slowly down on the settee. I couldn't even lie supine. That was the most painful position. It was like a piece of ember dropped into the marrow. However, I could not announce this to everyone. It's a suffering I must personally bear.

Then, this morning! To wit, the morning of the Battle of the Net.

Woken by a needling pain, I could find no position to suit a relief. Every other way I turned proved to be more inconvenient than the one before. I assumed the foetus position that offered me a moment's respite. But not for long. The ache returned. I laid on my back. I turned on my tummy. I sat on my haunches and curled up like a threatened armadillo. Nothing helped.

Half an hour later, I forced myself to forget the pain and snatch a few more sleep to recompense yester-night's loss. The sting began to generate heat and form a layer of sweat along the folds of my throat. It was December. Yet I couldn't help but grab the air-conditioner remote control and switch it on. At the same time, the ceiling fan was working furiously overhead. The air began to cool.

Speaking of mishaps, let me take you yet on another digression tour. A rather long one at that. To what something that recently happened to me. It was January 21, 2019. Monday.

I was back from office in the evening. Round about six, I reached Manovikas Bus Stand near Desun Hospital along EM Bypass. Traffic was moderately heavy. It was presently held up by the red light at Ruby Island several metres ahead. Few bikes, including mine, were inching in an ant-file along the right flank of the road to skirt the congestion. Movement was literally restricted to a snail's pace for a while.

In a moment though, the vehicles started moving again in a reasonable crawl. Just as I was revving up to tail the bike before me, something bumped me on the right side. Lucky that the vehicles had not sped up as yet. I tried to steady myself with my feet but couldn't as I was already in motion. I lost balance and fell on the road, face down. My scooty dumped herself on top of me, pinning me down to the ground. Traffic was about picking up. I knew cars would be coming on towards where I had taken the fall.

With the instant I hit the macadam, I raised my upper torso to avoid being run over by oncoming traffic. A car did come to me. Its headlights screaming straight on my face. It screeched to a halt a few feet away. I heaved a sigh of relief. Believe it or not, you die when your time comes. I could feel the shadow of the Grim Reaper towering above my supine body. But my time has not yet come.

I tried to push the scooty away to free my legs. But I was rendered too feeble by the sudden trauma. The driver who hit me came to my rescue with his passengers in tow. They moved the scooty to the roadside and picked me up. The ligament at the back of my left knee was painful. I tried to walk to the kerb on my own but faltered. Strangers around helped me steady. Except for the headlights of the vehicles, it was dark. I was not aware whether the overhead streetlamps were on or off.

The guys helped me to a concrete slab across the highway. I slumped on it and relaxed for a while. Somebody chirped, "Give him water, give him water...."

Will water heal me? I thought to myself. Aloud, I said, "I'm fine."

"Shall we take you to the hospital?" another guy offered.

"No, I am okay," I declined.

"Are you in pain?"

"A little in the knee," I said as I rolled up my jeans to see if any damage was done.

Fortunately, the thick denim had acted as a shield, leaving only scratch marks and a tiny reddish circle on top of the kneecap. In our local parlance, we call such injuries, 'chicken skin wounds'. A traditional first aid for such superficial wounds is the spittle. It is the best anti-inflammatory and fast antiseptic ointment. In natural reflex, this deeply ingrained custom brought my fingers to my lips. I spat a generously amount of sputum on them and applied to the open sore.

I was indisposed to talk much in the given scenario. The guilty party began to get panicky. They thought I was beginning to lose it.

Somebody even shook me violently as though I had passed out: "Are you okay?" He cried. "Are you really okay?"

I began to get irritated with the fussy attention. "I am fine," I said gruffly. "Please, leave me alone."

By that time, few cars had begun to hold up. Drivers and passengers poured out and began to form a tiny crowd around us. I was beginning to get uncomfortable.

"Where do you live, Sir?" the culprit-driver offered. "We can drop you home if you like."

"No," I said. "I can drive home myself. Please go your own ways."

Our quarter complex is right at the other side of the bypass. A spitting distance to be precise. But being displeased with the driver for the unprovoked assault, I was in no mood to accept sympathies for the moment. Yet I was in no position to pick a quarrel either. Hence the mute responses. After a few more offers and murmurs of concern from the building crowd, I could eventually persuade the driver and his friends that I was okay. They helped me up, of course not for my asking. They were practically dragging me up against my participation.

Having no power to resist, I got to my feet, tested the ground for a moment, and limped to my bike. I flexed my knees a couple times to see if they would hold up fine. Then, I fired up the *Maestro Edge* and began to roll again. From my rearview mirror, I could see the cars start up and come after me. Not in seconds, some of them overtook me and turned their heads to see if I was really doing good enough to drive myself home.

Let me add yet another tale.

One day, with my wife, we were visiting IGNOU Office at Bikash Bhawan, Salt Lake to collect materials for my history masters. By the way, I was not born to be a master. Every time I took up the course, nature seemed to conspire against me. One inconvenience or another would crop up and make me miss the dates. Or perhaps it is only an excuse to cover my laziness.

Well, that day, we were on our way back home with my newly collected study materials. As we were negotiating a bump at a traffic point at Sector V, the IT-hub of Kolkata, a small car in front of us braked suddenly. I am not a race-car driver. So, I had the habit of maintaining sufficient distance when driving, keeping such unexpected situations in mind. The habit proved to be a wise one. It presently stood me in good stead. I had enough time and space to slow down. A calamity was averted. The car skipped the light and zoomed away. The traffic light also turned green momentarily without switching to orange. Perhaps, the driver was anticipating it. Before I could bring us to a complete standstill, I had to rev up and move on.

I was on the clutch to shift gears when a dull thud from behind drew our sudden attention. Somebody has bumped into us. I wanted to pull over. But we were on the wrong edge of the road. I drove a little ahead and signalled for side. The driver of the maroon car had opened his door and stepped out of his vehicle. But seeing us drive on, he slammed his door and came up after us.

Pulling over, I went to the rear and checked the bumper. A slight dent. The maroon car pulled up behind us. "I've tried to say sorry at the spot but you drove on," the driver tendered his apologies. "Please, forgive me."

He was quite a gentleman, dressed appropriately in formals. Perhaps, he was one of the office-goers in this technology hub. By the way, who, in this infernal city, begs forgiveness after hitting a car in front of you? It is always the other way round. Had it been in the busy heart of the city, he would likely say, "Why don't you drive at a proper speed?" At such circumstances, everybody was right and nobody was wrong. And things are sorted out only with a nose-to-nose exchange of words, just an inch short of coming to fisticuffs. I was heartened to hear somebody ask for pity.

"It's okay," I said. "It's just a scratch."

The man mumbled more sorries but I brushed him away and bid him good day. I got in the car and drove away. The man took the next U-turn and wend his way. What I did not tell him or my wife beside me was that the knock had caused me a sting of pain on the very spot on the small of the back where the nuisance was yet to fully go away.

Let's pick up our narrative again.

On the bed, before long, drowsiness began to descend over me like a veil of mist. I began to slide into a state of half wakefulness. My eyelids began to kiss goodnight and my mind began to give way. Just then, I felt a pair of fingers press firmly on my forehead as though testing my temperature. The touch gave an amazing relief to my aching head. I took for granted that it was my wife taking pity for my loss of sleep and trying to help me get some. I didn't care to crack my eyes to check out the obvious. They had embraced only a minute ago. Yet, my mind couldn't stop wondering if it was really her.

Lazily, I pried my gooey-ed eyes a little. Through the crack I saw her in a blurry vision. Her bosom was rising and falling in a rhythm of deep sleep. I decided to return to my slumber. The fingers came back. The pain gradually subsided with the acupressure. The sense of relief was so pleasant I began to get drowsier than before. I laid my doubts to rest and surrendered to the pleasurable sensation. Slowly drifting into the *Sea of Somnolence*, I mentally hummed a long-forgotten rhyme to lull myself to sleep—

When I was sleeping,

Somebody touched me;

It must be the Hands of our Lord!

Before I realized I'd received a blessing of two precious hours' sleep. Then, I was reawakened with a lesser degree of pain. A thought nagged my mind the whole next day. Had the hands of our Lord really touched me?

Chapter 7

THE LAME BEGGARMAN

Around 5pm. Sunday. September 19, 2010.

The sky was hanging low with a fat promise of rain. River Yamuna had risen to its highest level since 1978. Way above the danger mark. News media reported that Delhi has been inundated for the past couple of days now. A warning had been sounded at Kolkata too for a possible similar situation. Presently, everybody was in a hurry to get back home before the skies opened up again. As though oblivious of the imminent deluge, my wife and I were riding the opposite direction. Down Gariahat Road. Heading for Beck Bagan Row.

Two hours ago, back from Sunday mass at the Salvation Army Chapel, Circus Row, we've bought a kilo-and-half of beef from a certain roadside meat shop. No sooner than my wife started rinsing the meat she began to smell something olfactorily offensive. No prize for guessing. The rancid odour emanated from the carcass. A man of short stature, I have a conversely proportionate fuse wire. My tempers flared instantly and blew over the roof. I told my wife to repack the meat for taking back to the butchery. And in a flash, we were off to stake a claim of cash refund or a replacement in kind.

A quarter of an hour later, we got caught up at the busy Ballygunj Phari crossing as we're heading towards Park Circus. Being a meeting point of five roads, this cross-section is always virtually logjammed. Sundays make it no better. All the while, the heavens maintained their menacing look, threatening to burst any moment.

Presently, all vehicles stood in an idle purr, waiting for the signal to go green. In the meanwhile, I could see up in a little distance a black object bobbing up and down between the cars in the middle of the road. Before long, it showed itself and I could see that it was a beggarman's head. He looked fortyish. I mean, he may well be thirty plus. The rocks of life could really rub hard on your looks and age you beyond your actual years.

The man I saw had his left leg amputated above the knee. And obviously so, he could only move either by pulling himself along with his hands or hopping with his good leg. Right now, he was crossing the road hopping between the vehicles. In spite of his disability, the cripple seemed to have a fiery temper. He was presently raving and ranting as he hop-hopped along the pavement with some three or four child-beggars tagging behind him.

Wait! They're not just tagging. They're literally pulling his leg: poking, mocking, knocking him around. By the way, the kids could not be more than ten years of age each. And one of them was a girl.

The little street urchins were on their naughtiest best as they shooed and shoved the poor one-legged beggarman, howling and shrieking in cruel joy. The lame man could only shoot harmless screams around, nothing more. He raved and waved angrily at the mini devil-incarnates. But they only seemed to derive more fun from his helpless protests. They would rather step up their taunt—jerking at the ends of his tattered shirt, pulling at his frizzly hair, jeering at his ungainly gait and giving him sharp thrusts until he staggered as though he would take a tumble.

Everybody in the traffic jam saw the goings on. Yet, all looked on in silence, some even sparing a wry smile as though bemused with the mindless heckling. No one seemed to bother the mendicant's plight. The well-off ones watched from their private cars. The common commuters in the crowded buses and cabs observed from their windows, stealing a little amusement under the oppressive heat. And those between the well-offs and the common-commuters witnessed the show from our autorickshaws and motorbikes. Not one voice rose for the defence of the helpless one-legger. Perhaps, we're far too calloused to spare a shred of sympathy, being witness to too many such theatrical events playing out in public places on a daily basis. In fact, a thing of such sort must be a mundane affair for the overcrowded mainland cities of India.

Frisking and frolicking in such a manner, the gremlins presently pranced their way in front of us. A twinge of discomfort tugged me somewhere inside the chest, making me release a grunt. My self-professed do-gooder nature made me want to chase off the brats. But my helmet came in the way. A convenient excuse. The traffic lights might also switch any moment now.

Needless to say, I was of no bigger help to the special man than those mute spectators. Only if I could slap some sense into the children's heads! But both my hands were engaged in steadying the bike to keep it alive. To admit the truth, I am not a tall man. My legs are reaching the ground only in tiptoe. Hence, the active use of the hands to steady the bike. That was an added bonus to my alibi though.

I croaked again from inside my headgear. Probably, the children didn't hear my muffled reproach.

No. They did hear me alright. They stopped short in their tracks.

Thinking they've had enough, I did not go on with my admonition. But then, eyeing me for no longer than a flicker, they simply picked up their cheeky ways again. The beggarman couldn't help but settle down on the roadside and ward off the intensified kicks and blows of the scallywags. Just then, the sea of vehicles began to move. The signal had turned green. I revved up the engine and let the clutch go, lurching forward. The other bikes were already roaring ahead in a mad race.

Unbeknownst to anybody, as I began to pick up speed, an urging thought nibbled at my mind. Why was I not yelling at the teeny brutes? They might have ceased their vile mischief. I wanted to tell them that the same fate could befall them any time. Not that they might listen. But at least to put at rest the nagging ghost that's beginning to eat me from the corner of my conscience. Perhaps, I was not fated to be a Good Samaritan. But at least I could try, couldn't I?

Too late. As always.

In my hesitation, time forced me to flow with the current and merge into the traffic.

Hesitation is not good for charity. Once I took a bus ride down the Eastern Metropolitan Bypass to run some personal errand. A teenage girl with a little kid-brother in tow hopped in at Panchannagram bus-stand. The girl had a shabby blouse on. The little boy was in dirty tatters. He was skinny but the sister did not look much ill-fed. She was chubby and quite fair, except for a few streaks of grime and sweat running down her no-bad-looking face. An old harmonium was hanging from her neck which she played with relative accomplishment. She sung quite well, too.

Hanging at the hem of his sister's skirt, the little boy extended a begging-bowl as they slowly ambled across the aisle, the big sister crooning all along. In a moment, I could hear pittances clinking into the aluminium container. But I was not done with my mental sizing. How could such a well-fed young girl be forced into begging? Where or how had she learnt to play the harmonium with such skill and ease? Many times had I tried my hands on the musical keyboard. But I got no farther than the basic major chords. In desperation, I simply complained why the keys had to be black and white and not all white or all black. I grumbled at the alternative arrangement of the short and long sets of ivory and ebony. I know it takes time and dedication, which I presumed at the moment, a mere beggar would certainly ill afford. I did feel pity that she had to run for alms in such a manner.

But what a waste of talent, I thought to myself.

I was still absorbed in my assessment when the bus began to slow down. The siblings got down along with some passengers. I and my big thoughts! I missed all the opportunity to spare a dime or two despite my sincerest intention to. With my self-styled do-gooder attitude, there could be no bigger hypocrite than I.

Back to the present.

I took a peep into the rear-view of my motorbike to see the poor cripple still fending himself from the little rogues. From that very moment, scruples began to whisper murmurs into my ears. Why didn't I let out a roar at those rascals? Why didn't I help that lame beggarman? I could have at least steadied him when the children gave him a shove. How did he get his one leg chopped off? Why, how, what? To which I may never get any answers. A fading memory relived in my mind's eye. It was fifteen years ago when I'd asked myself the same questions. Twenty-five years, in fact, as I am emending this story.

Let me jog you a little down my hazy memory lane.

It was early 1995. I was on my way to Murkongselek, the last railstop in Dhemaji District of Assam. I had landed my first ever job as Office Assistant at Jubilee Model School, Jonai. JMS was a mission school run by the then Evangelical Organization Church of Manipur. And Jonai was its largest mission field at the time. Jonai, a provincial town, is a few minutes' walk from Murkongselek. It is the east-end border township between Assam and Arunachal Pradesh.

On our way there, we had to take a halt at Guwahati and spend the day waiting for the night train. We—a team of fresh recruits and a guide—took advantage of the stopover and roamed the streets and alleys to acquaint ourselves with the city.

Just then, we came across a girl child who must not be more than seven. At most, eight, I guess. She was shovelling spadefuls of stone-chips into a wicker basket placed at her feet. A weather-worn woman, undoubtedly her mother, was waiting by her side. A baby in her arms. She was gaunt and emaciated. She was breastfeeding the baby while supervising the elder child. The little child was struggling with the spade itself, let alone lade the gravel. She was sweating profusely. And, I assumed, she must be hungry, too.

I stood there, transfixed. For some unknown reason, I couldn't take a step further.

Unaware of my presence, the child spooned tiny heaps of grit on and on until her basket barely filled. Her mother urged her on to load more. Adding a few more scoops, she then helped it to her mother's head who would carry it into the half-constructed mansion nearby standing on bamboo struts.

You must be so hungry, I wanted to say. But there wasn't a penny in my pocket either. I had five bucks with me some hours ago. But I had spent them on a bunch of bananas at Mao Gate for luncheon. In fact, that was all my mother could afford me when I came to join my first job. My heart was pounding. I wanted to spare something for the unfortunate girl who had to labour so hard at such tender age. I've had my share of struggles to see myself through high school and university while carrying along my family on my frail shoulders. For some reason, I connected with this tiny lady so well that it pinched my heart.

Now, the child must be exhausted. I believe the mother-daughter duo must have toiled at least several hours or so since.

"What are you looking at?" The voice of our guide, Pastor Zama Vaiphei, jolted me out of my trance.

Mumbling some nonsense to myself, I turned to take my leave. But my feet seemed pinned to the ground with leaden weights. I looked back twice. There was nothing I could do.

Well, I had carried you off too far. Let's go back to Beck Bagan.

At the Beck Bagan butchery, we turned our meat in. The vendors refused to hear of it. They insisted their meat was not smelling a fart. I picked a few spoiled pieces and applied them to their noses. In spite of taking deep inhalations, they still denied their underhand deception. They must've had a very bad case of cold, complicated with chronic sinusitis for they certainly did sell us foul meat.

In no time, we caught ourselves up in a bout of heated arguments. Under normal circumstances, we must have already broken into a brawl and created a scene. For I have brought with me a dadgum nasty temperament from home in the very first place. But the sight I saw at Ballygunj Phari had watered down my raging vehemence a great deal. The bile had leaked out. So, I merely requested another measure and told them to do whatever they wanted with their rotten meat. I pulled out a hundred bucks to pay for the fresh cut. Horse sense prevailed.

They are now refusing to accept the new payment. I tried to pay them somehow, haranguing them with sordid remarks such as I was not an unscrupulous crook as them. They flatly refused the offer. Well, if you really mean it, I thought. That's fair enough. We accepted the carrion 700 grams less from the original amount. Yet we're happy. Happy? For the loss of forty-eight rupees? No. I am not an idiot to celebrate with my own loss. Especially in pecuniary terms. I am happy that I am not a beggar, and a lame one at that. I could well have been him had the maker above decided so. But I am equally saddened that such infirmities and privations should happen to anyone. Even if such things should be inevitable, I often ask myself, why must they have to beg? By Jove! How miserable this world could sometimes be!

That night, sleep eluded me. I have seen lots of beggars before. Some armless ones, some legless, some with unimaginable disabilities. But they were let alone. Let to beg in peace. But today, why should a cripple be so tested? Were the kids his nemesis for his past sins? Was he receiving what's been rightly due to him? Was that the way the Just One dispensed justice? These naggings may never leave me alone.

I still could not reconcile myself with my unhelpful frame of mind. Even if I couldn't spare the beggar a farthing, why had I not at least driven the fiends away for him? I mentally traded places with him and pictured me with my children. I visualised my near and dear ones. God, how lucky I have been! Small tears escaped my eyes as I reminded myself of the days when I was a mere starveling. I rediscovered the bounty the All-Merciful has apportioned me and my family today. I cannot forgive myself for not helping the lame beggarman that day or the little girl in the yesteryear. But I cannot thank God enough for not putting me in their shoes.

Eventually, sleep caught up with me. Or I caught up with her, rather. As I shut my eyes and let them kiss goodnight, a poem I learned by rote during my schooldays came back in a veil of mist. The poet of course I do not remember.

I recite—

> *Each morning as I go to school,*
> *If I am not too late,*
> *I stand to watch the beggarman,*
> *Beside the temple gate.*
> *He always sits in that same place,*
> *He has nowhere to live.*
> *He sits and clangs his begging bowl,*
> *And cries to all to give.*
> *I must not poke the beggarman,*
> *I must not mock his cry.*
> *He has no friends to keep him good,*

And tidy; that is why.
He cannot see the city domes,
And clear blue sky behind.
He cannot see me stand,
Because that beggarman is blind.
And though his voice is hoarse and loud,
And though he cannot see,
God loves that poor old beggarman,
As much as He loves me.
Then, I slept like a log.

Chapter 8

THE DAY GOD SAVED US

God speaks in whispers. But when he calls, he shocks man out of his torpor.

August 29, 2010, Sunday. It was already towards dawn.

An hour or so before, I had had three sequences of bad dreams. I could not exactly recollect the dreams. But I know they were horrible ones. In normal circumstances, I would have shot up from bed, sweated and panted out of breath. I am a light sleeper. The slightest of noise or a tiny series of bad dreams would do more than enough to bring me to wakefulness. This morning though, even three consecutive nightmares could not wake me up.

August is not a comfortable month in Kolkata for those who can't afford an air-conditioner. The monsoon rains would have arrived by mid-June already. Days are sweltering and humid. Nights even stuffier. On rare occasions though, when it rained rather heavily, the heat would become a little more bearable. Perhaps this morning was one of those rare occasions.

It had rained during the night but not that heavily. Yet, it was quite enough to cool the sleeping hours. After the nightmares had failed to wake me up, a cold chill ran over my body. Goosebumps germinated all over my skin. I reached for the quilt.

We used to have the blanket folded neatly beside our daughter. She was sleeping to my left. But sometimes, a bad sleeper that she was, she used to kick and push it all over the bed. Truly so, when I reached out for the quilt, it wasn't where it was supposed to be. In half sleep, I groped around, fumbling about the headboard, the legroom, the gap in between us, and everywhere my hands could reach without opening my eyes.

I felt nothing.

Then, suddenly, something hit upon my senses. I bolted from the bed, sitting up abruptly. Disoriented. Could the blanket have fallen on the embers of the mosquito coils? My thoughts raced. My heart began pumping. In the dark, there was nothing I could do but prepare for the worst.

My wife would usually place the mosquito repelling coils nearby the bed. I used to remind her to keep them farther away. Or at least under the bed or a distance from the chair on which she would collect soiled laundries in an untidy heap. She never thought of taking precautions from my forewarnings. As usual, that fateful night, she had placed the smouldering loops close by the bedside.

Now, when I could not find the blanket where it should have been, alarm bells began to peal inside my head. I stepped down from the bed as swift as I could and looked for the placement of the coil. True to my fears, there it was! The blanket, crumpling over the coils. I jerked the fabric away in reflex action. Thank God!

Fortunately, the embers had been smothered out already. But not before melting a few places in the synthetic woollen to remind us of how close we've come to being charred to cinders. The stair-lamps of the building next door threw ample light for moving around in the house. But not bright enough to gauge how severe the burns were. So, I ran my fingers over the softness of the quilt. The charred patches had already gone cold. The jagged edges were sharp and stiff. In a certain place, it burnt the material entirely through.

I could see that the coil had gone out midway. It was indeed surprising the cloth had not started a fire. The cloth, being synthetic, was of a readily combustible material. Thailand-made synthetic wool, in fact. And the embers could have easily burst into flames instead of dying out. The dung-coils must've glowed red hot in their peak.

I looked up the bed. My wife and children were peacefully slumbering, unaware of the mere inches we were from being reduced to ashes in our sleep. I was almost angry with my wife. She never listened to my warnings. I chided her inside my head. Actually, she had not lent much credence to my fears and panicky attitude towards fires.

On second thoughts, I could only ascribe to the powerful hands of God that must have put out the embers before they formed into tongues of flames. I looked up to the heavens and murmured something like a thanking prayer. But I could not even pray properly. The thought of danger was too imminent. I was overwhelmed with emotion, fear, and of course, joy.

I felt we were given a second chance.

Chapter 9

THE ANNUAL DAY OF KOLKATA ZOMI CHRISTIAN FELLOWSHIP

The Chairman of Zomi Christian Fellowship, Kolkata, Mr. B. Lalzamang and the Secretary Mr. Lian Naulak, insisted that I write a report on the events of the Fellowship's Annual Day 2010 and upload it on the internet for all to read. I had a big misgiving on the task thus entrusted. For I had no prior experience in writing reports in such nature and style. However, once authorized, I started attacking the PC immediately, pecking at the keyboard as fast as I could. By five in the afternoon that day, we had a condolence meeting at Mr. Thongchinthang Khaute's residence in our Quarters Complex. Mr. Kevin Pausuanlal Hangzo, begotten son of Mr. Khaikhanthang Hangzo of Kestopur has unfortunately passed away the previous evening at Fortis Hospital, New Delhi. It was Dengue Haemorrhagic Fever.

To my good fortune, work was light in the office that day. By half past four, I had run over a five-page draft. I made a flashdrive save, took a printout as well, and hurried home. Then, I made a rush to the Khaute's. A number of mourners had already gathered to pay their last respects to Hangzo junior. The meeting was an episode that merited a separate narration altogether.

Not before late at night could I lay my hands on the draft again. I gave it a first reading. Made a tick here, penned a strikethrough there, added a point or so every here and there. Moments later, I drag-dropped the text from the pen-drive to my PC and started inserting the proofreader's remarks wherever appropriate. Having done so, I set the text aside for a while. Then I skimmed through the day's pictures to incorporate in the report. It was near midnight when I completed the selection. The Chairman and the Secretary were in a pushy mode already. In fact, every member of the Fellowship was keen to see their auspicious day come online. Unable to afford another reading, I skipped the second reading altogether.

Then, from the portals of my *Yahoo!* account, I started firing the materials off to *zogam.com*. To my dismay, the *Safari* browser-wheel spun forever. The clock lumbered to twelve. Yet, the spokes had no mind of winding up. After waiting for some more time, I realized that's not going to work. I aborted the process and thought of a way to fool the computer. I copy-pasted all the pictures into a MS-Word page, resized them to 2by4 inches, and tried to upload the main text with a string of photos. Didn't work, either.

I was baffled and clueless. So, I tabbed out *160by2.com's* homepage, signed in, and shot off an SOS to Mr. Ding Guite, one of the administrators of our pet indigenous website. In the meantime, the night had progressed to the wee hours. For now, I decided to call it a night and retired.

Early morning, a reply short message on the cellphone directed me to refer to my email. I checked the mail and found a guide on how to link and upload the pictures. Problem, however, was that I did not follow a shred of the technical gibberish. Unable to help, I placed a call to Mr. Guite who gave me verbal step-by-step instructions over the phone. My lack of IT knowhow was horrible. In fact, it only multiplied the confusion. I guess the online tutor must be appalled. Probably helpless with my gross ineptitude, he eventually decided to mail me the app itself with its online tutorial. Few minutes later, I refreshed the *Yahoo!* webpage and lo, there it was! The software and the tutorial. A complete package.

In a jiffy, I downloaded the .exe file of *batch photo factory 2.12* and installed it on my system. The tutorial was lucid no doubt. The software was also quite user-friendly. Yet, it was not before a few trial-and-errors that I got the things right. That was the first time I've ever used that particular application. Once acquainted though, I could compress a slew of photos with shocking ease. Then, I packaged the resized materials into the pen-drive.

One precious day lost for want of technical erudition! I could feel the Chairman breathing fire down my neck for this incompetence. I rushed to the office. Booted up the PC, drag-dropped everything onto the desktop, flung *in.yahoo.com* open and started uploading the report with all its accompanying JPEG's in a trice. Half an hour later, I saw in zogam.com's shoutbox, an administrator nicknamed TSM, calling me for the big trouble I had caused him. He was in a fix as to how to put together the material that had just jumbled up his space-traffic.

"That's the best I could do, pal," I exclaimed ruefully and apologized. TSM accepted my apology with an assurance to do his best to make the matter presentable. Few minutes later, the report on ZCF Annual Day 2010 came online, uploading....

To my pleasant surprise, even before the uploading was completed, several visitors had already made an access to it: *"Report on ZCF Annual Day 2010,"* the title reads. Anglicized, and of course a revised version of the report is reproduced hereunder.

*

Venue: Madhyamgram Badubazaar, Kolkata Outskirts
Date & Time: August 14, 2010, 8:30am—onwards.

So, the auspicious Day, long etched in mere ink and paper, looked forward to with unabated eagerness by all Zo descendants in Kolkata—the children and the grownups, the young and the old, the lads and the ladies, mothers and fathers alike—finally dawned!

By God's pure grace, there was no problem worth to disrupt the anxiously awaited day. That Nu Chiinching, wife of Pa Albert Munsong of Saltlake Sector III, got admitted to *Columbia Asia* due to severe loose-motion may not be necessarily mentioned here. And also for those who don't get our tribal terms of endearment, 'Nu' or 'Pa' as the case may be, are equivalents of Mrs and Mr in Western traditions.

A scare of sunstroke was looming large due to the cruel Indian summer heat. Fortunately though, the skies seemed to have heard our prayers. A light showers-of-blessing bedewed us in the early morning before we started off for the venue. An immediate relief! It was early morning. Of course not by our hometown standards. At 7:30, a rather swanky bus named *Sankhya* docked into the Custom & Central Excise Residential Complex to give a lift to those from farther locations and those who could not yet afford personal means of transport.

"Haven't you got up? Haven't you got up?"

Some time went wasted in the process of rousing those still in the bed. Every person who boasts of a cell phone gave calls to shake up their slumbering friends. Some more time passed. Ultimately, at around 8:15 *Sankhya* started to roll out of the Complex. "ZCF Annual Day 2010 has really begun!" cheered the first few passengers. The joy of the Day was quickly building: "Those at Salt Lake, be on your feet!"

Pre-signals went off as we're soon arriving the next pickup point. Members from Salt Lake area were also overexcited. Some of them caught the bus even before it could make to the stand. Shortly, Saltlakers were herded in from the Nicco Park bus waiting shed. "City Centre, get ready!" Forewarnings pinged again unceasingly.

Meanwhile, *Sankhya* happened to stray in circles for several minutes. It had been taking too many directions from too many people. Everyone knows every direction resulting in precious time-loss. However, we caught up again and arrived at City Centre waiting point in due time. From there on, we proceeded straight to Pa Lamlal's place at Baguiati off VIP Road, which was the extraction point for the day.

Some advance party, for instance, Pa Vungzamuan Valte, Pa Thangzamuan, and several others, unable to keep their simmering zeal, had already left for the location lest there should be anything unready for the event. In the meantime, the Chairman, Pa Lalzamang was in a fix. His family could not be accommodated in his car. The Fellowship guitar they had to bring along proved a little too large for their car's interior

At the same time, Nu Biakching & Co. from Salt Lake Sector V were also running well behind time. She has placed the order for *naasta* in the morning itself for fear the eats would go bad if she did the previous evening. On the other side, unmindful of his being the Secretary, Pa Kestopur Naulak [Oh! Pa Lian Naulak, I mean] got himself lost in a hunt for an old bicycle tyre and made a belated arrival.

All necks craned out to their farthest limits looking out for the latecomers. The clock struck eleven. But no one seemed to be in a particular hurry for the mere fact of a ticking time. Without any rush whatsoever, all those expected did trickle in eventually. Despite being from the farthest location, Pastor Biaka had arrived from Batanagar quite a long time ago. Whomsoever not hitched in the small cars were shoved into Sankhya like a flock of sheep herded into the slaughtering machine. The minister then said grace for a safe journey.

Shortly thereafter, the bus began to head away from the city, cruising along the concrete fencing of Netaji Subhas Chandra Bose Airport, swinging into Jessore Road like a beauty-pageant contender making the curviest gait. There were also members to pick up every here and there at several intervals before the vehicle could speed on and on and on....

Ahead of *Sankhya*, Pa Khenthang Naulak led the way with his silver *Santro* and Pa Lian Naulak brought up the rear in his deep-red *Wagon-R*. We thus proceeded sandwiched between the hatchbacks under the sharp vigilance of the Tughlaks, I mean, Naulaks of Kolkata. Those inside the bus were so overwhelmed with delight they simply sat mute and forgot to make any noise for almost the entire trip.

We were racing away from the hustle and bustle of the *City of Joy*...on and on...until we felt we might have gone too far. Had we lost our way? Had we swerved into the wrong track somewhere somehow? No one knows. What's assuring though was the never thinning population. Much to our astonishment, the plainspeople had not grown sparser even in the countryside. In fact, they are bursting at the seams of the outskirts as much as they do in the city. No wonder India is said to have a population explosion. However, natural vegetation and the general environment did begin to grow more bucolic. Rows of lanky betel-palm trees lined both sides of the road. A fair amount of greenery patched the country-scape, reminding us of the hills from which we come. Forest cover opened wider with every mile devoured. But the road, in contrast, grew narrower and narrower. In spite of the morning drizzle, the heat began to build up again.

Sankhya squealed and bumped and jumped like a frisky she-goat until the ill-paved road gave way to a dirt trail. On we drove down the mud lane till we came to a hairpin-bend that looked impossible to negotiate. The bus gave it a try or two. The bend was too sharp and unyielding. A try or two again. It seemed really unbeatable. The bus ultimately relented and rested its protesting wheels. Passengers tumbled out to stretch their limbs. Their butts had tingled from deprivation of oxygen due to prolong sedentary posture. Empty and lightened Sankhya then made a few more attempts. The pilot was about to give up when he suddenly, rather unexpectedly, managed to manoeuvre into the dusty lane ahead. Everybody cheered and reoccupied their berths.

The lane was layered with loose chipped bricks. The path was so narrow that the conductor/handyman had to walk ahead, waving on the giant automobile that followed him like a majestic jumbo trailing after its mahout. Everybody knew now that our location was not far away. Soon, we could see familiar faces waving at us in a distance. They were our forerunners presently acting as signalmen. A big relief after we thought we had been lost! Thus so we came to a place known as Madhyamgram Badu Resort.

Like a cast of crabs, the living scions of Zo spilled out like beans from the bus. The campus was set. Everybody hurried to the plastic chairs arranged in a circular fashion on the greens to relieve their legs and have a moment's relaxation. No rest for the mothers, though. No sooner than they alighted the bus, they unpacked the lunch boxes. In a trice, *Chowmein*, bananas, fruit juices, and a whole lot of eatables began to make the rounds. As if in a bid to outdo one another in courtesy and service, the caterers of the resort also sprang into action serving *veg-pakoras* in shining trays.

In the meantime, the Fellowship high-ups and members in charge of the day's activities had a spot consultation. Before long, a sort of roster was laid out and order of events were slated. Then, before enough rest could be given to the cramps, everybody began to yell in excitement: "To the football ground. To the football ground."

In a short while, all the members, except children as they were taken over by the Sunday School Department, got divided into two Houses. One of the houses was named *Power Rangers,* as suggested by its skipper, Pa Lalzamang. The other was House David with Pa Vungzamuan Valte at its helm. In a flash, out flew a new ball. The very ball used in the recently concluded African edition of Soccer World Cup. Original *Jabulani.* Hold on! Yes, yes! No one could stay put anymore.

"Let me touch it."

"How smooth it feels!"

"Let me test-kick it."

Everybody was on pins and needles. A veritable host of leeches reaching out for a warm-blooded prey! Then, with a "Kick into the Hole" the Day's activities, at long last, began to roll. Selected kickers from both the groups vied with enthusiastic vigour. But, what's that!

None could get the ball into the hole. True to the sharp criticisms on *Jabulani* in the last World Cup series, the Zomi soccer crème de la crème also had an impossible time with it. Pa Khenthang Naulak, probably the best-known footballer among the Zomis, a former Indian national player and better known as KT Paite, a left-footer, took the spot. But he was not even near the mark!

Oh God! What's going on? Let me, again!

But sorry! There were no second chances.

The competition grew stiffer as the day got hotter. Everybody was on the verge of losing the fuse for the treacherous *Jabulani.* Suddenly the ball slammed right into the bull's eye: "Who was that?"

That was Pastor Biaka, making the most out of his only-chance shot! The other contenders tried and tried, but none could get the fickle Jabulani into the circle even by the end of the allotted time. So, the first number of the day went in favour of the Power Rangers. The score: 1-0.

Next item! Next item!

Before the first item could be given a ceremonious wrap-up, everybody started shouting impatiently for the following item again. From his car-trunk, Pa Lalzamang dragged out a huge coil of jute twine he had specially ordered from the Calcutta Jute Mills of Howrah. Hmm! An old jute rope is quite a common sight. But a freshly braided one is a rarity. Everyone was eager to run his hands on the silky fibre that gleamed with its natural sheen. It exuded the aroma of raw hemp. It still smelled of the factory.

In a blink of an eye, a team from each House lined up at both ends of the rope. Even before the whistle could be properly blown, the rope strung taut. Traditional chants of encouragements filled the air: *"Heih-ha-heih, heih-ha-heih..."*

Daring each other, each team comprising of equal number of male youths and fathers, tugged with all their might, foreheads barely kissing the ground, faces burning red hot with exertion. Meanwhile, the womenfolk would cackle at the top of their voices to motivate their respective sides. A perfect match! In spite of the vehement yanks, the centre mark, a red ribbon, hardly moved. It just floated within a negligible area which made it impossible to pass a judgment. It was like a compass taken to the centre of the earth or to the pinnacle of North Pole.

Just then—

Thrakks!

The cord snapped!

"Who's the winner? Who's the winner?"

That's one hard question. The Entertainment Department took up the matter immediately. After a few seconds' deliberation, they decided that the winner was...the cord. We laughed our hearts out at the unusual decision. Such was the bonhomie that day!

Now, time for the womenfolk. Our female species were in no way any less brawny:

Heih, heih, heih....hoih, hoih, hoih....

The indicator moved from side to side. At times, it would slip into the territory of one team, about hitting the mark. But almost at the same instant, it would come back with a huge slide as though lugged through a lubricating tray. For a moment, both teams seemed to gain a firm foothold. The mark began to hover above the centre line. The compass was taken to the North Pole again. No movement at all in spite of extreme force spent on both sides. Eternity seemed to pass! Everyone was holding breath, curious as to which way the ribbon would move first.

And in a flash—

Thrakks!

The cord snapped again.

Regardless of weight, height and size, every woman fell to the ground, rolling on their backs, hitting the patches of mud and dirt. It was more like a shoal of fish splashing out of water with the explosion of a dynamite stick in the river. And the winner was—the cord, again.

—*Who's the winner? Who's the winner?*—

Nu Vungzakim, a rather good-natured and jolly lady, added spice to the already high-octane fun by passing a remark: "The jute has indeed turned out to be a *jhoot* [fake]." We all belly-laughed. The Chairman took this remark mock-seriously and wished that another "Tug-of-War Festival" be organized in the near future. In actuality, Nu Kim's comments and the Chairman's discomfiture were just for pepping up the convivial atmosphere. Nothing was taken in bad humour.

Coming up…cockfighting.

The jostling commenced in an instant. The cock-warriors would ram at each other with their folded knees, or chip with their shoulders, or some would even use their hands to shove around. As in a battlefield, warrior after warrior fell to the ground. Some of the women would be so skill-less that they would simply rub against their opponents' back and bring themselves down instead. That was a visual treat indeed!

Okay! It's time for the children to take the stage. Items like Sweet Race, Blind Hit, Musical Chairs, etc., blew over one after another.

Couples' 3-legged race came up within minutes. Watching life-partners hop-trot in three legs and bringing each other down or trundling like two unequal wheels, was an exhilarating sight. Hours passed. But no one seemed to be aware of it. Before long, it was time for men to go for the most awaited number: Football.

Owing to the substandard size of the ground, the teams were allowed to field only seven players each. That doesn't make the matches any less enjoyable. It was a rainy season. Several centimetres of precipitation had been added by the morning downpour. Fresh cow dungs and unkempt brushes interspersed the periphery of the playfield. The ground itself was soggy and full of puddles. No one seemed to mind the least bit though. Play got on.

Water sploshed all around. Mud clods caked every shank and shin. Some players got completely drenched while others would skip around like kangaroos trying to keep away from dirt and splashes. Some kicked the ball, some wallowed in the muck-pools, and some even slipped every time they moved. Different skills, different thrills. It was arts galore and a bountiful feast for the eyes. Zomis got talent!

In the meantime, as the matches were running in full swing, the hosts [caterers], in their impeccable uniforms, would scramble in the midst of the crowd serving *chicken-pakoras* and other eatables and drinks. To add to the abundance, the Fellowship would also arrange a free flow of *Thumbs Up, Coca Cola, Sprite, Fanta,* and other choice soft-drinks.

All the while, *Jabulani* would dash every here and there, sometimes airborne, sometimes ground-borne. On occasions, it would make sudden strays into the woodwork and score a chance goal. Then, the supporters on the stands would become even livelier, adding more charge to the already electrified sentiments and blowing the roof off the skies with renewed vigour and deafening cheers.

By the end of the contest, House David took the field with a score-line of four to three.

Unsatiated though we might be, a hall meeting was waiting for us. We could not help but round up the outdoor events with deep longing for more. We washed up and hurried to the auditorium for the second period of the day.

In the hall:

First part of the afternoon session kicked off with a worship service. That's the way most gatherings begin in our community. Tradition acquired with the light of Christianity since 1911. The Master of Ceremony, Pa Thangzamuan, led the order of events with ease and alacrity. Praise and worship and speeches and songs wound up one after another. Pastor Biaka delivered the main sermon of the day. He also presented a beautiful duet with his daughter, Miss Esther. Before they got into singing, the Pastor announced that they would be presenting a *"Kol la"*, meaning Hindi devotional song. By what twist of cerebral miscomprehension, the emcee did not get the meaning of *'kol la'* for a good moment and tried to expound it away as a *"Kawl la"*, a Burmese song. The gathering chuckled in their seats. A boisterous guffaw is not appreciated in a solemn mass.

Following, the Secretary of the Fellowship, Pa Lian Naulak, made a round of announcements to be noted by the members at large. In spite of the ongoing revelry, a grievous concern was weighing heavily inside our hearts. One of the staunchest members of the Fellowship, Mr. Kevin Pausuanlal Hangzo, by name, was treated for dengue haemorrhagic fever at Fortis Hospital ICU at New Delhi. This Hangzo junior was the begotten son of Pa Khaikhanthang Hangzo and Nu Niang.

The previous week, a mass prayer meeting had been held at the residence of one Pa Kamminlian Vaiphei at Saltlake, Sector III, IC Block, to exclusively intercede for the recovery of Kevin. Now, as our celebration progresses, we carried our fellow-member in our deepest hearts and decided to appeal God yet again to show His healing mercy. The minister led the mass prayer. The faithful prayed their hearts out. Self-consoled thus for a while, and our mental strain a tad lifted, we then proceeded with the remaining part of the programme.

Up came the introduction of the freshers. That year, ZCF Kolkata had ten newcomers to parade before the agog audience. They were made to offer their own introductions. The Pastor then prayed for their all-round health, safety and achievement of their objectives for whatever duration of their stay in the City. Then, he distributed handshakes around and the session wound up along with it.

Tea-break. Then, second part of the session resumed.

Entertainment in charges, Pa Lian Samte and Nu Vungzakim, and the Sunday School Department led by Tg. Lianthang Vaiphei, Lia Goungaihlun and Lia Zenbiaklun, kicked off the shift. They took their own sweet time, oblivious of the fact that the day was marching at a very fast pace. For those ignorant to our tradition, 'Tg.' and 'Lia' are acronyms for 'tangval' and 'nungak' respectively, poetic terms applied to unmarried bachelors and bachelorettes.

The Sunday School team started with items like Bible Quiz, Finding Verses, and many others more. These items are not only recreational but also educative and instructive. They are tremendously enriching to our spiritual insight as well as enhancing to our scriptural general knowledge.

A good while later, it was time for the adult members to take the stage again. The affair started off with the Fellowship Idol-10 Contest. Pa Lian Samte announced the names of the contestants from the list of preselected best-singers as nominated by their respective team captains. Judges for the contest were Nu Haunu, Pa Vungzamuan and Pastor Biaka.

The competition started in full swing. The singers were good, nay, excellent! The judges were excellent too. Their comments were as extraordinary as their decisions. And the audience was at its guffawing best, throwing up continuous laughter and encouragements. It was time for the ears to feast and the stomach to take a hard punch. Even in the second round, that is, the final round, the contest was shoulder to shoulder. The judges were in dilemma with their final choice. Ultimately, as a decision had to be made somehow, it was decided that there must be joint winners. So, Nu Boinu and Tg. Lunmuansang were proclaimed to be the Fellowship Idols of 2010.

Then followed "Exposition of Poetic Words".

Contentious and controversial explanations were offered for our profound poetic words and verses. Some of the elucidations would give endless tickles to the funny bone. Fresh yet outlandish perspectives were added at every turn of the lyrics and words. It was elating, indeed! *"Zodawn heisa bang n'ong pal..."* simply becomes "There was a flower in a certain village" which actually should have meant, "You've unfolded like a blossom in the wild." Pa Haupu would simply brush the phrase away as a lover expressing his yearning in an unnecessarily longwinded way. A kind of beating about the bush.

Pa Lamlal, on the other hand, was so confident that he chose to expound it in Bengali right away. It was later realized that the judges had not comprehended a word of what he said. The audience neither got it. And most delightfully he himself had not understood a word of his own! Never the less, he was adjudged the best expositor for his heroic attempt of the local language. That was truly funny yet most appreciable. We all grabbed our sides in hilarity.

Then there was a "Face Off Parliamentary Debate". The opinion of the House being: *It is good to organize our special days like today in an outing-type celebration.*

Once the ball started rolling, there was no stopping. Like true parliamentarians, all the debaters would rise in unison and voice their views and counter-views right then and there. Nobody listened to nobody. Everybody raised their voice to carry their own opinions across as loud as possible. Exactly like the Parliament House, I should say. The mock-parliamentarians took great pains rattling off huge measures of logical and illogical arguments, all worth pondering as well as regaling. The audience laughed their heads off, trying their best to keep themselves from doubling up on the floor.

Well, whatever be the case, there was one inconvenience that always faced us on such festive occasions. Time crunch. Today was no different. Darkness had set in over us. Dinnertime compelled us to wrap up in haste although the day seemed to be still in midway.

Outside, already set in line were the caterers keen to impress us with their most delectable dishes and relishes. The minister said a hurried grace and valediction, dismissing the Day. The crowd immediately filed out and lined themselves around the desk on which was laid all sorts of palate-teasing dishes. The table was rich and sumptuous, worth the proverbial meals of the Arabian Nights' tales. To cite a few, decking the epicurean board were juicy chilly chicken, firm fried fish, eggplant fritters (*bangan-pakora*), lentil soup (*dal*), sweet pickle (*chutney*), chickpea-flour flat pies (*papad*), unsalted cheese [*paneer*], etc. In short, all kinds of flavours and savouries, poised to tantalize our tastebuds. Some sweet, some sour, some salty, some hot, and some chilled.

In the meantime, the mosquitoes were doing their best feeding on us. We ignored them and fed ourselves with the luscious preparations. As though paying a visit to one's grandparents, we soon had everything to our heart's content. Our hands ran over our tummies that are threatening to burst at the seams from overeating. We've already started to miss the day. We wished we could hold time for at least a few seconds.

"A moment please!"

"Just a picture more!"

"Wait, wait, wait!"

But time had slipped away rapidly like the fine sands of Sahara escaping through the fingers of your little fist. We could tarry no longer. Thus taking with us a heavy heart and a lot of sweet memories, we climbed into the waiting *Sankhya* around 9:45. It was already dark.

And back we went to the way we came.

Chapter 10

SIHZOUPOK AND A FEW COOKBOOK TALES

Every nation has its own signature dish. The Italians have their pizzas. The English have porkpies and porridge. The Americans beef burgers. The Chinese chowmein and momos. In mainland India, they have their *dal roti* and chili chicken. Don't be misled by the fiery name of the chili chicken, though: Unlike its hot tag, it is more sweetish than peppery. But for us, in this tiny, unnoticed corner of the world, there is actually nothing that stands out as national cuisine. At least officially, I mean. Not that we are short of gastronomic delights or lacking in epicurean skills. It is rather the richness and profusion that makes it hard to pin down one particular fare as a representative dish.

In fact, there are a couple of dishes I would like to term as community delights on the basis of my personal predilection. In case any mainland friend would care to drop by, it may be a good idea to have a taste of these local cuisines. One day, in our office, we were engaged in a conversation about a picnic in the untamed hills. I was discussing how we would just go to the forests, collect wild vegetables and prepare them right then and there. "We clearly could not have your vegetables," the senior colleague expressed his doubts.

"A brinjal is still a brinjal in the wild," I explained. "There's nothing different in it."

"They may not be compatible with us," he still mistrusted.

"The only difference is," I persisted, "our brinjals are purely organic, unlike the fertilizer-reeking vegetables out here." I added, '100%' to emphasize my 'organic' argument.

Whatever the case, be assured these are not bizarre foods. They will not make you squeamish or queasy. Yet I dare say their unique and distinctive flavours could give you an experience of a lifetime.

The first dish I would like to call out, as the title suggests, is *sihzoupok*. *Sihzoupok* is a local term for a non-veg potpourri on which I shall dwell at length here. But before we go into the intricacies and technicalities of this characteristic curry and its preparation, I must give a bit of introductory description about the eponymous ingredient: *sihzou*.

The common name of *sihzou* in English is Tapering Leaf Eurya. Its botanical name is Eurya Acuminata. It belongs to the Theaceae or tea family. It is a small evergreen tree or shrub. It can reach up to a height of twelve metres. Tapering Leaf Eurya is found in the Himalayas, from Kumaon to North East India, Western Ghats and Ceylon at altitudes of 1300 to 2500 metres. Its florets are white and stringed along the stalks. They blossom from September to November. It has tiny berry-like fruits. 1 I don't know if the fruits are edible. I never tasted them. Yet I don't think they are poisonous, either.

It is rare to find a Eurya tree in these parts of the world that reaches a height of twelve metres. So, I prefer to consider it a shrub. Agreed, a tall one at that. The botanical community may not fully agree with me. I may be wrong. But that's where I stand. For I have never seen a sihzou tree as tall to qualify as a tree in the proper sense of the term. Perhaps our rampant and imprudent way of collecting its leaves for consumption is the reason they fail to gain full height and girth. Many of our tribal ways of food-gathering are destructive. But until we have a better way of doing things, that has to be the way. Sad, but that's it. A fact. And, as far as my knowledge is concerned, there are very few people in the world who use this particular shrub as a food item.

—*the sihzou shrub*—

[1] https://www.flowersofindia.net/catalog/slides/Tapering%20Leaf%20Eurya.html

Now, especially during Christmastimes or any other community feasting, if *sihzoupok* is to be the main fare, children would be assigned to gather the *sihzou* leaves from the nearby jungles. That would be one big source of excitement for us kids. Being abundantly available, it needs no huge effort to find a tree or two, even for little boys. We would wrestle a couple of trees down and bring back entire bushes, complete with trunks, twigs and barks. The elders would then deleaf the lance-shaped foliage as required and discard the wood or use them as fuel to feed the roaring firepits. Nowadays, though, due to our destructive method of gathering, it has become almost impossible for small boys to collect them. So, grownups had to do kids' work and hunt for the trees themselves.

In large-scale preparations, the leaves may be plucked and consigned straight into the cauldrons. They cook well from the intense heat of the giant pots. However, if you are preparing for a small domestic consumption, then you have to dress them more finely, splitting each and every leaf from the blunt vein that runs down the middle of the leaves.

Belonging to tea family, sihzou has a zesty, bitteresque taste. Much like chewing raw tea leaf. I believe it is the chemicals, tannin and caffeine, present in the leaves that give its piquant tang. I am no expert in botanical matters. But if its close cousin, the majestic tea leaf, contains the substances, why not *sihzou* itself? It may be in lesser traces. But I absolutely believe they do contain! It's the scientific community to debate it.

Sihzou is best used green. It can be dried, of course. But the sharp, bitter taste of fresh eurya is no match to the dried version. However, once dried, it can be stored for a long time without spoilage. And it tastes almost the same.

The drying process is most simple. You just dress them as you prefer—with veins or without—and air them in the open sun. Just a day or two will do. The leaves shrivel up and dehydrate. They are crispy. So, you should handle them with care. You don't want them crushed. That's simply not the way.

For those who don't know how to prepare it in the proper fashion, cooking *sihzou* can be a real pain in the ass. There was once a street joke doing the rounds at Thanlon village. It was about several valley Manipuris trying to prepare it without the appropriate know-how. That was a long time ago. And it is not a first-hand knowledge to me. Whether it even really happened at Thanlon or not, I cannot tell. I narrate it anyways because of its amusing twist.

As the anecdote goes: It was in the early eighties. The residential quarters of Thanlon Primary Health Centre were under construction, it was said. And these valley Manipuris, or Meiteis, had come to work as skilled labourers. How or where nobody knows, but these people somehow come to learn that the villagers are consuming *sihzou* leaves as food. And the trees were available abundantly around. They thought they should try it out too. So, without bothering to acquire the appropriate knowledge, they simply collected the leaves and stir-fried them in mustard oil. Needless to say, the high heat of the oil rolled up the thin leaves and dried them instantly. Just then, a gust of wind came and blew all the bone-dry leaves away from their frying pan. They were doing it the wrong way. And they never cooked *sihzou* curry again!

Let me add one off-note piece here. Whether it concerns these same valley simpletons or not, I don't know. But I think it somehow relates to them. Hence, the mention.

There is a wild leaf that is wide, large and often left untouched. It is very smooth and glossy. Very tempting to touch and feel. But mind you, there is a deadly danger lurking around it. It is the Devil's Nettle or more commonly known as the Fire Nettle. The locals call it *'Thakpi'*, the Super Stinger, to put it literally. The pain of touching it is devilish indeed.

Now, these valley folks usually used paper or leaves to swab their below after doing their morning thing. In those days, domestic bathrooms were a rarity. The entire country is open to everything. Why take the trouble of constructing one? So, it was standard practice to venture out into the wild outskirts to move the bowels at any time of day. Local folks traditionally scraped with the sharp edge of a dry bamboo slat. When the plain guys saw these large, smooth leaves, the temptation was too strong for them to resist. And there was nobody to stop them in their most private moments.

Now, now, I have warned you. And I repeat: *'Thakpi'* has a very powerful sting. A common nettle's burn is nothing compared to *Thakpi's* evil prick. It is itchy-pain. But the more you scratch, the more painful it becomes. You cannot dip it in water. Even a liquid's touch is like the grating of a hard wire brush. It intensifies the irritation even more. These people, blissfully ignorant of the hillman's way, fell into the trap. In no time, they would take short jagged breaths and make soughing sighs as though biting off a huge chunk of *bhoot jalokia*, the ghost pepper, the hottest chili in the world. They would jump into the stream nearby, only to worsen the situation. The reader may smirk to himself by now. Without an iota of doubt, they must be spending a few days and nights moaning and whining!

Okay, enough of this digression. Now, what is *mehpok*?

Typically, mehpok is a rice porridge, which is usually a non-veg affair. Not that it could not be a whole vegan fare, though. It can be prepared with any leafy or fruit vegetable. Most common being *sihzou*, mustard leaves, flat beans, green peas, bamboo shoots, bean leaves, etc. One could go as weird as one likes. You could even prepare a *mehpok* with potato leaves, chili leaves, bitter-gourd leaves, etc. In reality, the list is endless. *Sihzou* is mostly paired with meat. But every sundry vegetable can be prepared as *mehpok*. You throw in a handful of rice to the hotchpotch and mash them up until they turn viscous to a desired degree. Then, you add enough measure of lye and salt to it. That's all. Simple. But you won't believe the taste!

Sihzou may not necessarily be prepared in the *mehpok* format always. It can make a variety of soups and potage too. For instance, *sihzou* with tropical taro or yam with a dash of fermented soyabean can make a very delicious broth. Again, as I said, *sihzou mehpok*, or to shorten, *sihzoupok*, can be prepared in a hundred ways. You may prepare it on a very small scale for family consumption. Or you may prepare it on a large scale in huge cauldrons for community feasting. Normally, a large-scale preparation tends to taste better, perhaps due to more flow of juices from the ingredients. That is why sihzou belpipok (a giant-pot preparation) is always the preferred form and spoken highly of by *mehpok* enthusiasts like me!

The most important leavening agent of *mehpok* is lye. We tribals are an ingenious lot. There were many inventions and discoveries we made without scientific studies or academic motivation. One of them is lye. Lye is a chemical solution obtained from the distillation or filtration of wood ash. It is a primitive form of liquid soda. The process is simple yet very clever.

Take wood ash in a container. Any container will do as long as you can make perforations at the bottom. Our ancestors are said to have formed make-do cones from plantain leaves to serve the purpose. Then, you leave enough space on top of the ash heap and fill water to the brim. You may refill the water again and again until the solution runs insipid. As the water percolates through the alkaline slag, it drips down into a collecting bowl. That is lye. The intensity or alkalinity of the lye is heavily influenced by the type of fuel you use to make the ash. Bamboo ash is known to produce a very harsh solution. Straw ash also gives a strong extract. Some extracts are too potent that they are unsuitable for consumption.

Lye has multifarious uses. Apart from being a meat tenderiser and hue-inducing element in food, it can as well be used as soap, detergent, shampoo and several other purposes. Usually, a mild version would be used for shampoo. If it is too strong, it is diluted by adding more water to it before putting it to use.

On a personal note: It was still very common to use lye as a cleansing agent when we were children. I once happened to use an extra-strong dose to shampoo my hair without watering it down. Foam and fizz immediately hissed on my head. As we tended to carry hosts of lice in those days, our heads would greatly itch, and we would scratch ourselves vigorously. In the process, we'd often graze the skin with our long, unmanicured nails. As the brackish solution came in contact with the tender scalp, a high voltage of sting instantly flashed across the length and breadth of the crown. It was painful. A pleasantly painful kind of pain, I should say, though. Itchy-pain.

After the bath, I felt my hair very light and wispy. I felt it bouncing freely in the air, flowing along as the wind blows. I felt absolutely clean. However, much later, I realised that my hair had turned auburn and never completely black again. It became coarser and curlier, too, in course of time. And it never grew as luxuriant as before. Perhaps my skin was yet too young that the scalp and hair follicles got burnt by the raw chemical. I'd never had nice lavish hair. But I've lost all sheen and growth ever since.

Well, let that story be. Now, another clever use to which we put lye was as invisible ink. Who discovered the property, we didn't know. And what chemical composition it has we never contemplated. Just dip a stick into it or fill a fountain pen and write on paper. Let the ink dry. The letters disappear. To decode the message, you just wet the paper slightly. All the squiggles will jump back to your face, crisp and clear.

Well, from the preceding paragraphs so far, I believe the reader should have had a fair idea as to what *mehpok* is. I guess we need not make any more bones to expound it. Yet, let me still add.

Sihzoupok is undoubtedly the most common dish of the Paite-Zomi people. As stated earlier, it could be an entirely vegetarian course. But it is best prepared with red meat, be it beef or pork or chicken, if not carcass of wild animals. A medley of beef and pork is an all-time favourite, though. Festival feasts are special in that they are prepared with every part of the meat—flesh, bones, marrow, tripes and entrails. This is the ideal mingle of the porridge. Nothing can beat it. For domestic hearths, smoked or dried meats equally make ideal dishes. Pork smoked for a night is special. In our local parlance, this is called *'Voksa Zankhat Hou'*, meaning, obviously that. Beef jerky is also a common choice. Sometimes you get meats of wild games like boar, deer, wild goat, or other exotic animals and jungle fowl. If you are extremely lucky, you may even come across a porridge of the bovine gayal, more commonly known as mithun. Scientifically called bos frontalis, this bovine is mainly used as ceremonial meat for very rare and memorable occasions.

Now, regarding the origins of *mehpok*, nobody knows for sure. I remember a story, a very simple one, I heard somewhere and stuck away in the hoary layers of my memory. It was an anonymous account and unverified. It doesn't need to. Myths and legends should not be corroborated. Otherwise, they will not be myths and legends anymore. As for the story, it goes something like this: The Paites were poor people in the past. And they often had not enough grains to see them through the four seasons. So, when the rice stocks went down and vegetables became scarce, they would simply cook whatever is available throwing whatever little rice they could spare into the hodgepodge to increase the volume. Thus, the *mehpok* was born.

That reminds me of an adventure in which I was personally involved. I have already told the story in my first book, *The Good Old Days*. However, as I have talked myself into it, let me give a summarised version. It was in the early 1990s. We were logging into the faraway Zezaw jungles. Not before a few days into work, our rations began to run low. Many of us being new on the job and beaten to the bone, we soon turned into gluttonous monsters. The old guards had not stocked themselves up keeping us, extra hands, in mind. So, the provisions could not stand our voracity for long. We were staring hunger at close quarters when the head-logger eventually volunteered to go to town to procure replenishments, leaving us in the hands of his son named Kumar.

Despite measures to keep ourselves frugal, the remaining stock ran out in a matter of days. Kumar's father never returned. From where nobody knows we come to learn that he was caught up in a complete shutdown in Lamka due to some political unrest. In this part of the world, clampdowns are a common feature. It may not be an exaggeration to say that every third or fourth day of the week is a *'bandh'*. And they give fanciful names like General Strike, Public Curfew, Indefinite Bandh, Economic Blockade, and whatnot to prettify the drab Hindustani terminology. They still all mean the same.

Presently, we're left with only a cupful of rice to share among five or six grown men, dog-tired with low rumblings in the pits. The same thing ran inside everybody's mind: Dish the rice out in equal parts and chomp the grains raw so that the bellies fill at least with gas to see us through the night. Perhaps for being a male-only company, none of us minded the breaking winds, which we did with amazing frequency and noise levels, especially at bedtime.

As we rolled on empty stomachs, a lightbulb tings on somebody's head. Whose head none of us bothered to note. So, the bright chap lost an opportunity to be credited appropriately for his bright idea. We collected a few wild banana hearts and prepared porridge. We might not run our hands over our bellies, but our stomachs do fill somehow. That night, I realised how hard it would be to suffer the real pangs of famine. We logged for a few more days without food, always cupping our eyes to the southern horizon where the food-bearer would make his appearance. It was like keeping a constant watch on Mount Olives, looking out for the second coming of Christ. Nobody knows when it will happen. We finally left our work unfed and unpaid. But in the ordeal, we all learnt how to appreciate the humble *mehpok* that many of us may not prefer under normal circumstances.

Perhaps knowing the story of its rustic origin, the Hmar people call it *'Paihte mehpok,'* which denigratingly means the *mehpok* of the Paites. Not that they don't have it themselves, though. At our communal worst, out here, we have choice vocabs of derision to throw at one another. So, to return the ill-appreciated attribution, the Paites would accredit a mishmash veg curry prepared with fermented meat as *'Hmar sathu-bai'*. Not that they don't relish it themselves, though.

I think we can pretty well make out from the derogatory exchanges not how or where but who invented the dishes in the distant past. How it came to be invented, by whom, or where and when does not matter. All that matters is that these simple dishes are indeed a pauper's delights. In truth, they are no less delectable than the royal victuals of the upper society. It is even more agreeable to the tastebuds and the tummy, I think. Although not infused with a host of piquant peppers and spices, they are equally, if not more, flavoursome and aromatic. On occasions, they are nutritionally better fortified as the rawness of the vegetables is preserved and the nutrients are not adulterated or excessively tampered with. And it is a big plus that no cholesterol-inducing oils and indigestible embellishments are put to use. The natural taste of the leaves and fruits is consciously conserved.

There are multiple ways of preparing *sihzou belpipok*. However, the differences may be trifling or negligible. Yet, one may prefer one method over the other as a matter of choice. There is no ceremony or specified occasion for preparation of this common dish. You may freely prepare one at home any time you like. However, as I'll be concerning the general community feast here, I will describe the huger preparatory format. Let's consider the beef-pork hodgepodge.

After the desired quantity of pork and beef is mixed, you throw them into a giant pot. Usually, for a community feast, there are a number of such cook-pots lined on a battery of makeshift firewood stoves. Just for knowledge, the giant pots or cauldrons could be of brass, copper or aluminium. Unlike cooking in city restaurants or fancy banquets, you don't need marination or a mountain of spices.

You don't even need oil. You simply stir the minced meat into the pots and heat them up. Just prevent them from overburning.

—*the community feast, sihzoupok, cooking in rows of cauldrons*—

In a matter of minutes, the meats stiffen and turn light gold. Oozes of fat drip from the lard pieces in a while. As the meats begin to sautee and sizzle, you pour a huge amount of water into the pot and bring the flames up to their highest intensity. In the meantime, you throw in heaps of fresh *sihzou* leaves and stir them in. There is no measurement or any specified amount to be thrown in. You just follow the rule of thumb. That's where an experienced community cook comes in.

The cauldron is then brought to a boil, agitating the mix every now and then to avoid caking at the bottom. When the meat is cooked to an extent, it is time to add rice. Again, there is no specific amount of rice to add. Too much, and your hodgepodge turns out too thick. Too less, and it will be too runny. Here comes experience again.

However, it is not rocket science to figure out how much of things to infuse after you participate in the cooking procedure once or twice. If you are observant and perceptive enough, that is. Otherwise, simple though it may seem, it is a skill not easily mastered. Even in our communities, only a few people are left who can cook a perfect *sihzou-mehpok* today.

Now, the pot is allowed to simmer in medium flame for about an hour or until the rice softens up. You know the rice softens enough when the grains bloat and slightly burst without falling apart. It is time to add the first seasoning. Lye. Depending on the strength of the lye, enough amount is poured into the mix. Yet again, there is no preset volume to add. A practical rule of thumb applies.

The liquid solution serves three purposes: First, it enhances the taste, giving a hint of indescribable aromatic flavour. Secondly, it tenderises the meat and makes it cook faster and better. Much like vinegar, I guess. Thirdly, it gives a nice reddish-yellowish colouration to the entire mix, thereby heightening its visual appeal. Some people use turmeric powder to impart this colour, totally avoiding the use of lye.

Nowadays, with petroleum gas replacing most of the cooking fuel, it is hard to come by a good old heap of ash for the traditional production of lye. So, a powdery chemical substance called soda bicarb or more commonly known as cooking soda, is used. You'll easily find it in pharmacies or in your local provision store. Being a chemical product, this soda could not really replicate the authentic taste and texture of lye. Yet, for those who never had the taste of the original lye, the dish would taste no less delicious whatsoever.

As for our cooking, the flames must be brought to their lowest possible before adding the lye. Especially if you are using the chemical bicarb. The water will turn frothy and suddenly rise like a high tide approaching the shores of the sea. You must be ready to contain this sudden surfy overflow. It is not uncommon to see the slower ones, or those ill-prepared, let their pots flood over and sizzle into the firepit, sometimes even dousing the flames completely. By the way, why did the liquid suddenly rise when lye or bicarb was added? We never knew. We didn't care. Elders told us it was the heat of the fire. That's why they usually lowered the flames before tipping in the solution. They must have got it right. The strategy worked most of the time. But in certain cases, the pots overran all the same, no matter how low you put the flames. It was not before much, much later that I came to learn the reason behind this boiling-over phenomenon. It is the acids in the leafy matter and the meat reacting with the alkaline substance in the lye/bicarb. An uncontrolled chain reaction. Kicking off a mini-tsunami in the meat pot.

That's the hardest part of preparing *mehpok*. You have to be very alert and agile to contain the deluge. At the same time, you are mashing down the rice grains into a mushy mass until it starts to congeal to a certain extent. Round and round, up and down, this way and that you stir and agitate and squish with a *'gokeu'*, that is an extra-large bamboo spoon. An improvised wooden ladle could also well serve the purpose.

By the way, what is a *'gokeu'*?

Gokeu is nothing but an oversized spoon made out of hard bamboo. You take a desired size and length of bamboo with a node at one end. Then, from the node-end, you hew one side away, leaving four or five inches to make the scoop of the spoon. To form the handle, you shave the matter away equidistantly from both sides until you achieve the desired size of the handgrip. Smooth it down by scraping and scrubbing with your knife. Then, you give it a heat treatment on an open flame. This burns away all the furries and gives strength to the final product. Et voila! That's a new *gokeu*.

Now, with your new *gokeu* or wooden ladle, you keep on stirring your hotpot until the rice congeals to an intended consistency. In the meantime, you add salt. That's it. If you want a hot variant, then you add chilli pepper. Dried red chillies are usually used. These indigenous chillies are quite high in degree of hotness. By the way, chiefly cultivated in our region is the cayenne pepper variety. This chili is extremely high in hotness level. It is beautifully bright red in colour when it is time for harvest. This very variety is the main component of the world-famous hot sauce called *Tobasco*.

Now, some people may toss a stump of ginger or two into the mixture. That depends on the taste and liking of the preparer. One tip here. You must unseat the pot from the fire before the hotchpotch condenses too much. Or else you'll end up with a very thick porridge which is certainly not desirable. It is simple, clean, and unencumbered. No oil, no spice. Just plain. Yet very tasty and compatible with the tastebuds and the digestive system. That's a tribal's delight, indeed.

Now, there are a few more dishes which are very agreeable to the palate as well as purely organic and light. One such dishe is the *'gotuai-beteh meh'*.

This curry is prepared with fresh bamboo shoots and bean leaves. Chop the bamboo shoots into rough chunks and tear up the bean leaves. Now, let the bamboo shoot boil till it softens to the desired degree. You may add lye in the beginning itself or later in the cooking process. The bamboo shoot will turn almost bright crimson. You may put in a rather large helping of chili peppers. Green or dried as per choice. Then you add the bean leaves with salt according to taste. Put the lid on and just bring the water to a boil. You don't want to overcook the leafy vegetable. Slightly undercooking it is the main purpose, in fact. The raw, earthy taste of the leaf is what you want to achieve. Then, you remove the cooking pot and leave the lid open to cool. Serve warm.

Another version of this dish, a more intricate and delectable format, is by spicing it up with additional agents like fermented crab, fish or meat. By the way, fermented crab goes best with bean leaves.

A bamboo-shoot-bean-leaves concoction is best prepared with fermented meat. As for the procedure, it remains more or less the same. Yet, there are some ways that may differ. Suppose some people just drop in a tablespoon of the fermented meat into the simmering curry while others may resort to a more complicated style of preparation.

This is the way I usually do: Take the fermented meat. Fermented beef works better than pork. But that's my personal choice. Others may like it and vice versa. Then, add chili and lye/cooking soda to the batter-like non-veg substance and heat it up. It will give out a strong, putrescent fragrance. This is the smell that turns away the mainlanders, causing a lot many frictions between the cup and the lip among otherwise good neighbours. About a minute or so later, just add the bamboo shoot to it and fry it for a while. Then, add water and bring it to a boil. That's it. Simple.

Our traditional dishes are all simple. Even the most intricate ones are very simple compared to mainland or continental cuisines. Perhaps, that is why they are more hygienic and kinder to the stomach.

There is another fermented item which is very popular, almost the most favourite among the tribals but not at all a friend-making item when prepared in metro cities. It is called *'bekanthu'*. Fermented soyabean.

Fermented soyabean is extremely powerful. Some people even compare it with the smell of a turning human carcass. But for those who love it, the revolting analogy is not enough to put them away. There was a short indie move about this food item. You can watch it on *Netflix*. It is called 'Axone', pronounced *'akho-nay'*. It is a Naga word for fermented soyabean. It's a nice watch.

We tribals out here love foods with pungent stenches. Some of them are definitely not agreeable to the olfactory nerves. South-east

Asians have durian, the king of fruits, which is banned in public places in Thailand like restaurants and airports. I think some of our beloved food items would be no less stinky than durian. But there are no explicit bans on these items. Perhaps, that is because there is not enough promotion of the food items. We are not much into promotion of our things. We are a bashful people. We don't hawk our own wares. It could well be due to a lack of awareness and recognition of the wider mainland connoisseur community. And the peculiarly weird thing about smelly foods is that they certainly don't smell when consumed.

One awfully reeking food item is *'singthupi'*. Many people, even the tribal folks who love it big time, mistook the name to indicate the majestic nature of the tree. For, in local parlance, 'sing' means tree and 'thupi' means great. That is where most people tend to make inaccurate allusion. Here, 'thupi' stands for the mighty stink that emanates when the tender leaves, and stalks are prepared for food item. Literally taken, it means 'the great stink'. Hence, ridiculous though it may sound, the name taken in a factual manner means 'Stinking Tree'. I don't know the latinized name or scientific/botanic classification. It is quite a big tropical tree. I don't even know whether it is perennial or deciduous. As already mentioned, the tender stalks and leaves are the parts taken for consumption. These parts are, of course, not available year-round. They could be obtained only when the trees began to sprout new shoots in springtime.

True to its name, one cannot prepare the delightful dish in the privacy of one's home. You have to blanch it to extract the bitter taste. This coarse water is thrown away. This first process is what wakes up the whole neighbourhood with a pinch to their noses. For this very reason, we call it the roaming dish. The odour is so powerful that anyone nearby would enviously remark, "Somebody's gonna have an awesome side-dish today!" The more ignorant ones who could not make a difference would think some naughty neighbour has let off the cesspit.

Then, the partly-cooked matter is prepared in every possible way you like. Stir-fry it. Dust it with chili flakes. Or you may have it as it is without any seasoning whatsoever. The elders whose tastebuds had calloused due to age especially loved this unseasoned style. Have it in any way you like. This is a food as true, open, and unconcealed as our good-natured tribal hearts. You certainly cannot prepare it in secret.

There is one anecdote I knew about this food item. This time I personally heard it. It was in the eighties. There was one South Indian preacher who was very popular in our area. His name was

C.V. John. He once came to Thanlon village to address a religious satsang. His sermons were entertaining as well as enlightening. He knew how to pepper his speeches with practical humours. One evening, he was sharing his personal experience with the food item, which he found not much to his liking despite its high reputation. His wife was from the Hmar community. So, he knew it in the Hmar language. "When I come to Thanlon next time," he cried from the pulpit. "Please, don't give me *thingthupui* again!"

Later, a bit of googling turns out the following information: *Singthupi,* as we call it, is a flowering plant genus of trees and shrubs from the mahogany family Melieaceae. Its botanical name is dysoxylum procerum. The etymology of its name is derived from the Greek words 'dys' meaning 'bad,' which evidently is a reference to its bad smell and 'xylon' meaning 'wood'. In parts of the world, the wood has been prized for its rich red colour and is widely used in the furniture trade. The New Zealand species is even known as New Zealand Mahogany.[2] I am not writing about woods. So, interested readers may freely find further information on the internet themselves. By the way, much like the Greek derivative, the name, as we call it ourselves, is also a direct reference to its excessive foul odour. Any other food item is found to have hardly matched it.

Another smelly leaf many of us cherish is *'khangkhuh'*. Those interested in its Anglicised common name may look up for 'climbing wattle'. This is a thorny vine with fine leaves. Much like *singthupi,* this vegetable also cannot be prepared clandestinely. This goes well with river snails, especially those harvested from the local alpine freshwater river called *Tuivai.*

Enough of these malodorous foods. Let me turn to a more pleasing yet plainer dish. I mean, one which endlessly baffles my mainlander friends. The dish is called *'Antuimawl',* meaning 'boiled vegetable'. This *'antuimawl'* is so popular and widespread among us that a family banquet or a community feast is not complete without it. Even when it is not supplied on a large scale, families would prepare for themselves at home and bring them to the community dinner to complement the feast.

Stalks of mustard florets make the best *antuimawl.* You may also prepare it with bean leaves, aubergines, tender luffa, bottle-gourds, ash-gourds, snake-gourds, and all kinds of leafy vegetables. The combination is practically endless. And the preparation is extremely simple. Just mingle up all the items you want to prepare, toss them

---

[2] https://en.wikipedia.org/wiki/Dysoxylum

into a pot and bring it to a boil with a moderate amount of water. Simmer for a while with the lid of the pot on. That's it.

You may serve it either hot or cold. It tastes equally good. It is better served cold in the hot season. And inversely hot in the cold season. Too simplistic though it may sound, the pure and undiluted taste of organic vegetables is sure to take you by pleasant surprise. This is one dish our elders yearn for when somehow forced to make a living in the metro-cities. I, too, have made it a point to have it no matter where I happen to be.

In the mid-nineties, when I was working as a missionary-teacher at Jonai and Simenchapari, Assam, I would often demand the maids or the mess-cooks to prepare it. But without fail, they would somehow throw in a pinch of salt or a few pieces of green chillies to the decoction. In the latter part of the 2010s, I was posted at an outstation as a petty government officer. There, I asked my maid to prepare it for me. Even after hours of explanation, she still dropped a few red chillies to pepper it up. But without salt! Actually, it is not the process that the poor fellows do not understand. It is the concept that's virtually unheard of to them. I don't blame them for it, of course. For us, though, the simple dish is so popular and ubiquitous that a local songster named Chinzakhup wrote a beautiful song about it. A line of the lyrics goes—

> *Aw antuimawl na limpen hi; Ka duh pen e,*
> *Meh dang chi dang te teng sang in; Ka duh pen hi,*
> *Aw antuimawl...*

A rough translation—

> *Oh, a boiled dish is the best,*
> *I like it the most, of all other dishes,*
> *Antuimawl is the best.*

I don't want to be grouchy in the concluding part of our essay. But, having spoken about traditional values and faculties, I must decry that in our subservient aping of western ideologies introduced through Christianity, we have lost many of our own age-old skills and knowhows. For one, many of our poetic words and classic aphorisms have passed away due to non-practice and disuse. Bardic lingos and idioms are our linguistic and communal identity. They generally go with folksongs, romantic ballads, bacchanalian festivals and harvest ceremonies. With mundane and bawdy ditties, there's no mention. The advent of western-promoted religion has shoved these ballads and madrigals to the back bench. The younger generation has tried very hard to revive them. But in the face of censure and dim view from the church, there is very little opportunity to do so. Devotional songs in western hymnals and metres have become the norm. This is taken as a symbol of piety and spiritual devoutness. Those who sing love-songs are frowned upon, if not considered to be of loose morals. Especially women. So much so that when our local media house, *Angel's Vision*, called for entries for country/love songs to its first ever award ceremony in 2009, there was not a single nomination in the female category. No wonder many of our ancient folklores, native blues and rhapsodies passed down in songs and oral traditions have alarmingly declined. Only a few common and banal ones make it today.

Then, there is this traditional wine-making. Our forefathers were drinkers of wine without being dipsomaniacs. They brewed their own wines from rice they cultivated themselves. There were no added chemicals or elaborate processing. A simple malty fermentation was all they did. There was no evidence of hard liquor production. Whisky needs grapes. Rum needs sugarcane, etc. Out here, no fruit or cash crops are cultivated in abundance to sustain liquor manufacture. Not that there are no strong drinks. But that's mainly made from rice.

No country in the world is without its version of local brew. The Indians and the Southeast Asians have Arrack, a type of absinthe. The more advanced countries are also not without their spirits. The Americans called theirs moonshine. In Turkey, they call it raki. The Russians have vodka. France, Flanders and the Netherlands have gin. The Mexicans have the world-famous tequila. Even the Japanese have Sake which is very much similar to our popular neighbourhood distil called *Sekmai Zukha*, which, much like the French Champagne, cannot be brewed anywhere else but at Sekmai village.

Strong social mores and religious censures have spelled a bane to our traditional winery. Today, if at all, a handful of elders may still preserve the technique in the back of their heads. But with their demise, the secret and skill of good, salubrious beverage-making will die off. Instead of exploiting our ancient knowledge and know-how to our benefit, we seem to choose to de-conserve them in the name of religion. Losing revenue and rustic wisdom in the process.

The other day, I saw on YouTube an unrestricted sale of sticky-rice malt in a certain morning market in China. People freely bought and consumed it as if it were some common eatable or any other comfort food. This very same item has been made by our forefathers since time immemorial. It is called *Zuha*—malted glutinous rice. But it is sort of banned in our very religious society today. In the early days, even children and babies were fed with it. There were no known negative effects or undesirable spinoffs from this food product. But it was disapproved anyway. Extreme religious zeal and bigotry have intended to do away with it completely, touting and discountenancing its consumption and production as anti-Christian.

If the hard liquor is locked away in perpetuity, at least this harmless malt must be exploited for its beneficial values in terms of health, nutrition, and commerce. This is nothing but rice malt. Its alcohol content is relatively negligible. If properly explored, analysed, and systematically manufactured, it could be turned into a soft alcoholic beverage. Much better than the hop-suffused beer. I firmly believe it will go down very well as a dinner wine. It may be served in restaurants and diners in a restricted manner if we still could not agree to its open practice. This will help promote our indigenous product as well as help the restaurateurs save some money from importing fizzes from outside the state. It certainly could be an attraction to tourists. A unique selling point for our age-old ethnic produce. Who can say with the boost in tourism staring straight into our face, we may not develop it into a distinct signature drink?

Certainly, there would be more traditional and customary stuff to talk about. But the above two items should not be allowed to vanish. I hope our social elders and the churches rethink and give a second look at their aversion to it. It is indeed a challenge to revive and bring back many of our traditional values and practices. Many of them have been denounced and stigmatised for no reason but abject fanaticism and pure ignorance. Let's revitalise our established culture and traditions. This is one social campaign I would like to make to improve and propagate our ethnic values. It will definitely give big dividends in the long run.

Martin Luther, of all men, has aptly remarked: "He who does not love wine, women and song is a fool for his life."

Chapter 11

LIQUID TOBACCO

One rampant fix our people love to have is liquid tobacco. Locally known as *'tuibuk'*, this humble yet ubiquitous product is partaken in such a way that a little sip is held in the mouth until the decoction goes insipid. It takes around fifteen to twenty minutes or even up to half an hour to soak up the zing from the stuff. And, then the washy sip is spat out like mama-duck splatting wherever she wants. Let me take you on a little tour to this openly shared pastime.

Forgive me: This is a warning to the uninitiated in our tribal lingos. I might have to go into semantics every now and then to clarify the convoluted terms and linguistics which are not at all convoluted to us. You should also never take this as a doctoral paper. There is a big chance of you feeling being misguided. This is a simple armchair travelogue. A real scholar may give a completely different account. Mine is not a specialist's work. Hence, no authority. It is just a presentation based on what I see, hear, know and experience on a personal level.

Well, as already hinted, tuibuk is the indigenous term for liquid tobacco. However, if one were to literally break down the word as scholars do (I love to act scholarly, you know), *'tui'* simply means water, and *'buk'* is a vial or a container. *'Buk'* can also mean the apparatus for production of the final product. *'Tui'* can be loosely applied to the liquid product obtained from the distillation process of the *'buk'*. Thus, the composite term, tuibuk, stands for the final fluid yield at the same time meaning the device itself. In a sense, the term is interchangeably used to indicate any one of the two items.

Technologically speaking, *buk* is the apparatus or contraption used to produce the liquid tobacco. It is a rudimentary yet very ingenious device to perform the process of smoke infusion. In fact, it is a complete manually operated small-scale extraction machine. It quite resembles the Indian hookah in a much smaller version. It is basically a smoking pot or a miniature waterpipe. I could not find a proper terminology to squarely apply to it. Therefore, to make up this lack of knowledge, let me loosely use the term hookah or *'buk'* itself to carry myself across. Or we may even devise a term 'tribal hookah' to differentiate it from its mainland cousin.

So, this set of buk or tribal hubble-bubble can be broken down into four main sections. On top is the shag holder, the tobacco bowl. In the middle is the conduit or the connecting pipe. At the bottom is the water jar. Then, at the side, facing the smoker, is the draw pipe. Let's get a closer look into each of these parts.

The first part, the tobacco holder. This, in itself, is an ingenious tribal handiwork. It is made of high-quality clay usually collected from rivulet banks or some specific locations only. It is called vahaibuan in our language. It may be analogous with china in common parlance. A small lump of this wet, consistently textured black terracotta is taken and formed in such a way that it further constitutes three zonal features: The bowl, the shank and the spur.

The middle section of the bowl is the main zone. It bulges slightly at the girth. The extent of its protuberance depends on the artistry and accomplishment of the potter. Now, the main bowl bends away at the shank or shaft at no definite angle. It could be around seventy-five or a little less than ninety degrees, normally.

As the name suggests, the bowl proper has a deep depression with thin, uniform walls, slightly distended at the lower part, narrowing up to form a hint of a neck before it flares out into a trumpet. The shank or shaft, as you may please, may be the size of a small twig in circumference and about three centimetres in length. A hole is bored through it, surfacing into the hollow of the bowl. Then, at the bending joint, facing outward, a tiny pointed tip is created which looks like a rooster's spur. Hence the term. I am taking huge liberties in naming the parts. So, their preciseness and accuracy are not academically guaranteed. This spur is the thumb-hold when blowing air into the bowl to make the shag burn faster. Then, the soft clay is baked in the same domestic hearth on which you cook your daily dinners. No separate oven or baking kiln is necessary. The tobacco holder is ready in a day's time.

The second or middle part of the buk is a simple tube cut from bamboo stalk. Trimmed and shaved to its proper size and length, the stalk would perfectly fit into the holes where they are meant to be inserted. Stops are made at the terminals by cutting notches or simply winding threads around the desired locations so that the tube doesn't slip all the way through.

Then comes the bottom part: The water tanker. This portion can also be broken up into two parts. At the lower end is the tank proper or the jar which carries the water to be processed. The tank itself is made of hard gourd. A little more on the gourd.

There is a certain type of gourd which is very bitter, not edible and even touted to be poisonous. But it is not without a purpose. When the fruit grows to a desired size, it is plucked, hollowed out, and dried in the sun. Once dried, it becomes really tough and durable. It doesn't break easily. Some *buks* are said to have lasted generations. It is customary for a new bride to take a set of *buk* with her as a token of parental legacy or as a souvenir, if not an heirloom.

Another use of this bitter gourd is as water-mugs. The process is more or less the same. To make a mug, you slice a huge chunk off a suitable side depending on the curvature of the stem which will later make for the neck. The soft inner tissues are gouged out and the casing is simply left in the sun to dry.

There is yet another use to it. You cut the neck at a certain point and scrape out all the innards through this tiny opening. Then, you dry it out as before. This makes a perfect water urn, giving the water a peculiar, bitteresque taste which is very agreeable to the parching throat. It also keeps water cool for longer periods. It works with the same principle as earthen pots by evaporating through their microscopic pores. I remember my mother storing seeds in dried gourds. In spite of its humble look as a lowly creeper, its uses are manifold.

I digress because there is no much complexity in the making of the water tank. Now, back to our deconstruction.

The dry gourd is then fitted with yet another nifty contrivance. This is sort of a holder. It is carved out of bamboo stub or softwood. It is a Y-like structure with the main stem running up straight and an arm sprouting out at a certain degree. The stems are drilled to receive the tubes meant for drawing air and smoke. It's really hard to describe the ingenuity of this fabrication to trigger the visual imagination. It is best seen with your own eyes. This stubby piece of resourcefulness is married to the receptacle by using beeswax or any other natural adhesive material available around. This secures the two parts and seals them up in an airtight whole. The bottom part is ready again.

The fourth section, which is an outcrop of the bamboo stub, serves as the air intake spout. A hollow iron rod is inserted in the aperture of this branch-out with a stop made of wound threads again. At the base of this spout would hang a long metal pin to stoke the fire in the tobacco bowl. Seen from a distance, this pin, hanging at the base of the air-intake and leaning at a slant on the water-gourd, forms a rough shape of the letter 'K'.

Once the parts are ready, we can easily put them together. It's not rocket science. But no less in its ingenuity, I must say. Et voila, the contraption is assembled. Now, you stuff a handful of processed local tobacco into the bowl and apply a small flame to it. Butane gas lighters come much later. Yet, till today, the standard choice is a piece of glowing ember from the fireplace. Then, from the other end, through the shank, you repeatedly draw air with your mouth until the tobacco-leaves catch fire and light up properly. Once you drag enough smoke, you set the bowl on to the conduit pipe.

Oh, I forgot to mention. You have to fill the vessel to a certain level with clean, soft water. Who wants to swig hard water anyway? The good news is that you don't easily find hard water in this part of our world. And, finally, like any regular hubble-bubble, you drag from the draw-pipe and enjoy the smoke to your heart's content.

After smoking for quite a long time, the fluid is sufficiently infused with the fume. And lo, your tuibuk is ready. The liquid is then transferred out into small vials which I shall describe in a moment. Nowadays, glass bottles are more commonly used for their ready availability. Then, you pass around generously and have a good time.

—*a native smoking tuibuk*—

As for me though, I have stayed away from tobacco and tobacco-products all my life. The smell, for me, is too pungent and overpowering. For those not used to it, it may be easier to sip a glass of poison. And poison it is, in a sense. But, alas, for those fixated to it, it is nothing less than divine. Like any regular tobacco product, it is carcinogenic and injurious to health.

Another reason why I did not favour its use is that it is usually the womenfolk who are involved in its production. They have to smoke a lot. Even when they don't feel like it, in fact. For, the fluid is a traditional symbol of prosperity and hospitality. Sometimes, even young girls are encouraged to help in its manufacture, which is not at all advisable. And as all vices are wont, the ill habit catches on easily. Little girls are quickly hooked to smoking.

However, today, more imaginative people began to come up with crude machines to do the smoking by using hydro energy. Initially, they would harness the local streams. But most streams being non-perennial often dry up or overflood in seasons. Neither of which could be put to productive use. The last time I saw, a certain creative man had invented a smoking device which employs an electric motor to provide suction through the intake hose. And the rest, as they say, is understood.

Now, let me describe what the *'tuibuk-um'* is.

The tuibuk-um is also made from gourd. This particular genus of gourd is peculiar in that the fruit cannot grow beyond a certain size. It is beautifully spherical, although a little irregular as it is. And it has a tiny nozzle-like stem that makes a perfect serving spout. Hollowed out and dried like the water jar, this small vial is blackened with hearth-soot over the fireplace and polished to a shine. A flawless gourd-ampoule is a prized possession of the owner indeed.

As for semantics, again, *'tuibuk'* itself can be commonly used to denote this very bottle too. *'Um'* is added for sheer complementary purposes. It simply means, as it must've been clear to the reader by now, a container or phial. Whether you want to indicate the vial or its contents you can equally call out *'tuibuk'* only or *'tuibuk-um'*. As for the former, it is a generalising term for the liquid tobacco whereas the latter, if you wish, may be specifically used to indicate the decanter, no matter what it is made of.

It is not my intention to promote or endorse the use of liquid tobacco or any other tobacco products. I only wanted to highlight the uses and their effects, especially the disagreeable ones, due to its wide and unbridled consumption.

In the *buk*, there is a place where air leakage is not minded. That's the point where the conduit meets the Y-stub. Here, a by-product of the smoke would generously collect on the thread-stopper.

Nicotine dross. Actually, when in operation, that is, when the buk is being smoked, the smoker would every now and then lift the conduit pipe to blow out unwanted concentration of air or water around the fitting.

Now, this slag is a very good insect repellent, especially ticks. In the villages, it is not uncommon for children, and even grownups, to contract ticks in our wild outings. And ticks loved the soft inner portions of the ear or behind the lobes. So, if a tick sticks itself in such a place, this tobacco residue would work like magic. Take a small glob and smear it on the tick itself or around it. In seconds, the tick would be gone. Whether it has died from the strong chemicals present in the substance, or it has just walked away due to its disagreeable odour, we never tried to verify.

Needless to say, having liquid tobacco is a relaxant to the practitioners. It is much like smoking. It can be a stress reliever. But if you are kicked in the wrong way, then you are done for. It will force you to retch and vomit, spin your head and even knock you out of your senses for a while. I once personally experienced this so called 'high'.

As usual in every childhood gang, there used to be a bossy bully. And there was one in ours too. He was not that nasty or hard to put up with though. His only habit was that he had a way of encouraging us with mock flatteries to do his bidding. One day, he told us that salt is not salty but sweet. He took a little dip of his finger in the salt-container, licked it and exclaimed, "Ah, it's really sweet!"

With his dare, after him, we grabbed fistfuls of un-iodised salt and devoured them with a remark: "This salt is sweet indeed!" Bullies. I don't remember how much water we ended up drinking later.

And yet the other day, he would challenge us to try *'Khaini'*. *Khaini* comes with the brand name 'Golden Tobacco'. To me, there is nothing golden about it. It is a tobacco product packed in a tin container about the size of a hockey puck. Imagine a lump of horse shit coarsely grinded up and soaked in water and then packed in a tin. That's the best picture I can describe. You may get it or not. It's up to you. The smell was extremely strong and offensive. For those who don't like it, I mean. And it is a very, very powerful concoction.

The usual way of having this Golden Tobacco is to take a pinch of it and stick it somewhere inside your mouth: Between the cheek and the gums. Some people put in between the upper lip and the gum. Some put in below. Some simply put it on their tongue. Experienced users would not even employ their fingers. They would scoop a generous helping with the container's lid and lob it into their mouth. And much like liquid tobacco, the dash is held in the mouth until it goes relatively bland. Then it is spat or thrown out in a mushy splodge.

As for us, that day, knowing that we had not yet taken to the habit, our boss told us that wrapping the pinch with cotton fluff helps lessen the kick. So, we grabbed a cotton ball each, spread it out, wrapped it up, and shoved it down between our gums and cheeks. Until the cotton soaked through, nothing happened. Then, slowly, the saliva begins to seep in and ooze with the substance. Suddenly, the gums begin to tingle. Tiny electric shocks ran through the soft tissues. It is burning.

I quickly scooped out the boll and spat out vehemently. But I had already swallowed enough goop to send me into a tizzy. Did I throw up? Did I hit the ground unconscious? I did not remember. The next thing I remembered was I was completely drained and pale. I still continued retching inwardly although there was nothing left to throw up. The solar plexus hurt a lot.

This unpleasant experience kept me away from tobacco products ever since.

Now, why is this odious liquid tobacco so prevalent in our society? Like any other societies in the world, ours too love tobacco. Tobacco was once used by communities around the world as currency. We did not much use as money per se. But its worth is no less than gold. We could not live without tobacco.

In the olden days, having a constant supply of liquid tobacco is a sign of prosperity. It is sort of a status symbol. For a well-to-do family, it is a must to always have an adequate stock of it. It is an indication of wellbeing and affluence. Symbolical to abundance of household provisions. In local paraphrase, they say, *'annkhing tuibuk kiningching'*. That means, a family well provided. Probably, it must be like having an Apple product like iphone, ipad or a macbook in today's upscale urban society.

Even for families that may not be rich, it is a must to have at least a minimum supply of it. For, it needs to be served to guests and visitors as a gesture of warmth and openness. Not only tuibuk, even homebrewed beverages used to be served to special visitors or favoured callers. But with the advent of Christianity and the general vanishing of the art of winemaking, they are now replaced with common tea. Served with milk or straight out black, sugared or plain.

Today, if you visit the local markets like Old Bazaar or New Bazaar, recently rechristened as *'Nute Bazaar'*, meaning, roughly,

Women's Market, you can easily come across glass bottles with ember liquids on sale. With a quick glance, an inexperienced visitor may mistake it to be bottles of foreign made liquors. By just the look of it, it is no less beautiful and tempting as a sparkling scotch. Yet, to the unused, even a simple act of throwing the cork open can hit you straight into the chest, prompting you to cough violently. The best advice is, for those not in the habit, just admire it. Don't try it.

As it is very addictive. Even young boys and girls easily take on to it. And being not a banned item or not officially considered a narcotic, it is not looked upon with much consternation. When I visited Mizoram in December 2004, I was extremely surprised to see several young girls carrying tuibuk-ums freely and swigging openly. Even in front of the elders without a hint of compunction. And the practice seemed to have caught on by the youngsters of my hometown some years later.

One aspect I could not make myself reconcile is my hometown's unabashed imitation of Mizoram. Whatever happens in Mizoram happens in Lamka the next day. In fact, we are brazenly aping them from food fads to dress styles, from rock to roll, even from mannerisms to spirituality.

However, on the flip side, which is rather a positive note, it is a good revenue earner for the producers and retailers. It could be better commercialised and made to generate more income would the smokers invest more in brainwork to come up with better machinery. This would free the womenfolk from excessive smoking and prevent youngsters from taking on the smoking habit.

As for the fixation, well, it is impossible to stop a fixation unless the user decides to give it up himself or herself. I'm afraid I'm beginning to sound too pedantic. I am not fighting a moralistic cause here. So, let me hang up and move on to another subject.

Chapter 12

SOME COLD FACTS OF LIFE

Your joy is your sorrow unmasked.
And the selfsame well from which your laughter rises was oftentimes filled with your tears....
The deeper that sorrow carves into your being, the more joy you can contain.
Is not the cup that holds your wine the very cup that was burned in the potter's oven?
And is not the lute that soothes your spirit the very wood that was hollowed with knives?
When you are joyous, look deep into your heart and you shall find it is only that which has given you sorrow that is giving you joy.
When you are sorrowful, look again in your heart, and you shall see that in truth you are weeping for that which has been your delight.

—Kahlil Gibran

To make a living in the cities had always been my dream. In fact, in my younger days, I used to turn green seeing friends go away to the mainland pursuing their higher studies. When I was even smaller, I would look up at the sky and fantasise that I would one day ride that tiny floating thing, soundlessly zipping across the blue expanse, appearing and disappearing between the clouds. A dream I dreamed without actually believing in it. Dared not believe, should I say rather. The popular Mizo comedian, Mapuia, jested: "Dreams are not meant to be fulfilled. Once they are, they remain dreams no more."

Many years later, I really did happen to fly. That was when I struck a job and got stationed at Kolkata. My joy knew no bounds. It was indeed like a dream. The plane roared into the empty space and stayed there, airborne. I stared out of the porthole and grinned without any reason. I saw green swellings on the curved surface of the earth. It was awesome. That was the first time I saw the hills from top. They don't look as imposing as they did from down below. The aircraft cruised easily at an altitude. I closed my eyes and pictured myself, my wife and our two little children, and of course, my dad and mum, setting up a home far away from home. A small happy family.

The plane jerked. We're hitting an air pocket. The chain of my reverie shattered. The dream had to wait a little longer. In addition, the unforgiving weather condition and the notorious heatwaves of the mainland were a constant discourager to my ageing parents. They'd never left the cool climes of our hill country. Besides, with an ever-failing eyesight, my father could not step out without the guiding hands of my mother. She had indeed become his right-hand man. Well, right-hand woman, if you must. And a proud man that he was, he felt visiting us in our tiny government-supplied quarters would unnecessarily impose themselves upon us. So, even after marrying off all his children, he still chose to make it out on his own.

"I will not impose on you," was on his lips until his dying day. True to his word, even when he was fighting a terminal stage of cancer, he refused to come down for further treatment.

"I'm sorry Papa," I'd said over the phone. "I know your son's not making big money by working a government job. But at least you can come and we shall manage somehow."

"There's a modest nest egg in your little brother's pension. That'll see me through." He was adamant.

"The circumstance may be unfortunate," I reasoned hard to turn him around, "but it could be a good opportunity to pay us a visit, nah?"

"Okay, fine," he'd conceded at last. "Let me exhaust all the means out here. And if that doesn't get me anywhere, then I'll certainly come."

I had no more counterpoints to offer. You cannot win an argument with your father. We switched back to the usual tête-à-tête and other banalities to round off the trunk call. My father seldom broke tears in my face. But the crack in his voice that night was unmistakable.

Hardly four months after that telephone conversation, he left us for his final resting place.

Needless to say, I am from a family whose fiscal foundations are never sound. My ancestors seemed to prefer sand over the rock to build their future. I don't know much about my great-grandfather. The little I know tells me that he had led quite a peripatetic life. How rightly said it is that a rolling stone gathers no moss. Perhaps taking after his father, my grandfather accumulated no moss either. When it was time for him to pass on, he made his final bow from the hutch of his son, who was as homeless and penniless as he. I know my father all too well. He was doubtlessly taking after his father, who had, in turn, taken after his own father. The vagrancy of our family is still too raw to call it yesterday.

It's a bit shameful and self-demeaning, but I couldn't ignore the fact that there was no locality we did not move to in a village as small as Thanlon. Even in Lamka, the city of dreams, the Mecca of Zogam, we are driftwood, moving from neighbourhood to neighbourhood for more than fifteen years until we could send a semblance of roots in the mid-2000s. That too at the expense of my little brother's mortal remains that were never brought home by the Indian Army.

Now, after my father's passage, my mother was left all by herself in our decrepit mudhouse. The mudhouse may be just a battered tumbledown. But we cannot simply auction it away despite the thought being quite tempting for a while. It is our ancestral home. The only house we could call ours as far as I could jog down my memory lane. As I said, from my great-grandfather to my father, none of them had erected a house of their own. The only accommodations they afforded were mean dwellings and rented hovels. So, this humble rundown is the only abode we could come home to when we are a-home visiting. And my mother is extremely possessive over it. As she naturally should. It is the house she poured buckets of tears for the sake of her lost son. Now, it is where she grieved for her blind husband. So, it was not easy asking her to come out and stay with us in the baking ovens of Paschim Bengal.

However, there could be no eternal tug of war between us. I could not simply return home, giving up my only source of livelihood. I am not a small kid any more. New jobs would not be lying around. The scales of age had long tipped against my favour. As I write, I am pushing the fag-end of my forties. And it is time for me to settle down somehow. Besides, I had my own wife and children to look after. So, it must be she who must leave home and make a fresh start by coming over and spending her twilight with her eldest son and her two grandchildren.

With a heavy heart and grief still chafing, she, at last, agreed to fly down to the merciless heatlands of the City of Joy. Despite its heartening epithet, the name Calcutta (then) had inspired nothing but dread and terror to our elder folks. How the city happened to acquire such a grimy repute, I never knew. However, our elders seemed to be not alone in their aversion to the city. The grand old man of Indian literature, Mr. Khushwant Singh, himself was a victim of such loathe.

He wrote—

"My dislike for Calcutta has turned to dread; I am frightened of the city and its denizens. Every time I walk down the corridor of Grand Hotel and come face to face with the solid wall of humanity flowing down Chowringhee, I want to run back to my room. I have to muster all my courage to plunge into the smelly human stream, suffer jostling and buffeting, then stumble over uneven, broken pavements, avoid slimy ooze that is always there, dodge incoming, overloaded buses and cabs which bear down on me from all sides. I have developed all the phobias associated with filth and squalor, most of all claustrophobia—fear of crowds. No crowd in the world is more hostile than those in Calcutta.... I cannot understand why they have Calcutta. And if they can't do without it, why don't they do something about it, like, for instance, blow it up?"[3]

Moreover, Dominique Lapierre wrote in *Freedom at Midnight* that Calcutta, the second city of the British Empire, had been a metropolis whose reputation for violence and savagery was unrivalled. To generations of Englishmen, it was a synonym for Indian cruelty. Should I go even further, "Calcutta," wrote Robert Clive, the first British Governor of the Bengal Presidency, "is one of the most wicked places in the Universe..."

But those were days long gone. By the time we made our landing, that is, in the late 2000s, it was not as bad as it sounds. Or so it seems.

Well, let that be that. Not long before stepping into this accursed city, my mother began to raise complaints about her general health. She started scratching herself like a she-monkey. Literally. We did not pay her much heed. She could be suffering from pangs of nostalgia. Which is natural. Probably, she was going through the process of adaptive acclimatisation. Besides, my assignment to the outpost for the time prevented me from giving constant attention to her wellbeing. But do you scratch when you are homesick?

Later, she began to erupt into blisters as though boiling water was sprinkled all over her limbs and torso. The searing winds seemed to have done their worst. Medical treatments had no effect whatsoever.

Able to take the torrid waves no more, she began to pine for home. We tried to dissuade her in vain. Practical grounds disallowed us to retain her for long. Our mudhouse needed upkeep. Her little kitchen garden needed weeding. She had to prove to her bank that she's alive to continue drawing her pension. Her mental faculties

---
[3] 99 Unforgettable Fiction, Non-Fiction, Poetry & Humour, Khushwant Singh, ed. David Davidar and Mala Dayal, Aleph, p. 52

winged her to the peaks of melancholy. She was truly homesick. She must be in deep turmoil inwardly. I did not want to let her go. I had been spending too many years away from my parents. In fact, I could not properly live with them since 1995, when my first job called me away. I'd always felt that my parents didn't love me enough. Perhaps, that's a normal symptom of immature yearning for parental love. I wanted them to live with me now. Especially after my father had taken his permanent leave.

But that seemed a bit selfish of me. My mother is dying for someplace other than my house. She must be aching down inside yet biting her lips to keep it to herself. By tradition, it is expected of her to live out her old age with her eldest son. But she apparently couldn't get along with the feverish inland temperatures. That was clear from the skin bubbles presently germinating all over her body. And perhaps even in niches, we could not expressly verify. If I truly love her, I should not hold her back. Her happiness matters most. And she was obviously not happy living with us in Kolkata. So, it is my bounden duty to submit to her wishes, especially when she is walking into her evening days. Dusk would soon be catching up with her. And I don't want to be the cause of her heartache. So, it is purely out of love and care that I had to let her go.

Choice slipped from my hands at long last. I made time and dropped her home. And wonders upon wonders! The blisters and rashes went away in a day or two. I never thought about it before. But there must be some kind of healing properties in the air of this alpine country. Off with the tall claims of advancement in medical science. She didn't need a lop of ointment anymore.

I'd often come across as a callous, impervious brute due to my unappealing looks and darkish outer shell. To worsen, I love projecting myself as such—stoic, heartless, and insensitive. But looks can be deceptive. After my mother flew back, I began to feel a curious emptiness inside me. I felt abandoned. I became very touchy and vulnerable, unlike the suggestion of my physical appearance. Light sleep returned. I have been an insomniac since the mid-1990s. Now, I am back to spending nights wallowing in self-pity and revisiting my star-crossed fate on the high seas of darkness. Night after night, I would keep awake, fighting the devils of my thoughts and my endless wretched life. I could go days without sleeping with no telling effect. Except for a passing numbness and moments of dizziness that would briefly threaten to spin the head out of equilibrium.

Then it happened. You'll read about it in the chapter 'The Curse of Petrapole' if you are brave enough to plough on.

I never thought of leaving Kolkata until my retirement from service. But I never had the mind to settle in this strange land. Once I superannuated, I would definitely fly back home to start the second innings of my life. But now, my pathetic circumstances suddenly made me despondent all the time. As far as I take myself, I was quite a chirpy boy in any company I kept. And I had fought and won over a dozen bouts of depression. Yet, now, it seemed the ground was slipping under my feet. I began to ache for home, too.

Suddenly, a trapdoor seemed to open somewhere. I'd chanced across an office circular from Guwahati DRI, which was somewhat past its date. On random query, I gathered that the window was still ajar if I would like to squeeze in. Not once in my service career had I asked for a particular place of posting. But now, a tight spot prompted me to pounce on the opportunity. So, I shot off an application without any further delay.

Much to my dismay, though, the Big Boss precipitously rejected my petition and arrested its onward transmission. Clearly, he was not aware of the acute phase I was going through, which, in fact, was the real factor that made me yearn for the break. Now, without a cursory glance, my chance of deputation got swept away by the whims and caprice of one officer.

Luck seldom strikes twice in quick succession. But miracles do happen. I came across a bit of information. Current this time. Guwahati DGGI was requisitioning officers on deputation. Why was God so good to me? Without losing a moment, I shot off an application again. This time accompanying the application with a prayer for sympathetic consideration.

My Superintendent, who was kind to my cause, agreed to plead my case. Clutching a copy of my petitions, he represented me on multiple occasions before the High One. He rested not until the latter dismissed him with a 'Ho jayega' reassurance. That was heart-warming indeed. All we could do now was wait for the application to be forwarded to the concerned authority.

Before long though, everything turned out to be a mistake. The simple fact of pleading for sympathy being the first. I had not completed two years called the 'cooling off' period after my return from a sensitive posting. That was exactly why my previous petition was summarily thrown out. Actually, I had thought that my two years tenure at Review Branch, CCP headquarters, Custom House, was enough 'cool off'. And, presently, I was already running more than one and a half years at Review Branch in Kolkata North Commissionerate headquarters. I was hoping to be granted favour for these continued years under the same disposition, that is, Tribunal & Review. I couldn't be more wrong.

I take this as good information. A warning to all future aspirants that no application should be submitted without perfectly completing all formalities. I guarantee you'll be disappointed unless you have friends who could move mountains. As it happened, as though the original sin of submitting the petition was not grave enough, I happened to complicate it by accompanying it with a prayer for sympathy. I would not be surprised if the Big Boss cracked a dry joke on that impertinent beggary and got a good laugh out of it.

Despite my superior's failed intercessions and our misreading of the 'ho jayega' assurance, I still don't blame the Big Boss. The phrase 'ho jayega' literally translates to 'it shall be done". But one should not take it with blind optimism. I have spoken about Indian bureaucratic equivocation elsewhere in the book. So, in a more liberal rendition, it could very well mean, 'Let's see!' And 'let's see' means, well, you'll see. The only disconcerting fact is that it took almost five months to make known that neither of the wistful interpretations was true.

Moreover, there was no officer I happened to be in touch with who was not reluctant or outright unwilling to step into the Big Boss's presence. It was the talk of the town that he would be on the side of proud if his bearings were judged. But I don't judge anybody. I don't have anything to hold against him. He was absolutely within his rights to deny me mercy. He was fully justified in sticking to the law and repudiating anything and everything that goes against it. He was there to see exactly to that. I would have done the same in his shoes. He had the authority. Why would he bend the rules for my sake? He didn't know me. He never saw me. Well, I mean, he did see me once. Briefly.

I was standing in front of him. A bunch of folders tucked under my arm. I was waiting for a little tick of his signature on the files. Without much of a glance, he instead spared me a little unsavoury remark as though I was an abominable insect. It was about thirty-five seconds before he told me off. It could be less but certainly not more. That wasn't long enough to take the imprint of an unimposing face to one's memory. As such, there was absolutely no reason why he should show me a shred of sympathy. I am no family. I am no acquaintance. I am nobody in his ism circle. I am not even visible from his lofty perch. But I was still hopeful for a drop of kindness on grounds of my distressing state of affairs. That's utterly my fault.

Revenue officers, as the name suggests, are not there to listen to the plight of some lowly worker. They're there to generate government revenue at all costs. Shouldn't it be so bitter, the well-being of a worker does not make an item on their agenda. Enhancing revenue is the sole purpose of their (job's) existence. And you cannot blame them for not entertaining personal issues.

Prayers are answered only when there is a good reason to answer. Mine was never good enough. Merely appealing to somebody's fine sense carries no weight. In all practicality, accepting my prayers would send all the wrong signals to the entire rank and file. There's a fair chance that he would be perceived as a weak administrator. Bent at will by an inferior's supplication. A mere human with all its attendant susceptibilities. Who wants to be an ineffectual ruler, after all? A person who sits on the throne should never betray human frailty. Otherwise, what is the point of wielding the sceptre? Actually, I should have never contemplated tendering the application in the first place. Now, my only consolation was to blame everything on our wretched state of affairs that enflamed me to reach out for the unobtainable without first fulfilling the prerequisite conditions demanded by law. I am a lawbreaker in that sense. It is painful to know. But it is the hard, cold truth. A bitter pill to swallow.

For a man that nurses an embittered heart, all smiles are forced and pretentious. The lips may cut from ear to ear, but the inner core could be bleeding in misery. How truly had the poet observed:

Our sincerest laughter
With some pain is fraught;
Our sweetest songs are those
That tell of saddest thought.[4]

---

[4] Percy Bysshe Shelley in 'To A Skylark'

Chapter 13

BITTER-SWEET TALES

Life is not like the moon. The moon always shows its bright side, hiding its dark face forever. In contrast, life is a three-dimensional scape where all kinds of things happen on every side of the surface: The good, the bad, the pleasant, the nasty, the memorable, and the moments you wish you could leave behind forever. If you have a regular diet of sweetmeats only you will become diabetic, said somebody. How much this holds medically true, I don't know. But I am sure it won't be far from the fact either. Similarly, if I write on only the comical anecdotes of my life, then I would be a charlatan presenting just the amusing façades and pretending to be always having a fun-filled life. In my first book, *The Good Old Days*, to avoid this very pitfall and to add a tinge of sobriety, I had added a few ghost stories and a play on our traditional naming system.

It needs no elaboration that nobody wants to be given an unfair treatment. Yet all of us have had our fair share of it. Many of them may be harmless taunts that faintly linger on the fringe of the memory. But those deliberately meant to hurt could be so painful that even the sands of time could not blow the pains away. For instance, one day, in the early nineties, a mother of a friend of mine happened to accuse me of thieving their kitchen knife. What in the world would I steal a mundane piece of cutlery for? But the accusation was so pointed it completely deflated my self-image. In all estimates, the cutlass wouldn't have cost a fortune. But it was not about making the thievery good by buying them a new knife. It was just plain accusation without any proof. I myself knew not where the blade had gone. I simply had no explanation but to deny the charge. To no avail. Tail tucked between the legs, I walked away never to darken their door again.

Many years later, in a certain school where I was serving as a teacher, a debate competition was held. I was one among the panel of judges. The debate-hall was on the top floor of the school. I was given a simultaneous task of sitting at the back of the auditorium making my evaluations and tending to the students' discipline. That's how teachers work.

As the arguments rounded up, I rushed down to the staff room to have a glass of water before submitting my scoresheet. Just then, the headmaster happened to drop in and nab me by the waterhole. Where else? But that didn't prevent him from slapping me with the charge of unbecoming conduct. He insisted that I had scored the points from the comforts of the staff room without giving my ears to the proceedings. Am I really that good? A farfetched implication. But they say the boss is always right. And boy, he knew how to cling to that adage.

Many of the slights and barbs I've faced in life were due to the deep shit of penury our family was in. For us, the whole year is always a lean period. And, of course, for the unenviable looks I am blessed with. In fact, the shade of my skin comes as a point of contemptuous reference till today. Since childhood, I was literally branded the black sheep of the lot. The negro. Who says we don't have racism in villages!

Well, they are best forgotten now, I guess. Not that they ceased to happen though.

*

That there was something amiss with my heart was known to me since 2002. Limited means compelled me to take it as a minor issue, if not normal. A paternal uncle of mine was a practicing doctor at that time. He prescribed me some pills but charged me no fees. Yet he passed me a typical physician's remark: "You are a ticking time bomb," he said in suppressed alarm. "You can go off any minute!"

"Everybody can go off any minute," I retorted inside my head. Aloud I just murmured: "Hmm!"

I didn't mind the doctor's observation though. I had a good philosophy to not give a damn to anything: *Live life; Tomorrow may never come.* Even had I minded, there's nothing I could do about it.

Years passed and I had pushed the caution deep into the backwaters of my mind, until happened June 20, 2016.

Saturday is a general holiday for central government employees. But where I was posted, it was a seven-days-a-week routine and off-days had to be rostered. I was slotted for Fridays. So, on Thursday nights, I would rush back to the city to spend the weekends with my family.

On that fateful event, I had to overstay Sunday due to unexpected temperature. On the fine morning of the following Monday, I rushed to Sealdah Railway Station to catch the seven-something Bongaon Local. My office was about two-hours train ride and another half-hour autorickshaw drive away. It was then situated on the edge of no man's land across Indo-Bangla border. At the latter part of my tenure there, the office was relocated about half a kilometre inland from the old post to a swanky, newly commissioned, Integrated Check Post called Mukhiya Bhavan. Jokingly among ourselves (colleagues), we used to call it Murgkho Bhavan, the Abode of Fools!

Now, most unfortunately, my heart gave in while I was traveling in the local train. My wife and a good friend of mine picked me up from the third station. A couple of days in the hospital later, I was discharged with a certificate which confirmed what I had known for years but consciously refused to believe. HCM—Hypertrophic Cardiomyopathy!

For more details on the heart failure, please go to the chapter *The Curse of Petrapole.*

*

I should not have written this section. But the memory was always fresh and the pain of discrimination never recedes. Hence!

In 2013 three of us in the Accounts Branch got promoted to the grade of inspector under Estt. Order No. 57/2013 dated 15.04.2013. A subsequent Order No. 21/2013 dated 06.05.2013 got us posted at different places each. For the time being though, we were specifically *'retained in [our] place of posting till further orders'.* This, in official parlance, is called 'in situ' posting. Nine months later, we got released vide Relieving Order dated 26.02.2014 to join our respective units.

Another two months later, there was a buzz in the air that honoraria were given away to Accounts staff in retrospective effect. Reckoning myself eligible too, I went over to the cash counter to receive the incentive. To my astonishment, the cashier told me that my name was not included in the bill. Shocked was the kindest way of putting my reaction at that moment.

I crossed over to the accounts officer who was seated next to the cash cubicle. He had apparently overheard our conversation already. "Sir," I demanded. "Why is my name not in the bill?"

"You are already transferred," he replied, shrugging nonchalantly.

"But my friends are also transferred and posted out under the same order?"

At that, he got up and simply walked out on me.

To state the obvious: There were twelve staff members in the Accounts Branch for the material period. Of these, eleven of them were granted the honorarium. My name was starkly conspicuous by its absence. There must be a very good reason to so singularly bar me from it. Or I might have broken a serious law to disqualify myself so unceremoniously.

My fellow Inspectors did not want to dwell on the subject with me. I still don't know why.

*

Our office. January 6, 2015.

Around half past ten in the morning, the boss was coming around to give a look at the tidying-up exercise of the rooms. The cadre restructuring and reorganisation of field formation had suddenly come into force. With a coterie of officers flitting around him like butterflies, the boss strode into one room after another until he dropped into ours too.

We—a couple of inspectors—were actively discussing how to reclaim the corner space in our newly allotted room. In the northern nook was a rickety cupboard ready to come apart. Beside it was a huge Local Area Network Printer lying out of order. Even if it were in order, it won't serve any purpose. There was never a LAN connection in our section. But we could not simply chuck it away. There are procedures for proper disposal of official waste. Nobody may care as long as they sit where they are. But fail to trace them and your heads will roll.

It was at that juncture as we were contemplating how to rid ourselves of the redundant articles that the boss strutted in. "Are you not officers? You must work like officers," he jabbered in without slowing down his stride, excitedly pointing at the obsolete assets we were presently applying our minds to. "You should carry the cupboard and the printer yourselves. I must see them out of here by afternoon"

To us, it sounded like, "Move your butts! Move your butts!"

Overseeing the relocating process, the boss's refrain was: "Work like officers. Carry your own files. Move the computers, tables and almirahs yourselves. Sweep and dust your own rooms and furniture..." Did he mean we were hanging around waiting for all the stuffs to fall into place by themselves in a Potteresque magic? We could only murmur behind his back.

The process of restructuring was in full swing. The problem was that the basic infrastructure and arrangements were obviously not given sufficient attention. As a consequence, we had to function with skeletal facilities. The room allotted us was literally stark empty. No chairs. No tables. No nothing. Put in the plainest terms, not even a place to rest your arse. A bunch of dusty old files migrated from existing or abolished units were all that we had.

Those quick-witted ones took their computers with them to their new place of work. But those shifted from undissolved divisions like us had no such advantage. We had to leave behind the amenities for the next officers to succeed.

I made requisition after requisition to the relevant section until I became a laughing stock for holding hope. But without equipment, it was my work that was hampered. Nobody comes to your rescue when you land in real trouble. It was one for one and none for all. Is it any wonder that I took responsibility for my own resources and convenience?

Visually miffed, I went over to the Section one day. On a previous occasion, I had seen two sets of computers lying idle there in the corner. One of them was in working condition. The other was left to collect dust. I enquired if I could have the broken one to get it repaired and put to good use. The in-charge officer reacted as though I was making advances into his private estate. My entreaties fell on granite ears. Giving up was not an option though. You don't get computers from thin air. So, I went to our divisional command and requested him to step in. A long-drawn reasoning ensued that the computer was out of order anyways. The Section relented.

My room was on the eighth floor. Number 820. It was not a big joy carrying an inoperative computer up to it. I made requests to the computer section for a technician. They never sent one. Christmas came and went. Still no help showed.

My work started to pile up heavily. I could only discharge the most urgent files in long hand. It was embarrassing. I had to draw the letterhead by hand to draft the most immediate correspondences. As for the office logo, I am not an artist. It won't look near it even with my best attempt. So, I left out that part altogether. But our AC was really understanding that he signed on such handwritten communications without any hesitation.

I was beginning to get frustrated running from pillar to post, asking for computers and stealing moments from available ones to do my job. It was not easy getting a free computer. In the wake of restructuring, everybody had each a mountain of work to bury his nose in. And the computer section still failed to send me an expert. At last, I decided to take the risk and give myself a look into my new dysfunctional computer.

I brought a screwdriver set and soldering material from home and started tinkering with the PC cabinet. I found that the start button had shorted out. I twisted some copper wires together and welded them to the connecting points. Then, I powered it up. Lo! It worked. How happy I was to have a computer to work on! My own office computer.

But I still needed a printer. My requisitions for one were not yet met. So, I still had to hunt for free printers to get even a line or two done.

My joy was short-lived though. Not before a month, the machine went kaput again. After innumerable complaints to the computer section, a repairman did finally turn up. But only to tell me what I had already known: The computer was dead. "I know that, damn it!" I wanted to shout in his face. But he was already out of sight.

Days later, probably piqued at my persistent calls, the repair guy made an appearance again. This time he told me that the storage disk had crashed. How? Why? I had no answers. Neither had he. All he said was that their contract was for repairs and not supply of hardware. So, he offered me an easier solution: Purchase a new hard disk from your own pocket. He would be glad to help install it. I argued I was not authorized to make private purchases for official equipment and that I could not afford one personally. The technician simply disappeared. I took the matter to my supervisor.

Many days later, the computer section assigned a technician who told me to bring the PC down to him on the second floor. And more weeks later, I got it back with the HDD replaced. But I lost all my data and had to begin from scratch again.

The previous computer guy came to refit the machine and demanded a *'baksheesh'* of a few hundred rupees. He had done nothing much, in my opinion. He was simply jacking in a plug here, thrusting a cord there, flicking an electrical switch on, and ultimately powering up the system. I had done the same a thousand times with my home computer. Was that worth a reward of a hundred rupees? After all, he was doing his job. Is demanding a tip for doing one's own job fine?

I was not ready to cough up a single paisa. So, I told him to have a talk with my Superintendent, if he must.

Chapter 14

WINNING A FRIEND

When I was posted at the outstation, there was this colleague of mine who would treat me like a halfwit. Had he known me inside out, he would have treated me far worse. For, I certainly am not a halfwit but a full-blown fool. When he was in his elements, which was more often than not, he would be at his superior-attitude-best and drive me mad with irritation. Not a damn toot he gave to my protestations. I was not brave enough to express myself befittingly. Kenny Rogers' country hit *'Coward of the County'* would describe me best: *"He'd never stood one single time/to prove the country wrong...."*

I could only shrug off his arms he had 'lovingly' thrown around my neck. Or give him a cold shoulder for his courtesies for jest. I would non-verbally respond that my head was no more where it was meant to be. The more I took offense the more he seemed to enjoy getting on my nerves.

This annoying bloke had a way of constantly reminding me of my general lack of knowledge and ineptitude in workplace. He would order me around even for his personal errands. "Go, fetch me my bag!" "Pass me this file or that!" "Hey, *babu*...!" I don't think I have to explain the word *'babu'* in its implicative sense of the term.

We would often be together on our way to the train station. Our off-days fall on the same day. Then he would be at his atrocious best. He would fling his arms around my neck with a naughty laugh, for I was way shorter than he, and pass mischievous remarks to purposefully rub on my sensibilities. I felt like an idiotic flunkey of a gutter-don. He knew I wouldn't react. He would flash a contemptible grin at my face grimacing in discomfiture. The urge to lash out a sucker punch on his face was irresistible. But what is the point of raising a ruckus in a strange land? A land where you are a stranger even to your own countrymen? To meekly behave as a dimwit that I naturally am was in my best interest.

Stories of fellow-hillspeople coming out to the mainland with big hopes of making it but going home in wooden boxes are constant reminders to keep my tempers to myself. I might have fumed or ranted a couple of times. That's that. My docile appeals for a little respect had evoked no response.

However, as time went on, I realized that I was summing him up in a different perspective. I was reading him wrong for all this while. He's had this nature of throwing a dry humour with an attitude without really meaning it. He was a fun-loving guy after all. I was absolutely mistaken to hold him with bitterness in my heart at the time. I changed my perspective and we began to get along.

More time went on. And by the time we parted ways we ended up on good terms. We could not become bosom friends as we got posted in different places. And he soon got his promotion to become my superior. Yet, I am happy that we ended in a happy note and talked to each other whenever we happen to meet. I have won myself a good friend.

Chapter 15

BEATING THE NATIONAL FEVER (ALMOST)

In those days, friends in our residential campus would buzz with excitement when the Staff Selection Commission declared the dates for Combined Graduate Level Examination. SSC exams are a fever caught by every Indian youth aspiring for a government job. We are no exception.

I had long given up studying for competitive examinations. But I couldn't help being sucked into the vortex when every guy I knew started filling up the forms. Understandably, all of us were after a better job or higher entry level. Who isn't? So, I decided to join the bandwagon once more. I shot off an application form. That was 2011. I didn't let anybody know about it though. An admission certificate reached me on 1st June. My roll number was 4410516776.

From the animated discussions my friends used to have in our evening football games on the campus lawn, I could easily make out that I was no longer in their league. They talked about altered syllabi, convoluted question patterns, modified formats and all that sort. Such things were beyond my grasp. I have stopped following competitive examinations from the day I joined this service. Even when I actively pursued, I was always a below-average candidate. I had hardly made the cuts.

So out of touch I was that I have lost all track of the particulars. Nothing would trigger a sense of alarm even when friends went into a tizzy! A fool indeed knows not what to fear and what not to. It was not the expectation to make it but the refusal to be left out that forced me to jump into the fray. Going back to my old study materials was the last thing on my mind. I was simply daring to take the bull by its horns with an old stock of general knowledge. I just wanted to be in the crowd.

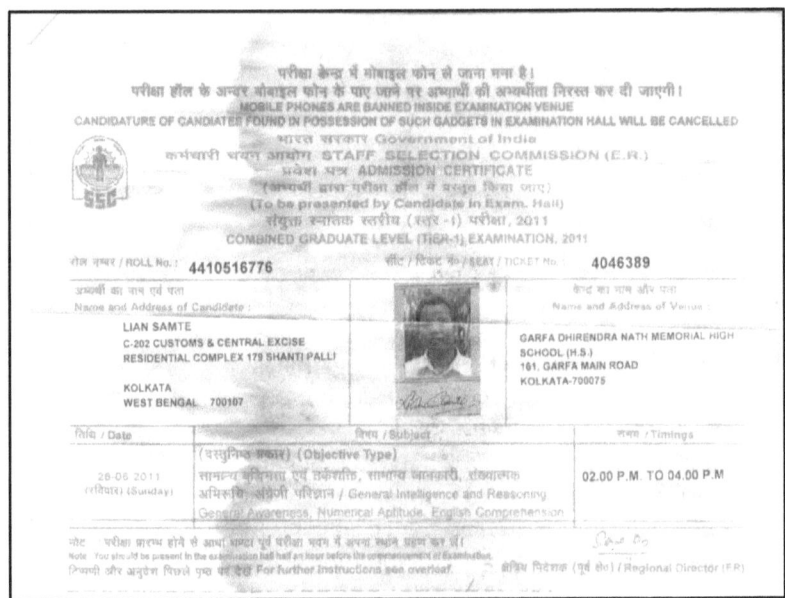

—*Admit Card to Tier-I*—

Lady Luck smiled on me rarely. But this was one occasion that she did. I made it to the first tier of the competition. The second tier comes up in a few months' time. Everybody, all across the country, must have burnt the midnight oil. For me, clearing the first hurdle itself was a fluke. So, I was certain I would bomb the next stage. Preparation was not an option. However, as the day drew nearer, a kind of tension gripped me from within. An ill-learnt man's fear of exams! I became anxious in the eleventh hour. I was nervous and thought I should have given my books at least a runover. I would make a couple of hours at nights. But sustaining became a problem due to the wearying day's work. So, it was only at the weekends that I could devote to reading.

The day drew nearer. Just a week's time. My friend in the section applied for a five days' casual leave. A last dash preparation. That was granted outright. Taking cue, I too prayed for two days. Fickle Luck played foul. The boss refused me. Not to blow my own trumpet but to only attest that accidental breaks could always come your way, I must reveal: Against the odds, I'd managed to scrape through the second level as well.

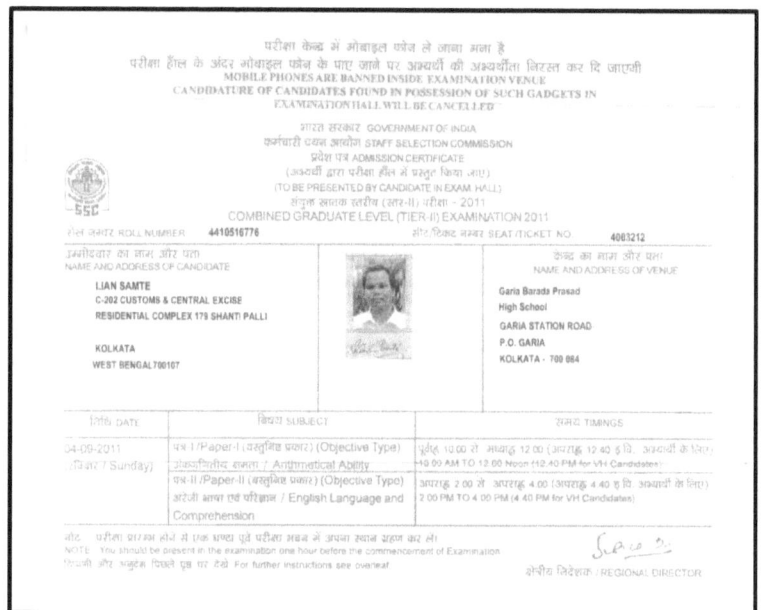

—*Admit Card to Tier-II*—

So sure to tank, I even refused to check the results when they were declared. I chose to be blissful in my ignorance until a letter slid under our doorstep on October 7, 2011. It was an intimation to appear the personal interview at the Eastern Regional Office, Nizam Palace, Kolkata. That was a pleasant surprise, indeed. Only two from our friends' circle made it to the vivas. One, obviously, being me.

Don't ask me how the personal interview went.

I had submitted writing, football, and singing, as my hobbies. Writing? I was clearly being presumptuous. I was taking huge liberties from a couple of my substandard articles that found their way into some obscure local media in the past. Singing? Well, I had come to learn from friends that Roshan, a Meetei colleague of ours, was once asked to sing a traditional song of theirs when he mentioned singing as a hobby. Anticipating the same treatment, I had learnt by heart one folk song which is very common in our community. I was prepared to sing it heartily.

Speaking of singing, a reminiscence presently struck my mind. Let me share it right away lest I miss it out altogether. The incident took place in Children's Training Higher Secondary School where I was serving as a teacher in the later 1990s. One afternoon, in the dispersal assembly, some students were rounded up for indiscipline when Jana Gana Mana, the national anthem, was sung. The assembly master paraded them in front of the gathering, himself strutting around like a slave-master conducting an auction in a slave-market. He bade them to attention.

"Sing," he barked.

The anticipation was that the boys would shy and refuse to sing. Or mess up in trying. Such an act would certainly call for a strict action. And corporal punishment was the norm in those days.

The boys sized up, clipped their feet, and sang with full confidence. Loud, proper and clear. If they had any inhibition, not a hint showed in their faces or in their voices. Taking everyone by surprise. The assembly-master gaped in amazement. Or was it in admiration? Robbed of the opportunity to dish out the cane, he could not help but give them a wide grin and let them go. The students saved their skins with their boldness and quick thinking.

Who says you don't learn from your own students? I was now minding to put that very lesson into practice should I be asked to sing. But the Chairman proved to be a shrewd one. "What is the size of the goal?" He asked me instead, skirting the song-question.

That must not prove a hard one either considering the fondness I claimed for the sport. But it was a curved ball nevertheless.

"I never measured it, Sir," I answered innocently.

The members broke into a peal of laughter. I couldn't help but laugh with them.

There was an elderly lady-member seated slightly to my right. "They say insurgency is rampant in Manipur," she chimed in. "What'll happen to us if we come to visit your hometown?"

"Well, Ma'am," I replied promptly as though expecting the question. "News are often blown out of proportion. Just come. I'll personally take you around. Nothing will happen to you."

A bigger peal of laughter.

Actually, I was not able to put myself across in a proper way. A lot of things, nice things, were going on inside my head. Boiling them down in a sentence or two was the problem. I don't want to say I was nervous. But in the face of interviewers, I must've been inwardly intimidated. It was a clear lack of expression on my part, to be honest. A sign of poor learning. I should have read more widely. Just early that year, a fellow northeasterner had released a beautiful travelogue called *'East of the Sun'*. He is a Guwahatian named Siddhartha Sarma.

He was a journalist working in Delhi at the time of writing his account, as I gathered from the book. There, Cid, that's how he calls himself in the book, has captured the exact words for me when I was bungling before the interviewers. Let me steal the concluding lines of the fourteenth chapter. "From a distance, reading the land (the Northeast) in a newspaper, you get all sorts of notions," rounded up Cid. Parenthesis supplied. "Just don't trust everything the papers tell you: they don't give you the usual, the ordinary, the commonplace, the normal…"

If it's not so unbecoming of me, I want to borrow the entire last paragraph itself. Please allow me to back-quote:

Someday, all the other unresolved problems in the region will be sorted out and the people will go on with their lives. But, otherwise, the place is just like any other on earth, maybe a shade more beautiful, a shade more naturally unspoilt, a shade more complicated and therefore fascinating in trying to understand, and totally worth travelling in.

Speaking of insurgency and laughter, they might be an odd combination. But I think one amusing instance that merits recollection here. A drama within a drama. The incident involved some colleagues of mine back at Jubilee Model School, Simenchapari (a branch of Jonai JMS, Assam), where I was sent to fill the gap left by Sir Zampu in 1996, if my memory serves me right.

The pleasant clime and easy weather condition of our hometown often made the subject of our daily chats. Some friends got curious and eager to come over to experience in person. In 1997, even after leaving the job, Sir Zampu managed to persuade an erstwhile local colleague, Sir Ranjit, to pay him a visit. He was probably keeping an old commitment. Unfortunately, that was when the Kuki-Zomi civil war was raging at its height. Poor Ranjit! On the very night he landed, the Kuki militants happened to mount an assault from the western fringe of our hometown, a few hundred metres from his host's residence.

Gunshots rang all around. Bullets whizzed past overhead like meteor showers. The petrified vacationer had no choice but to spend the night under his bed. No wonder, he never allowed himself to be taken around. He left early next morning. We never heard of him again! We couldn't help but spare a good laugh on hearing this hapless incident.

Even at the present time, given the undercurrent reality of our fluid socio-political environment, my assurances to the respectable lady were promising nothing better. Admittedly, her doubts were absolutely not misplaced. It's no surprise that the members did not hold back their merriment.

In the lounge, my fellow interviewees were anxious, thinking I had already clinched the deal. As I exited, they flocked around me like birds of a feather and flooded me with questions as to how I won over the members. I had nothing to say. The results came. My name would not be discovered even with a microscope. I had never won over the Board.

Athhs exthpecteth!

Chapter 16

THE CURSE OF PETRAPOLE

I was due for mandatory non-CCA posting after being recently promoted to the grade of inspector. As a rule, I had to leave station and serve in a rural outpost. I had never been posted away from Central Excise Bhavan, now GST Bhawan. I had been continuously stationed here for the last seven years or more. As such, even a slight thought of leaving the premises was inwardly intimidating. I do not have a big fondness for the office per se. But it has become sort of a comfort zone.

I always develop cold feet to be a first-timer in new surroundings. Despite my strong desire to make an adventure out of every turn of life, I could not find excitement in being a newbie in an unfamiliar ground. I always felt like a fish out of water. Awkward, embarrassed and uncomfortable. I've picked up this reversion from the frequent school-hops in my childhood days. I guess everybody knows what it means to be a new kid on the block. I am a diffident soul from the very start. I am a puny creature, innately built to command no fear or respect. True to it, when an imminent transfer was in the air and the time was ripe to go places, I was instead shuddering from inside. I did put up a brave face to the world but deep down I was lying to myself.

Serving non-CCA, as I'd already mentioned, was mandatory for the grade I was promoted to. So, knowing I could be relocated any time, I had asked around beforehand if there's any known face presently posted in the outlying areas. No much luck. But I did have a friend who'd always encouraged me to take the Customs option and join him in the outpost. In his words, he always happened to be the only person from the Northeast wherever he was posted ever since he joined the department. And he used to feel very lonely at times, he admitted, having nobody to talk to in his native tongue or at least in a language he was familiar with. I could share his feeling closely. I'd felt the same the first time I came out to the mainland. When he first mooted the idea, I had not given much thought. I had not anticipated my turn to come any time soon. Now, that it has finally come, he was the first person to cross my mind. In fact, I guess, he was as happy as I to hear the news. For, should I be posted with him, then we wouldn't be total strangers anymore with one another by each other's side.

To jump the gun, it so happened that I do get posted where I had wished for. Petrapole LCS where this friend of mine was presently posted. What more could I ask? My fears allayed to a large extent. The only fear that remained was but the remnants of my diffident attitude.

As I'd already stated, I was never in the outpost before. It is not my custom to drift on my way to office or back. Obviously so, my daily routine was from home to office and from office straight back to home. Unless I have a pressing concern, I never strayed from this pattern. A honeybee sticking to its dance-path. Moreover, never since I landed in Kolkata had I travelled in a local train. So, taking a ride on a local train and travelling up eighty kilometres north, that too all on my own, became the first challenge I had to face.

I think it's time to bring my friend to light. He is Inspector Songlawmthang Songate. A friend and colleague who encouraged me to take this opportunity in the first place. He had practically guided me over the phone all through my first local train journey. From the very point I was to start out, he showed me the way. The twists and the turns I should make when I stepped out from home to catch the train in time. How to get to Sealdah station. How to cut the ticket. How much to pay. Where to stand and wait. Even to the train timing. He was accurate to the last detail.

As prompted, I started out from our quarters complex at six in the morning. I caught a taxi at E.M. Bypass, a spitting distance from our residence. And headed for Sealdah station. At the station, the taxi metre displayed a fare of Rs. 160. But the driver insisted on an extra charge of Rs. 10 on the pretext of unseen added taxes. Taken for a ride on the very first day, eh! I realised that I was only beginning to face the real world. Having no time to haggle, I just paid up without a word. For my eight years in Kolkata, I had hardly seen a taxi driver sticking to the amount indicated in the fare metre. They somehow added some percentage to it to compensate whatever they had in mind. A daylight robbery nobody protests.

I seldom travelled local trains on my own. It was beyond my comfort zone. A crowd was swirling madly in the station like a host of locusts. I noticed long human-chains at every ticket-counter. I appended myself to one of these ends. Somebody said India is absolutely averse to spaces. A gap between two persons would be filled up in less than a minute. Truly so, I was sandwiched from behind by another ticket prospector in no time. My turn came eventually. I got a current pass for Bongoan Junction with twenty rupees.

A medium duffel bag, a backpack and a brand-new Milton lunchbox were my mere luggage. It was now five minutes to seven. The display boards had not flashed details of my train schedule which was due for fifteen minutes. That was a worry with me. Can an Indian rail be ready in fifteen minutes, I wondered. I walked over to a nearby helpdesk. The khaki-clad security apologized for being unable to give me any assistance at the moment. "Wait for the display," he simply said.

With absolute faith, I stood there below the board, never taking my eyes off the electronic panel. I rang up my distant guide, Songa, to make sure I was on the right track. He agreed with the security's advice: "The display won't come on until it's due for five minutes or less." My doubts were allayed.

With about five minutes to go, the red dots on the panel refreshed and bid to me to hurry to platform No. 4A. I briskly walked past platforms 2, 3 and 4. But where the hell was 4A? Why couldn't they just make it 5? Do they think I am Harry Potter and his friends going to platform No. 7¾? I cross-travelled between platforms 4 and 5 for several times until I spotted it. The signboard was a little off-way.

I made my way into one of the compartments and grabbed a window seat. In no time, the train hooted its last call before lurching for departure. It was seven-fifteen. In India, a train running five minutes late is considered exactly on the dot. The passengers began settling their arses when I asked a co-passenger if I was indeed headed for the right direction. He put my last doubts to rest. It is not my custom to take directions from strangers unless I was completely lost or unaware of my surroundings. But travelling after a long interlude kept me out of touch and made me a little nervous.

Blowing relief, I placed a call to Songa: "I am on my way."

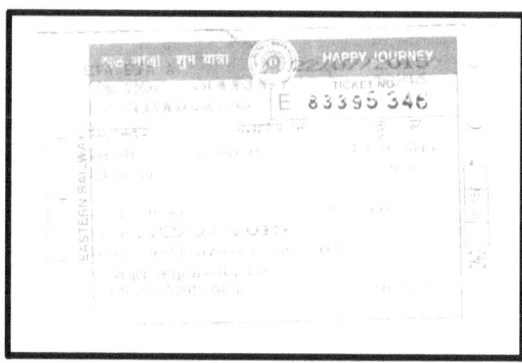

—*My First Local Train Ticket*—

The ride would have been a lonesome one had it not been for a string of live entertainers on the train. We were not far past the city. A blind singer ambled in and pleased our ears with a local number. An ampli-speaker combo hung from his shoulder, providing the accompaniment. Sonorous and mesmerizing was his voice that passengers began tossing him coins even as he sang. The train chugged on merrily. At every stop, swarms of vendors would swoop in with their assorted wares. Fruits, nuts, chips, local-made sweetmeats and eatables. Books, Chinese thingamajigs and all kinds of electronic gizmos at throwaway prices. A certain vendor touted that his vernacular cookbook contains recipes for everything under the sun. A middle-aged lady to my left fell for it. She paid ten rupees for a set of three books. But she couldn't seem to find anything the peddler had claimed to have been there. She called after him and asked what is where and where is what. The peddler cried everything is there in black and white. Curious madam! After a session of cross-questioning, the peddler's patience was tested. I think he just said, "Go home and read at leisure," before he left the lady to herself.

Thanks to this myriad company of entertainers and lively state of affairs, I could make the three hours journey without a hint of loneliness. Well, the train ride did not exactly last three long hours. Probably, my guide had reckoned the lap from the moment I stepped out from home. Actually, the ride was about two hours. However, I was not to learn about it till we had our pleasantries at dinnertime.

I was taken aback when the train whizzed past stops he told me were about nearing my destination. I sent him a short message to specify the second-last station. He called me back rather. But that was already too late. The remaining passengers had risen in unison and threatened to leave me alone. Taking cue, I picked up my bags and, as any remaining passenger did, pressed for the exit. When I took the call, I was already down at Bongaon Junction looking around like a lost puppy, unsure which way to proceed.

Following the crowd with my eyes, I saw, on the other side of the platform, autorickshaws my guide had pointed out to gun for as soon as I got off the train. I was not definitely fast enough. All the motor-rickshaws were taken when I made to the stand. I had to cross the footbridge above the rail tracks. Losing no hope, I waited for the next trip. A new line queued up in no time. It doesn't take long for another round of autorickshaws to appear. Then, we, six passengers, were taken away, past Bongaon town, to the Indo-Bangla frontier.

"Border," I called out as I boarded the auto. The driver nodded.

Ignorant of the location I was to get off, I requested the balding, salt-and-pepper driver to prompt me accordingly.

I felt it was about time we come to my destination. But our auto had no mind of slowing down. So, I reminded the driver where I was getting off. Before long, a big green signboard came into view. It says: *'You are entering India-Bangladesh border area. Always be cautious.'* A red skull-and-bones pictograph ominously smiled inside a triangle from each side of the margin. "I am alighting at Jayantipur Bazaar," I called out again.

The auto halted right by the signboard. I got down and tendered twenty rupees. The fare my guide told me over the phone. The driver demanded five rupees more, which I think, was for my taking extra help. I placed a call to inform that I had arrived and was standing like a fool beside a tree with a circular concrete around its trunk.

"Can you take the small alley down from there?" Songa instructed over the phone.

Which side is down, which side is up, I didn't know: "To my right or to my left?" I shot back.

It was not possible for him either to determine my right or my left as he didn't see which way I was facing. In seconds though, he walked up from the other side of the road, which I later learnt is Jessore Road, from where he waved at me. I crossed the road and followed him to his rented apartment. It was not even half-a-minute walk from there.

In his rented room: Songa introduced me to his roommate, Inspector Jayanta Kumar Mondal. Mondal happened to be a colleague of mine at Service Tax HQ several years ago. He also recognized me at first sight. That was reassuring indeed. What was sad, however, was that Mondal and Songa were leaving me in a short while following their transfer back to the headquarters. I was also introduced to the maid who must be in her fifties and spoke only Bengali. She was wrinkled and wiry. Her immediate worry was how to communicate with me once my two friends left us. For, I spoke not a smattering of Bangla.

A couple of hours later, we were at the office. Songa indicated a computer next to his table. I tabbed out a joining report in a jiffy. From the Canon copying machine nearby, I duplicated a few copies of my posting order to enclose with my joining report. Then he requested a contingent staff to submit it at the reception on my behalf. Kali-da readily took up the task. Later, he took me to the Assistant Commissioner, Mr. Shree Ram Vishnoi, IRS, for necessary introductions.

As we returned to his table, a fair, chubby officer dropped by. "Hey, I know you," he chirped in without any need for intros.

"I know you, too," I replied, instantly registering his face. But my weakness is still my weakness. His name hung on the tip of my tongue.

"Meet my Superintendent," Songa said and rose to greet the officer.

"You're at Service Tax, weren't you?" the Superintendent asked me as though to make sure his memory didn't lie.

"Yes, Sir," I replied.

We shook hands and had a fleeting session of pleasantries. Then, he disappeared again as suddenly as he appeared. As we were by ourselves again, I asked Songa what the officer's name was. Songa himself struggled to pronounce it. He even made a slight mistake when he wrote it out. However, the misspelling was enough to ring the bell loud and clear. It all came back in bold print. The officer's name was Sanjoy Kumar Batabyal. When we were at Service Tax, he was still an inspector. I had known him as a cool and level headed person. I was soon to experience more about him. Only time will tell.

It was completely dark when we came back from office. Masi, the maid, was already preparing dinner for us. Mondal went to the roadside stalls to come back with some vegetables and fruits. Before long, he was slicing up cucumbers and tomatoes for salad. I wondered why he didn't let the maid do that. Songa explained that he was a fussy man whose custom was sometimes bordering irritation.

Few hours rest later, we set down to have our meal.

There was nothing eventful in having a dinner. Perhaps, the only different thing was Mondal giving us a whole mango each for dessert. A practice I never did before.

Mondal was first to finish his plate. Then, he peeled his mango with his bare hands and took big, delicious bites. Yellow juice oozing between his fingers. I pinched mine and felt it a little too hard. I tried a bite. My teeth didn't sink. I thought Mondal had some special ability which I didn't. I presumed my fellow tribal wouldn't have it either. So, I rose to fetch a cutter from the kitchen. But before I could return, Songa had already followed Mondal's example, chomping rough chunks in his mouth.

Feeling left out, I quickly applied my knife to the fruit. To my shock, it was absolutely hard and raw. After a few strokes, a small crisp, white matter appeared from beneath the green skin. My two friends were already holding their sides in laughter. Unable to help, and also to console me for my bad luck, Songa patted me on the back: "That's the way newcomers are welcomed. Don't worry."

We all had a hearty laugh.

Thinking the fruit would be unripe and sour, I refused to take a bite. Dinner done, we stretched on our respective cots. And having nothing to do, and the night still being young, I decided to test the green mango somehow. To my pleasant surprise, the stuff tasted quite sweet and aromatic. Bite after bite, I relished the unexpected delight until it was time to retire. "You see, it isn't so bad after all," I challenged my friends. "I still have it while yours have gone."

My friends couldn't help jesting at me although I felt it was I who had the last laugh.

About a year later, things began to change. For better or for worse, that I couldn't tell. It was June 20, 2016.

As I did many times by now, that day too I boarded the train at Sealdah Station. And as is my wont, I grabbed the window seat immediately. No sooner than the train chugged out of station, I suddenly felt a strong rush of heat overpowering me from within. Sweat gushed from every pore, drenching me from head to toe. Yet, I did not remember running my hands or a handkerchief to mop the perspiration.

In no time, the train picked up speed and everything became a smudge. The wooden sleepers along the tracks, the slums and tenements alongside the railroads, the highrises, the ponds and the scrubby vegetation by the rail line, everything began to whizz past in a fast motion blur. The guys sitting opposite me began to dissolve into the shadows. I must have sunk into a momentary slumber.

When I opened my eyes again, the world outside was still zipping in a hazy speed. Heavy beats tortured my eardrums. The back of my shirt grew slippery against the metal-leaning of the seat. I was completely soaked. Sharp punches pounded the sides of my temples with a threat to bust the arteries. My head grew light and woozy. Dull aches throbbed mercilessly in the veins behind the earlobes. Through misty half-cracked eyes, I could make out a substation coming up in a distance: Dum Dum Cantonment. Probably the third stop in line. Pulling myself together, I strung my backpack and staggered across the floor to get off as soon as the train should slow down.

The train for Bongaon would already be crammed at this time of day. But I could not recall brushing against any shoulder on my way across the door. Had I staggered all the way eyes wide shut? And I hardly remembered the rush of passengers trying to force themselves in, which is also a normal at this time of day.

The train hooted and moved on. I did not know when I got down or took the unoccupied concrete bench on the deserted platform. It was probably vacated by the persons who had just boarded the train. Consciousness threatened to take leave of me again. My head reeled wilder than before. The muted ache stepped up its tempo and intensity. I was lying prone. I thought a little rest would do me good enough to continue with the journey. But something felt strangely wrong inside. So, after biding for a moment, I pulled my weakened nerves together and placed a call to my better half. I always had my wife's number on the homescreen of my cell phone with a direct dial facility keeping such an emergency in mind. It turned out to be quite presentient.

Now, having placed the briefest call I've ever made to my wife, I blew a sigh of relief and phased out with a peace of mind. Somebody would be collecting me in a while. Help seemed to take forever. My wife, along with my close friend, Mr Romeo Vaiphei, had to squander many a precious minutes scouring the platform until they could identify a motionless bundle that resembled my description. They shook me awake.

My wife gathered my backpack. My chum offered me his back for a piggy ride. I of course turned it down despite my draining energy. The big ego had not abandoned me yet. Dangling me between their shoulders, they half-dragged me to the waiting yellow cab. I'd never walked such a distance before in my life. I felt we took ages. I must be in and out of it. I didn't remember being piled into the taxi. But we were soon on our way. I could, every now and then, make out vague building-tops through my half-drawn eyes. I was laid on the rear seat. My head rested on the lap of my bonnie.

My rescuers said their taxi had taken almost an hour to reach here and a good additional time to negotiate the choking bylanes into the station premises. It was rush hour. Yet, I felt we hardly took ten minutes on our way back to drive into the Apollo Hospital off VIP Road. I doubt my time-keeping could be fully trusted at that moment though.

After a battery of tests in the vestibule, we were verbally advised to get admitted by depositing two lakh rupees upfront. Had I heard that first hand, I think I would've gotten well at that very instant. The sum was unheard of to us and way beyond our means. Left with no option, my wife requested a referral to Desun Hospital. Desun Hospital is literally located at a stone's throw from our residential complex. Spitting distance would be more like it. Besides, it is one of the most prominent heart specialist hospitals in town. The discount benefit they offered to the staff of Custom & Central Excise Department under a central government health scheme was a cherry on the icing.

Request granted.

We instantly zoomed away in a medically armoured vehicle. In a slightly offbeat note: I had always wanted to hear that ubiquitous siren up close from inside the ambulance itself. Amusingly though, I heard nothing of that sort that day. Was our ambulance not pinging that piercing, discordant ditone? Bad luck upon bad luck!

Straight upon arrival at Desun, I was trundled into the emergency entrance from behind the hospital. A backdoor entry, eh? In haste, cursory examinations were conducted again in the foyer itself. A short while later, I was packed off to the intensive care unit. I was kept under observation for the next twenty-four hours.

Before long, a few friends had collected to enquire after my welfare. One of them was Lalboi Doungel, an all-time good friend. I took his name because he had this rib-tickling anecdote he told my wife later. I shall relate it presently:

I was wheeled out of the ICU to the testing room for angiography. Seeing me prone and senseless on the gurney, Lalboi turned around and faced the wall, choking with emotion. As he told my wife later that day, he was truly terrified because that particular doctor and the test I was going through had a very low rate of success. He even knew somebody who had never woken up again from an exact similar procedure. And, as he had to say, he was afraid that that could be the last time he would ever see me alive.

I did make the ordeal alright. But never as fit and bouncy anymore.

Now, as though the commendable care the nurses gave me wasn't enough, a man who appeared the least bit of a medical type, joined to prep me for further manoeuvres. He placed himself at the foot of the bed and fished out a razor from his kitpack. Then, non-verbally, he commanded me to rid myself of my knickers. I was already stripped to the bone under the sheets. Why was I not allowed a personal dignity, at least? Left with no choice, I saw my inners away with a scalding blush. No prizes for guessing. How they must've smelled with the day's toil and sweat! I was yet to have a proper bath.

The man positioned himself. Then, he took my limp manhood in a pinch between his thumb and index finger as though he was retrieving a piece of rag from a privy pit. That was the second time my member got such a preposterous attention. First time it was at a certain hospital in Gurgaon in the year 2000. The doctor rolled it between his fingers to determine my medical fitness to join the Armed Forces HQ at South Block, New Delhi.

The cold touch of steel brought me back in a vicious start from my brief reverie. The blade slid swiftly into the pubic province, putting itself to the least conceivable use. The master-shaver was dexterous. Mowing down my private vegetation without any hint of mercy. When he was done with, my lower front felt like the smooth bottoms of a freshly bathed baby. Even the slightest whiff of air made the entire estate tingle.

In the days that followed, the doctor advised me not to put myself to excessive physical and mental strain. Most importantly, he advised me to give up rigorous exercises and sporting activities. And I must absolutely abstain from unaccompanied travelling. I took the counsel in a humorous stride. I never believed I could give up the sport I loved most, football, for one inconsequential illness. And I certainly couldn't take my wife to office every day!

I should have requested him to put down the advisory on the discharge certificate. Having not done so proved to be my grave undoing. He only noted: *Restful life at home.* However, even had he printed it in glowing letters of gold, it may not necessarily serve any purpose. So, it's better to shake it off.

I am a jolly fellow, at least to the people I am comfortable with. So, I never took the medical condition seriously. It was not before I came to a news item in a certain national paper that I began to consider it as a situation. One Anwar Ali was the cynosure of all eyes in the Indian football world when he played every minute of India's campaign in the FIFA U-17 World Cup, 2017. He was in a league of his own for all the three years he was with the Indian Arrows. The high point of his career arrived when he inked a lucrative contract with the Mumbai City FC to play in India's premier soccer league called ISL. However, his dream of a super career began to crumble even before it kicks off. He was diagnosed with a congenital heart condition, an extremely rare form of the already uncommon Hyper-cardiomyopathy. Now, his future hangs in the court of the All India Football Federation that was not so keen to take any risk in fielding him. Anwar wrote AIFF a 57-page letter pleading not to ban him from playing in the league as he was the sole breadwinner of his family. "Your disqualification of me will be a death sentence for me and my family," he implored. "I beg you to let me play." The governing body however refused to relent and felt that he should refrain from any form of physical sport.

My curiosity was further roused. I went to the World Wide Web to check things out. The synopsis and symptoms were not unknown to me. So, I skipped over the introductory passages with a cursory glance. My interest was in how to make it well.

Much to my disappointment, a couple of medical sites I visited had more or less the same thing to say when it comes to its treatment. They simply repeated what my doctor had to say. 'There is no known prevention for hypertrophic cardiomyopathy,' ran the beginning of one paragraph. I switched over to the next webpage. The same thing: 'There are currently no disease-specific medications for hypertrophic cardiomyopathy.'

Disgusted and disillusioned, I clicked 'X' and left the pages. Google is not a doctor, I said to myself.

Chapter 17

IN LOCKDOWN PHASE-I

'All work and no play makes Jack a dull boy,' goes an old English rhyme. In the wake of covid lockdowns, the rhyme better go 'All sleep and no work makes all a dull guy'.

Everything suddenly becomes boring and insipid. You craved for a day off before. Now, you are having all days off. From dawn to dusk. Twenty-four hours a day. Seven days a week. In utter contrast to what one believes, it is not always wonderful to have all your wishes come true. The only places you could safely visit are your sitting room, your bathroom, and of course, your bedroom. All other places are out of bounds. It is a veritable prison. I never knew staying home could be so arduous and patience-consuming. You've truly got to have the nerves. You sleep in the day and wake in the night. The day has indeed turned upside down. The hours and days become absolutely dismal. *Youtube, Netflix, Prime Video, Hotstar,* et al seemed to run out of content and variety. All of a sudden, nothing excites you anymore.

Then, on 5 April, 2020, as though to pep up the nation one small bit, Modiji, our Prime Minister, decreed that all electric lightings be switched off at 9.00 PM. In their place, one should light candles, *diyas* (a miniature oil lamp made of mud with cotton wick dipped in ghee), mobile torches, or any light other than domestic circuits, to show solidarity with the medical fraternity that was fighting the pandemic day in and day out.

Many people grumbled at having no power for about an hour. That's too much. But people like us, who come from a land where there is perpetual loadshedding, we took the opportunity to brighten up the mood with natural sources of light. Yet the idyll didn't last long. The depressing spirit returned as quickly as it is dispelled. It's been hardly two weeks since we were ordered into our caves. We still had ages to go. More news of lockdowns splashed across the morning papers. Nation after nation, country after country. The world is going into a shutdown spree. Observed from an imaginary bird's eye view, the world is going off grid section by section, plunging earth into the depths of darkness.

Shops closed. Portions of the city fell into containment zones. Roads were abandoned. A sense of after-the-end-of-the-world feeling pervaded the air. You couldn't think of the thoroughfares of an overcrowded metropolis like Kolkata ever falling vacant. Yet it did. They do really go empty. It was literally like a ghost city. The world has truly gone quiet.

—Empty streets of Kolkata—

On the flip side though, which is rather the good side, the air began to clean up. The haze that constantly blanketed the skies opened up. It was a long time since you see a clear blue sky. As for the lockdown, we were only on the thirteenth day. But everything had already gone haywire. Everybody seemed to complain of excess sleep and respite. I wonder if human beings were originally meant to be nocturnal creatures. It's easier to wake at night and sleep in the day. Naturally so, I lost sleep, yet again.

April, the seventh, twenty-twenty. It was hardly past three in the wee hours. I had had an erratic sleep pattern since lockdown fell into place. My wife also seemed to have fitful nights. Presently, she had just returned to bed after a sip of chilled water from the refrigerator and taking a middle-of-the-night pee. She tossed and turned for a while. Then she went still.

"Are you asleep?" I murmured on her back. That's my customary way of checking her out. She didn't answer. She has got her sleep back. Mine was not that easy.

I squeezed my eyes and rubbed them hard with the base of my palm until they hurt with a burning sensation. I popped them wide, ogling into the dark nothingness. None helped. Sleep has left me for good. I am no stranger to such nightly plights though. I'd reiterated the umpteenth time that I am a poor sleeper. So, I grabbed my glasses that I always kept by my side on the bed. Then, I cracked the Kindle Reader which I also kept ready for such situations. In fact, my laptop and e-reader are my constant companions. Always on standby to give me company in case I lose sleep. Which I do more often than not.

Presently, I was squinting at the home-screen of the e-reader, looking for the book I've purchased online the previous day. C. Sankaran Nair's, 'Gandhi and Anarchy'. It had not shown up in my reading list nor in the library. I was pissed. But I instantly realized that I had not synced it with my tablet on which I've read the preface earlier in the day. I did that and the book showed up fine. I am a slow reader. It took me well over an hour to plough through the first two chapters.

By the time my eyes tired, the clock had travelled into the wee regions of dawn. Folding up the e-book, I started stretching, curling, faking sleep, legs spread-eagled to allow the a.c. to blow as much air into the main point as possible, rolling up, simulating a few sleepy yawns... Nothing fooled Lady Somnolus.

In normal days when I'd lost sleep, I would crank up the TV and watch insipid documentaries or some frivolous DIY's on Youtube till the droning voiceovers lulled me back to sleep on the sofa. But this morning, a new idea hit me. I had always wanted to film the breaking of the dawn. So, I grabbed my Alpha-6 Sony 4K-camera and climbed the terrace to capture the morning skies unfolding in real time.

Owing to reduced pollution in the wake of lockdown, the cityscape was much clearer. The skyline was breathtaking. The northern skies were squeaky clean with only few streaks of semi-transparent clouds scudding across the firmament in a thin veil. An aeroplane glided gently in the far horizon, a long track of plume trailing behind it. In a span of minutes, another plane followed. Its white trail parted in the middle like a watery path cut by a vessel on the ocean surface. Perhaps the planes were cruising deliberately slow to kill lockdown-time. This lockdown has afforded everybody a lot of time. Nobody was in a hurry. Or was it distance playing tricks on my eyesight?

Yet another incoming craft, much closer this time and flying low. It was lining up with the landing lights. It's a beautiful sight to behold.

In the meantime, the east began to blush with the hue of dawn. The heavens gradually bathed in reddish tincture. The sun started pushing from below the skyline. In no time, the dark purplish haze gave way to a suffused golden glow. Progressively, the eastern sky turned whiter and whiter until dawn broke into a resplendent morning. I looked around for a place to place my camera. I found a loose brick somewhere. Then, setting it up on the water-tank, I pulled the lens to capture Mother Nature. Now all set to unfold her morning glory before my eyes.

Cawing crows and chirrups of mynahs and other common bushbirds added to the pleasing ambient noise. Cool breeze wafted gently in the air. A colourful kingfisher flitted past. That was the first time I ever saw a kingfisher in close range. I had always wanted to sight one but no luck until now. I quickly plucked the camera off its brick-pod and followed it. The majestic bird tantalisingly slowed down its flight for a brief moment. It was preparing to make a perch on some overhead wire beyond my line of sight. My thumb was ever ready on the record button. But before I could train my lens, it gave a shrill call, abandoned the landing plan and fluttered on its way, disappearing behind the urban jungle as swiftly as it appeared. A surreal moment. I believe it was flying to a place where there is no fear of coronavirus or the languor of lockdowns. Free soul. I envy thee!

I returned the Alpha-6 to its former position and took a time-lapse footage till the sun glowered above the telecom contraption planted on the roof of *Shrachi*, the *Emami Building*. This medium-rise multistorey has appallingly blocked the view of the eastern rims. Otherwise, my clip would have made a splendid panorama. Not what I captured was any less splendorous though.

Leaving the camera to do its own work, I roamed my eyes around to admire the picturesque view three-sixty degrees. A mysterious urge inspired me to look down to the terrace of our next-door neighbour. There, I saw two metal meshes left to the elements. One of them was about two square feet. Crumpled yet whole. The other was smaller in size, ripped and torn. From the layer of rust on them, one could easily gauge that the meshes had been lying there for years. However, mental assessment told me it was good enough to serve the purpose I had in mind at the moment.

Since the last few days, I was on the lookout for a mesh-wire to fashion into a brush-cleaner. To elaborate, since the last couple of days, I had embarked on a painting escapade to take on the lockdown monotony. I had my materials bought years ago. The mood never struck. By the way, I happened to buy oil paints that I've never worked with before. I don't work with watercolours or poster colours either. I am more comfortable with acrylics. But I am a man who wanted to experiment everything. My curious nature had more than once cost me dear and pushed me to tight corners. Understandably so, buying a medium unfamiliar to me was not totally unintentional. Despite the lack of knowledge, I wanted to try my hands on it, whatever the cost. The mistake, however, was that I didn't know what to use as a cleaning agent.

There was a bottle of thinner I bought for wood paint. I am in the habit of undertaking amateur plywood projects. My son poured some amount into a thin disposable plastic cup and brought it to me. I dipped my brush and agitated it. Suddenly, the solution ate through the cup-material and spilled diluted paint on the floor. That's a harsh solvent indeed.

Then, I looked up Youtube for a DIY brush-cleaner idea. That's how I ended up retrieving a corroded pile of mesh this morning. It was not an easy engagement though. The terrace was a good ten paces down below. I looked around and found a length of nylon cord lying on the parapet. It was desiccated and brittle due to extreme weathering. Obviously, it had been there for quite some time. The other end was purposelessly tied to an iron pipe. I undid it. Then I tied the other end in a bulbous knot. Then, I threw it down to the netting with the hope that it would somehow pick it up.

Nylons don't attract metal.

Now, I skimmed the area for something that may act as a gripper. Just then, I saw a plastic cable-brace nailed loosely on the parapet. I plucked it out with a little struggle and modelled it into something of a hook. Then, I threw it down again to the pile. And, hallo, the fixture latched on to in the first try itself. My luck's improving.

I roped in the mangled mass gingerly till it rose to an arm's reach. But I was too slow. My movement had caused an imbalance. The mesh slipped and tumbled away to a spot farther than where it was before. I am not a man to give up so easily. I tried, and tried, and tried. My luck has gone back to its previous condition. Had somebody seen me from afar, he would certainly think I was practicing for some kind of robbery. The thought pinched my conscience. I better stop the stupid act. But I feel I must give it a last shot. So, I gave myself as many last shots as necessary till I hooked the material up again.

Not ten minutes later, I finally made it. This time, I moved as swiftly as a lightning. Giving equilibrium no chance to upset. Did you ever feel joy in reclaiming somebody's junk? But I was fully satisfied and happy. The rusty net has become mine. Mission accomplished.

I took down the camera and filmed some of the campus area in a bird's eye angle. Under normal circumstances, the campus-paths would have already teemed with morning walkers. But only the brave ones ventured out now.

The sun had mounted high. It had begun to grow too warm in spite of the gentle wind breezing through the lush greenery of the campus park. Picking up the prize of my treasure-hunt, I slung Sony across my back and clambered down the ladder. To begin yet another day of lockdown. That is, indoors.

Chapter 18

SICK TALES

It was early 1976. Just around time for torching the newly cleared jungles for the year's jhumming cultivation. A small sampan, a Bengali dhow, was sailing down Riverrun. The river is officially known as the Barak. The locals call it *Tuiluang,* meaning, simply, the running river. Thus, Riverrun. Not to be confused with the Riverrun of George R. R. Martin's magnum opus *The Game of Thrones.*

In the sampan, under the low curved canopy, was a young father with his even younger, unmarried sister, escorting a two-and-half-year-old child. The child's mother could not give them company. She was held back home by a newborn babe. A brother to the child. The child in the boat was very sick. Years later, his mother would recall with failing memory that it was an affliction of the liver. Presently, he was taken to a medical facility at Alipur, the town nearest to their village. Far from home.

The *maji*—boatman—was squatting on the brow of the boat. The paddle was lying idle by his side. The water current had done all the rowing for him. They were cruising in autopilot mode. The sky was clear, and the moon was up. But the waters were black, simmering in dark silver ripples. The tiny tot coughed violently. Then he held his breath. Deep. For a long time. His face turned blue. His lips went purple. His young aunt, who had given him company, fanned him frantically, knowing nothing to do more than that. The child did not let out his breath again.

My mother used to tell me that I was brought back from the dead. My escorts, she told me, thought they would lose me for real that night. Did they pray hard? Perhaps not. Prayers don't come when you are really desperate. You set into motion instead. But what course of action can a helpless young aunt or an absentee mother far away home launch into? Yet I was pulled back somehow. The blue receded. A palish hue reappeared as blood began to seep slowly under my facial skin again. I'd often call myself a miracle child for that! Just kidding.

I wonder what the *maji* was doing all this while. Perhaps, he was kneading weed in the cup of his palm to build a toke to enjoy with the moonlit night. Ah, speaking of weed, I am reminded of a certain misadventure embarked upon by my father and his band of brothers. I heard the story from third-party sources. So, I cannot vouch for its veracity or non-veracity, for that matter.

As the story goes, in a bid to make a quick buck, my father gathered a small band, and they ventured into a smuggling enterprise. They sourced their contraband from the Kaihlam hills, they said. They took huge sackfuls down Riverrun to vend off at Silchar. Silchar is a small frontier township of Assam, bordering the Vangai Range of Manipur. It is where Pu Rochunga Pudaite met the clever Bengali merchant before he went abroad to study theology during the pre-independent days of India.

Now, to avoid detection, the smugglers had to row their boats, or more probably bamboo rafts, as quietly as possible. But not all smugglers had the knowledge of watercraft. Oars, needless to say, are always wide at the paddling end. So, if you hit the water with the wide flat, it makes a big splashing noise that easily travels to the shore in the quiet of the night. My father was born and brought up in the riverine village of Thingpuikuol. Riverrun and its banks were his haunts as a boy and a youngster. Not to exaggerate, but in the water, he was nothing less than a river otter.

I once saw him in action as a small boy when he took me to the Tuipi River to the east of Thanlon village. We were fishing with dynamite explosives. Following the blast of the gelatin sticks, fishes would splash up dead on the surface of the water in a silver flourish. But they would quickly return to the bottom if you are not fast enough to collect them. Now, I was just a child and in no way capable of rendering a helpful hand. And my father could not pick the fish all by himself. So, they started sinking back right in front of our eyes. That didn't bother my father the least bit, though. Looking around, as if assessing the depth of the dark bluish-green pool, he would strip leisurely and throw his clothes in a pile on the huge boulder we were standing and watching the fishes go down. Then, he took a swift plunge. If I were not to overstate, he made not a sound at all. Just a soft 'swissh'. And a negligible splatter.

Later, he would tell me that in order to make minimal noise when rowing, you strike the water with the slim edge of the oar's blade, then twist it slightly to thrust forward. And repeat the cycle with utmost attention.

As for their trade, though, it seems they did not make a bumper sale. A damp squib, after all.

I've stated ad nauseum that poverty is our family's constant enemy. Needless to say, this poverty can easily arm-twist you to take the most desperate measures. Even the risk of a dishonest recourse. Most probably, my father was driven to the wall by this wicked force when he had decided to form his band of brothers. I am not justifying their illegal trade. I am only asserting that he was not an evil man per se, although he may not be an angel altogether. That being said, I disagree that poverty is the biggest enemy of mankind.

Guns, cannons, rockets, and atomic bombs are also not man's real enemies. These are too bulky and noisy. Our biggest enemies are not these gargantuan weapons or the hostile nations we make for ourselves. Rather, our worst enemy belongs to the most minute microcosm. The invisible world. The microbeverse. Virus and their ilk.

For no reason known to me, I happened to be a very unhealthy child. Even to the stage of post-pubescence, I used to be taken down with one sickness or another at least once in a year. A slight attack of seasonal flu, a mild cold, or an infinitesimal rise in body temperature would lay me prone for days on end. Every once in a while, diarrhoea or chronic typhoid would rid me of the bed for weeks.

One day, in the early 1990s, I was down with a serious case of typhoid. Or was it cholera? Or diarrhoea. I don't know. They all appeared the same thing to me. My medical knowledge is pathetic. I am naturally not cut to be a medical practitioner.

Presently, I was endlessly passing fluid from both ends since early dawn. By mid-morning, I was already too weak to visit the restroom by myself. I had thrown up all the solid matters hours ago. Down to the watery residue. All I could puke now was yellowish-green bile which was very bitter to the taste and unpleasant to the olfactory nerves. Perhaps my eyes rolled, showing a white ball. Alarm bells went off inside my father's head. There was no strength in me to lift my voice and assure him that I would be okay. Did I pass out?

The next thing I recalled was being roughly jarred on my father's back. He was piggybacking me down the town bus stand. He meant to take me to the District Hospital. The District Hospital was a good mile away from our residence. But I did not remember by what mode or by what time I was spirited away. Perhaps, I was passing out for real this time.

Years later, a friend of mine got nastily thrashed by some village youths. They said he was caught in the act of thievery. What he stole or who apprehended him in the first place was never made known. Was he framed? I don't know. Nobody was coming forward to lend us a helping hand. So, I had to carry him alone till their house, which was a good hundred metres away. If not the same height, he was slightly shorter but much stockier than me. Not that I could not take his weight. But carrying an unconscious man is like carrying a dead corpse. It seemed much heavier than a wakeful person.

In the meanwhile, his parents booked an autorickshaw to take us to the District Hospital. I still could not let my senseless friend out of my hands even inside the conveyance, although a couple of his family members were giving us company. So, I laid him across my lap and cradled his head in the curve of my elbows all through the way. That was utterly a tiring exercise, to say the least. The things we do for friendship.

My father was a strongly-built man. But I now realize he must have been quite exhausted carrying me to the hospital that day.

By the time I opened my eyes again, I was already hooked to a network of intravenous tubes. My eyesight was immediately restored. Why do patients in movies always have unfocussed vision when they come around? I don't understand. And, despite having no memory of the ride or flight and all the moments following up till now, I did not mutter, "Where am I?" "Who am I?" or "What am I?" I could clearly discern the plastic tubing running to the upended bottle of 5% dextrose Ringer's lactate solution.

Not in seconds, my attention was drawn to the drip chamber. The fluid was filtering in way too fast. I thought it should be trickling drip by drip, slowly and steadily, as I often saw with normal patients. I thought the V-Track Controller must be out of order. Or the nurses had forgotten or deliberately neglected to regulate it. I shifted my eyes to the track-wheel and, to my horror, saw that it was set to the extreme spectrum of the groove: The hose was not subjected to any tension. It was a free-flowing stream! I could have gone...

I tried to communicate the situation to my father, who was seated by my side. Or was it my mother? I don't remember. My voice seemed to trail away. And the people around me seemed to pay me no heed whatsoever. But, as I turned my head to the side, several bottles of 5% met my eyes. There must be at least five of them. They had their contents clearly discharged. Had all of them been emptied into my veins?

I passed out again. By what time or in what condition did I regain consciousness is not the subject of interest here. So, let's move on.

If I am there, will sickness be far behind? Apparently, sickness and I were linked together. Like winter and spring. But I am not relating every sick tale of mine. Except for ones that mattered! And here's one right away.

One winter malady mainland folks have a phobic dread for is dengue. In the hills from where I come, we'd hardly heard of such a thing. Probably not because of its absence or rarity but for a lack of medical awareness. Perhaps, that is why I and many of my kinsmen do not catch even the proper pronunciation of the pathogen. We would pronounce it as deng-goo, deng-gew, or whatever. That doesn't reduce the hazard a bit, though. Personally, I was not even closely familiar with the more common malaria when we were living in the hill villages. Certainly not beyond our hygiene textbooks.

In our childhood days in the villages, we had no need for mosquito nets. It was much later that they were introduced to us. At least to our family. At the first time, we felt very uncomfortable being tucked inside the meshwork. We felt like encaged tiger cubs. We would often complain that there were not even midges, let alone mosquitoes. However, I must admit that we would have bedbugs in abundance. I later learned from our wizened elders that chicken mites could transform into bedbugs. I do know that caterpillars transform into beautiful moths and butterflies. But mites into bugs? Well? It is not unusual in villages to have our chicken coops hanging next to the kitchen or by the bedroom wall. But the metamorphosis of mites into bedbugs needs further research, I think. In a more scientific temperament, if possible.

Thanks probably to global warming, nights began to get warmer indeed. And by the time we left the village and came down to the plains, I began to get a full measure of the mosquito menace. But still no dengue. I got bitten much, much later. Perhaps, twenty-twelve or 13. That was not a pleasant experience, at any rate. My head felt like it would split into smithereens. It was terribly painful and hard to bear.

My wife would tie a traditional Meitei *gamsa*, a soft cotton sash used as a towel or a simple wrap-around, across my head. As tight as possible. It felt like a hundred rubber bands strapped across the girth of a watermelon fruit. I believe my head definitely twisted out of shape. That lightened the head a bit. Yet the pain lingered. At my wit's end, I even let my wife climb onto the side of my head, right above the temple. Had she put on a little weight, she would have crushed it like a watermelon indeed.

It went on like that for days. So excruciating was the pain that I wept out loud once, thinking I would not make it. My wife gave me her typical nonchalant response: "Don't act like a child!"

That was my first brush with dengue. I hate it.

The bug came back the next year. And we went over the same procedure again. The difference this time being that I still recalled my wife's indifferent riposte. I stopped acting like a child. I bit my lips and spared the tears. The protozoan took to its heels, tail tucked between its legs. If protozoa have legs or tails, that is.

For the next half a decade or so, I was not bedridden any more. It seemed I had attained proper health at last. Except for the slight miss in the heart, which I had narrated elsewhere in the book. That was not until the world turned topsy turvy and God pressed the hard reset button.

It all began with a lady shrimp vendor named Wei Guixian in Huanan's wet market in China, developing cold on December 10, 2019. From there, her cold spread all over the world and came to be known as the novel coronavirus. In short, covid-19.

It is hard to believe that a pandemic of a global scale could still occur in this highly advanced world. The earth is no stranger to plagues and pestilences that leave trails of death and destruction in their wake. For instance, one of the most deadly plagues in the world, the Bubonic Plague, better known as the Black Death of the 14th century AD, had claimed almost sixty per cent of the European population. The Spanish Flu, or the Great Influenza Epidemic of 1918, took an estimated 50 million victims. But these are events at the time the world was relatively backward. Lack of scientific knowledge, primitive medical practices, unhygienic living conditions, general poverty with its attendant social ills and evils, and of course, mass ignorance and illiteracy, if one were to add.

In contrast, today, the world is apparently at its peak of scientific advancement, medical know-how, widespread awareness thanks to the universal coverage of the World Wide Web, education and enlightenment down to the individual level. There seems to be no scope for a thing so insignificant as a virus to wreak havoc and create such a scare.

But, still, it happened!

A twenty-year-old woman, a medical student from Kerala, was recently traveling from Wuhan to Kunming, in China. She noticed people having respiratory symptoms at the railway station and the train. She came back to India on 23 January 2020 due to covid-19 outbreak situation in the city of Wuhan. Four days later, she reported to the Emergency Department in General Hospital, Thrissur, Kerala. She had a dry cough and a sore throat. She was subjected to various standard tests before she was referred to the Government Medical College on 31 January 2020. There, she was admitted to an isolation block designated for corona infection. India's first covid-19 patient was detected. On February 20, 2020, she was discharged after being tested negative.5 That very day, a section of hill tribes in the far corner of northeast India was celebrating its national day, the Zomi Nam Ni, oblivious of what the world was portending for them.

By the first two months, China had registered 1772 covid-deaths already. However, that was not enough to trigger alarm in us Indians. We carried on as usual as if nothing had happened. Our southeast Asian neighbours had already gone into lockdown mode. But it would not be before three months and a universal spread of the virus that we decided to put a nationwide restriction into place. About the ides of March, a ban on public gatherings was issued.

In total disregard for the ban, the Tablighi Jamaat religious congregation took place in Delhi's Nizamuddin Markaz Mosque. More than nine thousand missionaries from various states of India and nearly a thousand attendees from forty foreign countries joined the conference. Not surprisingly, the conference turned out to be a super spreader event. More than 4000 confirmed cases and at least 27 deaths were linked to this hotspot. That represented a third of all confirmed cases in the nation till that time.6

Eventually, the government decided to take some concrete action. March 24, 2020. The first nationwide lockdown was promulgated. But for a mere 21 days, as though it were a probation period. None in our family was infected. So, we took the news as something blown out of proportion.

Not much of a necessity, but hoping it would serve some informative purpose, let me throw some light on what really is coronavirus:

Coronaviruses are a family of viruses that can cause illnesses such as the common cold, Severe Acute Respiratory Syndrome (SARS) and Middle East Respiratory Syndrome (MERS). SARS and MERS are a handful of human coronaviruses that are known to be deadly. Coronaviruses are a large group of viruses that are common among animals. In rare cases, they are what scientists call zoonotic, meaning they can be transmitted from animals to humans. Scientist Leo Poon, who first decoded the virus, thinks it is likely started in an animal and spread to humans. The currently prevailing covid-19 is a new strain of coronavirus that has not been previously identified in

---

[5] First confirmed case of COVID-19 infection in India: A case report (nih.gov)

[6] 2020 Tablighi Jamaat COVID-19 hotspot in Delhi - Wikipedia

humans. It is a contagious disease caused by severe acute respiratory syndrome which is medically coded SARS-COV-2.

Now, I hardly watch television news broadcasts. However, thanks to the lockdown-induced tedium, I happened to switch on a certain news channel the other morning. The newsreader was excitedly chattering on a particular news bite. I did not pay much attention to the commentary. Just as I was about to skip to some movie app, I saw a number of unconscious or perhaps dead bodies scattered haphazardly across the ground. A man was about taking a woman into an autorickshaw, or was he just bringing her out? I cannot say. The woman simply collapsed in the man's arms and fell to the ground. Bodies seemed to drop dead like flies.

Being holed up in the comforts of your home, there was no way of verifying the news flash. Everyone you called seemed to be no wiser. Very few people seemed to watch the news indeed. Ridiculously, one news segment that brings a smile to your face was the Republic's Arnab Goswami, who was constantly barking at his clueless panellists: "The nation wants to know! The nation wants to know!" His poor experts would have nothing to say but follow him with a boisterous squabble and verbal duels in vain attempts to hammer their own pieces of mind into one another's. They were loudmouths, much like their anchorman. Nobody listened to nobody. The nation is watching.

Then, somebody started a gossip: The dead corpses were covid victims. That's how lethal the virus is! The positive effect of this dark rumour, however, is that it drilled some seriousness into the public's heads.

The following day, dailies would carry the news of a manmade disaster: A gas leak from the LG Polymers industrial plant situated at R.R. Venkatapuram village, six kilometres from Vishakapatnam International airport and around ten kilometres from the city's main railway station. People and animals died due to inhaling the toxic gas. It was said that there was a malfunction in the cooling system of the styrene storage tanks due to years of neglect. Twelve people died, and hundreds were taken sick. This came to be known as the Vizag Gas Tragedy of May 7, 2020.

Phew! The deaths were not covid related after all. But was that any relief? Sickness and deaths were all around. Covid casualties increased by the day. The only street noises were sirens and alerts from ambulances and emergency transports. The year 2020 was an awful year indeed. Towards the end of the year, though, things began to look up somehow. Lockdowns began to lift in a phased manner.

Shops began to roll up their shutters. Offices began to run albeit with half-strength and staggered attendances. The streets began to hum again. Things seemed to normalize eventually.

Mass religious festivals like Durga Puja, Diwali and Christmas were dreaded to end in super spreader occasions. They came and went. We ploughed on. With a huge sigh, cold December made a quiet and unceremonious exit. Yet, the dawn of the New Year seemed to promise nothing better.

With bated breath, the world moved on. It was like treading on a minefield. When will the virus strike your home? We were in constant awe and fear of the unknown and the unseen. A painful and distressing time to live indeed. On the one hand, we are at the peak of advancement in all walks of life. Yet we are in the worst of situations man can ever get into. Dickens has proven right till today with his opening lines in his 'Tale of Two Cities': It is the best of times. It is the worst of times!

However, the world seemed to limp back with the inching of time. Fighting back and never giving up. The resilience of the human race is amazing. The other day, I saw a video clip on social media which is quite comparable to our prevailing situation: A squirrel caught in a fit of seizure was nursed back to life by an unknown animal lover. Similarly, we are slowly resuscitated. We are slowly revitalized. We are resurrecting. Slowly yet surely.

But all these are to be undone by one massive event: the Maha Kumbh Mela at Haridwar in May 2021. A religious gathering again.

The Tablighi Jamaat conference had allegedly sparked off the first wave only yesterday. Now, the Kumbh Mela is poised to snatch that credit away. Religious gatherings and covid propagation go hand in hand. And India is a very religious country. In fact, it is the birthplace of three major world religions. No wonder we soon galloped ahead of everybody with respect to covid infection and casualty.

An 80-year-old Hindu priest, Mahant Sankar Das by name, arrived in Haridwar to participate in the Kumbh. Covid was raging across the country. On the 4th of April, just four days after the festival was officially thrown open, the priest tested covid positive and was advised to quarantine in a tent. However, instead of isolating himself, he secretly packed his bag, boarded a train, and travelled more than six hundred miles to the city of Varanasi. Varanasi is one of the most sacred cities for the Hindus. It was believed to be the home of Lord Shiva. The priest reached his village 12 miles from the train station on a shared taxi. He said he was hale and hearty and quarantining himself at home. But within a few days, his son, who had picked him up from the train station and a few other villagers began to develop covid symptoms.[7]

More than nine million pilgrims flocking in from all corners of the world took a dip in the Ganges in that Maha Kumbh Mela. Now, consider this massive multitude dispersing. One mental graphic comes to mind to represent the statement: a giant drop of water burst and spattered all around. At least a few hundred of them could be as irresponsible as the Mahant, the chief priest. Who says they wouldn't turn out to be covert agents of the evil microbe? The Kumbh was 'maha'—great—indeed from all angles and perspectives.

About a month later, in faraway Kolkata, a totally unconnected incident took place.

Six days before Mahant Sankar Das arrived in Haridwar, a very unexpected call woke me up. It was early. About seven in the morning. 9 May 2021.

Despite being a Sunday, nobody seemed to mind getting up and start observing the holy day. The year had had a dreary start. The West Bengal government was dead against imposing another lockdown due to its adverse impact on the economy and the lives of the citizens in general. Yet not many people are seen roaming the streets either. Everybody had taken caution. Except for medical emergencies and eventualities like accidents and bereavement, it was wiser to stay put in the safety of your home. The second wave was on the rise.

Some people are so rude that they switch off their phones at night or decline late calls. Or any call at any ungodly hour, for that matter, including early mornings. That's not my habit, though. The morning was extremely early for mainland standards. So, with sleep thick in my voice, I croaked, "Hallo!"

It was my upper neighbour, Mr. Khanthang Paite. Yes, you guessed it. That famous Indian footballer. Not to be confused with Mr. Khenthang Paite, aka KT Paite, who was also a former Indian national player. The latter being the former's uncle.

Khanthang seldom called me. It must be important. He was passing me a general information. He and his friend, Mr. Pauzakham Ngaihte, a revenue officer, were going to a funeral service. Nu Chinglian, aged 74, a staunch member of the Evangelical Baptist Convention Church, Kolkata, had bidden her final farewell in the

---

[7] India Covid: Kumbh Mela pilgrims turn into super-spreaders - BBC News

wee hours of the morning. She was the mother of our old mutual friend Mr. Lian Naulak.

Without hesitating, I requested them to wait up for us. I relayed the news to my wife, who was already half awake with the astonished tone of my response. Since our informer and his partner were already on standby mode, we were afforded no time for the normal morning ablutions. We just threw splashes of cold water on our faces, slid into the nearest clothing, and without applying brush to our teeth, hurried to the campus gate by the Eastern Metropolitan Bypass. The two guys were seated in a car with its engine running at a low purr. They looked like Mossad agents about to pull off a kidnapping stunt on an unsuspecting old Nazi war criminal. I smiled inwardly.

By the time we reached Mr. Naulak's residence in Keshtopur, some friends and church members had already gathered. The mortal remains of the house mistress were still under regulation and medical clearance. Some of us headed to the nursing home to lend whatever helping hand we could. The rest were left to coordinate the upcoming mourning service at home and offer solace to the few family members staying back to entertain the small ensemble of empathisers. Medical clearances take time, thus leaving us ample time to kill. Having nothing particular to do in the intervening period, we started engaging ourselves in chatters and asides, gradually pandering to mild jokes and harmless banters.

As is our custom, the few women in the house started serving tea around. Some local baked cookies were also served for those who missed their morning refreshments. I picked a cup and removed my facemask to take a sip. Mindlessly, I laid the mask on the settee by my side. Actually, that was a reflex action of which I was hardly aware. Before long, as I was about finishing my tea, I started groping around for it. The mask had simply vanished. I looked everywhere in vain. Some guests even joined in in the search operation. Not in moments though, we located it under the far back of the couch. The strong overhead fans had blown the flimsy material away. I returned the mask to where it should belong.

The team from the nursing home returned quite late in the afternoon. It was not before, deep in the night, that we ended the funeral service. Flights were restricted due to the pandemic situation. So, the Naulaks had to take their beloved matriarch home in an ambulance and their family car. By road.

Incidentally, the day coincided with International Mother's Day. In his speech to the small gathering of mourners, the host, Mr. Lian Naulak, aptly remarked: "I'll be remembering Mother's Day differently from this day onward..."

Several days later, I began to feel weird sensations going through my body. My back ached. My nose ran. I had a sore throat and a dry cough. Slight temperature. Yet I still managed to attend office. I was not allowed full homestay in spite of the raving virus and a nationwide catastrophic situation. In the meantime, my neighbour, Mr. Paite, had ordered a TV stand from an online store. When it was delivered, he requested me to put it together for them, which I did obligingly. The next day, he booked a barber, and we had our hair cut on their balcony. That was the sixth day since the funeral ceremony.

On the seventh day, God rested. Not the viruses. Instead of keeping the Sabbath, they broke out and launched into their most virulent depredation. I fell victim at the drop of a hat.

Doubts abound. Could I really be infected? It was like making yourself believe you would never die despite knowing that you would surely die one day. It was only later that we learnt that some of the aforementioned bereaved family members were covid symptomatic. Yet nothing was known for sure. To put all doubts at rest, my wife took me to Genesis Hospital, a mere walking distance from our quarters. I was already feeling weak and feverish. So, she had to slow down her pace to keep abreast with me. She is a fast walker, just to note. It was a Sunday morning: 16 May 2021.

The medical assistant poked deep into my nose and the back of my mouth with cotton swabs. I gagged. My hands involuntarily went up for his as though begging him to stop. The entire process took just a few seconds. But it was like hours to me. The interiors of my nose hurt a long time after the procedure. I think the swab collector was deliberately being vigorous. Perhaps, he had an old score to settle with me.

The following morning, a call came from the lab. The voice was detached and dispassionate. As though conveying a normal medical report, it said: "It's positive!"

A stroke from the blue. A pall of gloom descended. It was really ironic that a positive result turned out to be so negative. It was almost ridiculous. Suddenly, it was all downhill. The mood, the spirit, the health. My condition hurtled downward like a piece of rock chucked from the top of a mountain. Alarmed, my wife and my son also got themselves tested immediately. Positive! The only one spared was our daughter, who's staying with her maternal family back in our hometown. At least.

We quickly hived off our son into his private room. However, it wasn't easy to always stay apart. Every now and again, we had to come together to partake in dinners and confabulate in general. It was not the time to be cloistered and pine in the lonely confines of your own. No wonder, many people sank into depression in their isolation. Probably for age and feebler immunity it seemed I took the blow more severely. It was made public that the second wave would hit hard on middle-aged people. I was a ripe target.

My wife had undergone much discomfort herself. She would cough violently and complain of mild aches everywhere. But she could not afford any respite due to my fast-deteriorating condition. The viral attack was unpredictable. It could come in the day or dead in the night. So, basically, she could not leave my side even for a minute. And she definitely couldn't allow herself to be taken unawares. Stories of abrupt covid-deaths floated aplenty. She dared not grab a snatch of sleep lest I take her permanent leave at the most inopportune moment.

In a sea of pain, I would be alternately in and out. Sometimes it was noon, and the next thing I knew would be the midnight hour. Sometimes a day would have lapsed before I could gather my wits around. I could not visit the loo on my own anymore. My wife set a small pail by the bedside and actively facilitated my relieving rituals. And even bathed me, which I felt awkward at first but had no strength to protest. By the way, which fool would dare to object to his wife bathing him?

The weather was exceedingly hot and stuffy, exacerbating the torment which I already found very hard to put up with. But I could not take the cold whiffs of the split air-conditioner either. It would readily shake me up with fever. So, we had to manage with the ceiling fans. May is known to be the cruellest month in Bengal. A mere act of reliving the memory today brings back the sweat on the brows.

I craved the cool natural air. So, we shifted into the sitting room, which was much more airy and more spacious. Every now and again, my wife would rouse me to administer one pill or another. I never had problems popping pills. But when you are really, really sick, every pill seems to be too big to swallow. I gulped each pill as though that would be the last pill of my life. Then, she would also force me to take regular hot vapour inhalations. She would not listen to me when I reasoned that hot steam treatment is only apocryphal and medically unproven. She believed what she believed and refused to be shaken. Her faith is set in stone.

Ever since I was taken down, my phone rang incessantly. Evidently, I was not in a position to entertain the calls myself. So, my wife had to do all the honours. Well-wishers and sympathisers were gushing care and concern for which I would always be indebted. My mother-in-law would ring us at least thrice a day—morning, noon, and night. Amongst the host of callers, I would like to make special mention of Mrs. Hau Ciin Tungnung of Howrah and Mrs. Vungngaihkim Simte of Mukundapur. They were the ones continuously monitoring me through the line. These guardian angels are nurses working in different public hospitals in Kolkata. Let alone their concern, I shall never forget the assessments, prescriptions, and general measures passed over the phone without any need for us to consult the doctors ourselves. I must also not forget our good neighbours, Mr. Khanthang Paite and Mrs. Rosie Tombing, for selflessly delivering medicines and whatever supplies we would call for.

All this while, a good friend, Mr. Kaplunthang Simte, was undergoing a torturous trial of nerves. His son, Master Eric Hauminlun, had been admitted to the Calcutta Medical College for the last few days. Eric had been invalidated with postnatal complications and was presently very sick. He had been under intubation for days now, wrestling with the last vestiges of life.

Eric was a sweet, angelic baby. We had seen him in his mother's arms, making his entry into the world from the maternity ward of R. N. Tagore Hospital in October 2018. Now he was in the grip of a merciless malady. Had I not been pinned down myself, I would have surely been by his side. My body was tied to the bed. Yet my spirit soared to him as he was fighting for his very existence.

Despite his own war of worries, Kaplun still made time to arrange a medicine we failed to obtain in our vicinity. That's not all. He even came over and delivered it himself. I will always be indebted to this amazing man.

A few days later, 21 May 2021 to be precise, a dark piece of news populated my Whatsapp message box: At ten minutes to two in the early afternoon, Eric lost his battle.

I was appalled. My spirit sank. I grew restless. I was too weak to even express my condolences. I called Kaplun and mumbled my sympathies. That's all I could do. Deep inside, I felt like I have lost my own son. An unbearable pain constricted my chest. My condition moved down a notch. All I could say to myself, as the young man made his last journey home, was: "Fare thee well, my son. We shall meet again someday somewhere beyond the blue where there would be no incapacity or fighting for one's life."

Eric was interred with full traditional honours in the land of his forebears.

I had not fully recovered from the gloom of Eric's demise when another bad news circulated in the air again. Much like us, Mr. Vungzamuan Valte and his family members were taken over by the virus. They were living in Delhi. His wife Mrs. Kimte, and his son Mr. Sangboi Valte had to be taken to the hospital. His daughter, Miss Momoi, was symptomatic but milder, as I guessed from hearsay. In fact, Mr. Valte was still recovering himself.

Mr. Valte, whom I address as U Muan ('U' being a customary honorific for a person older than you), is a high-ranking revenue officer. I got acquainted with him and his family in the later part of 2007. Of course, I knew U Muan long before I met him in person. He is one of the best-known officers among our people. In fact, he is our community pride. Furthermore, he is one of the most distinguished personalities in our society that I hold in very high esteem. Not only me, I dare say. He is the inspiration to many of our aspiring youths.

As for Mrs. Kimte, his wife, I must count her as one of the best human beings I've ever met. Despite being the spouse of a highly notable officer, and herself being the daughter of a top-class police officer, she never minded stooping low to share a word or two with lesser souls like us. She would deign to address me with the customary honorific 'U' although she was junior to me by hardly a month. I was absolutely floored by her humility from the very first moment I met her. It was in their Salt Lake quarters in Kolkata in 2007. Out of deference, I never dared to address her by her name. She was also very beautiful. A consummate woman. Her kind heart and sweet demeanour made her even more charming. I was completely shocked to hear that she has fallen victim to covid-19 on 26th May 2021. The pall of gloom re-descended. I felt as though I've lost a very dear friend.

That's not all. Barely two weeks into it, even more ominous news floated in the atmosphere. Sangboi was in the throes of death, battling with the dreaded coronavirus.

I've had no opportunity to know Sangboi very well. He was a mere boy when they were living in Kolkata. As far as I know, he was a gentle and obedient boy. My observation was corroborated in 'Memories' written by Kevin Hauzel, one of his childhood friends. In his eulogy titled A Warrior Who Fought Till the End Kevin wrote: "He was a momma's boy and I would poke fun at him about it, but he didn't seem to mind it at all. Instead, he smiled and said, 'Who doesn't love his own mother, man? I'm not ashamed of it, neither should you be!'"[8] For all that I knew, Sangboi had grown into a perfect gentleman.

Then, suddenly, he let up the fight. 15th June 2021 became yet another dark, heartbreaking chapter in the history of the plague. And one most awful tragedy to have ever occurred in our community. Our entire tribe was shocked and shaken. I was benumbed to even contemplate what U Muan had to go through. I had followed the funeral service of his wife live on Youtube from my own sick bed. Now that I was on my way to convalescence, I followed Sangboi's from the comforts of my sofa. That's all I could do to show my empathy and solidarity. How insignificant human beings could be.

I truly admire U Muan for the brave face he put on and the addresses he unfalteringly gave to the mourning crowds. Had I been him...oh, I couldn't even think of it. That's the stuff this gentleman is made of. May God lead him from strength to strength in the wake of his loss!

I realized I could be next in line. Not because I am afraid to die. But who would take care of my wife and children if I leave them behind? The future was bleak. Not even a flicker at the end of the tunnel. I broke down. This time, my wife, who was herself down with the infection, had no words to comfort me. She could only say, "Where is it written that you'll lose the fight?" I called up my mother-in-law and asked her to make arrangements to bring my wife and son home and leave me to fight my own battle. I was that desperate. I had completely lost the will. But I could not allow my small family to follow me suit to the lake of no return. I had to save them somehow. Whatever it takes.

Second wave was raging at its height. Rumours are fraught that anyone taken to the hospital never came back alive. The buzz was that treatments meted out to the patients were perfunctory, and the survival rate was dismal. The dead were bundled off by the medical personnel themselves without allowing even the family members to see their beloved's face one last time. Forget your time-honoured cultures and religious traditions, you never know with what rituals your departed were seen off. These terrible news stories dissuaded me from seeking hospital admission despite strong advices to do so.

By the second week into the sickness, my wife had also started developing body aches and high fevers. She is a petite lady. But looks are deceptive. Belying her frail appearance, she is a tight pack of spirit and mental fortitude. Had it not been for her fierce love, she would

---

[8] https://www.covidtales.org/a-warrior-who-fought-till-the-end/

have certainly complained and bidden herself to bed. By the time I started lumbering up the slope of recovery, she was wholly wearied, lack of sleep screaming in her bloodshot eyes. In fact, she would sometimes fall off on the sofa and sometimes right on the floor without herself realising it. That was totally uncharacteristic of her. To say the least, she was over-exhausted.

I couldn't sing enough praise of my wife. Her taking care of me without flinching devotion needs no mention. She seldom slept. She tended to me without slacking a moment. I doubt many wives would go to such lengths as mutely as she did. The sore over her body had no time to lessen. She administered her her own medication. And not to forget our son, Dik. It's truly a wonder she still could make time to wait on him without any divided attention. Literally, I owe my life to her. The worth of a mother reinstilled in my mind. The pandemic, although evil in some ways, taught me one of life's great lessons: I came to understand what a dutiful wife means only after seeing how much my wife was ready to do for me. She would gladly sacrifice everything to pull me back from the jaws of the Devil. I have no iota of doubt that she will willingly lay down her life for me, should the occasion demand. Her devotion is beyond compare.

Let me add one stray titbit here. As a consequence of my visits earlier to help assemble the TV stand and have a haircut, our neighbour, Mr. Khanthang and his family had also caught the malicious bug. Evidently, from me. There's no hiding. Fortunately, though, they were not as hard hit as us. They got along well with minimal medication and indoor confinement, as they told us later.

All this while, the sun was beating down mercilessly. Nights were as hot as days. Had I not been comatose every once in a while, I would have died of heat stroke, I am sure. By the end of May, we were utterly deadbeat. I strongly believe the torrid weather was heavily responsible for my slow rate of recovery. I felt like a fish trapped on land, panting, desperately gasping for air. Then, suddenly, the rains came. Cool air drifted into our casements. Mists of vapour dampened my makeshift bed on the floor. I did not mind at all. Rather, I gulped the cold air as much as my lungs could take. Nature had given me the elixir of life. The process of my recovery started kicking in that very day.

At a snail's pace, things began to look up around the mid-first-week of June. I could now muster some strength to pull me up in a sitting position. For, to be on your back for such a long stretch could be truly a pain in the ass, I mean on the back. Sitting upright may be as simple a task as taking a breath. Yet it turned out to be quite a challenge. Not in minutes, I would slide back into a reclining posture.

I could now occasionally check my mails and Facebook wall too. But my eyes were still too weak to strain. And I was not strong enough to update my status and announce my sorry plight to the world. As if the world would care! Some people do care. A couple of calls came from my office. The Headquarters Branch called to know how I got along with the stages of improvement. A few colleagues called to enquire about my general health. The call on the 7th instant was imperious: "Come to office!"

That was the new Assistant Commissioner, Mr. S. J.

I was still struggling to even sit for an hour. But the entire burden of the office seemed to fall on my shoulders. My Superintendent Mr. Soumitra Bhattacharyya had, tested positive on 2nd May 2021, two full weeks before I did. He was on medical vacation since and was yet to recover. I don't know if he, too, received the totalitarian call. The call came without a decline option. Your sickness doesn't matter, be it Covid or David.

I had wanted to get well myself as soon as possible. I had ingested a ton of antibiotics and paracetamol tablets. We practiced every conceivable cure and treatment suggested from all cardinal points of the earth. When I described the signs and symptoms to my monitors, they suspected some comorbidities. But I couldn't wait to get tested again. Twelve days is a very long time to undergo a sickness you really don't believe in. That's the longest twelve days of my life. Although still weak and anaemic, we requested a phlebotomist to come and collect a sample. Thank God, it turned out negative this time.

Now, I had expected everything to look up and go overdrive. In reality, though, regaining health is not as speedy as one would like. I refuse to say this, but I did seem to have comorbidities owing to complications in my heart and artefacts from previous bouts of dengue. These considerably reduced the pace of my recuperation. It was not before months that I got back my sense of smell. The tastebuds seemed to have shrivelled up. It took them aeons to give a new lease of life to the exciting world of tang and flavours. I think some patches had died out completely and never revived. This resulted in poor intake of food and nutrition. Be it in the body or in mind, there was no vim and vigour for a long time. I seemed to have lost all interest and fervour. The zest for life was simply gone.

I jokingly told my wife as I started recuperating, I would be able to join my duties in a couple of days' time. She didn't find the joke funny at all. I mock-protested. It was the truth that I told. Lounging on the bed or on the sitting room settee for whole days is too boring and rather tiresome. I needed fresh air. At that, she lectured me on a certain incident that had recently taken place.

Ankur Bhatia, the owner of Indigo Airlines, IBIS Hotel and Roseate Hotel, of the 1990 batch of Modern School, Vasant Vihar, passed away at the tender age of 48 due to sudden cardiac arrest as he was on a cycling ride one morning. He had just recovered from Covid-19 a few weeks back. This is a grim reminder, my wife totally agreed not to overdo it till three months after full recovery.

That was the ideal medical advice. But who takes medical advices seriously? I am exactly the same age as Bhatia. And I, too, had a tricky situation in the form of hypertrophic cardiomyopathy. All these bolstered my better half to discourage me from stepping out of the house as yet. I couldn't help but laugh at her innocent concern and oversolicitous angst. Away with the three months recovery period. These medical people did not know anything about the urgency of our office works. "Report for duty tomorrow," the call was officious and insistent. "At least for an hour."

Whether I was fit or not is not a concern. Calls from the bosses are sacrosanct and cannot be violated. A boss is a boss. Whether you are sick, recovering or dying doesn't matter. If the call comes, it comes. And you have no choice but to abide by it. That's what subordinates are expected, nay, unfailingly bound, to do. It is called duty.

I turned up the following day, i.e., 8 June 2021, and reported straight to the boss. He was in close consultation with a certain officer over, I guess, some official matter. All the while, I was bathed in my own perspiration. The effort I spared to maintain a mere upright position was profusely bleeding me with inward sweat. But I did not want to appear sickly. My hands trembled. I gave all my might to steady them. My heart dashed madly against the ribcage, wracking the body with internal vibration. The boss told me to wait on the settee across the floor. In a safe distance.

I waited for about half an hour. He had no time to talk to me. So, I decided to walk out on him. I was feeling faint and dizzy. The old sore in my ankle had re-inflamed due to reasons unknown, preventing me from taking normal strides. I even perspired for the simple task of taking the stairs and walking the corridor. As I was by the doorway, the boss called behind me: "Come back after twenty minutes."

The twenty minutes I spent catching up with work I had left out for the last few weeks. Although I felt recovered to an extent, resuming work proved to be much more trying than I had anticipated.

A small exertion, like holding a pen, became a striving effort. My hands began to tremble fiercely. I persevered and completed a few jobs that needed immediate attention. Pending works had piled up heavily. Despite being very weak and tired, I was not allowed to stay home anymore. I was not even allowed to work from home. My superintendent was not to turn up till the next month. The link officer was also affected and quarantined. So, most of the time I was alone, except for our contingent staff Mr. Pappu.

More times than one, I would be called up before nine in the morning and not let go before working straight 12 hours, all the while being lambasted as an incompetent nincompoop. There was no chance to make any excuse for my sickness. I often felt faint and vertiginous. But what I felt was not the concern of the boss.

Work had so stacked up that, on occasions, I was not even allowed to break for lunch. Thank God my wife at least served me morning tea with two pieces of baked cookies. That's the only breakfast I could have on such days. Sometimes I felt like protesting. I felt like I was being denied a basic right. But when you have a boss breathing fire down your neck, foods have their own way of losing appeal. Forget a fire-breathing boss, after a spell of covid sickness, you lose your appetite anyway.

Now, so intense was the pressure that, one day, I started to work from home by dawn, at four O'clock, and was still not permitted to leave the office by 9.00 in the evening. Many days, in those days, I had to have cold dinners for missing family time. Drained from top to bottom, I would often prefer to rest on the sofa for a while and hit the bed straight away instead. Only to lose sleep in dread of the next morning's sunrise.

Not long before, I began to have that familiar sinking feeling. I didn't feel like going home after office. What would I tell my wife if she asked how my day was going? Not that she frequently asked. It's not her nature to poke her nose into my professional life. But slipups could happen. Fathers are the mighty lions of the house. What do they say? Ah! Head of the family. But in the office, where you are an insignificant subordinate, you are nothing but a mewling kitty. This is one secret I kept to myself. Prestige and dignity of a father, the 'head of the family,' is at stake. It's embarrassing. Many times I had mentally given up the job. I had a couple of resignation letters typed out, ready to turn in as soon as I mustered the courage. Night after night, I lost sleep.

One fine midnight, I climbed the terrace of our four-storeyed building. Looking down into the quiet campus, I saw the tall decorative plants and the sycamore tree beside our apartment. Awash with the overhead lamps, calm and composed. The world was asleep. Gently running my hands on the coarse gravel of the parapet, I contemplated the height of the building and the distance to the concrete path. A thought flitted across my mind. A very tempting thought. But I lost nerve and went back to bed. Only to rue until the sun rose over me again.

Then, I would be back in the office as though nothing was running inside my mind the previous night.

My immediate superior may not do much to protect me. But in his total absence, I was like a stray satellite without an atmospheric cover. The verbal deprecations of the higher boss were getting worse by the day. I was like the earth with its ozone layer stripped off and the cosmic rays blazing straight into its face. More down to earth, I was a dung-beetle rolling an excrement ball without a head upon its shoulders. Given no time to properly recover, I would often fear a relapse due to overexertion. But something held me up. Shame. The shame of being called 'lazy' is too much to let myself down. I must not break down. I cannot break down.

I shuddered. I sweated. The solar plexus hurt. And my hands quivered. But I refused to be beaten. I have fought the vilest virus and won. I may be weak. I may not be afforded time to heal and repair. I may be alone in the office. But the next war is for the preservation of the moral ethos. I must not lose. Ugh, that's all too distressing. Let's have one light moment to cheer us up.

At the onset of the covid outbreak, a standard operating procedure was put into place at our office entrance gate. Everyone passing through had to be thermal-scanned. The normal range of the reading should be 36-37 degrees. A reading of 37-38 would ping a warning. And 38-plus is a red alert. I made it a point to note my temperature every time. It usually ranged between 36.2 to 36.7. Normal.

The other day, the security personnel trained his thermal gun on my forehead as he always did. However, unlike other mornings, he would totally refuse to show me the reading. I was annoyed. I insisted I was shown it. It's my right to know my own temperature. But he simply waved me on with a remark: "You don't have a temperature." Did I hear him right? How can that be? A man without temperature.

"You mean I am dead?" I shot back as he was about turning to another person making his entry after me.

—*You have no temperature!*—

The security guy didn't get the humour. I snatched the device from his hands and checked the digital display myself. It read 33.1. Well, I thought, I am not dead after all. At least there is a slight heat left in me. But I did not feel anything. No cold. No fever. No nothing. Although the scanner boy told me not to worry, a tinge of wariness crept into my mind. What if there's something really wrong? Hesitating for a bit, I went ahead into the foyer. Another security guard stood there with another scanning device. I asked him to take the measurement again. He obliged. The reading registered 36.9. The thermal pistol at the gate must be faulty. What a relief!

The virus is an intelligent being. It transmutes as fast as humans can learn to develop a deterrent. It has mutated into various forms of which, the most predominant and currently prevailing being the Delta variant. However, another variant, as deadly and fast-spreading, was detected in Botswana and South Africa as I write. The World Health Organisation named it Omicron. Naming of the variants after Greek letters were done to avoid public confusion and stigma, said WHO.

Now, India is watching the third wave beginning to take shape in the horizon. As I drop these lines, India has already registered more than two thousand cases and its first Omicron death in Pimpri

Chinchwad, Maharashtra, on the fag-end of the year 2021.9

A number of vaccines have been developed and approved across the world. In India, the two most common are Covaxin and Covishield. My wife and I are vaccinated with Covishield. Whether it really shielded us remains to be seen, though. By the time I started recovering in June 2021, India had already registered more than four lakh covid-deaths. In fact, the second wave was considered to be the worst tragedy since the partition of India in 1947.10

As I write, West Bengal has been rising to be the worst hit with the new strain Omicron and the third wave. In spite of that, the State government was not in favour of banning the Gangasagar Mela, which comes off in a few days' time. Not again!

I was not even dropping the curtains when another ill-omened news started claiming a corner in the morning papers again. Scientists at Wuhan University have discovered a variant that is only a mutation away from infiltrating human cells and carrying the risk of MERS and covid-19's transmission rate. They call this type of coronavirus NeoCov. It is spreading among bats in South Africa and may pose a threat to humans if it mutates further.11

Is some great body living in the nebulous skies above hell-bent on wiping out the human race again? This time not with a great deluge of water but with germs. The vicious cycle seems to go on and on and on.

---

[9] The Times of India, Kolkata, Friday, Dec. 31,2021, p. 11

[10] 2nd Covid wave was India's worst tragedy since Partition, saw up to 49 lakh excess deaths: Report - Coronavirus Outbreak News (indiatoday.in)

[11] The Times of India, Kolkata, Saturday, Jan. 29, 2022, p. 14

Chapter 19

IN HIGH SPIRITS

I would often pass off as a teetotaller because I don't drink openly. Some friends even thought I do not touch alcohol. Far from it. I am never alien to the taste of spirits. And I am no stranger to the torments of a family that had a drinking father. Memories of my inebriated father threatening to fling my mother off the window and we, tiny kids, clinging to her skirt-ends, could not fade even with the shifting dunes of time. In actuality, he would have never done that. But every word, especially when it comes from the mouth of your father, who is often your first idol in life, sounded very real.

My father was a very resolute man though. He ran into God. And once he met him, he took no time giving up the unholy ghost forever. In religious parlance, he was 'born again'. I don't run into holy spirits. So, I never gave up drinking. The only good thing is that I never boozed enough to lose my sanity. Or is it in contrast that I had not drunk enough to gain the good sense? Whatever. Let me take you on a zipping tour down my bender trail.

It was in the 1980s. I had a friend whose parents happened to be the village moonshiners. We would often play our children's games around his grandmother's brewing apparatus. Being just kids, we did not much know or mind that an illegal activity was going on around us. One day, a lightbulb flashed above somebody's head with a bright ting. "Let's pilfer a sip from grandma's distillation!" A bright idea, indeed. "That we may know how the drink really feels and tastes like."

Biding our time, we played our kids games around, constantly keeping furtive eyes on the bamboo spouts. Condensed vapour soon trickled from it like crystal pearls into the small receptacle below. Once the drips reach a certain level, we meant to swipe it away. And sample the notorious draught which all the world's men and women are mad after.

As though sensing the secret mission inside our little heads, grandma seemed to be extra careful that day. Unlike other days, she never took her eyes off the tiers of mud-stained pots with tubes running in and out of them. She seemed more zealous stoking and tending the fire that, to us, was already blazing unnecessarily bright.

We tried to distract her with our innocent, kiddy ways. But she seemed to always see through our intents. Her eyesight may be failing but her aural nerves were sharp and snappy as a squirrel's.

After what seemed ages, vapour did start to concentrate and slowly squeeze through the glazed bamboo tubing. *Dri…i…ip! Dr..i..p! Drip….*

We stole glances from the corners of our eyes as the container gained measure by its micro-millilitres. The level rose painfully slow. We kept on kicking our mud-pucks around while we conspired in hushed tones and eye-cuts how to get away with the glass once it achieved the desired quantity. I could not recall the finer points of the plot or how we executed it. But we did end up with almost a quarter of the glass, that is about an ounce or 30 ml, to be precise. We rushed to the nearby tea-orchard to get a sip each of the little precious liquid.

Thoo! Thwack! Awrrrgkh!

Whoever gets the first taste spat out in disgust. The fluid was warm and insipid. It had just cooled to mouth-temperature or do they say body-temperature. It was a little blandish-sweet on the tongue before it hits the tastebuds. As the real taste kicks in it was pure bitterness. It was not a mouthful each that we had. Not even enough to wet the tongue. But the entire palate was awash with the smell of pigswill and acidity. Needless to say, not one of us agreed with the pungent taste. At least me, I mean. That was the first time I tasted local made liquor called *'zukha'*. The very name translates to 'bitter drink'. But I or we didn't know what to expect at that time. They say seeing is believing. For us doing is believing.

It was only much, much later, when I grew well into manhood, that I come to know that the first few drops of the distil are skimmed away as slag or dross. No wonder our booty tasted so awful that day. But I don't think I would like it either if I were to have the final product. All I could hope for, on hindsight, was that those undesirable drops were not poisonous!

That was a bad start for drinking. In fact, I never touched that type of bootleg anymore. It's too far from my liking. The next time I tasted alcohol was in the early 1990s. This time, it was a real deal. Rum. I'll tell you why or how I came across it.

Like any boy of my age, I too was a fitness freak during those days. I may not boast of the heft and height of a towering man. But I too was dying to gain brawn and puff the flesh as any fitness freak would. Although not eons away, gyms were unheard of in our side of world in those days. We did see them in the movies, especially in Hollywood action flicks. But to see them in reality was not even in our dreams. It is indeed recently that gym culture came to our hometown. With no irons to pump, the only way to add matter to your muscles was to do raw physical exercises. Countless push-ups (we called them 'bends'), carrying pails of water on both hands, pull-ups on horizontal bars or door-jambs, and whatever that could benefit the tissue in an inflating way.

And of course, we are aware of the existence of dietary regimens that could rapidly enhance one's mass and bulk. Only that we, or rather I, could not afford them. However, there are a couple of inexpensive alternatives. One of them was soaked Bengal gram.

Take a handful of Bengal gram, or red gram, or *'chana'* as you may call it. Sometimes we jokingly call it *'kel-ek'*, goat's crap. They looked exactly like it. Only different in colour. Then, put them into a bowl of water overnight or a couple of days. The chickpeas will soften to an extent. Then, remove them and chew them raw. You may also drink the liquid extract if it is to your liking. Otherwise, you may simply throw it away. Personally, I never drank it because I believed no nutrients would seep into it.

Now, you may pocket a handful of soaked pips and chuck them into your mouth every now and again, chewing along in your stretching or jogging sessions in the morning. I felt it slightly bitterish and not much agreeable to my taste. It also has a raw, earthy flavour which I do not like. Yet I forced myself on them in my blind passion to build a lumpy body. I don't know if it really helped. But I am certain it easily builds gas. And for those with weaker digestive powers, it is very easy to break the wind as you sprint down the highway. Just make sure there are no dainty damsels exercising around or simply present within hearing range.

The second alternative is eggnog.

How and where had I arranged the alcohol-base, I could not remember. I could not have stolen it from my father's stock. For he had given up drinking long, long ago. Probably, I got it from some friends by way of purchase or persuasion. Or begging. That's not important. What's important is I did manage to get nearly half a cup of rum to make an eggnog.

After having a mouthful, I feel responsible to sound a warning: Don't try this at home!

It was stinking. The mixture of rum and egg is simply incompatible. For me, at least. The odour was awful. Extremely awful. I could not swallow even the first sip. And it was very, very bitter. Bitingly bitter, in fact. The nearest comparison would be an extract of aloe vera saturated with neem juice and infused with a badly turned batter. I pinched my nose, drew my tongue as far back as possible into the mouth and closed the lips to allow the least amount of the fluid as practicable. Still then, the slightest touch of this vile concoction could completely overpower the tastebuds.

I never turned back to rum. And abandoned the dream of six packs and meaty biceps that would have helped me lure the female species like moths to a flame. Hah!

They say a man is known by the company he keeps. I keep weird companies. I am a free soul. I don't mind my company as long as there's no intention to sway me in a way I don't appreciate. I could rub shoulders with the local high society. And easily hobnob with the riffraff too. I could chum up with alcoholics and hit off well with junkies. And I could boast to have known a few home celebrities, notables, and who's who of the town. In short, I gel with all rank and file with equal ease—top to bottom. The bottom side more often than not. I could sit out with friends for their entire binging duration. I could also sit out a humdrum politician droning on and on.

I even once had a friend who claimed himself to be a police-wanted. He was an ex-soldier seeking vengeance on a man who had wronged him. In his own account, he espied this man about boarding a bus. He ran up to him and buried a dagger into his arsehole. He was captured. He flew. He was still on the run when we struck friendship. I often accompanied this felon to his drinking den because I wanted to see how wanted men behave! He knew I was averse to drinking. So, he respected my choice and never forced to offer me his glass.

I may never qualify as a proper tippler. But, I repeat, I am not alien to the taste of alcohol. A very unlikely guy once said, "He who loves not wine, woman and song is a fool for life." I said unlikely because I never thought a wine or woman remark would come from a theologian like Martin Luther. I do love the latter two: woman and song. Whether in the true sense of the term or whether the Reverend really meant his words, that I don't know though. I did love a woman. And she became my wife. I still love her and she still stays my wife.

As for songs, I could not even remember the first time I fell in love with them. Songs fascinate me. Especially the tuneful ones. Since my very early boyhood, I loved country ballads. There was one particular love song I could not stop humming when I was just a little boy. In vernacular, it runs thus:

> *Aw I khen kei ding ka sa ngaih aw,*
> *Simthu I lelsa te,*
> *Kei di'n pakbang vulta;*

Aw I khen kei ding ka sa...
Let me try a rough transliteration—
Never thought we'd be through,
The words that we've shared,
All blossoms but withered,
Oh, ne'er thought a breakup we'd do....

It was in the early 1980s when I first heard a certain Hindi song called *'Apne pyar ke, sapne sach huwe...'* (Your love has made my dream come true) from the film *Barsat Ki Ek Raat*. A lady neighbour of ours had a gramophone. We called it 'Record Player'. The lady was a spinster, I guess, although I had no way of telling it. From a big black vinyl, she would often play the song to which I would stop in my tracks wherever I heard it. Even from a distance. The spinster was a kindly lady, fond of children. And whenever I happened to drop by her house, I would always request her to put that particular number on. The lilting tune and soulful vocals of Lata Mangeshkar, the Bollywood Pop Queen would invariably carry me away to unimaginable heights. It was not many years later that I came to know the cast of the movie—Amitabh Bachchan and Rakhee Gulzar.

I don't much like Rakhee. But I did fall in love with her for that very song. And I was completely head over heels with her for the song, *"Ae ri pavan..."* in the movie *Bemisaal,* starring Amitabh Bachchan (again), and Vinod Mehra. Rakhee has now become very charming and stunning in my eyes.

As far as alcohol goes, especially the strong ones, I think my hands are clean. However, I know a few names from the many friends I kept. Whiskey, Rum, Vodka, etc. They say 'etc' shows that you are pretending to know more than you actually know. Well, that might be true in this context. I admit, I don't know many names.

I was diagnosed with HCM in the mid-2010s. In my quest for a home remedy or an easy cure, I came across many suggestions. One of them being wine. They said wine could do wonders. It burns fat and reduces bad lipid. I was entranced. There is no medical credence on its therapeutic use. But even a *Medlife* website sings praises to its benefits to the heart and cardiovascular ailments. You are taken by some belief or another for once in a while. I was taken by this. The Bible said a man is enticed by his own desires.

So, I started looking for wines that may agree to my taste. I researched on the internet. I asked personal friends. I asked anybody I trust. One very sweet wine they suggested was Port. I remembered the name because of the cute, bulgy bottle in which it comes. I immediately bought one and tried a lidful: *'Thooey!'* Definitely not to my taste. And not sweet at all. That's when I had this bright idea.

I started adding spoons and spoons of sugar to it. Even jaggery. But surprisingly, nothing enhances the sweetness of the Port. Rather, they seemed to increase its bitterness. And the odour was turning even more offensive. I soon gave it away to a friend who finished it right away and remarked, "It's indeed very sweet!"

Did I miss something?

I went on a wine hunting spree. Sometimes, I would go directly to the wine-shop and ask the keeper for the sweetest one they had. The keepers would eye me dubiously or throw me out right away. The keepers in the 'Spirits Section' in shopping malls are more helpful and polite. They would pick a few bottles and give you a choice.

But I could not come to terms with their bitterness. Some of them are even acidic. That was technically called its dryness. Being not a fan of alcohol so far, it is very difficult to force it down the gullet. I would take a little sip, not even a peg, by measuring out with the lid of the bottle. And when it doesn't suit my taste, as it does eventually, I would give it away to any friend who has the liking for it. I tried about four more types of wines. Some red, some white, some dry and some even like soda. Nothing suits me. I did not even remember their names despite the high prices I paid for them. And I tried to sweeten them every time. Wine did not get sweeter by adding sugar. That is what I learnt from my experiments. And I always ended up giving the expensive spirits away to some lucky fellow.

Thinking I needed to first cultivate the habit, I once invited a friend over to my house for a wine party by lying that I was always drinking on my own in the confines of my home. And I couldn't sleep without a nightcap. I drank two glasses that day. But my chest hurt so much that I could not think of nurturing the habit any longer. A week later, I got coronavirus! I think I better give up trying. Indeed, drinking is one habit which did not come to me at all. Much like smoking, I guess. I won't promise I wouldn't drink again. But as things appear, it may take me some time to get used to it.

However, there is one wine I would like to test for sure. The one our pastor serves in our church as communion. That was sweet indeed. The closest I could compare it with is the draft of our homemade sticky rice wine. Many times I tried to ask the pastor to tell me what kind of wine it was, where to get it, or how much it costs. But each time I try my courage failed. Perhaps, godmen have some kind of aura around them to ward off evil thoughts.

Chapter 20

THE MARRIAGE FEAST

The other day, our boss, Shri Alok Kumar Sen, the Assistant Chief Accounts Officer at Service Tax Headquarters, handed us a card each. He was soliciting our presence in the send-off/marriage ceremony of his daughter. With a bright reddish-brown rough-wooden-bark finish sprinkled with a generous dose of gold dust and a golden silk thread running around it, the card certainly showed no low class.

I've received a number of invitation cards. Of various sizes, make class and quality. The oddest card I'd received so far was a leaf of *paan* (betel) and two unpeeled green betel nuts. That was in 1996 at Simenchapari in Dhemaji District of Assam. The ceremony was as unique as that of the card. It was not that of marriage, birthday, or of any other known occasion to me. My colleagues, then, had already known of this local custom and were not as confounded as I. But to me, that was a completely new thing. It struck me with a pleasant surprise.

The great fanfare to which we were invited was a salutation or rather an induction of a new female adult into the youth fraternity of the society. A certain virgin, in whose sake was the celebration, has had her first natural purgation. She had announced this dawning puberty to her parents, who later broke the good news to the community leaders. The merriment seemed to have gone on through the entire night. Young boys and girls dancing hand in hand [like *Thabalchongba* of the Meeteis back in Manipur]. We could hear loud modern dance tracks from Bollywood movies blaring from the P.A. systems all night long. The ritual [if there was any] was certainly not just a family affair. Rather, it was a social business, as could be seen from the bright lighting that illuminated the entire night sky. In what or which manner they carried out the rites, I did not know. We had unfortunately not honoured the invitation (perhaps out of reservation). It was teasingly said among us that when such invitations come, we—the unmarrieds—ought to present ourselves without fail. To rejoice at the first menstruation of a lady.

The community I am referring to is a certain tribe, perhaps the Bodos, of Assam. Which sub-tribe or sub-clan I know not. I had been a big ignoramus to have avoided such a peculiar observance. In fact, I have missed a big opportunity to witness a ceremony that comes very rarely in my life.

In our society, though, openly making known one's natural cycle is considered impudence or brazenness. Most first-timers take it as a disgrace or shame. For instance, my younger sister once used our *gamsa* (a soft fabric common to the valley Manipuris) as padding the first time she bled. I never noticed the hand towel was missing. I was looking around for it to dry my face. Days later, I found it under the bed in a dark pile. It was smeared with dried blood. Something's not right, I thought to myself. I sniffed the congealed redness. It was disgusting. It smelled human. I confronted my sister with a gentle query. She turned herself in. Things became clear instantly. Then, I ran over to the nearby provisions store. That was my first time ever buying a lady's tampon.

1998. It was in Children's Training Higher Secondary School. I was passing a question around among class VI students. A fair young girl dropped something between her legs as she rose to answer me. From the plopping sound, I could easily guess that the material was saturated with some kind of gooey. Upon cursory glance, I realized it was her flow. She nimbly moved her left foot over the soggy mass to keep it from view. Without wasting a second, I told her to sit down.

Embarrassed, she cuddled her burning face in the cup of her hands. I walked up to her, telling the class to read their books as I did. That was a ploy to make a noise so that nobody would overhear what I had to say to her. Close to her ears, I whispered, "Got a spare?"

"No," she meekly replied, sniffling gently. Almost in tears.

"Don't mind," I comforted her. "Just pick that up and head home, girl."

I saw her off to the doorway, watching her back. A patch of blotch had already started growing behind her dark-lavender skirt. I pitied her. But there's nothing I could do to help her any further. I recalled the Simenchapari festivity. Had we been more enlightened about the functions of our body, a thing as natural as a period would not have been such a harrowing experience for this beautiful child.

Now I understand why such natural cycles of the human body must not be stigmatized even if it involves a repulsive discharge. That I had considered strange and ancient now earned my respect for their awareness and appreciation. Even the so-called highly civilized societies today have a very primordial view and understanding of things as basic as a menstrual cycle of a woman. I once heard that certain Hindu societies locked their menstruating women in until they abated. They were totally disallowed to touch utensils and cutleries, let alone prepare food. How primitive and superstitious! And demeaning to the womenfolk. To corroborate, I must mention a first-hand account of Madeleine Slade, a close associate of the Father of the Nation.

Ms. Slade, the daughter of an English Admiral in India, was rechristened with a Hindu name after she became a disciple of Gandhiji: Mirabehn. The Mahatma had very close companionship with her during his experimental days of *brahmachaya* (celibacy). In one of her correspondences with the Mahatma, Mirabehn wrote about the discrimination she encountered from orthodox Hindus during her menstrual periods. She was revolted, she wrote, because, in the ashram in which she happened to be staying, she and other women were expected to live in rags, in miserable quarters, during menstruation. They were considered unclean and, for all practical purposes, untouchable, so they were not only segregated but also forbidden to go near places where food was being prepared or served.[12]

Enough of this *bloody* nonsense. I wasn't exactly starting out to preach about superstitions or menstruum or any inglorious appellative to it. So, where were we? Ah, we were talking about cards—invitation cards. No, I was actually trying to tell you about the send-off/marriage ceremony of Miss—never mind—to which we were invited.

Come December 9, 2009. Everybody was busy with his own allocated work in the office, as usual. Nobody seemed to remember anything. Everything seemed to go fine until...

The bustle began once the clock struck three. Everyone was in a hurry. Everyone was afraid to not win a place in the limited transport vehicles arranged by the office staff. Initially, two service cars were allotted—both Gypsies. I, too, was crammed into one of those cars. The car's capacity was seven or eight, including the driver. We were twelve. There was hardly space to move your knees. Why knees? You'll know it down the line.

In the beginning, there was no problem. It was a tight fit. Not uncomfortable. However, once we set off and started bumping along the uneven roads, I began to feel discomfort in no time. Mondal's legs were too long. His knees have butted straight into mine. I spread my legs a little to let them go between my thighs. But they still reach the groin area. The only way to avoid this obtrusion is to block the jutting

---

[12] "Mahatma Gandhi and His Apostles" by Ved Mehta, p. 222, Penguin Books

kneecaps straightaway. Knee to knee. Mondal just seemed to feel nothing. His kneecaps must have ossified with age or something else. Others were chatting away like caged birds. Mondal being the most garrulous of them. He was blowing his own trumpet about his days in the Indian Navy. As was his wont. Around 7:00 pm we came to Sankrail, our boss's village. Our arrival and participation attracted no special attention. In our tribal society, every guest would be properly ushered and chaperoned to their seats. I mean, everyone is given some kind of attention, at least. Here we we're just another black head in the milling crowd. To satisfy my curiosity, I tiptoed to the doorway of the bride's preparatory room and stole a glance. She was heavily bedecked and bejewelled and installed on a thickly mattressed bed, jewellery chiming and clinking every time she turned. A painted doll. I wonder what she would look like in the morning when all those layers of makeup are scrapped away.

The only thing left for us to do was wait to be served dinner. Guests were swarming around like flies. Some had had their feast, some rushed around to grab seats, and others, like us, simply stood around, clueless, waiting to be escorted to our dinner tables.

Our time arrived eventually.

First, an empty plate would be laid for each one of us. Thermocol disposable plates are as light as a feather. The weather was hot, and the stand-fans were at maximum speeds. So, some of us had our plates blown away before we could place our hands to pin them down. Then comes buttered fish fritters. I think they called it *mach-pakora*. It was juicy and smelled of pleasantly burnt oil. I asked for an extra piece and filled myself up even before the proper course came around.

Boiled rice, flat bread (*rotis*), shredded potatoes (*allu bhujia*), lentil soup (*dal*) and all sorts of delicacies started arriving in their hordes. But what I believed to be the main fare never appeared. Mutton. Except for mutton, all items were easily repeated as per your call. I was already filled to the brim and about to give up when the main course came into view. It was broiled in a thick, spicy gravy. But my mouth did not have the strength to water anymore. I took the gravy with my fingers and licked them off. Then, I popped a piece in one go. I nearly retched.

Then came the surprise.

A tiny bowl of greenish liquid was provided to all those still at the tables. Some of us took a sniff at it like a dog testing some unfamiliar food. We gingerly looked around to see what others had to do with theirs. Nobody seemed to bother with them at the moment.

We shrugged at one another, none the wiser. Even our local friends could not tell us what to do with it. Had we not been so full, we would have lapped it up, taking it as a soup. Then, in a far corner, we espied a certain elder dipping his oil-stained hands into it.

Aha! That's it. It's a finger bowl!

We followed the stranger's example. Only then did we understand why no water place was to be seen around. We wiped our hands with our own handkerchiefs and made way for the remaining guests to take the table. I wanted to see what they would do with their little bowls of green liquid. But we could not simply stand there and watch. We had to leave for the night.

Our way back was absolutely uneventful. Except that I reached home with an extremely sore knee.

Chapter 21

A TEAM OF BAICHUNGS

Déjà vu. This chapter reminds me of the bumbling volleyball match we had at Madhuripathar, Assam, in the autumn of 1995. We had participated in a certain volleyball tournament as staffers from Jubilee Model School of Jonai, Assam. You'll find the story in my first book, *'The Good Old Days'*. To briefly recap: Being players from an outside state, that is, Manipur, our name happened to precede us. Promisingly, our opening match ended with a thumping victory for us. The audience was all praise and adoration for our 'stylish moves and classy touches'. We were highly expected to beat all teams hands down and effortlessly decamp with the winner's trophy. But Lady Luck had a totally different idea. We got a good drubbing in the next match. We're out of the tournament. Just like that.

Once out of the race, the organisers engaged our best player, Mr. Lemthang Khaute, to referee the final match. It so happened that he had to take a close call on a certain fault. The losing team boiled up in strong displeasure. They protested and nearly turned violent. Their sense of respect for being us outsiders, was our only saving grace. But we could not stand there and wait for the air to turn sourer. We had to make a run then and there itself.

We caught a local train under the bright moonlit night. I was about to reach the bogie when an iron cable strung across the ground to hold the concrete poles caught me in my steps. I fell flat, face first, bags, bearings and all, thudding mightily on the dusty gravel. No time to fret, I picked myself up, dusted, and jumped into the bandwagon. The journey back to our campus was uneventful. Just that the moonlight made us all wistful, yearning for the safety and comforts of our homes.

Sixteen years later, it happened again.

Quite a number of us from Manipur and other Northeastern states have congregated at the Customs & Central Excise Department, Kolkata. And most of us availed government quarters, especially at the complex off E.M. Bypass at Shantipally. Now, as is our wont, we would soon get into playing evening football matches on the campus lawn on weekend afternoons. Unmindful of the gathering dusk, we would kick around as long as the ball would be visible.

Being the first among us to avail of the quarters, I took the initiative and bought the balls. Friends decided to chip in and share the expenses later. About a year later, the floodlights around the lawn were repaired. Now, with the brilliant lamps powered up, we could enjoy ourselves even more. We no more needed to start the games in a hurry. Many of us used to get home late from work. And we often had to give up the day's match for that. That's not the issue any more. Now, we could meet up and kick-off at our convenience. Sometimes, we would horse around till late into the night.

We began to attract notice. Every now and then, some local boys would join us in the games. In the process, we started striking up some sort of friendship with them. One day, some local guys invited us to play in a local tournament organised not far from our residence. Govinda and Shibu, workers on our campus, became our managers. It was August 23, 2008. According to my diary, players of our team that day, apart from a couple of mainland residents, are: Thongkhohao Kipgen, Kamlianthang Vaiphei, Khaigindam Hatlei, Helun Haokip, Lalcha, Ravi, Victor Doungel and I.

Govinda is a player quite well known with the locals. He was our designated manager of the day. There was a spring in his step when he took us to the ground. No doubt, he was bringing a dream team. We could hear astonished gasps as we marched towards the playground. The locals were at once awed and intimidated. Our leaders, Govinda and Shibu, were puffing their chests with pride. They started blowing their own trumpets. I did not know what they said, for they boasted in Bengali. Yet, from smatters that I could put together, I think they said something like, "Beware, we come with a team of Baichungs!"

Murmurs rose from the stands: "Baichung, Baichung...*sudu* Baichung...." *They have indeed come with all the Baichungs in the world!*

The first eleven, which actually was seven in number, geared up in a moment's time. But it was not before we stepped into the pitch that we were told, 'no spikes allowed'. We all grimaced. The ground was nothing but a field of dried clumps of mud. It had rained days ago. But these local guys are used to playing in the rain. Like us. The ground had been kneaded into a soft slush. Now, baked under a strong sun for several days, the soft mud clods had burnt into lumps like unformed bricks from the kiln. As the rule stipulated, we had to remove our shoes. None of us had ever played without boots before.

Now, with our tender soles, we were like stepping on a field of thorns. More like walking on a bed of burning coals, I guess. Ooh, ahh, ouch! We were not even walking. We are hobbling. And the match is yet to kick off. Then the whistle blew. All we could do was hop around gingerly, trying to avoid the hard-baked clods and find a footing somehow. We curled our big toes for support. To no avail.

Our opponents were like a herd of stags let loose on a soft green meadow. Nothing pricked the calloused bottoms of their feet. Or is it hoofs that they had for feet? Far from tackling them, we were simpering and ouch-ing behind them, not even touching their tails. They struck their first goal, not in minutes.

Our friend, Haopu Kipgen, would always have a cap on his head. He's not a hippie. He's not a male fashionista. He's just prematurely balding. So, unless ultimate honour demands, like having a prayer, he would never remove his cap. But a player running around with a cap in the middle of the pitch is perhaps too peculiar for the officials. They insisted he remove the cap or sit out. Is there any rule that disallows you to play with a cap? But there was no choice at the moment. He removed his cap and wrapped a red scarf in its place. Such was our devotion to the beautiful game.

There was a huge pool of rainwater left over in the corner of the ground. And the grass was wet and soggy on that side. So, we always tried to kick the ball that way for obvious reasons. But our rivals were not stupid. They would compulsorily bring the ball back into the centre where the mud is most hardened and ragged.

All the while, the sun was beating down mercilessly. Whether it was my poor vision, I do not know. But that day, the sky was extremely clear, and the sun was scorching. I saw everything in a dark-bluish tint. Sometimes, it was even dim, although we were out wide in the open. The team of Baichungs was far from making goals. Instead, they were eating goal after goal. Every time a goal was scored, roars from the audience would get louder. I think there were at least fifty people watching the game.

The match wasn't a standard one. So, we took a break at twenty minutes. But switching sides doesn't mean anything to us. It was the same pitch. The same hardened mudballs. And our soles are extremely sore now. We had not even come close to their goal once. Our manager, Govinda, was immensely displeased with our performance. So, he decided to switch some players that he thought were underperforming. Just for the sake of fun, let me narrate. I apologize if I offend.

Being the senior-most age-wise in the team, our manager would often pick me, perhaps as a mark of respect, to pass his words around. Consult if you must. From accepting the invitation to the moment when we were required to take off our boots. Govinda was now ready to make the changes. For all his previous consultations, he simply ignored me now. He had made up his mind without any grand ideas from my head. Agreed, I did not deserve to be consulted after such a poor performance. Indeed, he was in an incendiary mood. Better not interfere with his decisions any more.

Much to the bad luck of Helun Haokip, the manager picked another player from the bench, giving the cold shoulder to another Baichung. That must be mortifying indeed. I empathize with him. He immediately raised an objection, accusing me of intentionally unselecting him. He even accused me of poisoning the manager's ears. That was far from true. But all my reasonings and pleas that I was not taken into confidence in that particular matter fell flat on his ears. For a long time, he held the grudge to his chest. But, looking back today, I think he would have a nice chuckle at the folly of youth and our mad dash for adventure.

By the time the match ended, we were richer by ten goals to nil. Or shall I say poorer? Call whatever you must, nothing makes a difference. The fact remains that the team of Baichungs had a sound trashing. We had given our national soccer hero a blazing embarrassment. Please don't tell this story to him.

On our way back, Helun was constantly chipping at my back, blaming me for conspiring against his own hill brother. The inner truth is, at the back of my head, I envied him. I should have never stepped into that accursed playground. I should have been him, sitting out on the bench and taking the liberty of hurling choice profanities at my teammates for their underperformance rather than carry the cross of that stupendous defeat.

The weather was so extreme that day that we could not even sweat properly. Whatever moisture the skin produced seemed to vaporise the moment it came into contact with the external heat. The epidermis dried and peeled like flakes of dandruff. Thin layers of salt deposited across the neck and arms. I did not much remember our way back home. My head was hurting a lot. I felt giddy and dehydrated. In the evening, I was down with a fever.

Then, a storm hit. That was the only relief we had after being pounded to a pulp. The possibility of being drubbed 10 goals to nil would have never occurred to our local acquirers. The team of Baichungs had never been a dream team, after all.

Chapter 22

AN EXCELLENT WIFE

"An excellent wife who can find? She is worth far more than rubies." Proverbs 31:10.

All my life I've never bought jewels. Much less rubies. I don't even know how they look. I don't know how much they cost. The reason is simple: I could not afford them. Yet, when the Bible makes comparisons in such glowing terms, I couldn't help but check out if my wife is indeed worth "far more than jewels." Particularly rubies.

As of today, as I write, we are pushing nineteen years of our marriage. It seemed just the other day when we gave our words and decided to take on the world together. We are still young today. Younger still at heart. Sometimes, we feel we are yet too naïve and inexperienced. Obviously, we still have a lot to learn. We are untested and childlike in the ways of married life. We are still too unready to commit ourselves. Yet we did, binding ourselves in an oath of loyalty: a vow we both hold sacred and inviolable. So, like it or not, for all these years, we have braved the rapids of life, together. Stood by one another through thick and through thin. Climbed the ups and downs of adversity, hand in hand, never letting us go.

As the man of the family, I was often afraid we could really pull through the challenges. A poor man that I am, I had an even poorer heart that my wife would have certainly felt difficult to put up with on most times. What amazes me is that she never complained: Not about my childish eccentricities. Nor the stricken life I have ended her up for marrying me. Besides, I am a difficult man. Radical and unorthodox. I doubt she would give me her hand if I were to woo her anew. Yet, not once did she threaten to pull back her vow nor poison the ears of my in-laws. I couldn't help but stand in awe of her for putting up with a man the world so loves to hate.

For all these nineteen years, my wife never gave me the opportunity to raise my voice nor my hands on her. Not a single opportunity, I must boast. Sometimes, I would pick a fight purposefully to normalise our relationship. For I feel too much calm and tranquillity augurs no good. On such occasions, except for a mumble or two, she would choose her silence thus effectively neutralising my phrenzy. And when she decides to hold her peace, there's no point going on yelling and ranting. It makes you the fool.

One mantra of a happy marriage is to never get angry at the same time. I've learned this precious lesson from my wife. Whenever I happened to mess up with her mood (which I often did knowingly or unknowingly), she would make me melt away with a harmless grumble. Being the older in age, I should have been the wiser. But the contrary seemed to be the fact. For all these forty-eight odd years of my life, I've never uttered a word of wisdom nor lived a life of prudence. Till today, there are bits of goodness to discover in her to imbibe. Such is my ignorance and lack of intelligence in the ways of man. But she would never point out the fact lest I feel emasculated. She had accepted me with all my shortcomings and oddities. And I could never express enough gratitude for that.

Although much younger, my better half is way pragmatic and sensible than I am. Be it family matters, finances, keeping relations and general maintenance. Admittedly, I lag miles behind in all quarters. For instance, spending mindlessly is one preposterous habit of mine. Any wonder that remained poor all my life? I would make bold to expend to the last pice on what strikes my fancy, not what I need. That would invite grim countenances from my wife. But I know her resentments are fully justified. I tried my best to mind my spendthrift ways. I believe I have made big strides although far from being mended.

I said she's a practical lady. Take this for instance: If our children would fall sick, which children do more often than not, instead of wasting nights in prayers or holding self-inflicting fasts, she would rather force bitter pills down their throats, which, unable to ingest, they would often throw up as they tried to swallow. Yet, I believe that produced more desirable effects than going into the deepest sanctum of your room and supplicate. She's certainly no Gandhian.

However, if I were to nit-pick for some flaw anyways, I would definitely find multiples. She's a human being, after all. But no vice of hers is capable of exciting my displeasure. She does have a pitchy voice even when she speaks normally. She's not necessarily agitated. I had misunderstood that for quite a long time in the early days of our wedlock. She's just being garrulous and cheerful—the very reason I'm enamoured with her all the more. Perhaps for her clean heart and pure mind, she is seldom taken to bed sick. She had, of course, undergone a course or two of common cold. But that's all she's got for bodily illnesses. A sound mind in a sound body, they say. I disagree. I rather say, a sound body in a sound mind.

For all the circumstances above and more, I believe there could be no spouse better for me in the world. We may not be made for each other. For I know she deserves a much better, abler husband. But she is certainly tailormade for me. Had I married any other girl, I suspect our marriage wouldn't hold out with my weird propensities, irreligious faith and immature ways. Maybe all women are the same in character and calibre and I didn't know because I am married to only one of them.

Or perhaps my wife is truly special and way above the worth of rubies. She is, without a shred of doubt, a priceless and noble wife to me.

Chapter 23

GRANDPA AND HIS STORIES

Like any village boy, I too loved grandpa-stories. I could remember my grandfather cuddling me in his arms by the fireside or on the bed and tell me stories that would hold me in endless awe and wonder. My father used to tell me that my grandfather was one well educated fellow for his time. He had done his primary school, which might be equivalent to eighth standard or matriculation today. And probably people of that time, that is, the early 20th century, must have studied quite widely. He knew a lot.

One story Grandpa loved to tell was Reddi Ding Hoot. It was a story about a small village boy by that very name. This Reddi Ding Hoot used to pay regular visits to his grandmother who was living alone in the deep jungle. And there was a big bad wolf who wanted to eat the delicious snacks and fruits he would bring his grandmother. So, he would often trick him into telling him when he would be visiting again. One day, he ran ahead of the boy and killed the old woman. Then, disguising himself as the old woman, he laid on the bed pretending to be very sick.

Reddi Ding Hoot observed that his grandmother looked very different that day. "How long have your eyelashes grown, Grandma?" he remarked.

"They have grown so long looking at the forest path expecting your arrival," the wicked wolf replied.

"How long have your nails grown, Grandma?" Reddi Ding Hoot continued.

"They have grown so long pointing out the way you are coming." The wolf was always ready with an answer.

Here, the story begins to mix up with our traditional folktale called *Tomi and Nantal:* a monster that carried away the beautiful sister of the Seven Brothers.

Anyway, did the wolf really eat Reddi Ding Hoot too? Did Reddi Ding Hoot succeed in hoodwinking the big bad wolf and make his escape? I don't remember how the story ends. Perhaps, I had always fallen off before Grandpa came to the end of the story. Or I had completely forgotten it.

When I grew up and could read my own stories, I came across a quaint European folktale called Little Red Riding Hood. The tale bore uncanny resemblances with Grandpa's story. A slight, or rather major difference was that the protagonist in this folktale was a young girl. Not at all a boy as Grandpa would have it. But the elements and the flow were basically similar nonetheless. I think Grandpa had learned the story in their school English reader that must have contained the fairy tales of Brothers Grimm and he had paraphrased for his grandson to grab it more easily.

Then, there was another story he loved to tell to encourage me to keep fit and healthy. There was a man, he would tell, who could easily carry a full-grown cow without any difficulty. And how did he manage to do that?

This man—Grandpa never named him; it was always 'once upon a time, there was a man'—had a calf. He would lift it every morning and carry it for a distance. Slowly the young cow grew. But the man did not notice the difference as he carried it each and every morning without fail. A few years later, the calf had fully grown but the young man could still carry it easily as he did not feel the weight added little by little over time.

It is absolutely possible to carry a full-grown cow should you start taking the weight every day. I think it must be something like adding a barbell every now and then when you hit the gym. It is very logical too although it may not be practicable in reality. Actually, it is not the possibility or rationality of the tale that had me astounded. I rather wonder where Grandpa must have heard the story. Had he made it up himself? Perhaps he had read it in a book somewhere or in their school syllabus. I grew up believing the story nevertheless.

One day, around the onset of my middle-age, I happened to come across a story as I read a certain book about the early Greeks. There, there was a very famous athlete by the name Milo of Croton. He was a Greek strongman who flourished around the 6th century BC. He was said to be a six-time wrestling champion at the ancient Olympic Games. And this is how he built his incredible strength.

There was a newborn calf near Milo's home. Milo decided to lift the small animal and carry it on his shoulders. He did the same the next day, and the next, and the next. Milo continued this simple strategy for the next four years, hoisting the calf onto his shoulders each day as it grew until he was no longer lifting a calf but a four-year old bull.

My grandfather might have forgotten the name of his hero. But he still remembered the tale and used it to impart lessons to his grandson. That's what's commendable about him. I couldn't help but admire that he must be quite a well-read man in his time.

Then, there is this story that very much sounds like an indigenous folktale.

Once upon a time, there were two sisters. And these two sisters went to their paddy field every day. As all myths go, there was a huge snake, most probably a giant python or an anaconda, living in the jungle beside the field. Let's call this a python. It is more commonly available in our area. By all mysterious means, this python is said to be very old and had a long mane down his back.

Local belief goes that pythons, especially the aged ones, have magic abilities to lure their prey or perform feats to serve their purpose. Elders would often warn us to keep distance from these great snakes. They said they could hypnotize you and make you slowly drift towards them all the while thinking you are walking away from them. Moreover, killing a python is not encouraged. Not that we did not kill them and have their meat once in a while. But killing pythons, it is believed, could summon up tempests and thunderstorms to avenge themselves, bringing natural disasters and untold miseries to the perpetrators. Whenever a nasty squall hit our village, elders would scratch their chins and wonder aloud if a python is hunted down by our own villagers or by someone in the surrounding villages.

They say trading in python skin fetches big profits. I don't know if this is true or not. Forget skin-trading, in our childhood days, it was popularly believed that rendered python fat is a great ointment for burns. As they are rare even in the olden days, such fats are carefully stored away in glass or gourd vials. Pythons are attributed with mysterious abilities and capabilities. There was a mountain not far from our village which was said to have been beaten down in the middle by an enraged python. As children, we would be filled with terror hearing these stories. Today, on retrospection, I think the tremendous wound on the mountainside could have been a landslide in the wake of monsoon. But our capacity to build myths and mysteries around such natural phenomena is staggering. And we believed them like gospel.

Much later in life, a friend of mine who is quite steeped in ancient tales and beliefs told me that a python keeps increasing its nostrils as they age. A python with six or seven nostrils are the most potent and dangerous, he said.

Now, back to my Grandpa's story:

In course of time, as the two sisters worked their field, the old python would begin visiting them during their lunchbreaks. The younger sister was so scared she would hide away as soon as the python makes his appearance. But her sister was instantly hooked by the beauty and sweet words of the great serpent. She would let him rest his head on her lap and stroke the hair down his back as they exchanged sweet nothings for the entire afternoons. They were in deep love in a short while.

When the big snake turned up late or missed the tryst for some reason, the elder sister would send her younger sister to summon him. Fearing consequences, she would walk to the edge of the field with a trembling heart and sing aloud:

"Tuisanlui a gulpi samnei,

Ka U in zuan roh ati..."

Roughly rendered, that means:

"Maned serpent of the Red River yonder,

My smitten sister for thee beckons...."

My grandfather would sing the song with folkloric refrain. I tried to get the tune to hum to myself later. But the flow was so peculiarly melodious that I could not make out even after I grew up. Being a child, I never gave a thought to the wordings. However, as I began to understand the meaning, it began to strike me as an intermingling of our own language with that of the Duhlian-Lushai dialect.

Is this a Mizo folktale? Is it our own folktale? In a sense, it is a tale that evidences our affinity and homogeneity. For our historians had us believe that we shared a common ancestor. The song was neither purely Paite nor purely Mizo. It's a comingling of hill dialects nobody seems to speak anymore. Did our ancestors speak that way in the olden days? Much later, with the advent of social media, I've come across a certain post in Facebook of an aged woman speaking a jumble of words that very much resembles this patois. One comment below suggested that it was the Ralte vernacular. Are the Raltes the original Zomis? They still speak this medley of dialects.

To complete grandpa's story: The younger girl ceased to partake lunch out of sheer dread. She'd hardly touched any food ever since the great serpent came. Apparently so, she began to grow thinner and thinner until her parents began to notice the change in her physical appearance. When their parents asked her the reason, she would resolutely keep her silence. For her sister had given her a stern warning. At last, their father decided to find things out for himself.

When he came to know the truth, he took out his big machete and butchered the python. That's it.

I never tell stories to my children. Telling bedtime or fireside stories have somewhat gone out of fashion. Storytelling in general, even seems to have lost its charm and practice. My children could read by themselves very early. And all I could do for storytelling is to point them out or buy the books I want them to read. Besides, the wave of *Youtube* has washed them over before they could even reach their early puberty. Telling them stories is kind of a fading fad.

I wish Grandpa was still here to spin his old, irrational, yet spellbinding yarns to me.

Chapter 24

THE FINAL FAREWELL

"Come back soon!"

I had set my mind on leaving the national capital for good. The autumn break I had intended to take was a mere excuse. So, when the Big Boss asked me to come back soon, I did not give him any answer to give me away. I was walking out of a job: a Central Government job. Not that I disdained the clerical post but it was certainly not a job to die for. A paying, guaranteed, pensionable job nonetheless. Friends and families, and anybody who happened to know me in general scoffed me at the back. Not a few of them openly called me a damned fool. That's not a new thing to me though. I am used to it. I had decided to bid the last farewell to Raisina Hill for reasons more than one. I stuck to my guns.

The parting was final but not painful. There was nothing that drags me back in New Delhi. I'd revisited it seventeen years later and still had no regrets. I was taking my family on a trip to the historical places and monuments of national importance that my children often come across their school textbooks. I'd just wanted to show them that they do exist in flesh and blood. Or rather, in marble and stone.

When I was freshly back from the capital, years ago, I was in no mood to take up any competitive examinations for a while. In fact, going for another Central Government job was the last thing on my mind. Not because I do not want to have one but my first job-experience had me too miserable and demotivated. The mere thought of it was sickening. Central Government jobs usually require you to leave home and start a new beginning in the mainland which is more or less a strange and intimidating place for us. Homesickness was and is still my Achille's heel. I would not be surprised if the young Robert Clive wrote home at the end of his first year in India in 1744 that he had not enjoyed one happy day since he left his native country.

I could look for a state service. But that's as good as out of question. One reason being that job opportunities rarely come up in Manipur. Even if one slips through, it would be up for grabs to the highest bidder or the best connected. Lack of dough would certainly deprive me of the chance anyways. Furthermore, nobody in my family ever had the necessary connections. Say, even if we had the pelf, I am not shrewd enough to figure out the right palms to grease. Perhaps, I am not wired to perform such underhand stunts.

Having said that, when every friend of mine was gripped by a national fever called SSC's Assistant Grade Examination, I could not help but allow myself be bitten by the bug once more. The prevailing passion melted my determination to stay away from job-hunting. I was easily carried away in the flow of the day. Woe begone me, the fear of being left behind has always been the cause of my embarrassing self-defeats. However, with my half-hearted resolve, was it any surprise that I came out with no flying colours? Albeit, the examination stood out as a defining moment in itself. For, the next time I heard, it came by a rechristened name: SSC's Combined Graduate Level Examination.

In those days, and still today I guess, you had to go to Imphal to participate in the exams. The exams would usually be conducted on Sundays. I don't want to talk politics here. But roadblocks or *'bandhs'* would have the tendency of coming up on such very dates. Whether they were deliberate attempts I do not know. But that was exactly why I would make it a point to see myself a night in advance to the city whenever I'd decided to go. To avoid last-minute eventualities.

Now, I had a colleague at Rayburn High School named Mr. Nangchinkhup Guite. Actually, Khup, as I call him in our traditional way of addressing, is way more than a colleague to me. I want to call him a best friend. Even if he is not keen to be besties with me, he would still be a very special chum. One quick fact that makes him special: He's the one who taught me how to work arithmetic in simpler yet more practical methods. And he's the one who rekindled a dying spark in me to take competitive exams again. That makes it two facts. Never mind. He's got a compelling vibe. Unsurprisingly though, I didn't make it as far as he does.

In the school, teachers and staff go by their acronyms. Khup's was Sir NC. He was teaching maths. He was a resident of Imphal. I mean, at least his parents were at the time. He is smart and diligent. He has an infectious aura around him. I'd often joined his preparatory studies to learn from him. I was, and still am, a dull and lazy boy. In spite of having such a good teacher-friend by my side, I could not add any more intelligence to what little I already had in my vacant head. But that did not prevent me from drawing inspiration from him. Truly so, I ended up deciding to follow his footsteps.

It was December 11, 2004. Saturday. As I've mentioned in the preceding passages, we made it to the state capital a day ahead and put up at NC's parents for the night. We had had our dinner and were relaxing in the study when a lady next door came calling on me. That was truly unexpected. I knew nobody in the city and nobody knew me in return. Except, of course, my friend NC.

"A phone call for Lian Samte," the young lady announced.

There were no mobile phones yet. Landlines were afforded only by people of affluence and status, especially that of the official nature. Unless the news is extremely bad and cannot wait, phone calls did not follow you around when you travel. It was ominous and unnerving. A tingle ran down my spine. NC walked me across the neighbourhood.

It was my wife at the other end. She was calling from our neighbour's telephone. They themselves were rung up from Shillong. In those days, it was said in a teasy way that whoever owns a telephone is a runner in the locality. Apparently so, many phone-owners refused to take unsolicited calls unless they were life-threatening emergencies. By the way, our neighbour, Pa Thangson Naulak, who is a local business tycoon, seemed to not mind running our errand that day. I take this opportunity to thank him as well as offer my apologies since I was not in a position to do so at the time.

And the news? My youngest brother, Paukhansiam alias P.K. Siama, was taken comatose to the ICU of a military hospital at Rajouri, Jammu & Kashmir. He was unlikely to make it, I was informed.

My heart sank. At that time, my parents were living at Sihphir village in Mizoram. Whether they had been informed or not, I did not know. Everywhere I turned, my eyes grew dim. We were informed that we must find a way to make to Jammu & Kashmir before it was too late.

Jammu & Kashmir was one place in the world I was dying to visit. Hindu mythology has it that Shiva was so enchanted by the beauty of the valley that he chose it for his home, making it a paradise on earth. I was long enthralled by the snowcapped peaks and breathtaking landscapes I often saw in calendar pictures and old Hindi movies. I had always fantasised about the romantic environs of Dal Lake and the breath of chill from the layers of snow that crowned the distant mountains. In sum, J&K had always been my dream tour-destination.

But the news of my brother's illness shook me so hard that the name immediately spelled dread and gloom. We were hardly making ends meet with a humble private-teacher's salary. How on earth do we arrange to fly to the country's northern tip in a day's notice? It was way above our minds and means. I could not even start thinking about it.

In the meantime, I pictured my little brother in the intensive care unit. He was, we were told, on life support and utterly indisposed. Later, his friends who'd brought his meagre belongings home told me that he did move his finger once, if slightly. They could not make out what he wanted to communicate. He must be thirsty. He must be longing for company, for someone near and dear. He must be definitely yearning to be comforted. He was sending a message! But not a soul around him to listen. And I was thousands of miles away. How useless I was!

I did not know when we went to bed or when the sun rose the following morning.

At the examination hall, I was still in a daze. I had not slept the whole night, tossing the picture of my sick little brother over and over in my mind. I had a terrible ache and an interminable hum inside my head.

The first paper was General Knowledge or do they call it General Studies. It was in a multiple-choice format. I perfunctorily ran through the questions and marked my answers without much thought. My mind was bombarded with schemes and plans and estimations on how to reach out to my kid brother. The exam paper on the desk was nothing but a white blur before my eyes. I was fighting back silent tears all the while.

What did I do in the break between the shifts I could not recollect. But I remember being very busy inside my head, calculating how to get back home as soon as the closing bell peals. The regular line-bus service between Imphal and Lamka would be available all right. But I had to walk to the stand quite a distance from the exam centre. I would be losing precious time that way. If I got one, it must be the last bus or almost it. And being a public service bus, it would be a fit and start journey at best, halting and hurtling to drop and pick passengers along the way. It would definitely be nightfall by the time I reach back home.

Now, I had come to learn that there was a bus arranged by *Tongluang Enterprise* specially for the candidates of this examination. It was docked a little distance away from our centre. Needless to say, only those with valid tickets were allowed to board. I did not have one. How do I get myself in?

In the meantime, the second paper of the exam was distributed. It was conventional arithmetic. Working sums had never been my forte. I've passed my high school math with a grace mark. Was it because I am inherently weak with numbers? I don't know. But I know for sure that we hardly covered three chapters—graphs, algorithms and a little mensuration—for the entire term of the crucial matriculation. Had it not been for the extended sittings with NC, there would have been no calculations left in me. Close sessions with him did burnish my keenness. But they never really helped sharpen my brain that has long rusted and gone blunt.

The invigilator came around giving away the answer sheets. I received one and mechanically filled out my particulars. Then, I skimmed over the question-paper. Not one computation registered. The grey cells, my Random Access Memory module, had gone kaput. That in no way meant that the brain was dead or frozen. Or no activity was taking place inside the cranium. Far from it. The intellectually-hollow space was smoking with a thousand thought processes. How do I get into that bus? How do I get to my family in Mizoram? How do I get to Jammu and Kashmir? My head was spinning at the rate of more than 7200rpm although not for any academic excellence.

I was simply waiting for the final bell to clang.

The writing-time must have lasted longer than the ice age. The bell did ring eventually though. I rushed to the invigilator's table to handover my paper even before the bell ceased pealing. The invigilator glanced at it and winced, wondering for a while. The sheets carried nothing save the essential personal details. He looked at me twice. But I was already on my way to the door. I felt his eyes waving for me behind my back. Perhaps, that was my wish playing tricks on my sixth sense. I did not turn around. There was no mistake that the pages were blank. The invigilator would have no choice but to stacked them as more papers started to pile in.

I hurried to the chartered bus and talked my way in. It was plain luck that the organisers were well known to me. As luck would have it, they even refused to accept my payment for the return trip. Some aspirants had opted to stay back in the city for reasons of their own. So, I even won myself a comfortable seat towards the rear of the bus. In a short while, all responded to their rolls and the transportation eased out into Tiddim Road.

Even before we hit the main road, the bus was already filled with animated discussions. Everybody chipping in from every nook and cranny, chittering about their performances or non-performances. Some expressing hope, some lamenting, some disappointing at their misjudgements and some even gloating over their hits and misses. Under normal circumstances, I would have joined in without reserve, peppering my dialogues with dumb jokes and lusty bragging about my sterling performance. Only to fail when the results are out. Presently though, the uproar was nothing but white noise. I sat with myself in stoic silence yet no less busy with my own thoughts.

When I reached home, I was told our parents had been duly informed. And we were directed to wait for more instructions from them. That was not comforting in any way. But there was nothing we could do except to hang on for further news.

The following day dawned. It was a Monday. Regular school was closed for the winter recess. But prospective matriculate candidates were in their preparatory studies. Concerned teachers were engaged in special classes. Both students and teachers were therefore busy as a bee. My younger sister, Lulun, was one of the eligible candidates at that time.

I was taking my class when the peon knocked at the door. The Principal was sending for me. It was not before I entered the Princy's chamber that I was told to wait for a phone call from Shillong. Not long before, the phone jangled. The Principal allowed me to pick it up myself. I did.

My brother was no more. He would be taken to Mizoram. To our parents.

What more was communicated, I did not remember. I nearly broke down. I told my boss about my plight. He offered to collect my sister himself. A minute later, brother and sister, without a word to one another, we walked out of the campus in deafening silence. That was the loneliest day for me leaving the school. It was not before we reached home that my sister gave up and broke into an ocean of tears. But I could not afford such a luxury. Being a family with not many kith and kin, I had to run my own errands, even a death-call, in fact.

I took my bicycle and pedalled down to Rengkai Muolhlum where my elder sister lives with her husband and family. It was hard but I had to tell it. We could only fall into each other's arms and cry our hearts out. Then I left her to dry her own tears. I had to rush to the cab counter to make arrangements for our imminent travel to Mizoram.

By the time I reached back home, my sister and her children and a few friends and a relative or two had gathered. We hurriedly bundled our things up, trading mutual consolations as we go along. We did not even have time to weep properly. Mr. Langkhanpau Guite, our Principal, had come by in the meantime and brought me several months' advance salary as financial assistance. That helped a lot. I could never thank him enough for that.

The *Tata Sumo* I had hired for the purpose arrived and moored itself in front of our ramshackle CGI-sheet gate. We boarded and wend our way in short notice as quiet as we could. We did not want to raise a heckle in the neighbourhood with our plaintive cries and grief.

It was not before we reached Mizoram that we learnt that the mortal remains of our brother would not be dispatched. So, home they never brought our warrior dead. According to army authorities, the corporal had died of rabies and the virus could spread from the fluids of the cadaver. They later sent us a video recording of his burial ceremony. The audio-track did not work. The image however shows the chaplain interring him with Christian rites: A Holy Bible in his hands and a semblance of prayer on his lips. From the footage, one could see the body properly wrapped in plastic sheeting. We could not help but perform a token funeral roughly in conjunction with the service being conducted thousands of miles away.

We may be in mourning. But there was no staying away from my classes forever. So, we had to head back home. At that time, we had a little puppy named *Thangboi*. It was a real child to us. Pampered and doted like a true son. We left him in the care of our friend, Haupu. When we returned, he informed us that the pup had completely given up food and always ran in the direction we had departed. He told us that he would not touch even a piece of meat. Quite uncharacteristic for a dog. Probably, he had come after us while his keeper was unaware. He never came back. That was an added pall of gloom for a house treading a rough patch already, dragging the phase of our mourning to an extended period.

Much later, we gathered that my brother's local guardian was hosting some kind of a party in their Shillong residence. A birthday party, perhaps. He was, like me, an animal lover. And being a cheery and fun-loving youngster, he was toying with the host's little puppy. In course of their frolicking, the canine probably grazed his heel with its teeth. Around the ankle they said. So slight it was that he felt no pain. Not even a prickle. There certainly was no discomfort. No wonder he was not aware of it.

He re-joined his unit in Jammu & Kashmir as his furlough came to an end. Not long before, his friends noticed that he was not keeping well. But he never seemed to complain. Whether he skipped his duties or ran from any obligation on that pretext, nobody ever told us. He was a persistent lad. If it was in his capacity, shirking work was the last thing he would do.

One morning, or was it evening, I wasn't sure anymore, the duty-master found his post unoccupied. He had informed nobody that he would be absent or running late. Probably fuming, the duty-master hurried back to the barracks to give him a piece of his mind. But, as we were told, he found the corporal shivering in his charpoy. The sick soldier was then taken to the medical facility. From the tales we heard, he was not stretchered but taken dangling between the shoulders of his mates. And they said he was breathless and scared of wafting winds and water puddles. That was one big factor that determined his illness as rabies.

Two days later, he was no more.

That was the hardest farewell I ever had to say in my life. Not only being our youngest male sibling, the fact that we never received his mortal remains made the reality very hard to sink. We could not accept that he was gone for real. Every now and again, we would look over our shoulders, across the doorway, hoping he would walk in somehow: A bedding roll on his shoulders and a rucksack on his back, grinning in his greenish combat fatigue and a tilted beret cap. It was very hard to give up hoping for a miraculous reunion.

It was three years before that I had seen Siam in person. We never knew that that would be our last time together. On my way back from Guwahati for a certain errand, I had decided to drop by to see him at his camp. So, I caught a taxi and headed for Shillong. I met him up at Assam Regiment Cantonment. He took me to the barracks and showed me his cot. I had to turn around seeing the spartan cot with nothing but coarse black army-issue blanket on it. How could he beat the nights with this scant covering in a place like Shillong which is famous for its freezing cold? My eyes moistened before I realised.

Seeing me losing it, he reassured me. "I am a big boy now, brother," he said with a tender smile. "Don't you ever worry about me."

Then, he took me to places across the hill station. We visited Hydari Park and saw the animals there. He also took me to the famous Ward's Lake. We had not seen each other for a very long time. In fact, I had not seen him since 1999. Even when he joined the army, he was with our parents in Mizoram. So, that was our congratulatory meeting as well. We talked about the past and dreamed the future. The day was too short. The sun had begun to set on us before we could have enough of each other.

"You should not stop writing exams," he'd encouraged me. "I'll save as much money as I can. And when you get a better job, we shall really start building our family."

Verily, we had been in dire straits for too long. We dreamed. We romanticised. We envisioned a future where we would be doing better and living a more comfortable life thanks to his job and mine that I was yet to strike. He never criticised my decision to give up a job hardly a year ago. Perhaps, he trusted me too much. He was always an obedient little brother. Perhaps, he had high hopes on me to bag a better one. But then, before we could meet again, fate had decided otherwise. I imagine he would still be pondering on his ICU berth whether I could really pull off the feat. I imagine he must have wanted to whisper his dying words in my ears.

It is too painful to even visualise how he must have suffered bodily and mentally. I have miserably failed him as I could not establish our family properly even after he left us. But life must go on. Time and tide began to draw us apart. And the pain began to subside gradually. The hope to see him turn up suddenly lingers yet till today. However, there is some sense of acceptance with the passing of time.

Days rolled into months, and months into years. Our tears seemed to never run dry. But we have to make ourselves understand. We are not the only ones losing a loved one. We had to move on with the world. It took us many years though to begin leading normal lives again. I could see my mother's eyes still wet on the decade mark of his exit. In the meantime, I had clinched another job on the strength of peer and family pressure.

Oh, I nearly forgot the fate of that exam when the bad news had hit. It was quite a surprise to receive a call for the skill test after all what happened. As we had known already, I had not scrawled one squiggle on the math paper. However, I seemed to have done well in the first paper. So, I was summoned to Guwahati to face the practical exam.

This test was one of the easiest I had ever taken. In the actual typewriter, you had to manually return the carriage every time you start a new line. As for the word processor, everything is done by the computer. To add to the convenience, a plain text came scrolling across the top of the screen. You don't have to turn your head to see what you are keying in. Besides, the text stops should you miss a key or make an incorrect stroke. So easy that before I could really warm up my fingers, the running text ceased and a dialog box popped up, giving me an option to submit. I clicked 'yes' and decided to type again. But there was nothing to type again. I called the invigilator and enquired if there was any problem with my system. He told me that I had completed the task. I had taken not even one third of the stipulated time. It was hard to believe.

In the mid-1990s, when we would go for Clerks Grade Examinations, we had to type on typewriters supplied in the examination hall itself. Those who could make an arrangement of their own were allowed to do so of course. In my first such test, I could complete around four to five pages, which, I think, was not a bad speed. There were quite a number of candidates who even struggled to complete a single page. The condition of the machines also mattered. If you're out of luck, your machine might not work and badly reduce your performance. I was in luck. I got a Godrej. I was already familiar with the model.

Despite my sterling performance, at least according to me, I did not make it in this first attempt. I blame it on the written part.

In my second attempt, Pa Zakai Thomte was very kind to lend me his portable. But, as luck would have it, I need not use it as I managed to win a better machine in the hall, again. I did not do as well as in the previous effort. But, when the results came out, I made it with flying colours. Fate is fickle, indeed. And if one is to go by the literal meaning of the Employment News that carried the results 'in order of merit', my roll number came first among the Scheduled Tribes category. Does that mean I have topped the scheduled-tribes category? I don't know. Doesn't matter. It took quite a long time for me to join the job though. That was how I landed in Delhi as a clerk in the Armed Forces Headquarters.

Now, as for the computer skill test, I clearly did not make it due to zilch in my arithmetic paper. However, the next year, there came a special drive for SC/ST categories in the grade of Tax Assistants. This time, I answered at least a few questions in the arithmetic paper too. And the skill-test was altered a bit. The scrolling text was discontinued. A paragraph of running text was supplied in hard copy which we had to key into the computer. Those who could not 'blind' the keyboard came to be seriously disadvantaged. As for me though, it posed not a speck of a problem.

Obviously, that's too much bragging of me. The absence of on-screen rolling text did make me take a little more time. But being used to 'blinding', I was not as crippled as those that cannot. For the cursor would still stop moving if you happened to hit the wrong tab. A convenient indicator. Peck the right key and the cursor began to blink and move again.

I beat the exam this time and am still yoked to the consequent job as I pen this anthology.

Now, fast forward to eleven years later.

Somewhere in the weeks of August, 2015, a phone call came for me one late night. Yet another phone call, indeed. But unlike when my brother Siam passed, this time cell phones were present everywhere. So, I received the call from the comforts of my bed in my rented apartment at Petrapole, about eighty-seven kilometres away from Kolkata. It was my wife, yet again. She sounded alarmed. Again! And the news was, well, not good. Again!!

My father was detected with a very late stage of thyroid cancer. I was shocked. I never thought cancer would come to our house. I had always considered cancer and diabetes the rich man's ailments. I suddenly realised that there were no such discriminations. I was instantly dispirited and distraught. Impending death was casting its long shadow into our house again.

Just a few months ago, last Christmas, in fact, we had visited home. My father was not much in a bad shape then. Or so he seemed, at least. He did have mild symptoms which we believed to be of cold or seasonal flu. His throat seemed constantly parched though. His coughs were dry. Everybody, even he himself, blamed it on his prolonged habit of smoking and endless consumption of a green betel-nut concoction called 'kom kuva'. Taking it as casual flu or mild pneumonia, he would treat himself with homemade remedies like gurgling warm salted water and cutting down his tobacco and betel intake. Nothing seemed to relieve him but there was no room for suspecting such eventuality. By the time it was for us to leave, his voice had begun to turn raspier though.

He had recently given up smoking. But he found the temptation of raw areca nut impossible to resist. That was almost like a staple diet to him. I had many times told him to kick the butt and forgo chewing the cud. He did give up the former. As for the latter, he could not beat the habit and took it to his grave.

When I got the call, I was newly posted at Petrapole Land Customs Station. So, I could not afford to take another leave. I asked my father to come down to Kolkata for further treatment. But he turned me down. He felt he would only be imposing upon us. "Let us first do our best here," he would say over the phone. "You don't worry. I'll definitely come down there should the need arise." He was a real man till the last moment.

I had seen my father shed tears only twice in my life. The second time was when he gave me his blessings with his hands rested on my head. He was praying to God to put all the burden of his sins and of his father's and his father's fathers on his shoulders and let it not pass on to me. The first time was when my brother Siam passed away.

Now, in the latter part of his treatment, I could hear his voice cracking over the phone. Every time he called me, he would always say, "My son, don't ever worry about me. I will do fine." Yet, from the feeble ring in his voice I could clearly tell everything was not fine at all.

I was only a couple of months old in my posting. But by any means, I had to arrange a quick leave for the winter. On earlier occasions when we visited home, he would always receive us by the gate. He might not see us with his eyes. But I believe he did make out our hazy images in the daylight's luminescence. This time though, he could not even step out into the open. He must have been quite eager when everybody rose agog at our arrival. When we entered the house, he came staggering out of the bed, tapping the ground with his walking-cane before we could step into his room to meet him.

I had never seen my father so frail. He was quite a big man. About six feet tall. Swarthy and huge-boned. I, with my little more than five-foot stature, am not a pale shadow of his. As he slowly walked into the study, he was looking skyward vacuously with his pupils turned greyish and sightless. And with his right hand, he was feeling the air, groping around for hands to shake. With his croaky, hardly audible voice and staring blankly into space, he rasped, *"Hong tung uh maw, bawi!"* You have come, my son!

Bawi is the most endearing term in our language. My father seldom called me that. My voice hit the Adam's Apple. A crack had started developing inside me already. "Yes, we have, father," I could only say as I grabbed his hand and gave it a gentle shake. I didn't want to show unmanly emotions in front of my children. My small family followed my example. They took his hand before it fumbled aimlessly in the air. Then, he groped his way to the hard, wooden bench in the sitting room, by the brazier. The winter days were getting cold.

"Do you feel any pain, father?" I asked as I sat with him, "anywhere, whatsoever?"

"No," was his straight answer as always. "Only that I could not take food as I should have."

For the following few days, we spent time together basking in the pleasant December sun. There would be no much exchange of words since to even vocalise was a struggle for him. Sometimes, he would exclaim that his vision was restored and everything appeared to him as clear as daylight. He was simply talking in delirium. We would ask him anyways what he saw just to indulge him. "It's the wall!" He would exclaim as though he could really see.

He would then go on describing the bench, his old creaky chair and sundry objects he was familiar with years ago. At that we would express our joy to cheer him up. I knew that was the last waver of the flame before it blows out for eternity. I was filled with melancholy and indescribable loneliness deep down inside. My only assurance was that my frequent queries whether he felt any pain were returned with a stoic negative.

As all cancer patients do, and as doctors advised, he had undergone a chemotherapy course. But, in the latter part he would adamantly refuse to continue. He would prefer the organic traditional decoctions and herbal amalgamations over the allopathic treatment. We insisted. Yet we did not want to displease him in his last moments. He was a hard-headed person in his heydays. So, to humour him, we just went with whatever he wished so that he would not leave us with a gripe.

Christmas and New Year came and went. It was not much a joyous occasion for us. But we surmounted the yuletide with a subdued festivity. I had no mind of extending my leave. Instead, I secretly planned to avail it again to revisit sooner or later. As for now, I had to report back as soon as possible.

My leave ends on January 5, 2016. We had to take our leave by the third so that I could make a day's allowance to prepare myself for a further journey to my station. Our return tickets were already confirmed. And a cab had also been booked to drop us to the airport on the morning of January 3. As for my father's condition, things did not seem to be looking up. But it didn't seem to be looking down either. In a sense, everything was in a state of equilibrium. There was nothing to trigger immediate alarm. Or so it seemed. The year's Christmastime may not be the best one for us. But there was no reason to take it as the worst either. We're still in the same square. There's nothing to upset our peace of mind. Nothing to bother for the moment. We may not spend the vacation with laughter and merriment. But we were not drowned in a sea of tears, either. So far so good. Status quo, I should say.

On the night of the 2nd instant, I called up my brothers and sisters and held a small family council. As the eldest son, I spoke to them on how to carry ourselves forward, what to expect and what not to, etcetera. Even if we're to face the most undesirable eventuality, we must be ready, I'd said. It was easy making the utterances. Something deep inside refused to accept the worst-case scenario I myself painted. Yet, I was kind of setting our family in order. Apparently, my father was listening on his bed, being unable to join us in the study. Then, we all went to our respective beds with the hope to part the next day and meet again hale and hearty.

The sun was peeping from the eastern horizon with all its regal splendour. The day was sparkling and promisingly fine. Being a parting day, everybody was up early and freshened for the morning tea and bites. But my mother unusually overslept. Perhaps, she was exhausted with all her night vigils. Perhaps, she could not sleep last night minding my father.

"Lian...!" A shriek pierced through the morning chill. It was my mother. "I could not wake him up!"

She shook and stirred my father to no avail. He was already on his way. To his eternal abode.

How was that my father chose to move on in the very morning we're leaving? Did I hurt him so much? Was he displeased with me? Had I missed something? Had he suffered during the night? Or was he at peace on seeing me willing to shoulder family responsibility? These questions will haunt me forever. Willy-nilly, we had to defer the return trip with all immediacy. I had to extend my leave for several weeks till we are over and done with the customary rites and rituals.

—*My Dear Father*—

On the night of my father's interment the earth shook. Literally.

As is our custom, a few relatives were sleeping over to afford us mental and physical comfort and assistance. As the night approached the small hours, the rafters of the house began to creak. I was still awake figuring how to lead a life without a father. I could see the trusses and girders beginning to sway gently. Then the ground moved.

"Wake up! Wake up!" Everybody cackled in unison. "Run out of the house. It's an earthquake."

I grabbed my undergarments and found my way to the open patch like all the others. It is shameful to mention here. But fact is fact. When the tremor subsided, we realised not one of us had the mind to rouse the children. Natural fear factor. The children were sleeping through the seism peacefully while we, the abled grownups, all chickened out in the moment of scare.

Perhaps, that was my father bidding us his final farewell. In fact, Pi Zam, my maternal auntie, thought it was really his ghost getting back at us before we learnt it was a quake. In a lighter note, I think she fled more with the belief that it was his spectre. But I wish my father could really stir us that way. The only other person who shook the earth with his death was Jesus Christ, our Lord. Then, it would have been a truly ground shattering demise, indeed.

Or was it his way of letting go the pent-up frustrations of his lifetime? To tell the truth, I have never been a good son to him. Not only am I a poor son, I am an abject underachiever. I had never done anything to make him proud. On many issues, I did not see eye to eye with him. I would often call him old-fashioned for his age-old beliefs and outdated wisdom. I would often brand him incompatible with my generation. I often wished I had a better father. Only today I realise how much he must have suffered putting up with all my impertinences. Unlike standard apologists, my father never believed humans have consciousness after death. I wish the conventional preacher is right because I want him to look down from heaven and forgive me and all my unconscionable acts. But, lo, he would often say the dead are transformed into spiritual beings that neither have earthly cravings nor physical awareness. There would be no pain or suffering in the arms of Morpheus, be it bodily or mentally.

My relationship with my father could be described as bittersweet at best. They say there's many a slip between the lip and the cup. We have a traditional adage to suit the bill better: Even the tongue and tooth bite inside the mouth. So true. Which father-son duo has not had their quarrels between them? We fought a lot. Of course not the physically engaging type. Most of our ideas, ranging from social issues, family matters, personal outlooks, and even religious views, were polemically oriented. I am very argumentative. Admittedly, I could argue to the point of nagging myself. Once I set my mind to a thing, until and unless proven wrong, I would hardly see the necessity to change my stand. I take myself as a modern-man with a very forward-thinking and scientific-tempered mind. Apparently so, many of my views ran against the grain of his 'in-those-days' opinions. I never had a good ear to lend his clarified prudence and raw intelligence much to my own loss and undoing.

It was not before he bade us adieu that I realised I should have been all ears even when I had not subscribed to his insights. I had nothing to gain by talking back but everything to lose by not hearing him out. I could have been more patient with him and later sift his words in leisure to obtain those that give a good ring.

Like any other kid, there was a time when I thought my father knew everything and could do everything. I once pestered him to buy us a tape record player to play a video cassette on after listening to his vivid drawing of similarities between the two devices. He never knew the workings of the magnetic tape or the principles of electronics. But his practical and colourful description of the mechanisms completely bowled me over. It's hard to realise that your father did not actually know everything or could do everything.

In spite of my poor description of my father, he was no less a source of inspiration and constant support to me. Let me take a few steps back in time. My education, be it in high school or graduation, was mediocre at best. Apparently so, it has never inspired confidence in me to dream for a job. It was extreme necessity that arm-twisted me to look for a means to make the ends meet. For that very reason, I happened to have my fingers in many odd pies till I could settle for one good one in 2007. In my later life, this admixture of endeavours earned me the label Jack of all trades and...you know it. However, the truth is, my experiences on these multifarious vocations are what taught me the hard realities of making a living, not my academic qualifications.

I once saw an advertisement in a local paper, probably in December 1994. But so conscious with my middling education that I dared not write it. It was my father who challenged me and persuaded me to shoot for it. He even offered to take the application to the office on my behalf. My stars smiled and I bagged the job. Years later, the chief recruiting officer confided in me that it was my handwriting that impressed him and what determined my selection. I was never recognised for my penmanship though. Strange are the ways of irony, indeed. But that's not the subject of interest here.

I did not know much about my father's youthful days. Some people said he had a good sense of humour and was an amuser to any company he kept. But I do know he loved music, especially religious hymns and choruses. They said he even used to be the village choir-master in his days. I never really saw him wield the chorale wand but often saw him in community singings at Christmastimes and other church occasions as a lead-drummer. Perhaps, by our time he had given way to the younger boys and became less involved. However, I did often hear flattering remarks that the community singings would ramp up when he took on the big drum.

And, oh, that nervy act he pulled off as a young soldier. I had faintly heard the story on prior occasions as apocryphal street legends. I heard it first-hand only at the launch of my book, The Good Old Days, in September 2013. The charming anecdote was shared on-stage in passing by one of his young maternal uncles, Pu Kamgin Thanglun.

A certain year, Pu Kamgin retold, a big football tournament was held in the front courts of Borobekara Government High School. There was a Home Guard garrison in the village at the time. They also fielded a team. My father was one among the players. (Not once had I seen him play football in my life though!) As with village competitions, this match also unsurprisingly ended in a free for all.

Their Sector Officer who, I suppose, must be their captain on field, happened to be a trained boxer. And having lost his cool, brought down an opponent with one fell swoop. The audience, obviously supporters of the local team, took offence and began to invade the ground. Seeing them mobbed and their skipper hemmed in with a sinister intent, my father dashed to the side-lines only to return with his service rifle, cocked and ready to discharge. The mob receded at the point of the gun. The visitors then whisked themselves away at the fractional moment. Such derring-do may not qualify for bravery awards. But I should not call it an act of idiocy. The quick thinking had saved the team and his commander from mob fury by the skin of their teeth.

My father was never known for moderation. Whatever he did, he did it to the hilt. When he drank, he drank. When he gambled, he gambled. He listened to nobody but his own heart. You could not put advisories or new concepts to him unless he was willing to open up himself. He would simply retort with I-have-graduated-all-those-things and I-don't-need-your-advice remarks. That was very irritating especially when you confront him with proven facts like the ills of smoking or consuming tobacco products and wanted him to cultivate new, healthier habits. Truly so, it was equally impossible to get him around once he turned the other side.

Now, he would decide to cut the temporal flab and embark on a spiritual journey. He would then metamorphose into a hard-headed dogmatist and theologize to the point of being pharisaic. It was in the early eighties that he chose to turn around and make a religious commitment. In that particular church he attached himself, the members were few yet utterly casual with mass timings. He was coming from a straightlaced and pedantic denomination. This laidback attitude was absolutely alien to him.

One evening, he was appointed leader of the worship service. Being small in numbers, the leader was usually entrusted with additional duties of ringing the bell, dusting the pews and conducting the songs. It was well over half an hour since he had started singing all by himself. And he was down to the fifth or sixth hymn when a scatter of the faithful started streaming in. His nerve was already frayed inwardly. His patience wearing thin. Then, a few more batches of hymns later, he looked around and saw the numbers good enough to proceed with. He walked up to the podium and asked the gathering to rise. The congregation thought they're having a mass prayer or some harmonious liturgy.

At that, my father, with his typical impatience, bowed his head and began to recite the Lord's Prayer. Like it or not, the assembly had to intone after him. In normal practice, the Lord's Prayer is the valedictory invocation. Ending the common prayer, the worshippers lowered themselves to take their seats again. But my father dismissed the mass and the faithful could only disperse with helpless laughter. Those joining the service that day still talk about the story to this day.

I may never make my father proud. And I certainly hurt him more often than not knowingly or unknowingly. But a father that he was, he never grieved at my insolent talk-backs and effronteries. He did yell at me a couple of times. But he was only a human with limited patience. I never believed I would be missing his grumbles and grouches as I do today. Obviously, he never had an axe to grind against me although I do not know many good things to say about him. Yet, my shortness of adulation doesn't mean he was not worth it. It was rather my lack of understanding of his true nature and my failure to comprehend his sublime nobleness as a father. He might have had a dim and less appreciable personality especially in his earlier days when he was more dynamic and fuller with ambition. But who doesn't have a moment of weakness, a dark leaf somewhere in the annals of one's life-story wherein shaming memories refuse to die?

Despite his many mortal frailties, he was still a complete father to me. The best father I could ever have. A beautiful doggerel with which I wanted to drop the curtain encompassed everything I have to say about my father. It never fails to moisten my eyes whenever I go through it. I utterly failed to find the author for acknowledgement. So, I may just borrow it with folded hands for pardons. They say a version of the poem appeared in an Ann Landers Column for Father's Day in 1999 with the author ascribed as 'unknown'[13]. So, with an acknowledgement to 'Unknown', here it is in a slightly adapted version:

A Father to His Child

At 4 years — My Daddy can do anything!
At 7 years — My Dad knows a lot. A whole lot!
At 8 years — My father does not know quite everything.
At 12 years — Oh well, naturally Father does not know that either.
At 14 years — Father? He is hopelessly old-fashioned.
At 21 years — Oh, that man, he is out of date.
At 25 years — He knows a little bit about it, but not much.
At 30 years — I must find out what Dad thinks about it.
At 35 years — Before we decide, we will get Dad's idea first.
At 50 years — What would Dad have thought about that?
At 60 years — My Dad knew literally everything!
At 65 years — I wish I could talk it over with Dad once more!

That, quintessentially, is my relationship with my father. May his soul rest in peace!

---

[13] https://www.fatherville.com/index.php/2016/03/06/my-daddy-when-i-was-four/

Section-II
Fiction

"If a nation loses its storytellers, it loses its childhood."
- Peter Handke
(Nobel Prize in Literature, 2019)

Chapter 1

INTO THE FIRING LINE

Looking out from the vantage point of my office in downtown Lamka, I could see the distant mountain slopes surrounding the tiny *Tuitha* valley, where my hometown is snugly nestled. Even from this far, I could see that the rolling hills had started to wear a tinge of the gathering fall. Patches of brown adorn the deciduous forests. The last monsoon clouds had blown away, giving way to the nippy gusts of the approaching autumn.

My office was located in the heart of the town, on the top floor of a four-storey building. That was the tallest building in town at the time. I was allocated an airy corner which was meant to be a stockroom in the original blueprint. The grabby landlord had converted it into an occupiable space to let out to our small real-estate company called *Lamka Real Estates Pvt. Ltd.* The windows on the three sides afforded me a spectacular view of the mountain ranges that encompass our little home town. My room was tiny and rather congested. But cosy.

Presently, I was swinging on the two rear legs of my old wooden chair, producing terrible creaks like the first notes of an aspiring violinist. That's my custom when I am in a bad mood. Our petite lady-typist Miss Manniang would always complain about it. As if that helps! You cannot kill a bad mood and an old custom with a grouch.

I was piqued. Sulking. We had somewhat run thin of clients lately. The tribe of people running after real estate seemed to suddenly dry up from the face of the earth. Ironically though, for the last two or three quarters, our business had never been better. It was sort of a boom, I must say. And for that, I had applied for a raise which, in my unsolicited opinion, was long overdue.

My boss, in the briefest summation, was the type of man that needs a lot of convincing. Not that he was a bad man. But he was not particularly generous either, especially when it comes to dipping his hands into his pockets. It needs an extra-strong reasoning to persuade him to do so. Not that he didn't know how dedicated and hard I worked for the company. Not that he held my integrity in doubt. He was simply a demanding type. And I hated him for that.

"Give me a break, Sir," I had pleaded. Unnecessarily, in my opinion. "Has not my service proven my worth enough?"

"We're a bit lean lately, you know," he said as though the ever-shortening line of clientele was my fault. "Prove your salt again. We'll see in a week."

Back to my corner, I was sullen and grim. Rocking on my chair, my mind was vacant. Yet inwardly engaged in rumination, ruing my predicament in general and roiling in discontent for the current plight. There's no question of walking out. Jobs are not lying around like candies. I just wanted my boss to feel that he needed me more than I did him. Shall I threaten to quit? But what if he simply agrees to it? What do I do? I mentally weighed my options and opportunities. Lamka is a land of abundance. You find whatever you seek. From the vilest crime to the loftiest virtue. In between, however, you have to struggle as hard as anywhere for survival.

I made a mental survey of the town and my circumstances. I was already off the bracket for competitive examinations. The widest doors of local employment are the schools. Lamka is generously dotted with educational institutions run by private enterprises. However, I never liked teaching. It's not my cup of tea. I didn't hate teaching kids, per se. But every fresh graduate in town seemed to aspire to be a teacher. Do they think any graduate makes a teacher? I was disgusted with the lack of ambition and drive of the youths of the day. That was an awful turn-off to me.

Or I could start my own—

I was in the middle of scheming when the phone on my table jangled, bringing me up with a terrible start. I cursed myself for always forgetting to put the ringtone at low volume. Anyways, I am glad it pulled me back to the firm ground of reality. Daydreaming is not good. Scheming worse. Expecting a new buyer, I jumped to the receiver and pressed it to my ear. "Hello!" I chimed sweetly. "Lamka Real Estates. How can I help you, Sir?" That's the introductory questionnaire. The first bait. I sang it in the sweetest tenor I could manage.

"Still the same old job, huh?"

I could hear a suppressed chortle at the other end. My humour darkened. The suppressed laughter could be from some hangers-on close by the caller, I thought to myself. Had it been our better days, I would have certainly slammed the hook down and forgotten all about it. But the tide has recently turned, and the boss was looking for a scapegoat. I mentally stroked my bristling feathers. My voice calmed a bit.

"Excuse me, Sir," I said in a crisp, formal tone. It's almost impossible to hide the irritation. The voice on the other end pretended to sound too familiar. I didn't like that. "May I know who's speaking, please?"

That was an absolute no-no. The boss would have fired me instantaneously had he heard me put it across the line. It was against company policy and decorum.

"Never ask the caller's name until you're sure you've got him," the Boss would never tire of reminding the staff. "There's nothing ruder than asking a man his name over the phone. He won't give it unless he is committed. Real estate is not an investment you commit over the line. Everybody is testing the waters..."

Judged from our general tendency, the Boss was extremely right. Unlike in the West or more advanced nations where it is impolite to start a conversation without introducing yourself, out here, we are not so forthcoming with personal tags. Giving it first or without being asked is considered a mark of subservience. We are not being rude. We are just embarrassed and uncomfortable with spelling out our own names. A humble lot we are. However, this practice of civility was beginning to take baby steps thanks to the active campaigns of the better-educated people of the society.

I am digressing.

"Still stuck with the formality, eh?"

The voice refused to identify itself. But a little search in the archives of my memory produced an amazing result: "Yito Riba?"

"Yeah, man." The voice opened up. Then, it's all warmth and ease. "Seems your job has eaten your brain like hell."

"Never call me up like that again!" I gave him a long-distance punch. He chuckled as if he really felt it on the tender flank. "What a surprise call, by the way!"

"Surprise?" He was surprised by my surprise.

"Why not?" I shot back. His eyebrows must have been raised to their highest arch. "I thought you've disappeared into nowhere."

"You mean Rajan and Sunil didn't ring you up?"

Let me race you down old memory lane to acquaint you with where all this began.

We—Rajan, Sunil, Yito and I, the most unusual combination of ethnicities—had agreed to someday tour the pristine hills of the state where Yito hailed: Arunachal Pradesh.

Well. Let me start from even the more beginning.

Yito Riba, Rajan Das, Sunil Kumar, and I were bosom pals. We were studying Management together in Pune. I was always at the bottom rung. The *five-point-someone*, as the Indian novelist Chetan Bhagat would write ages later. Being from a very laidback and unorthodox society, I used to forget the general manners and propriety protocols when going out on field surveys and practical exercises. I had to be constantly reminded. Thanks to my three chums who'd always steered me clear from coming across as offensive or ignorant.

When we had completed our courses, as agreed, we visited Rajan's and Sunil's places—West Bengal and Orissa, respectively in quick succession. Then, we wended our ways, landing different jobs in different places in different capacities. Rajan and Sunil got themselves quickly established in private firms in mainland metropolises. The advantage of being city denizens, I guess. Sunil even rose to the rank of Deputy Manager in the Oberoi Group of Hotels in Orissa. Yito involved himself in the timber trade and did just well. It was I who was stuck in square one. I still had to wrangle for a measly raise. Nevertheless, I was not doing that bad either to be in my place.

Actually, I was the third to host my buddies in my home state, Manipur. However, much to my relief, the city-dwellers had no guts to test the waters out here. Risky adventure is certainly not in their bucket list. They were, to put it mildly, too petrified by extensive reports of insurgency, rampant abductions and homicide stories that invaded the state and local dailies every morning. I'd proposed Yito's homeplace in my turn. I didn't need to press. Everybody readily agreed.

"You still there, dude?" the nasal twang in the earpiece intoned.

The chain of my reverie broke. I think that will do for calling back things to mind.

"Yea...yeah," I stammered, shaking off the nostalgic mental rerun.

"You've got a day to make to Guwahati," Yito informed. "Rajan and Sunil had already arrived. Any problems?"

Yito's communication was a flash reminder of an old proposition, as the reader may be aware by now. And I think it came at the most opportune moment. Why not make myself scarce for a few days, if possible, without notice? And see if the boss really dared to fire me. It will be fun, I thought. However, I am not the kind of guy to vanish into thin air without a trace. My scruples did not permit me. Moreover, I really had no nerve to piss the boss off, to admit the truth.

As for now, though, without minding his opinion or permission to leave, I just spat a *No problem* into the mouthpiece, hoping the boss won't miss me for a few days given my demand for the unappreciated raise.

*

It was very late at night when I got off the *Blue Hills* night super at Paltan Bazaar. The shops and stores had long closed. It was only the neon lights from the signboards, the advertisement hoardings and the orangey streetlights overhead that greeted my arrival.

I had not stopped cursing the bus when it broke down for the second time at quite a distance from Dimapur. A wild brook was crashing down its narrow bed at the bottom of the hill. Sharp rocks and boulders jutted out everywhere across the riverbed. The rapids were crystal. Dazzling off golden rays from the setting sun. The rush was a noisy burble. The strident calls of cicadas reverberated, comingling with the night buzzes that were beginning to get louder with every slip of the sun.

It would soon be dark. The sights and sounds would have been breathtaking had it not been for the predicament we were in. I suggested we turn back to wait out the night at the village we had just passed, which was not that far away. Perhaps, an hour's walk. The bus crew laughed at me. The sun was not even near down, they said. It must not be uncommon for them to get stranded in the jungle and spend nights in the middle of nowhere. But for infrequent wayfarers like us, the prospect easily shook your nerves. We are not used to it. We soon grew anxious.

The crew redoubled their efforts. I could not describe the snag. Mechanics never roused my curiosity. I could only mention that the handymen would slide under the bus every now and then with a sledgehammer and slam hard at whatever it was. Loud clangs resounded through the jungle air. A wildfowl, probably wakened from her early sleep, fluttered away in protest.

Much to our relief, the vehicle got fixed in a couple of hours. And we started off again in the peace of the young night.

When I eventually alighted at the bus stand in the abandoned city bazaar, the night, as I feared, was well-ripened. The thoroughfares were deserted. The streets were so quiet that ghosts would love to roam in gay abandon. In no time, my fellow passengers drifted away. To their respective destinations obviously. Nobody cared to ask where I was headed. I simply stepped off the bus and looked around like a lost soul. Before long, the bus lumbered away, too.

Nobody was there to receive me, and knowing not which way to advance, I just threw my oversized portmanteau to the ground, raising a small cloud of dust. I sat astride it and held the smaller *Adidas* airbag on my lap, waiting for my pals to show up.

Half an hour passed. Nobody showed up. Waiting was not a business I was particularly good at. I'm a naturally impatient man. But having nowhere else to go at that time of night, I was left with no choice but to wait. A Bible verse hit me on the head. The gospel of Luke chapter nine, verse fifty-eight. I mentally recited it: *Foxes have holes, and birds of the air have nests, but the son of man has nowhere to lay his head.*

It was eerily calm. Even the gods seemed to have gone aslumber. So, I waited and waited, gnashing my teeth with impatience. My jaws hurt. Not long before, the exhausting bus ride began to take its toll. My head began to weigh a ton, getting heavier with every ticking second. The night winds had swept away the day's heat. The warmth of my body began to dissipate, and the skin switched on its automatic adaptive mechanism. The eyelids drooped slowly, threatening to kiss themselves good night.

To keep myself from falling off, I perked my ears and made friends with the night noises. Wild jackals howled in the distant outskirts. I cracked my eyes to every whimper of a stray dog lazing around the trash heaps that littered the street sides. All of a sudden, I felt a tingle creep up my spine. A movement behind me.

The sense shifted to my left. A scampering squirrel. I held my head in its place, fearing the mugger would take on me before I could make any defence. The figure closed up in calculated moves. I could feel the weight of the shadow falling upon my back. In reflex, I tensed my sinews, tying them up in knots for action at the slightest hint of provocation.

A furtive tap on the shoulder. The knotty ligaments uncoiled and sprang to life. My right palm instinctively went to the offending hand, caught hold of it, pushed up the elbow curve with my left to form a twist, and threw the heap of enormous meat to the ground with an easy *aikido* move—a Japanese art of lock and release. All in one sequence. It was sudden.

A heavy grunt emanated from the fallen carcass. At the same time, I retraced my steps, weaving my hands in a basic martial arts move. Bruce Lee flashed across my mind's eye. Never had I thrown an opponent with such ease before. Martial art was not even my hobby. I was keeping it up only to please my friends of early youth who were crazy to learn it. It eventually paid off, I guess.

Emboldened by this rare success, I braced for a second offensive. But before I could leap to the next action, a shrill note of laughter sliced the still night air.

"Yes! The same old Northeasterner. Ha, ha, ha!"

The laugh sounded more like a clap in the absence of city noises to dampen it. Nobody was known to have a worse falsetto than Yito when it comes to laughing. In a moment, he and Rajan detached themselves from the shadows to make their appearance. Sunil was squirming to his feet as though his bones were a pile of broken ceramic ware.

Coming to a realisation, I apologised and extended a helping hand. Sunil, of course, slapped it away with utter rage, groaning in pain and misery. Actually, I had overdone it thinking he was a real snatcher trying to mug me in the hope of decamping with a rich booty. I wanted to prove the crook wrong and send a message not to mess with me. A desperate mouse can be dangerous.

"Doubting Thomas gets his evidence..." cried Yito, holding his sides with laughter.

Rajan pointed a finger at Sunil as the both of them couldn't help themselves but take the humour off the roof and scrape dust as they walked up to us almost on all fours. "I always told you not to touch the Northeasterners..." Yito continued, still in a guffaw.

"...for they're mostly good in this type of..." Rajan broke into Yito's speech. "—what do you call it...?" He deliberately let it hang there for Sunil to figure the answer out for himself.

"Don't tell me it's *gung fu*," Sunil completed with a thick pout. He never wanted to 'not know' anything. He limped with a perverse gait as though he would never walk normal again.

After all, men will be men. We ended the scene with a burst of laughter and pleasantries. Yito and Rajan picked up a luggage each and led us to a nearby lodge.

Now, it was my turn to sulk. The proximity of the put-up made me a little upset. They should have had a bit of a sense of responsibility, I complained. That would have saved us from all that embarrassment. We walked into the foyer of the low-cost hotel. Sunil was still licking his injury. They should at least know, I continued grumbling, although no more needed. I was in dire straits, all alone in an unknown world. Yes, 'world' was what I put for that tiny city at that moment. I was getting even more livid to learn, from their own words, of course, that they were observing me all the while, sharing snickers among themselves as I was nodding off in the street with wide sleepy yawns.

We continued our conviviality into the night. The night steward came and reminded us that it was late.

"By the way," I changed the subject to quieten us down. "Where are the *bhabhis*? Nobody bringing your madams?"

They said they'd left their wives behind to spare me from jealousy. To mention, all of them had married and sired a child or two each. Despite hitting the upper ceiling of my thirties, I was still not in luck in the romantic department. I was a poor lady hunter.

*

We didn't tarry at Guwahati. We hit the road the very next morning on a chartered *Tata Safari*. The expedition might be a hell of an experience for us. But it would make a dull narrative for the reader. So, let me just give you a run-through of the bare basics.

We traversed the hills and valleys, roamed the jungles and villages, sipped the local brew called *'apong'*, saw the black nose-plugs of old Apatani women, and came across a farmer whom we believed to be a Mishing gentleman sporting a crewcut only on the lower half of the head, in traditional attires. A tiny loincloth pulled up between his crack. He had a curved blade sheathed in an ingeniously made wooden casing. The narrow strip of cloth reminded me of the favourite G-strings of the Hollywood striptease hotties. In L.A., it may be a fashion statement, but out here, it is our culture. Move over, Hollywood. I prided myself inwardly.

We even saw a couple of fair Adi damsels as we passed Itanagar and its suburbs. In no time, we circumnavigated the length and breadth of Arunachal, stepping into temples and caves and visiting every place worth visiting in the whole of the Pradesh. Captivating natural landscapes, bubbling brooks with icy fountains, snow-capped peaks of the Himalayan appendage and the blue-green mountains speckled with copper as if it were a mink cloak of autumn.

Needless to say, we were entirely overwhelmed by the pristine glory of Tawang. Our brief drop into the enormous and enthralling Buddhist Monastery there was a spiritual experience indeed. Mere fixing your eyes on the peaceful face of the giant Buddha could transport you to a surreal world. I wonder if a goddess of seduction must have lived on this hilltop once upon a time.

By the way, the monastery was built in the seventeenth century, as Yito enlightened us. The fifth Dalai Lama commissioned one of his trusted lieutenants to visit and build an abbey there. The lieutenant, on arriving there, was completely taken by the beauty of the area. So taken that he could not decide where exactly to start laying the foundations. Everywhere seems marvellous and fit. While he was left in a dilemma, his horse simply walked away and vanished. Only to be found a day or so later standing on top of a hill. Taking this as a sign from above, the monk made up his mind. And so, on that hilltop was the temple built. And he named the place *Ta Wang*, which means 'Selected by the Horse'. The place is even more remarkable in that the sixth Dalai Lama was born here.

Moving down to the exquisite riverbeds. No word seems to have yet been invented to describe the splendour of River Siang with its white sandbanks. None of us would have guessed that the blockbuster hit of Shah Rukh Khan–Madhuri Dixit starrer *Koyla* would be filmed here ages later. Somewhere down its majestic onrush is situated the rock-strewn picnic spot of Ranaghat, a few kilometres from the border town of Pasighat. We tarried there for a few days to stretch our legs. I jotted down in my journal the indescribable cool ambience of *Tsang Po,* the source of the mighty Brahmaputra. To be expressed later should I ever find an idiom to match its grandeur.

After thrilling adventures in Ziro, Bomdi La, Bhalukpong, Hapoli, and many more hill stations, we came back absolutely refreshed and rejuvenated. From the tour, I learned two lessons:

Yito could be an excellent tour guide. He seemed to have devoured the history of his homeland. He never kept us guessing. And second, all of us spent generously, probably adding a minuscule percentage to the state revenue. That might be insignificant in real terms. But it could've mattered a lot to the money-strapped people of my home had we been there.

*

We took a ferryboat ride on the Brahmaputra on our way back home.

We had not steamed off the harbour for more than a quarter of an hour, but my dog-tired body had already given up. My head soon bobbed in snatches. I had lost a good amount of sleep over the last few days in exhilaration. Now, it seemed to come back in hordes. It took no time to overpower me.

The waterbus rocked gently like a cradle, making me exceedingly drowsy. I shifted over to the far corner behind the captain's cabin, where I could catch a few forty winks without any disturbance. There was a huge coil of rope and tarp beside some junk stacked in the corner for emergencies. I plopped on this pile as though it were a bouncy mattress in a five-star hotel.

Snuggling myself into position, I threw some furtive glances around, looking for any unfriendly face. That's unnecessary. Just habit. Animal instinct, I guess. I saw none except that of Sunil's. He was training a straight gaze into my eyeballs. He was apparently still nursing a grievance. Or, perhaps, he was already eager to get away from the magnificent mountains we had not yet left even properly behind. A little snigger escaped my lips. I didn't mean to. I tried to stop it. It escaped somehow. I could only smirk a sign of regret and apology.

I am not a proficient fighter. Forget the adjective. I am not even a fighter. I didn't dare to fight even when driven to the corner. But that night was a different setting. There was nobody to fight for me. I had to let instinct take over. To my good fortune, the right moves came at the right time. And the opponent was not a fighter himself. But I couldn't tell that to Sunil. Yito had had me too highly acclaimed. Letting out the cat would not be the wisest thing to do. It would be a question of prestige and undoing all the adulations bestowed upon me.

My friends at home, back in the days, would've hooted in disbelief had they witnessed the feat I had pulled on the unsuspecting fatso. But for a pudge like Sunil, who doesn't know how to roll even a proper fist, much less deliver a blow—he was a gentle giant—I could well come across as efficient and rough. He shouldn't have doubted my ability, I thought. He had led me into the temptation of imagining myself as a real martial artist. At least, that was the best I could grant my dream of becoming a kickboxer one day. The dream that never was to be. In reality, it was I who would always take the beating in our more playful, sparring-loving younger days.

Contenting myself with a couple of clucks, I gradually slipped into a pre-noon nap.

*

I had not let my guard down for a few seconds, or so I thought when a soft bundle of what-I-know-not was dumped onto me. A piercing shriek stirred me into instant wakefulness. There was no time to adjust my groggy eyes and take a guess. My nerves were benumbed. My orientation in disarray.

Through a bleary vision, I could see three pairs of bellicose eyes receiving my dozy squint. One of them was brandishing a *khukri*, the iconic Gorkhali combat knife, a spark glinting off its sharp edge where the sun hit directly. His brother-in-arms to his left was holding a country-made Sten carbine sidewise at waist level. The third man had a handgun. Probably a police issue dispossessed of the rightful serviceman in an unlawful manner. I think it was Webley & Scott.

The awakening was so abrupt and unwarned that I could not decide whether to cower in fear or stand up in defiance. My mind went blank for a moment. My pulse stopped racing. The leaves of the trees that were still visible on the distant shores seemed to droop all at once with the sudden cessation of wind movement. Or were they too scared to flutter in the breeze? What's going on?

One of them, which one I had no time to notice, grabbed me by the collar, dragged me to my feet and shoved me to the end of a file. The passengers had already been forced into a line. From the powerful thrust and downward glance, I guess the guy must be much stronger and a full cubit taller than me. He was huge and not at all friendly-looking.

The passengers were split up on the lines of gender. While I was blissfully unaware in my power nap, all the male passengers had been rounded up to the far side of the deck, ordered to lock their hands at the back of their heads and fall in a single file. The women were brazenly misbehaved with even as they were herded to the other flank. Like cattle to the tinning machine.

Next by next, the man with the *khukri* was prodding the men to part with their immediate belongings. A lady's handbag of imitation leather, probably snatched from one of the ladies, slung down his front. He was using the long strap to carry it so that his hands were free to thwart surprises that could spring from anywhere. He was pacing up and down like a Royal Bengal Tiger in heat. The bag continuously slapping the groin area.

One or two of the voyagers seemed to have hesitated to let go of what the villains demanded of them. They had large black circles around their eyes. I could see my three chums in the early part of the line. I winced inwardly.

Yito knew the futility of remonstrating in such situations. He readily parted with his fake platinum-plated *Rolex* and a wad of cash he had strapped in his pocket. Rajan was yet to come to terms with this particular, unexpected Northeastern hospitality. He had won himself one black eye before acknowledging the reception upon the sea. Once persuaded, though, he needed no further urgings to volunteer whatever he's got in his pockets.

Sunil seemed to say to himself, *so this is what they've bragged about tribal generosity?* He was too scared to even hesitate. Perhaps, he was even glad that Rajan took all the demonstrative violence. He suddenly developed a malaria-like fever. He jiggled his hands into the buccaneer's offering bag and dropped even his wedding ring, trembling all over his body. Actually, I didn't know he really had a wedding ring. I was just guessing. All his fingers were adorned with rings bearing different kinds of gems and stones. He was a very religious person. He believed in superstitions.

The revolver man was holding the passengers in check. In the meantime, the Collector and the man with the Sten gun let their hands roam free on the better-endowed female folks. The Carbine-man even once went to the extent of thrusting his hand under the *saree* of one Assamese beauty, groping up between the thighs. She grimaced more in impotent rage than in pain. Her long legs were trembling. She bit her lips so tight a drop of blood oozed from the bitemark.

I shut my eyes to the gross disrespect. But I could not shut the picture out. It has already been etched on the granite slab of my memory. Never to be defaced again. Gall injected into my arterial system and converted into adrenalin, rushing into the bloodstream in a mighty whoosh. Sunil's blended look of resignation, indignation and accusation could never be forgotten. It has scraped my feelings too painfully deep. I mentally begged his forgiveness on behalf of my fellow northeasterners who did not realise the wickedness of their deed.

Father, forgive them, for they don't know what they are doing. I wished I had a little more faith. Then I could be happily waiting for a retributive miracle from above. But I was also told that faith without action is dead. Well, it doesn't actually say 'action'. It says works. If I don't work now, I may as well be dead. I hope fighting back counts as works under certain circumstances. The question is, how do I begin?

Presently, the raiders were only two persons away until they come at me. That gave me a moment's time to finalise my course of action and set my belief in it.

They are dealing with a Mishing gentleman right now. He was of a respectable age, quite handsome and elegant. The modern version of what we saw in the hinterlands, certainly. His haircut did not take after the traditional style. The bandits didn't care to show him any respect, though. Vile men are never known for their sense of etiquette.

Immediately beside me was the gorgeous lady who was thrown on me a little moment ago. A quaking mess. She was hauled up along with me and queued in the gentlemen's file. She was too scared to demand a transfer to the lady's rank where she must belong. I had not had the opportunity of laying my eyes on her. In fact, in my imploding wrath, I was totally consumed and oblivious to her presence. Now, in the peace of a ticking moment, I suddenly realised she was indeed a paragon of beauty.

Her skin was so fair and smooth I wondered if she must have bathed regularly in the purest untoned milk. Her cheekbones were lifted just the right degree to please the beholder's eyes. That's mine only at the moment. Her face was pinkish-pale, flushed with fear and anger. Her cheeks were plain sheets of paper, colourless, when I saw them out of my abrupt wakefulness. Now they are apple-red. Embers of rage and horror from within. Or it could be fate in store for her in the immediate future that enflamed her with revulsion. A nauseating expectation. Unless I acted in time to pull off an impossible feat.

I prayed for Killmaster's luck.

The untended hands would soon shift their location.

My heart missed a beat. For a moment, I threw all caution to the wind, unmindful of the danger crawling up every ticking second. Which man can tear off his eyes from such a bewitching face? I was drawn against my will.

She seemed to feel my stare. Psychologists say looking at the same place on a lady's body for more than three seconds is groping. To admit, I was visually groping her all this while. She wanted to ask me to look the other way. She shyly eyed me twice. I didn't get the message, though. I was that dumb. True beauty could really deaden your sense. Something deep down forced me to ignore her gestures. My neck seemed permanently twisted that way.

I heard a babble of unfamiliar tongue before I saw a hairy hand switching over to the partly uncovered cleavage of my lady. Her pale-yellow *dupatta* had fluttered away when she was chucked on me. Now, it dawned upon me that she must have resisted their moves which they took as an offence. And pushed her away for a moment, only to deal with her later.

And I was wakened up.

The dirty fingers now landed on the fatty lumps, slowly squeezing close on the perfect pair of assets. At that very instant, one of the devils, which one I could not determine presently, got down to his knees and gingerly lifted the hem of her skirt.

I was spared precious seconds in the heat of the moment as they paid full attention to the lady. Should I now call my lady?

I tried to move.

A second too slow.

Cold steel rubbed against my left temple with a metallic click.

No one spoke. There were around thirty-five passengers, including the crew. All were huddled to the far corner of the deck and held up by the carbine-wielder.

The *khukri*-man was beginning to tug at the flimsy frills of the lady's skirt until it tore in places. She grabbed hold of the molesting hands and pleaded not to outrage her modesty. *Not in public, at least,* she entreated with folded hands. Tears streaming down her face.

Actually, I did not know what she said. I was just making up what I believed she would have said in the given situation and from her wild gesticulations. Yet, I think I heard her language somewhere before. I couldn't place it straightaway. Perhaps, that's Yito's mother tongue, or at least close to it.

The lady screamed, tears burning fiery trails down her matchless cheeks. The horny scum had not listened to her pleas. She begged with clasped hands. But her implorations seemed to arouse the monster's animal passions all the more. He became even more aggressive.

Her dresses were in complete tatters now. The molester then placed his palm with a strong grip on the vee where the succulent thighs come to a common point. The *Beauty* yelled in shame and disgust. The *Beast* yowled in pleasure.

I couldn't take it anymore. My eyelids bit themselves shut. My head was still stuck with the abominable Webley & Scott.

If I made a move, only a slight press on the trigger would be required to set the powder ablaze. It may miss me. The pistol man would certainly take a fraction of a second to act. But one of us had to take the bullet. And I could not afford to put the lives of my co-passenger in jeopardy. I should not even think of moving a muscle if I wanted everybody alive. And I dared not take accountability of any casualty that's bound to be there. There was no guarantee that things would go perfectly right. In such eventuality, instead of singing praises to my bravado, everyone would be baying for my blood, nails drawn to skin me alive for the stupid responsibility I took upon myself.

But the lady's agony was sending out undeniable SOS signals. Actually, not to me in particular. I was merely being presumptuous. I had to act, though. Not only for the girl but for me. To save my own face from my trusting friends, who must have felt cheated and gravely misguided. I must at least give it a try so that things would go easier on my conscience later. I know I am not a hero. But I couldn't run away in the face of my buddies. I must save them or die trying. There was no better scheme of things at the moment.

The dame in distress was now sobbing piteously, her voice broken and gone in screaming for the entire duration. The brute had eventually undone her, leaving her just in her inners. He let her free, untouched, for a moment. For extra erotic effects, perhaps.

I couldn't take the sight anymore. But I could neither not take a look to take in how things have progressed. I rolled my eyeballs. She was even more striking undressed. She must have made a perfect model for the European Renaissance painters. I couldn't help but notice. Perhaps, I am innately a pervert!

I studied the scene and extrapolated the radius of my reach. From the corner of my eyes, I caught one anomaly in the setting: The rapist had left his big knife on the floor but haplessly out of the girl's range. He was not careless, I could see. But, with my capability to roll, it could be easily within my grasp, I calculated.

The molester turned his gaze to the man who pointed the gun at my temple as though seeking his permission. The gunman bobbed with a soft chuckle, scratching his three-day-old stubbles with his free hand.

That was their mistake.

That momentary lack of attention was the millisecond I was praying for. Taking risky decisions had been part of my career as the Chief Sales Agent of a real estate baron. I sprang to life like a lightning bolt with a textbook precision. Well, I am a bit over-romanticising. But I have to exaggerate the ordinary fight for better visual effects. I hope the reader indulges me. In reality, I did manage to pull the surprise because the gunman took longer to react. To my good fortune, he was way slower than I estimated. He was probably rusting. That's good to me.

Dodging a fraction is all it took to have my skull away from the line of fire. Not a big deal. N3's luck was on my side. For now. I don't know how long it would hold out, though.

With the gunman still in disbelief, I grabbed the hand that held the revolver and crushed the tiny knuckle-bones without any trace of mercy, disarming him in the process. I let him go for an imperceptible moment and gave him a butterfly shove on the chest to make room for my legs to flail. Then, leaping into the air, I swung a powerful roundhouse back kick at face level. He had no chance to duck.

A sweet snap connected to the hard sole of my shoe. I could hear a vicious crack as he twisted his neck almost three-sixty degrees. I am blowing the picture out of proportion again. In actuality, the crook was staggering backwards and was still taking the steps when I hopped into the air, spun around, and slapped him on the cheek with a simple back-kick.

The gun made no sound to rouse the horny beast at my feet.

Half staggering in the air, the gunman flipped over the railing of the deck and disappeared into the cold waters with a mighty splash.

The man-with-the-carbine was too stunned to move. He could only stare at my moves with a dropping jaw. He didn't know that Lady Luck was smiling at me. The *khukri* was to my advantage now.

I rolled across the floor, retrieved it, and whipped it while still in motion. The knife homed snugly into the Carbine-man's ribcage, missing the solar plexus by a centimetre.

He slumped to his side in excruciating pain. He couldn't sound a warning to his rapist comrade. Only a wheeze escaped from his mouth. He coughed noiselessly. A spatter of blood spurted between his clenched teeth. Then he went limp.

Not a single shot fired till now. So far, so good.

It is not possible to battle without commotion. Landing thuds and shuffling feet produce natural sounds which are beyond your control, no matter how much you try to muffle your moves. So, the *khukri*-man was eventually aroused. The soft thump of his comrade hitting the floor gave me away.

Leaving the disrobed lady where she was, he scampered like a harried hare, scooping up the Sten gun as he darted away. His fly remained untended in his haste. Nothing poked out to hint at his manhood which must be a ramrod not seconds ago. If there was any trace of urge left, that must have been induced by a mixture of fear and anger, not sensuality. Or if he was an insatiable sadist.

Taking advantage of that fraction of a second, I removed my jacket and flung it to the lady to somehow restore her honour. That was my mistake.

That precious millisecond was enough for the *khukri*-man to prep the gun for a shot.

The lady found her feet jerkily. She gave me a weak smile of gratitude. Indeed, a small yet fatal smile.

A staccato report split the quiet noon sky. I caught a flicker of flames in the corner of my eyes. Instinctively, I dove into the line of fire. Everything became weightless.

Heavens began to grow brighter and brighter until I could suffer the brilliance no more. The last thing I remembered was my body leaning ominously towards the beautiful lady. The space exploded into a blinding burst of light. I hope she caught me in her arms. If she does, that would be my ultimate dream come true. I would be so satisfied that I would never wish to wake up again.

I passed out.

*

My brain didn't register a thing when my eyes cracked open again. Confused bits of thoughts swam inside. My vision was hazy. My sense organs seemed to serve me no more. I could not move. Perhaps I was too used up in that brief exertion. I tried in vain to draw from my *chi*. The mysterious source of inner power in the human body discovered by those equally mysterious Buddhist monks in China. Unbreakable chains of metal seemed to fetter me to some immovable pegs. I gave up struggling. I blacked out again.

There was no light outside the window when I came to the second time. It must have been already dark. My head cleared up a bit, although still dazed. I could see the intravenous tubes going in or coming out of my veins. I must have been on drip for quite some time. My thoughts were still disorganized. Am I in the bunks of the ship? Nobody was beside me. I was too tired to look around. My eyes were still heavy. I slept once more.

The next morning, I was suddenly woken up by a circle of unfamiliar faces, chattering and jabbering like a troop of monkeys. I didn't comprehend a single word they said. I could see the flaking concrete of the lime-coated ceiling. I was in a hospital. I felt like caged in a zoo for public display. I was lost. Really lost.

Not in a moment, Yito came to my rescue, calming the excited hosts down. "Local news reporters," he whispered me. A couple of them being correspondents of national papers even. Which papers we could not point out right away, though. Then, he began to sing a litany of praises on my daredevilry. I didn't know what he said. From his mannerisms and indicative gestures and from the laudatory looks on the faces when they turned to me, I presumed that my audacious exploit was the subject of discussion.

Audacious? That was the border of stupidity. I myself am amazed no end. I could be equally the object of expletives rather than adjectives had the wheels turned the other way. So, I could confidently assume that the majority of the adjectives and adverbs Yito employed to lionise me were sheer exaggeration and absolutely unwarranted. In fact, the bravado he so effusively commended was not worth the ado and admiration. I was simply defending the honour of a fellow human being who happens to be of the fairer sex. Anybody in my place would have done the same.

I mean, not necessarily losing their heart as I secretly did at that very instant. It was not at all a conducive atmosphere to lose one's heart. But I'd lost it all the same. I am like that only. But what I did was not necessarily compelled by amorous consideration alone. Rather, I took it my duty towards humanity irrespective of race, caste, or gender. Not that I am a do-gooder or a saint. In fact, let the truth be told. I am a sinful normal human being hanging around every possible corner seeking my selfish motives and gains.

The vaunting praises, the encouragements and congratulatory remarks not only from my own friends but from the doctors, nurses, inmates and a stream of visitors I never knew reminded me that I am alive. By the way, how and when had the story made the rounds and what kindness of heart made the people gather here escaped my power of reasoning. Humans could be really good when they wanted to, I thought.

But I was dismayed internally. The face I secretly longed to see never turned up. To add to the pain, I dared not enquire after it. But my heart protested loudly for her.

My friends had constantly jeered at me for not getting a better half till today. They used to call me heartless or worthless. Perhaps, I had not yet come across the right person. But they would never subscribe to my theories and had their fill of jokes at my expense. Frankly speaking, no one had so far captured my fancy. Perhaps, I was not looking around hard enough. Why, I don't know. Or maybe I really didn't have a heart. And nothing so far has betrayed my emotions.

However, some change in my face seemed to have given me away. Yito whispered in my ear: "You miss her, don't you?"

I certainly would have hit him on the head had my hands not been tethered in I.V. tubings. He had accurately adduced my innermost feeling. I hissed like a helpless cobra played by its charmer. At that juncture, the doctor walked in and showered me with a splash of praise which I still considered superfluous and unmerited. He asked everybody out. Then, taking the bed-head card, he scribbled something onto it and flashed me a naughty grin. "There's someone to see you in private," he said casually.

He gave me a pill that I popped right away without much thought.

I was too exhausted. I needed more rest. My eyes grew heavy. The tablet must have been a sedative. I was dozing when the doctor left me. I counted.

Before I got to ten, though, I felt a warm breath across my face. I had already closed my eyes. The odour was feminine. Perhaps, Chanel. Expensive.

I wrenched my eyes with a huge effort. Sleep had almost overtaken them. But the mind was still aware. Through a tiny, struggled slit, I saw a facial feature out of focus. Holy cow, it was her!

I wanted to scream in joy. But all my strength was gone. Sapped. I cursed the doctor. What has he given me? Yet, I also feared to scare her away. I pretended to sleep. The pretence was absolutely unnecessary. I was too sleepy to even feign it. Now, I was hoping she would plant a kiss somewhere on my face. The lips, most preferably. That I would gladly take to paradise.

But no!

She moved away after feeling my breath. She took my wrist and felt my pulse, and hummed: "Hmm!" Nodding satisfied, she turned to me again as I shut my half-cracked eyes almost too late. She came to my face. Again!

"By Jove, just do it!" I cried inwardly.

She bent down but to my earlobe. And whispered, "Thank you, my saviour," and a few sweet nothings.

Wonder how I knew her language? She spoke English! Stupid. A slight accent but educated nonetheless.

That's all I got for saving your life? I scolded her inside my head. I wanted more. More of what, but I didn't know. Oh, Lucifer, why didn't we take the bullets together and walk into the city of Necropolis hand in hand!

I didn't know when she left. The doctor must have given me the sleeping pill on purpose.

*

No more visits from her. No more news. Even Yito zipped his mouth about it. And I dared not ask anyone.

Before long, I began to develop a very bad temperament. I pestered my friends to leave, especially Sunil and Rajan. They did leave reluctantly after much persuasion. They hated to see me off in this state of affairs. But I stood my ground unmoved. Actually, I had begun to feel a liability on their shoulders. And I could not think of them wasting time on me anymore. Especially with what treatment we had meted out to them. They tendered a tanker full of apologies. Yito would not submit to my will, though.

We talked very less for the last few days. I was brooding and listless. I did not know what had happened to me. Yito seemed to just avoid me. I wanted to leave, but the doctor won't let me go.

One morning, a Thursday, or probably the fourth day or the fortieth day of my medical confinement, I don't know, Yito simply did not turn up. Had he gone too, after all?

In fact, I had insisted he go too. But when I didn't see him turn up, I wished he hadn't been really gone. Why did he leave without informing me? I know that's unreasonable. I was just picking a nit. I was furious and wanted to stomp away. But I had nothing with me. The doctor had told me that I would be dropped home by the authorities after all the formalities and proper discharge.

It was only eight in the morning. I turned around, popped a fistful of sedatives and waited for the sun to sink. It took me no time to drop off. The man with the pistol swam behind the steamer and clambered onto the deck. I fired at him with his own firearm. The slugs flew harmlessly through him. He lumbered forward with ominous outstretched arms. Then, he snatched the lady away from my arms and thrust out a heavy blow at my stomach. I buckled. My face came down to the perfect level for him to perform a strike with his leg. In a flash, he lapped my chin with the flat of his foot, sending me down, down into the sea.

A violent shake woke me up as I splashed into the water. I sat up on the bed, trembling viciously. Yito threw me one more blanket and comforted me with a manly hug. I composed myself in no time. But I could not hold my tongue any longer.

"Yito," I said in a tone so meek it did not behove the egotist me. "I don't know if I am in love—"

"You are." Yito cut me out, matter-of-factly.

I hated him for so quickly making out my sentiments. I hated him in a good way, though. But to dampen my spirits, Yito broke the news that the lady had been airborne that very afternoon. For Vellore.

A dark curtain drew before my eyes.

I told Yito that I needed more sleep. I slipped under the quilt once again.

*

A few days later, with a proper discharge certificate and a lot of useless appreciative notes from whomsoever-they-are-I-don't-know-or-care, I was back home to my dear Lamka.

But, of course, with a missing heart! And a newfound haunting nightmare that won't leave me in peace.

*

Several months eroded.

Yet the whirr of the engine still rented the peace of night as the steamer kicked up a meandering silver trail on the majestic Brahmaputra. The landscape was bathed in bluish mercuric beams emanating from the phoebe on yonder.

I flung my arms around her tightly and murmured a language understood only by hearts that beat as one. We looked out from the deck, neck-and-neck, leaning on the rails, admiring the moonlit night. The silent observer in the skies above had grown to its full size. It was brilliant. She looked at me and smiled. I smiled back. I was in seventh heaven.

But nothing lasts forever.

The Webley-&-Scott-man rose from his watery grave, dripping wet all over, the handgun in his shaky hands. He raised it in slow motion, perhaps to intensify the psychosis of fear. Then, he pulled the trigger, sending a series of shots our way. The night was ripped apart by the deafening reports. I screamed at the top of my lungs as I lunged forward to tackle the dead gunman.

Hearing a creepy howl, my sister-in-law rushed into my room and stirred me awake. Then, she showed me a white envelope that reminded me of the white panty of the lady of my dreams. I secretly smiled. My sister-in-law teased me. "So, you found her in your tour?"

"What're you talking about?"

"This came in right now."

She did not answer my question as she left the letter there on the bed and retreated.

I tore it open. In just a single sentence, it says:

My dear saviour,

How can I not lose my heart to him who bothered to risk his life for me?

With true love,
Dr. Bess Panyang
Arunachal Pradesh

—*A special version of this story is published in the Siamsinpawlpi Annual Magazine, 2003, 38th & 39th Vol.*

Chapter 2

PERFECT STRANGERS

Twenty-three Christmases isn't too early for a sane young man to fall in love. At least for the first time in my life. Even for an introvert counselled a hundred times that love doesn't reside in the loveliness of the face alone but rather in the inner charm of the heart. And who believed that innocence and virtue are not the only qualities that count. Yet, Eric wasn't a guy moved with such high-flying theoretical notions. For what he sees in everyday life often proves reality in perfect contrast. True love, in the first place, doesn't exist, he would often contend. Girls aren't much different from moths. As long as you have glitter to show, he would maintain, much to the chagrin of his girl friends.

Whatever be the case or his belief system, it took him just one rainy day to rip the gates of his inner self open.

It was a fine sunny morning. A fine sunny morning is nothing to cheer about in a typically unpredictable Indian summer. It always coincides with the advent of monsoon. The sunrise might be clear and shiny, all right. But without warning, the skies would, in a moment, wrap themselves up in a cloak of dark clouds and dampen the rising spirits of the little people on earth. Before you realise it, the moisture-laden clouds would swell and give the town a torrential bath.

That certain fine day was no exception. The monsoon had decided to show that its gloom was not an empty threat. A heavy discharge unleashed over the town of Lamka without any forewarning. The rolling clouds are a monsoon normality and not counted as a warning. No thunderclaps, no growling heavens, no lightning streaks. The fluffy rainclouds simply parted and poured buckets on the Asian terrain below.

Shoppers in downtown districts started running helter-skelter, seeking the nearest shelters. Marts and stores worked their asses off to save their merchandise from the spontaneous precipitation. Eric, too, was busy cradling bosomfuls of fabric laid out in wooden crates across the promenade. He was far too engaged when two damsels ran into the safety of his shop.

"How careless of us to not have taken our umbrellas with us in this uncertain monsoon," one of the girls remarked, giggling casually as she brushed raindrops off her matted hair.

The voice seemed to have a very peculiar ring. It struck a unique chord somewhere inside Eric's being. He had heard hundreds if not thousands, of voices every day. Never before had a timbre had such an impression on him. Needless to say, there was something about this Mary and her tonal quality. Or was it his unwariness that took him by surprise? Could one ring of a voice really throw a person off his feet? How did that little thing called love really work?

The struck chord inside Eric vibrated violently as the girls indulged in more titters between themselves. A titter that changed his life and set of beliefs forever.

He turned around to find its source. He was caught off guard. He nearly dropped the grey T-shirt *Bon Jovi* boldly emblazoned across the breast he'd just removed from the peg overhead. His nerves sprang into involuntary twitches. He was literally bowled over. And deprived of speech. He was simply gawking at his guests as though they were unwanted aliens or zombies straggling into his apartment.

The girls were unnerved by the mute stare of their host.

"W...we are really so...sorry mister—er-" the girl with the giggle stuttered.

"Eric." Eric provided even without realising he had spoken.

"So sorry to wet your floor," the lass went on, blurting out the apology, ignoring the name anyways. "But we can't help, you see," she continued, shrugging at the slush that was beginning to brim the gutters and overflow into the streets. The peaking monsoon can rain inches in a matter of minutes.

Never mind, Eric wanted to say. Only empty words formed inside his voice box, sizzling away like droplets of water on a heated pan. His lips fluttered, but the audio came out in muted mode, to his utter embarrassment. The belles stopped their laughter midbar as they saw their host welcoming them with nothing but a dumb gawk. They were tempted to move over to the adjacent shop. Something stopped them from going over, though.

The rain ceased as suddenly as it came. Sunlight broke through the clouds. It was brief but harsh and bright. The laughing lasses turned to express their gratitude. That was absolutely unnecessary. But they felt ill at ease and kind of obliged because of their host's uninviting courtesy.

"Thank you for allowing us..."

The thanking was lame. It trailed off as they stepped out into the sun, away from the oppressive silence of a stranger they never knew.

They walked away without looking back once.

Their host, however, was still robbed of his speech. He couldn't help but gape at his unexpected guests taking their leave. The giggling one walking away with his heart right under his nose. In fact, he was staring long after they had gone.

—*Eric, the dumb host*—

It was yet to sink in. His thoughts were still vacant. But the images were lingering. He still saw them swaying into the crowd but never out of sight. In the meanwhile, a lady shopper was dropping in, but she had to move on as there was nobody to attend her. The shop owner was still fixing his eyes in one direction until somebody bumped into him and cursed him for standing in the middle of the path. He, startled out of his stupor, mumbled nonsense to return the blame, accusing him of running into him on purpose. That was truly not himself. Was that the first sign of losing his mind?

Eric knew his peace was invaded. He easily lost his grip. His already short span of attention was further shortened. He suddenly lost interest in waiting on prospective buyers in his tiny retailer.

Something has gone into his mind. Something is very wrong. Or was it very right? He was confused. He had never had that experience before. He was even terrified that he was going senile. What? Going senile in the early twenties?

Probably he meant going soft and mellowing to a common human emotion called love. He would often assert that he never felt the desire for it. But every man needs one. Perhaps, it's time he admitted and accepted the realities of life.

He was uncertain. He was sceptical. He was not a love-at-first-sight kind of guy. As he said of himself. Or was he simply self-conscious? His inner self told him to go out and live a normal love life. He hesitated because he never trusted himself in matters concerning the heart. He had generally regarded it a girlish pursuit. All these thoughts running amok in his head held him up for a long time, although, in simple terms, he strongly wanted to run after the discovery and find out what it really portends.

A week passed. He was still undecided. The enchanting voice refused to go away. Trilling clear and audible on his tympanic membrane. Her wet hair and innocent look still traced a clean image on the surface of his mind's eye. Something about her was overwhelming. Tempting, in fact. Even a slight re-thought of the moment formed goosebumps on his arms, sending pleasant chills down the spine. He might have had his qualms, but he had definitely taken the tumble.

Then, one day, he made up his mind. He decided to look around for the angel, whatever it took. For over a week, he had waited for her to drop into his shop again. That never happened.

Opportunity seldom knocks on the same door twice. He realised he had to run after it, grab it, and own it. But making up one's mind is easy. Working on the resolution is not. Eric ran into a wall.

He's got no friends.

Friends, well, he did have scores. But not one he thought he could take aside and confide in. Not that all his pals are fair-weathers. Only most of them. Which ones, he could not or would not point out, though. Truly so, when it comes to matters of the heart, he was spoilt for lack of choice.

He was scared and a bit ashamed. What if they make him the butt of their jokes? What if they label him girlie? He was known to be a hardliner. The moralist, the stoic. He could not lose his reputation. But love doesn't go well with keeping reputations. One has to be a little crazy and unabashed when it comes to opening up one's heart to someone one likes.

Will Eric dare take the risk? Was he crazy enough to fall in love?

Much to his own disbelief, Eric would frequently lapse into a pensive mood and pine away in deep thoughts. He began to forget to up his shutters and make a living. How could an unknown soul, with just one little laugh, blow his mind away so hard? It was really stupid of him. He would often reproach himself to no avail.

In spite of making up his mind, he was still stuck at square one: Lack of ideas on how to take the first step. It was uncharted territory. He had not once whistled at a lady. Laying out a scheme to seek out an unidentified angel who stole his heart and make an approach is way beyond his capacity. He needs help. Fast.

Till the second Sunday since he ran into that girl, or rather that girl ran into him, he was indolently languishing in his abode. Taking himself to be a good Christian, he'd hardly missed masses, especially on Sundays. Naturally so, on that second holy day, a friend of his called in to enquire about his well-being. It took a few raps before Eric answered the door.

"Hello, what brings you here, Mike?"

Eric was pleasantly surprised. He was lately longing for a shoulder to cry on. Throwing buckets literally if need be. He was that helpless.

Mike didn't wait for the formality of being invited in. He simply nudged his way and walked in as though it were his own home. Eric followed and offered him a seat from behind. Mike plunked on the fat sofa without saying thank you. He was tame and certainly no stranger. It was his regular haunt here.

Mike was on the talkative side. Talkative people are normally not known for their ability to maintain secrets. Can Eric lean on such a shoulder? The padre would love to say that he was God-sent because he turned up at the most unexpected yet fervently prayed-for moment. Is Mike the one to show him the way? His Messiah? Or at least to share his burden and lessen the weight? Eric was in a dilemma. Did he have a choice, anyway?

"Closing shop, missing services, skipping youth activities..."

Mike prattled, automatically reaching for the TV remote control. He depressed the green button. MTV came on. Mike loved Hindi songs and Bollywood chicks. "Anything ailing you, buddy?" he asked casually.

That's not a concern. It's a taunt.

MTV croons—

Chhuimui si tum lagti ho;

Phoolon jaisi hasti ho...

Roughly rendered, the ditty may mean something like—

A touch-me-not that you are;

You smile like a blooming flower!

Eric was mindlessly doodling circles on the sofa arm with the tip of his fingers. He was not sitting with Mike. The soulful tune and the coy starlet in the song sequence from the TV had carried him somewhere to an ethereal world. He was mentally serenading his 'Lady with the Giggle'.

"I am talking to you, man," Mike jostled Eric out of his reverie. "Anything wrong? You seemed lost and disoriented. You're not going mad, I hope?" He chuckled at his own joke.

"Indeed, I am," Eric replied tersely, being so shaken out of his daydream.

"Joking, man! Somethin's buggin' you? Just tell me. Why get worked up?"

Actually, Mike had called Eric thinking him to be down with flu or something like that. Not serious. But now, he slowly came to think that the illness was more than skin-deep. A long shot. Not that there's any risk in taking it.

He was about to spell out his mind when Eric, probably unable to suffer the phase of silence, spoke up: "Are you good with secrets, Mike?"

"I hope you're not planning to loot a bank," Mike quipped.

"Worse than that," Eric came snappily. "It needs super secrecy."

"A super-secret of a mid-twenties guy is usually an infatuation," Mike took the pot shot. "Call it love, if you must. Mate, you're having a bad fall, I'm sure."

"You nasty little brat."

Eric threw a punch at his friend's fleshy biceps. It was not gentle. It landed with a loud smack. Mike returned with an equally sharp knock. Eric dodged, and the fist landed sidewise on the chest harmlessly. He gave it back. Mike exchanged it with another. They soon came to blows. That's boys' way of dissipating tension. Just a kangaroo fight. Trading a few more blows, they ended up locked in each other's arms, grappling across the floor.

Before long, though, they gave up wrestling and slumped on the settee, panting and sweating, filling the house with a peal of laughter. Eric had found himself a friend he could trust. A stooge.

Now that Mike had given him the oath of silence, Eric began to narrate the turn of events. He was not a storyteller. Despite the rare and exclusive features he attributed to the giggling angel, he could not put them across as such.

"Any girl would fit into your description, pal," interjected Mike, dismayed at the ineptitude. "Tell me something that'll make her stand out. Easy to notice."

Eric tried again. The voice and the looks were very clear in his mind. Crystal. But putting them in words, he fell miserably short. Wordsmithy was certainly not his calling.

"Okay. Leave it," Mike stepped in eventually, resigned. "We'll scour. Ours is not a big town. We'll rake it with a fine-toothed comb. From tomorrow."

"Why not from today?" Eric jumped, over-enthused.

"Ah, well. Why not, of course," agreed Mike and rose to his feet. "Laughing Angel, here we come!" he yodelled theatrically like a Shakespearean thespian.

Lamka is not a small town. It is a big village. Hardly a square mile in size. It won't need a Herculean effort to scout the entire length and breadth. Or so they thought.

Not before they started out did they realise that it was a proverbial case of being easier said than done. There must be at least a few thousand womenfolk to scrutinize. In a way, their expedition was undertaken with only one pair of eyes. For, the other pair that belonged to the more energetic searcher was as good as blind. He was absolutely unfamiliar with the face they were looking for. No amount of Eric's verbal portrayal could print a picture with clarity on Mike's mental screen. The only thing he understood was the hair. It was brownish black, perhaps recently coloured or hennaed, shiny, and of the length between the shoulders and the hip.

Well, Lamka is a fashionable township. Almost all the ladies sport a mane of that length. That was the most common and conservative hairstyle in those days. Except for those with a bob popularly known as Momoko-cut. And there might be a few with curls and waves. But Eric's girl was certainly no frizzie.

And the evening and the morning were the first day. And Eric saw that it was not good.

They started out from the north and ended up in the south. Traipsing every lane and by lane. Peeking into every casement near and far, high and low. Studying every girl-face, they came across like a mad anthropologist going overdrive with a project of profiling facial structures.

To Mike's eyes, every girl they met fitted Eric's description. Down to the hair. To Eric, none of them did. Some girls laughed at them. Others abused them. The rest just ignored them.

And the evening and the morning were the second day. And Eric saw that it was still not good.

Now, they started from the east and rounded up at the other end. The angel-with-the-wet-hair was an elusive eel.

"I think you're high that day," Mike charged at last. "And hallucinating, obviously."

"Stop it, Mike," Eric's gaze was arrested by a tiny speck of human figures coming down Tipaimukh Road.

The westing sun glinted in his eyes. He shaded them with his palm above the eye line. He looked like a US private saluting his captain. Something out of the Hollywood movies. Mike chuckled at the analogy.

"Did you see that?" Eric said.

Mike followed Eric's gaze. They're looking out from somebody's terrace, which they climbed without the owner's knowledge. He also saluted.

Two ladies were walking down the grey, simmering road.

"The eagle must be shamed before your eyesight," he remarked, squinting hard. "It's a mirage."

"You don't have mirages out here," Eric started down the stairs. "I know it's her."

Mike could only wonder aloud after him. "Is it her gait that gives her away?"

Eric didn't answer. He need not. His heart knew. Just knew.

They scampered to the roadside and waited under a random jujube tree. Eric's heart pounded vigorously. What if she's not her? What if his heart has lied, after all?

The ladies were strutting along unmindfully, preoccupied with their own girly chat.

"Come on, you need not pull me that close," Mike complained, shaking off Eric's grip.

"Look, look—" Eric whispered in a tremolo, his breath growing more rapid with every approaching moment of truth.

"I am all eyes, man!" Mike said gruffly, hitting him on the back of his head to slam calmness into it. "She's just a girl. Not a ghost nor a goddess. Take it easy."

The same two girls Eric claimed to have known. Chittering like monkeys engaged in their own talk. Punctuating their dialogues with giggles that blew him away. Unaware of the two Peeping Toms hiding under an overgrowth at the edge of the highway as though trying to bushwhack them.

Eric's hand went to his heart as he fell onto Mike's bosom, eyes wide shut. A stupid grin playing on his lips.

"Hey, bud," Mike shook him awake. "Tell me which one?"

"The one with the giggle, you silly," Eric said without prying his eyes.

"Both of them giggled, you sillier!"

"The one whose hair is between the shoulders and the hip."

"Both hairs are between the shoulders and the hip."

"Don't you have eyes, you stupid?" Eric hissed at his friend for his inability to pick out the better-looking one.

"I like the one to the right better," Mike opined.

"Whose right?" Eric growled. "The one on your left? The one on your right? Be specific, man?"

"The right on the left," Mike got mixed up real good now. "The left of the right. Well, I mean, the one on the far right."

"That's the wrong one."

"Hmm!" Mike hummed. "Then, I think we both have an interest here."

For a moment, the bug seemed to have bitten Mike as well. By the time they came up with a proper identification, the ladies had already turned the corner and ambled out of view.

And the evening and the morning were the third day. And Eric saw that it was beginning to good.

To cut to the chase, they sought out the epitome of beauty, offered acquaintances, and made the indecent proposal. And the rest, as they say, is mundane tale.

The lady in question made herself known as Sherrie. She was a blank sheet. A vacant courtyard. Eric waltzed into it and drew his own line of control. Sherrie took no time acknowledging it.

It may be revealed that Sherrie, too, had kind of left her heart in the garment store on that rainy day at the same instant Eric lost his. She had not ached as hard because Eric's outer shell was a bit of a put-off to her. She had wanted to visit the store again. She did visit it a couple of times. But it was lately shut. And her friend had discouraged her to give any further thought.

Now that they had opened their inner selves to one another, they found that they were rather mutually agreeable. And they hit off quite well before they realised.

Eric was yet diffident to perform the home courting: The traditional ritual of wooing a girl. He had never done it before. It was uncharted territory. He needed some time to pull his courage together to take the formal plunge. Moreover, he's got a lot of catching up to do in the commercial department. He had wasted a good number of days mooning and manning the town. Only good thing is that the wastage paid off eventually.

"I'll pay you a proper visit in a week's time," promised Eric. "I'm a bit daunted to meet your parents although looking forward to it at the same time."

"My parents may not approve," Sherrie demurred. She was simply being straightforward to pre-empt any later misunderstanding. "They wanted me to finish college before I take any step into personal relationships. I'm afraid my father's not a kind to easily change words."

"Uh, oh—" Eric groaned. "Not so promising, eh?"

"There's good news, though," Sherrie chirped gayly as though to lift the sagging spirits. "I'm finishing college this year itself."

So, they decided to let their parents be for the time being and spent the remaining days happily together until Sherrie had to leave for Mumbai to wrap up her studies.

And the evening and the morning were many days. And Eric saw they were all good!

*

Now, there happened to be a vainglorious timber tycoon somewhere in the town where Eric lived. He was arrogant and extravagantly given to drinking. One day, when the sun was mild, and the shadows lengthened, this Mr. Tycoon took his new sleek *Maruti* car on a long countryside drive. The rustic highway was serene and empty.

Sozzled as he always was, it took no time for mists to swim before his bloodshot eyes. He kept shaking his head to clear. In a short while, the highway forked into three blurry thoroughfares. And, being a self-professed believer in no extremities, he took the middle path.

From the other end of the road, Eric was riding his *Devil* bicycle, town-bound, back from a visit to his grandparents at a certain suburban hamlet. All of a sudden, he heard a nasty crash somewhere ahead. He pedalled at full speed. A little distance later, he saw a deep reddish hatchback at the bottom of a gentle slope, kissing a eucalyptus tree.Cables popped out from under the mangled bonnet, smoke rising with a steamy hiss.

Without properly dismounting his bicycle, Eric hopped to the ground and trotted down the gradient to see if there was still a soul to be saved. His bike's wheels were still spinning on their sides as he made out that the vehicle had just one occupant. The driver. A deep gash ran across the forehead from which blood was spurting copiously. And he was out cold.

Eric yanked the door open without difficulty. He was almost knocked out by a powerful stench. The whole interior of the car was reeking with alcohol. The tubby occupant was not easy to wheedle out. Eric huffed and puffed, testing every tilt and turn to no avail. The victim's flaccidity added a good deal of weight to it. He struggled for what seemed ages.

Suddenly, Tycoon dislodged, throwing Eric off the ground with himself on top. Eric pushed away the unconscious face that seemed to give him a French kiss. That was the foulest odour that ever assailed his nostrils: Alcohol, a cud of green betel nut concoction called *tamul*, lime-red slaver oozing from the sides of the mouth, and a natural bad breath, all blended into a strong brew of halitosis.

He thought a stinking gas bomb had just been lobbed at him. He nearly fainted. He retched for a moment. Then, he took a few deep breaths before starting over again to haul the victim to safety.

He had barely dragged the man away when a gas leakage sparked a hungry host of flames to engulf the car. A deafening explosion occurred. Eric could hardly believe his eyes. He had never seen death up so close. He shivered with the afterthought.

In the heat of the moment, he totally forgot to seek help or cry for one.

Now, the problem is how to take the victim to the hospital. Apparently, his bike was too insignificant for the purpose.

As luck would have it, he was spared from further worry. A *Tata* lorry lumbered into the scene without any prelude. The truck was laden with bags of charcoal and various other farm produce. Eric waved it down and signalled for assistance. The driver instantly alighted from the *Pilot* cockpit, followed by his handyman. A couple of passengers in the cabin offered more hands and made space by moving over to the laden back carriage.

They threw Eric's bike on top of the bulging sacks and let him accompany the injured man. They drove straight to the *District Civil Hospital* and dropped their fares. The driver volunteered to inform the police on their way back to the truck stand in the market. That's tribal altruism.

The tycoon was immediately taken to the hospital on a creaky gurney. Two nurses wheeled him towards the operation theatre. Meanwhile, the duty doctor pulled Eric aside for a few formalities.

It so happened that the doctor had known the victim quite well. He quickly filled out the forms. In the process, he asked Eric for his identity in a casual manner. Eric hesitated. He knew the police would soon be on the trail. He was uneasy about getting himself into police records. He requested the doctor if he could pass him off as a simple, unidentified Good Samaritan. Perhaps, a good friend, if he insists? The doctor understood.

No wonder Eric refused to disclose himself unless forced. Getting your name in the police files was considered a blot on your personal standing. A character assassination. That's a misapprehension, of course. But in those days, it was a currency on people's minds. Simple folks. Not a surprise that everybody was scared to feature in the police logbooks.

Further, upon arrival, Eric found that the gentleman was quite a known person around, although he himself was ignorant about him. One of the beautiful nurses came forward to inform his family before he could ask who he really was. From the flutter of attention he was given, Eric could easily make out that he was quite a somebody. Or at least known very well to one of the medical staff. So, he did not want to be someone who appeared to be hankering around for favours or some monetary reward.

Tycoon was pronounced out of danger, although he was yet to come around. Just a bad cut on the forehead. Nothing more. Despite their nasty look, the injuries turned out to be minor and superficial. Eric heaved a sigh of relief and decided to make himself scarce.

*

That morning, Tycoon had gone to drop his daughter, Sharon, at *Tulihal* airport. Sharon was leaving for a certain mainland metropolis where she was studying. She's a cheerful girl. That morning she was even chirpier. Cheeping all along like a red-breasted robin.

"Papa," she tweeted animatedly, sipping from a *Frooti* mini tetrapack. They were approaching the aerodrome. "I've got something to tell you when I come back for Christmas."

In truth, Sharon had recently fallen in love despite her father's strictures. Tycoon was, of course, not a harsh father. He was a bit of an old-school and a self-made man. He had known struggle and learnt the hard lessons of life on his own. Not unlike any typical father, he did not want her only daughter, that he treated like a son, to undergo what he had. He could not see her fail in life. That's why he was sometimes too concerned and overprotective, coming across as a control freak. Otherwise, as they say, he was wax should you peel away the outer crust.

Tycoon simply hummed and tooled the little car into the entrance of the airport.

In a short while, after all the formalities had been covered, the father-daughter duo waved and parted ways. Nothing unusual.

On his way back, Tycoon saw an aircraft flying past over him at a low altitude. He downed his window and peered out, waving, as though his loving daughter was looking down from it. He was somehow missing her already.

It was afternoon when Tycoon reached back his hometown. He had no mind of going directly home. And it was kind of late to visit his business establishment. So, he drove straight to his watering hole. Needless to say, drinking was his weakness, and in his own words, there was no temptation he couldn't resist except booze. So, booze was what he went to get.

After having a few neat shots, Tycoon decided to take a motor ride in the countryside. To clear his head, he said. As it often was, the few pegs turned out to be a little too much already. Regardless, he took a spare bottle with him from which he swigged straight away. Drink-driving is not much of an offence in this part of the world. He soon swayed and swerved along the meandering single-lane alpine highway.

The sun was mild, and the shadows had lengthened.

Sharon had missed her father's accident by a fraction of a day. Actually, her holidays had expired days ago. She had made an excuse to overstay for the sake of her newfound boyfriend. When it was time for her to fly, she was no doubt cheery. But once she got on the plane, she suddenly felt melancholy. Sharon, a bright, intelligent girl who used to be quite effusive and sprightly, was brooding for some unknown heaviness in her heart.

Was she already homesick? Was she already longing for her beau's embrace? Not only because her father had advised her against it, but she herself never wanted to get involved in a love affair. She knew that once she gave herself, she would be so committed that it would come in her way one way or the other. But blame it on nature and age. How could she fight the urges of youth forever? Now, she's madly in love. And she couldn't help it.

They say love and motion come at will. It must be true, she thought.

*

A couple of days later, Eric learnt from the local dailies that the police had closed the investigation as a case of personal negligence and ill luck. Feeling safe now, Eric decided to pay his accidental acquaintance a visit.

Only then did Mr. Tycoon come to know the angel who pulled him back from the jaws of death. So overwhelmed with gratitude that he was at a loss for words. When he eventually overcame his emotions, he asked Eric to name anything he wanted as a prize. "I'd be glad to fulfil anything you may ask, should it be in my capacity," he vowed. His near-death experience taught him a little lesson on humility. He sounded different already.

"My philanthropy isn't for sale, Sir," Eric said. "But if you could," he added with a wince of doubt: "Give up your drinking. I'm sure you'll be doing yourself a big favour."

That was a bit too didactic and out-of-place for a man like Eric. But we might not say so if we know him inside out. He had himself lost a father to alcoholism just as he was pushing his teens, the moment he needed a father most.

"Noble soul!" exclaimed Tycoon, moistness of disbelief in the corners of his eyes. "I'll surely live up to your wish." He placed a gentle grab on Eric's arm and continued, "But you won't leave me without naming a gift." He insisted.

"What can satisfy human desire, Sir?" Eric replied. "Everything perishes. But your words of praise and resolve will please me forever. Thank you." He declined and decided to take his leave. He was always uncomfortable with strangers. Had it not been for his sense of moral responsibility, he would never have paid him a visit in the first place.

Tycoon reached out and motioned him to tarry. Eric would have walked out anyway with one pretext, or another had he not seen the film of unshed tears coating the cornea of his eyes. He couldn't say no to tears. His mother had cried a lot during his father's lifetime.

Taking cue, Tycoon lost no moment in contemplation.

"My wife and I have decided," he said in a near whisper, "to repay your goodness of heart with a gift that'll last you for a lifetime."

At that moment, the ward door groaned open. Tycoon's good-natured wife walked in. Tycoon immediately gave way and allowed her to make the announcement.

Tycoon's wife shuffled a bit, putting the prescriptions lying haphazardly on the metal tabletop into the box below and quietly settled down on her husband's side. She began in a subdued tone. "We thought of offering you Sharon's hand"

"Who's Sharon?" Eric ejaculated, raising his eyebrows.

Sharon's mother clarified. "She's our begotten daughter."

Eric was not amused at all.

"We're not in the movies, Madam!" he remarked, taken aback. "Even if I were to accept, there's no guarantee your daughter would agree to such an absurd arrangement. She's not a toy."

"She's our baby," Tycoon supported his wife from his supine position. "She never goes against our will. She's a darling indeed."

Eric was horrified by the feudalistic mindset of these parents. He was even shocked that such people still exist.

"You want me to play baddie with your daughter, eh?" He nearly smiled in exasperation. *I've got a girlfriend of my own,* he thought of giving himself away but held his tongue in time.

"But, please listen —" Tycoon's wife continued.

"No buts please," Eric cut her bluntly. "Have mercy on your daughter."

"Well said," Tycoon intervened. "We're truly sorry to have offended you." He propped himself up, leaning against the wall. "We thought you'd be interested. We just wanted to show that we're ready to give everything out of gratitude. I could have offered you my own life would it be worth it." He paused for a moment. "May I ask for another favour, then?"

"Go ahead," prompted Eric, more in frustration from the outrageous proposition than in approval.

"I'd like to introduce you to my daughter anyways." That was more a plea than a request. "I want you to be friends with her at least, that we have talked you into this." Eric hesitated for a long time. Then conceded: "That's fair enough."

*

Sharon got a phone call in her hostel.

"Baby," it was her father on the line. "I need you home for a week."

"Anything wrong, Papa?" Sharon was alarmed.

"Nothing's wrong, don't worry," Papa continued. "There's some obligation of mine that needs your attendance. I'll talk to your teachers."

In a sense, Sharon was eager herself to get back home. Her yearning for her swain was yet to subside. But to fly back at such sudden notice filled her with nervousness. "Is mother okay," she said after an extended pause.

"She's alright," the answer from the other end reassured her somehow. "It's both our wish to have you back for a moment, dear."

Sharon couldn't stop wondering what was so pertinently requiring her presence at home in the middle of her academic session.

It was not before she reached home that her wonder transformed into anger of volcanic proportions. Instead of feeling empathy or astounded for not being informed of her father's mishap, she even wished he had better been dead. She had never gone against her father's wishes. She was known to be a complete daddy's girl, and she didn't mind it. She's put her full confidence in her father's judgement in everything. But, the idea of meeting up with an alien bachelor and, if possible, impress on him so much so that he would swoon and get down to his knees with a ring in his hand was too bizarre. Even for the wildest fantasy. It may make good stuff for typical Bollywood love stories with all their unrealistic plots and subplots. But this is not Bollywood. The very thought was sickening.

Had her parents gone mad? Yet they won't budge an inch.

A smile on her father's lips somewhat soothed her frayed nerves. Still, then, her fury had not abated completely. "What's that smile for?" she demanded irascibly.

"But for my insistence, he was not even ready to meet you," he said slowly.

Sharon heaved a huge sigh of relief.

His father continued: "Your boy must have got a girl of his own. Otherwise, how could an available young man not agree to a blind date? After all, we are only saying thank you to the person who saved my life. And I wanted you to be friends with him. Of course, a marriage would have been better. For who finds a young boy anymore in this self-seeking world risking his life for an unknown victim of a car accident? I thought it was destiny. A divine ordination. But that's most unlikely, seen from both ends, now," he said ruefully, pacing the floor with thoughtful strides.

Sharon's eyes widened. She was now more curious than

infuriated with the twist of the tale. She almost did not hear her father as she began wondering what a guy who refused to meet her would look like. Not her pride, but a boy would naturally agree to meet a girl, especially if that were with her parents' approbation.

"Can you be at least friends, for my sake?" Papa implored. "Remember, he saved my life!"

That was emotional blackmail. Sharon didn't mind any more, though. Her curiosity got the better of her. She wanted to see how things panned out. She nodded absentmindedly. Now feeling guilty and rather sympathetic to her father. She didn't mind making new friends.

It's just a meeting, after all.

*

Sleep had eluded Eric for several nights altogether by now.

What had he gotten himself into? Why had he accepted Tycoon's proposal? What would he say, and how would he conduct himself in the face of a girl he never knew? Will he be taken by her charm? For beauty is one temptation no man could successfully stand. Not that he would be so easily swayed, though.

It took more than twenty years to find one lass to blow him away. But it's not a matter of falling head over heels. It's the principle. How could he guard his frail heart that belonged to Sherrie? And to Sherrie alone had he pledged his faithfulness. Is meeting another girl a sin when you still have a girlfriend? He looked up and prayed. He was a devout Christian.

That damned appointment. Promises are indeed easier made than kept.

Let's get done with this in the morning, Eric thought. Lest the entire next day would be wasted again pondering, vacillating between keeping or not keeping his words about socialising with an unknown opposite sex. Dawn had already thrown a pinkish hue across the eastern sky. Daylight would soon be breaking from the jagged Saikot mountaintops.

That's just a call for tea, after all. Why bother about the girl so?

He hit the pillow once again to catch a few more winks before the cursed morning cracks.

*

The young glimmering orb of the east heralded a beautiful daybreak.

Sharon was still asleep. She was tugging between herself for the whole night. At times, she wouldn't mind entertaining an unknown guest. Yet the very next moment, she would brim with shame and self-reproach. How would she explain the situation to her lover? Would he take it as immodesty? Would he regard her too wanton?

Her mother barged into her room and yanked away the imported Thai quilt from her skimpily clad figure. Then she pulled the window curtains apart, allowing sunbeams to flush into the chamber. The instant brightness shone on Sharon's face. She cupped her eyes instinctively to protect them from pain. Her mother threw the windows open. She shuddered but not from the cold gust of wind that whipped in instantaneously. So unusual was the morning air that she couldn't get herself off the bed for a full minute.

Knock, knock!

"That must be him," Mother paused for a while. Then she harried Sharon off the bed. "Up you lazybones! Mind the door. I'm busy."

The cursed hour had arrived.

Sharon lazily trudged across the study, rubbing sleep away from her eyes with wide pretentious yawns, taking her sweet time. The slower, the better, she thought. She deliberately fiddled with the knob for a while. The latch seemed to give way too easily. The door creaked ajar. Sharon turned away as it swung open. She was not yet ready to meet a stranger.

Eric took a deep breath. Contemplating for the final time whether to beat a retreat or to go ahead with all the stupid idea. He mentally kicked himself in the shin: "Be a man!"

With that self-motivation, it became much easier to make up his mind. No retreat. No surrender. He moved his strong foot forward, stepping into the gap between the door panel and the frame.

Into hell.

Two pairs of eyes brushed past for a fraction of a microsecond. But that fleeting glimpse was enough to make Sharon turn around to make sure her eyes were not playing tricks on her. The hostile eyes were now locked in a dumb stare. Two hearts beat in frenzied synchrony. Eric once again lost the power of speech. He couldn't even let out an exclamation. Only a wheezy gasp escaped in spite of his jaws dropping as wide as the Gateway to Hell in Turkmenistan.

Sharon was better known to him as *Sherrie*.

Chapter 3

FRIENDS, THAT'S ALL

Somewhere on a nonperennial pier by the sandy shores of River Brahmaputra.

It was a sultry day. The sun was beating down mercilessly. Sand particles were simmering like granulated pieces of glass strewn across the beach. Dry khamsin was blowing in occasionally, kicking up small clouds of sand dust. It was going to be one hell of a summer day. As usual.

Seated on one of those crude benches in a makeshift fast food joint, Richard Zoukhankhual was leisurely munching on a chunk of greasy seafood. He was amusing himself with the restive seafarers milling around to kill time. A little less than an hour was due for his ferry to hit the water. Every now and then, he would pull back the collar of his shirt to allow trapped body heat to escape, fanning himself frantically with a hand fan.

Just for trivia, the handfan was a local handicraft made from palm leaf. He had bought it on his way here this morning at a certain bus stand where a peddler had popped in to hawk his wares in between the brief stoppages. The fan caught his eyes immediately. The peddler named his price. But he at once felt being taken for a ride. He had no skill or sense of bargaining. Seeing his hesitation, the peddler dropped his price to a decent range without going into the haggling process. Now, being agreeable to him, Rick bought a piece each for him and his partner, Basumatary.

Basumatary was a friend of his who had come to see him off despite his declining the gesture. More on him as we go along.

Presently, Rick's attention was drawn to an old wartime jeep overburdened with a load of passengers. Shrouded in a cloud of dust, the jeep was careening into the quayside, leaning dangerously as though it would tip over one side or another. The vehicle skidded to a halt in an open space. The passengers jerked forward in unison. A thick blanket of dust descended upon them from all sides.

Hardly had the passengers got off and dusted themselves, then the ever-ready porters swooped down upon them like vultures on a dead buffalo. They bleated noisily in nasal twangs, calling attention with their quirky voice modulations. The dust was yet to settle. And the passengers were barely able to touch their luggage. But they were snatched away from them as though they were bearing somebody else's property. Unwilling though they might be, the passengers were not given a chance to protest. They could only scuttle behind the coolies for fear of losing sight, crying after them to wait or slow down. Belying their potbellies, the portly coolies were unbelievably agile, appearing and disappearing in the midst of the crowd like the brown river whales diving in and out of the mighty Brahmaputra.

Rick smiled gently before shifting his gaze to the majestic river rushing along the complimentary seascape. He squinted at the gleaming stretch of sand, blowing air to his chest every now and then. He seemed to be in a thoughtful mood. It was about an hour ago that he forced his friend to return home despite his insistence to stay on until he departed.

"You know how rare vehicles are around here," Rick had said as though he was more the local. "What if you don't get one back?"

Basumatary had said nothing. In a way, Rick was right. Transportation was few and far between in this part of the world. And unpredictable. Not that he couldn't manage to get back home. It was his home turf. But he was tired of quibbling with his friend like immature teenagers. Moreover, Rick was above his equal. He should be the one obeying and not arguing.

"I have nothing to give you as a parting gift, Sir," Basumatary said. "It's really bad..."

"Am I a child to be pampered with gifts?" Rick shrugged, throwing up his palms. "Are we lovers going their painful ways? Oh, come on, you...your coming to see me off is the biggest gift I've ever had!"

B gave him a warm hug. Rick reciprocated with equal warmth. With extra blubber and size to boast, B was not called 'the Bear' by his colleagues without reason. To add to the epithet, he was not on the fair side of skin colour. Rick was not one bit handsomer, but a lot slimmer. So, when B gave him an embrace, it was literally a warm one: A warm, damp, sweaty bearhug.

Having done with the farewells, B caught the same bus they came in. As the bus eased out of the stand, he leaned across the lap of his co-passenger on the window seat and waved Rick his final bye.

That was about an hour ago.

The day was still young, hardly noon, to be precise. But the mercury was already hitting the roof. Typical Assam summer, his good-natured friend, Basumatary, would remind him time and again when he complained of the excessive heat. In spite of the mob swirling around, Rick felt a bit alone, having nobody to talk to and tell how extremely hot the weather was.

In the meanwhile, the stall boy had cleared up his spoons and platters and swabbed the table with a piece of rag stained with grime and perspiration. Rick asked for a bottle of Coca-Cola. It appeared in an instant. The bottle was wet from the melted ice cubes. But it wasn't cold enough to chill its content. Without a bite or fizz, the drink was but sweetened, tepid water. He spat out his very first sip on the dust, pushing the curvy bottle away. Disgusted yet unable to help, he simply gazed at the panoramic view, which was like a photograph with a blown-out exposure. He checked his watch and saw that he still got ample time for excursing the riverine scene. He looked around and mentally assessed which way to go first.

As he was sweeping the bucolic landscape with his eyes, a lone bulb of sweat surfed down the ridge of his nose, hanging at the tip for a moment like a tenacious cliffhanger refusing to let go. In a while, his eyes travelled up to a spot where there was a patch of beach grass overhanging the seaside promontory. A laburnum tree was in full bloom, with its yellow pendulous blossoms hanging profusely down its branches. He thought he saw a lady leaning on the trunk. He blinked his eyes several times. Squeezed them tight. His visual senses did not lie. He looked again. The figure poised demurely on the edge of the sandy ledge did not go away. Was it real? Was it a life-sized statue of a Greek goddess?

Venus, he thought.

In a moment, though, he realised that the perfect sculpture closely resembled the beauty whom he had lost his heart to. His pulse raced, burning extra calories. The heat suddenly seemed to intensify, permeating through the palm-frond roofing of the stall. If distance truly didn't deceive his eyesight. Goosebumps germinated over his arms and all over his body.

"It can't be true," he rubbed his eyes and looked yet again. What, for Christ's sake, is she doing here? Am I dreaming? He pinched his arm and felt the pain all right. His heart screamed her name.

Anita Saikia!

"Kimaan dibo," said Rick to the stall-keeper. How much do I pay?

"Babu," the slovenly stallkeeper replied with no hurry. *"Bis toka."* Twenty rupees.

Rick shoved a fifty-rupees note across the counter, taking off at the same instant without collecting the change.

"*Babu, babu...*" the stallkeeper cried after him.

His client had already made his way into the bustling crowd, drawn by the dictates of his heartbeat. He waved after him in vain. He could only scratch his head and murmur to himself. It's like he was sucked by a powerful oppositely-charged magnet hidden somewhere in the midst of the throng.

Rick sweated profusely but seemed to feel no exertion. His shoes were covered with cakes of dirt and sand. The back of his shirt was completely drenched in perspiration. As he got to the grassy patch, away from the host of passengers waiting to board their launches, he pressed his eyes together once more to make sure he was not misguided by a delusion.

A little far from the madding crowd, alone, there stood Anita.

—*Venus! Is she real?*—

She seemed to be lost in thought, mesmerized by the rolling waves gently lapping at the feet of the nearby islets. She folded her arms across her bosom, her silken tresses swinging freely across her face. A balmy gust of wind puffed in from the sea as though to drive away the strands of hair mindlessly playing on her matchless beauty. Or was it taking advantage to have a field day itself, caressing the tousled silken mane? Rick was nearly jealous of the sea breeze. She was certainly no less lovely than Helen of Troy, the face that launched a thousand ships. The yellow laburnum garlands paled pitifully in the presence of the lady leaning on their trunk. Despite the hypnotic scenery around, there seemed to be no joy writ in Anita's dark-blue eyes.

Rick stopped in his track, unable to bring himself forward to approach any nearer. Anita stared far into the empty horizon, unaware of the lover-boy swooning in her immediate surroundings. Stillness reigned. Rick struggled for words to break the ice.

Erm! At last, he could clear his throat to shoo away the uneasy spell of silence.

His heart missed a beat. His soul shivered like an aspen leaf blown about by an autumn zephyr. Anita turned around and expressed herself with that killing smile of hers, sending him head over heels. As always.

As always!

"I...I..." Rick stammered with jaws wide open, "...didn't see you come?"

Anita turned away abruptly. She bowed her head for an imperceptible moment before lifting it up again to stare out into the empty river line once more. Rick thought he saw a sparkle of wetness in her eyes.

"You should have..." he was about to continue.

"I'm going to Dibrugarh," she said, nearly dropping her delicate masquerade. She's fighting some invisible force of emotion strongly welling up from within. "For eye check-up."

"A coincidental coincidence, eh?" Rick fumbled for words, blurting out incongruous adjectives. "It would've been nicer if you told—"

"How can I? You didn't—"

"Please, Anita," pleaded Rick. "Don't bring that up now. You're here, and that's all that matters."

His heart screamed her name.

*

Anita!

That doe-eyed Barbie of Hiralal Saikia, his boss, the manager of the Jonai Branch of the State Bank of India.

Three autumns ago, Rick had landed here as a Probationary Officer.

Nobody recognised him when he walked into that nondescript one-level building to report for duty. In faded jeans and a badly creased shirt, tucked sloppily beneath a faux leather belt, he stood in the customers' lobby for a while, looking around, reading the signs hung, pasted or printed every here and there. A backpack on his back and a medium-sized airbag in his hand. He had come straight from the station as his train had run late for reasons never known to him. And the rickshaw-puller was not in his prime. He was gravely behind time, which was very uncharacteristic of him.

Presently, he took a seat beside a random customer and began rummaging through his backpack. Not in seconds, he fished out a windowed banker envelope. As he was unfolding its content, a burly, middle-aged guy tapped him on his shoulder and asked, "You're Richard Sir, I presume?"

Rick looked up. "I am," said he without a smile.

"I am Basumatary," the man introduced himself, "the errand boy of the bank."

Rick stood up and offered a handshake to his first acquaintance. "Just call me Rick."

"All the staff are my Sirs and Madams," said Basumatary, shaking the hand lightly. "I'll take you to the manager. After me, Sir." He bent down to pick up the baggage to carry it for him.

"No, I'll carry it myself," Rick said, reaching out before B could grab it. "Just lead the way."

B did not insist. It's not good to differ with a 'Sir' on a first meeting. So, he let the baggage go and took the lead forward. "Follow me, Sir."

The rest is official work.

That's how Rick and Basumatary hit off at the very first encounter.

In course of time, Rick came to know more about B. He was a local unskilled labourer initially engaged for menial jobs in the Bank. Basumatary turned out to be a fine, perceptive young man who always proved himself to be indispensable. One day the Bank needed a local errand boy. Without looking further, the Bank decided to upgrade his services. That was almost ten years ago. And the Bank was not once disappointed by him. That's how B, despite being a mere semi-literate, came to be part and parcel of this reputed Bank.

However, with time, things changed. People changed. Staff changed. At times, an officer or two would be put off by his guileless straightforwardness, especially if they had something to keep from the Bank's knowledge, which was not uncommon in those days. It's not possible to please everybody. So, when Rick showed signs of over-friendliness with him, some colleagues told him not to fraternise too much with 'the subordinate staff'. But Rick was not a man to operate on terms dictated to him. Until he was proven false, that is. As for his acquaintanceship with Basumatary, he knows where to draw the line.

And the two became fast friends.

There was yet another friendship Rick was to make very soon.

It was only two days since Rick joined here. Presently, he was perusing a bunch of documents. Jonas, a South-Indian guy, a colleague assigned to assist him, was standing by, pointing here and pointing there to familiarise him with things, explaining this and explaining that all along.

Despite his deep concentration, his attention was suddenly drawn to the door that was opened and shut for a brief moment. It was still a quarter of an hour to open to the customers. All the staff seemed to have made their entries already. His curiosity was naturally aroused.

In came a lady adorned in a light salwar kameez, a sunset-yellow scarf to match, draping down her front, which, he noticed, was bulging with just the right amount of endowment. Her hair hung loose on her back, silky and smooth, perhaps still wet from her morning shower. Gently greeting her colleagues around, she marked her attendance and, without a word, disappeared into the teller's cubicle in the far corner. Rick was transfixed. Mesmerised. The Hindi lyricist, Gulzar, had perfectly captured the essence of the moment with his couplet in the 1976 Rishi Kapoor-Neetu Singh starrer *'Kabhi Kabhi'*:

Tere chehre se, nazar nahi hatti;

Nazaare hum kya dekhe.

Tujhe mil ke bhi, pyasi nahi ghatti;

Nazaare hum kya dekhe...

Let's roughly paraphrase it for those who don't speak our national *bhasa*:

I can't take my eyes off your face;

Oh, what a sight I have seen!

Even having met you my thirst hasn't' slaked;
Oh, what a sight I have seen!

Basumatary was bringing in some folders when he saw Rick's mouth gaping. He followed the gaze and saw nobody. Jonas was busy rifling through another bunch of documents and was, therefore, not aware of Rick's distraction.

"You may swallow even a sparrow-like that, Sir," remarked B casually as he plopped the folders down on the table. "And your buck teeth tend to go dry that way."

Rick jumped as though startled out of a deep trance. He gulped down a huge dose of air, eyed at B for an awkward moment, and blabbered something before returning to his exercise. B didn't get what he said. But unwilling to make him repeat, went his way to bring him a cup of tea.

In spite of being in his late twenties, Rick had not yet followed a woman with his eyes, let alone court. He had never looked at a woman that way, let alone give a second glance. Not that he was not interested in women. Rather, he never thought a woman would ever fall for him. A sheepish diffidence had always come in the way of his previous enterprises. He was simply not gifted in the art. He never thought of trying a hand at it. Perhaps due to his lack of attention, he found no woman to turn his head twice till that day. And he had never met a woman who caused his heart to flutter. Till that day.

As for that day, the lady who last walked in seemed to have a very different touch. Not necessarily love. And certainly not love at first sight, to which he was totally immune. Or at least so he thought. It could be a click somewhere deep down, portending something very good or very bad in the days to come. Perhaps he was simply fascinated. He struggled for some time to return to the task at hand.

Customers who had already queued outside started pouring in with the iron grill being pulled back. Everybody soon got busy with their own jobs. In no time, the lounge was filled with people chattering and shuffling around. The day had begun. And there's nothing exceptional about that. Rick, too, had regained his composure. And everything that had taken his concentration away seemed to be a thing of the past.

However, the hours seemed to crawl too slowly that day. He had wished the day to end swiftly so that he could get back to his quarters early and do...well...nothing. His eyes had furtively darted to that far corner at least a dozen times. But there was nobody except a line of customers to withdraw cash. Despite his conscious reluctance, an unseen hand seemed to twist his head in that direction every now and again. It's indeed hard to fight with nature, especially if that nature is acting within you.

For the following days, his eyes automatically strayed over to, nay, riveted on, that fair teller who would tantalisingly come into his line of sight when she bent over to hand over cash or collect tokens. His colleagues occasionally reminded him in jest where his attention had drifted to. He would vehemently deny the charges. But his denials were sheer eyewash. For denial is a sign of admission. His heart sang a different tune, betraying his intentions at every turn. In fact, it had already engraved her name in glowing letters of gold. In secrecy, of course.

And how did he come to know her name? She was a colleague, silly.

Wait, it's not that silly, after all. The Bank may be small, but asking names around, especially if you are the new guy, is not a nice thing to do. It could easily come across as rude and idiotic. You cannot just go over the attendance register and run your finger down the list. That's even more unbecoming. Except for the staff that are immediately related to you, it does take time to learn names and get familiarities. Basumatary being the exception, though. But you did manage somehow. With time, of course.

Since that day, days seemed to be too long for Rick. Nights even longer. Every dawn broke with joy and vague expectation. But the day would always end more frustrating than the one before. The way to the restrooms was across the teller's cubicle. But how many times could you go to relief yourself in a day?

Speaking of restrooms, Rick even roamed over to the ladies' once. His eyes were certainly taken off the path. He almost bumped into a lady colleague who had just come out. He apologised but had no quick words for getting lost in such a small region. He simply admitted: "I was distracted!"

"You certainly were," shot back the lady, not at all amused.

Was it meant to be sardonic or sympathetic? Rick couldn't make out a thing.

Rick might be a man of few words. But when he had fallen head over heels—well, if it was love remains to be seen though—he could hardly keep his predicament noticed. Not verbally, though. He was fidgety and seemed to be always preoccupied with something other than his job. The only saving grace was that everybody thought he was sort of a nervous wreck.

Jonas, his assigned trainer and guide, was a little baffled. He was alright for the first few days, he thought. How did he suddenly become so edgy? "Everything will be okay, Rick," he comforted him one day, thinking it was work pressure that daunted him so. "I am with you, alright?"

Rick simply nodded and smiled inwardly. He realised he must take control of his outward manifestations if he wanted to avoid an early scandal. He tried to stop stealing glances, no matter how hard it was. He also fought the urge to rush to the men's room. He did significantly reduce the adventure. Before long, things seemed to resume normalcy. Adrenaline would rush to pester his heart. But once he's made up his mind...well, let's see how long he can make up his mind!

Suppressed emotions of the day, bottled up to the chest, would often burst forth in the ripe hours of the night. Rick would toss and turn in his bed, beginning to have sleepless nights. He would sit up wide awake in the dead of night, having nothing to do but being unable to lie. Sometimes, he would grab a notebook and scrawl nonsense, meaning obviously nothing. He never liked poetry, forget writing one. But now, his pen seemed to traverse across the pages on its own accord as if trying to capture the travails of his heart that presently ran like a fever. Not in minutes, his trashcan would fill up with crumpled balls of paper.

Dreamy days and restless nights soon became a new norm. He gave his best charade to keep his feelings and external indications under wraps. He did largely well. But what's within cannot be hidden forever. And not everybody was fooled or blind to the tumultuous internal war he was fighting against himself. There was one guy who was especially observant and could not be pushed aside as easily.

A certain day, the weather was rather gloomy, and the skies were churning with ominous clouds. Rain drizzled just enough to put off people from venturing out but not enough to stop staffers from going to the office. Still, attendance was dismal. Few customers who defied the looming thunderstorms hurried their steps and tarried not when done with their transactions. It was not uncommon for visitors to catch up with acquaintances and get carried away in casual conversation. But today was not a good day to strike up a chat and get caught in the nasty whims of the elements. By noon, the office was already shorn of customers, and the business of the day, more or less, concluded.

Cloud people up there began rolling their giant canisters to decant at select locations. Deep rumbles could be heard in the distance. Streaks of lightning occasionally lighted up the sky. There was a strong hint of a gale or a tornado. Are they the same thing? If not a super-cyclone.

It was about four o'clock now. Most of the staff, having no customers to attend to anymore, excused themselves and fled for their homes before the skies opened up. Under such climatic conditions, Rick invited Basumatary to his home. And by the time they got to his quarters, which was about half an hour's walk, the rain had started to increase considerably.

In a short while, Rick brought a steaming black coffee to his guest. Basumatary never visited his superiors. He was a bit uncomfortable. But Rick, despite his reticence, had quite a way of putting people at ease. So, his uneasiness was soon dispelled, and they began to engage in a gripping tête-à-tête. In the meantime, the heavens let up their fury, pattering down on the small village. It was deafening.

Basumatary knew that Rick was simply beating about the bush. He was not unaware of his odd demeanour for the last few months now. And he was pretty sure why he was invited to dinner today. Rick was not a good cook, at any rate. The pretext could not justify the gesture.

"Sir, don't you think we should zoom in our gossip on one particular subject?" Basumatary brusquely suggested with a naughty grin. "That way, we could waste less time and be more productive."

"Come on, dude," Rick was almost taken aback by his guest's candour. "There's no particular subject in my mind. We're just suffering out the elements."

B felt he's got to take the lead again. Being married had its uses sometimes. It makes you less inhibited about, like, talking about youthful obsessions. They looked nothing more than stupid escapades once you said 'I do' and merited nothing but a light joke. But he sensed that his friend was badly in need of its 'uses' now.

"If you don't, I do, Sir," said B, sipping his piping coffee.

"Don't sir me," Rick said, a bit embarrassed that a man his senior had to address him that way. "Not at least out of office. And what do you have in mind, if I may ask?"

"It's a habit, Sir," replied B. "It's hard to beat it. And it's behoving me. Please don't mind the address. It has become a second nature to me." B took yet another sip with a loud slurp to show his like. Then he spelled out his suggestion in the most casual manner: "What if we discuss our wives?"

Rick spluttered, spilling droplets of coffee on the centre table. B knew very well why but didn't say a word. Rather, he simply added, "But I'm sorry, I can't pick on my wife," wiping his lips with the sleeves of his shirt.

Rick went silent for quite a long moment as he had nothing to contribute when it came to better halves. So, B had to continue again.

"Ah, well!" He remarked as if a realisation had dawned upon him. "I did see your marital status in your papers."

"That's right." Rick nodded mug to his lips.

"I could suggest one," Basumatary feared Rick would take offence to this offhand pushiness. But he took the risk to see what transpires. "If you don't mind, Sir?"

Rick showed no reaction. Was he offended? Was he amused? Was he interested? The rain was really noisy on the galvanised tin roofing. Basumatary thought he heard a grunt or something. But he dared not push on. He only eyed him cautiously. Then, after a brief pause, Rick drained his cup, placed it on the table and threw himself back on the sofa. "Go on," he simply said.

When Rick reacted nonchalantly, an alarm went off inside B's head. He must tread carefully, he thought. Else, the dinner could be their last, if not the end of their friendship. He could not afford both.

"I mean," B stuttered. "I am just joking, Sir. There's nothing...in...my—"

"No problem, just shoot it," Rick cut him off, prodding him instead. "I am game."

"Time to shut your big mouth, big guy..." his inner voice sounded the bell louder. But B had already landed himself in a hot soup. He must say something. Could he speak his mind? He better do. He's not good at fibbing. But he just couldn't hold his tongue now. "I'm just trying to tease you, Sir," he said aloud.

"Tease me," Rick offered himself matter-of-factly. "The rain would need some more time to subside."

"Well, then, that you are talking me in," B cleverly shifted the blame on his host and repositioned himself to take the chance. "At least I am not blind when you set your eyes on..."

"Et tu Brute?" exclaimed Rick. Then broke into a guffaw.

B's heart leapt. Was that the villain's horselaugh? Was Rick truly amused? Should he join the laughter and get himself shot in the middle of his merriment like Kaalia in the Bollywood blockbuster *Sholay?* Should he make himself scarce under the pelting rain? He was helplessly undecided.

But before he could offer an excuse or an apology, Rick continued. "You've got me, pal," he shivered in hilarity. "You've hit the bull's eye!"

"I'm sorry, Sir..." B tendered weakly. "I don't mean to..."

"Not at all, B," Rick patted him on the arm as he saw him squirming uneasily. "That's what I'm asking you to dinner for. Actually, I had no courage to come straight to the point."

Basumatary regained composure and seated himself more comfortably, releasing a long breath. "What are you scared of, Sir?" he moved on.

"Put my fears aside," Rick leaned forward. "Now that the ice is broken, I want you to tell me everything you know about her. But—" He raised his forefinger as authoritatively as possible.

"But what, Sir?"

"This is our little secret."

"Fine."

"Now, tell me all about her."

"Anita!" began B in right earnest.

And that was how Rick learnt everything he wanted to know about the lady in the teller's cubicle in the farthest corner across the restrooms.

Well, almost everything, I mean!

*

It was hard, but Rick kept all his sentiments bundled up deep inside him. Sometimes he kind of relapsed and took a peek before he realised. However, he performed largely well to keep his feelings under check. Basumatary did occasionally prick him when he was in his naughty elements. Otherwise, there was nothing much to betray his inner turmoil. Before long, a year passed quite uneventfully.

Then, one day, good news came. Not for Rick, personally. For the office. Their Branch had won the best performance award of the year for the North East India Region. And to celebrate, the office biggies decided to have an outdoor picnic party somewhere in the countryside. Suggestions were collected, and a majority agreed on one picturesque location. So, they went to Ranaghat in Arunachal Pradesh, by the icy waters of River Siang.

Everybody was like a little kid going on a class outing, excited and hysterical. The child in them came out after all these years. In fact, it was one helluva day. They all enjoyed themselves to the hilt, to say the least.

As things were, Rick had known for some time now that his secret feelings were not nursed by him alone. And they were only holding themselves back. Today, he somehow felt Anita wanted him to take the ultimate plunge. Or was he merely imagining things? Perhaps he was only superimposing his own sentiments on her. Or was he seeing things as they really were? As he always did, he refused to acknowledge the inner truth. His heart protested from within. But he forced it to believe that Anita's suggestive hints were nothing more than circumstantial stimulus effected by the serene vibes of the captivating Siang. Anyone would have easily fallen in love in these romantic environs. The heart was only half-convinced. Rick, too wanted the sight and the fantasy to be real and not merely tricks played on him by his over-imaginative mind.

In truth, Rick and Anita had already developed a friendship in course of time. A close one. Very close indeed. But they just stayed there. They were late entries into the game of love. That said a lot about their inhibitions and doubts about taking the relationship any further. Apparently, both waited for the other to put the first foot forward. Not that they were not aware of their hearts beating in sync. For they gelled so well in their likes and dislikes.

In retrospect, Rick sometimes thought Anita gave him clear indications to take matters into his hand and move to the next stage. Especially at nights. The darker the nights, the clearer the signs would appear. He would often practice how and where to begin. He would even speak out like a lunatic conversing with himself. His voice would often come out louder than he expected due to the stillness of the night. He would lay out stratagems, embolden himself and hit the bed again with a smile on his lips. But the sun would rise, and all his nocturnal bravado would melt away like dew in the morning. This soon became his daily ritual. With every nightfall, he would regret not having taken action on his plots. But it would be the same thing the following day.

Presently, with glances stolen at simultaneous moments, the covert lovebirds would shy away when their eyes met, pretending that nothing was going on between them. Anita would often blush and coyly smile as her peeks met his midway. Rick battled a burning urge to take her aside and spill everything.

He weighed the chance of winning the queen of his heart. Improbable, he thought. His soul cracked. He inwardly swore never to go to such an enchanting place with a lady again. Unless to fall in love. Even if he were to win her heart, there are many things that would certainly come their way. Better play safe than embark on an impossible voyage, he reasoned. He's a pragmatic man. But his heart begged to differ, revolting, twisting the veins and arteries until Rick felt a pulsating grip inside his chest.

True, the hushed lovebirds were in denial mode. But they were not unaware of their hearts beating as one. It was only the cursed social barriers, customary differences and religious variances that kept their feelings in check. For they were not kids anymore. They put up a show of casual friendship, which was often (mis)taken by their colleagues to be more than just friends. Of course, they need not scream to tell that they were struggling to keep their hearts in their proper places.

The other day, in a local café where they used to meet up, Anita told Rick that her father had smelled the air of their close-friends affair. Her heart gave a false beat as she broke the bad news. She was visibly in pain from the inside, where you cannot exactly point. Rick had no words. Sometimes, it's definitely not a blessing to be a man of few words. Embarrassment was cooking him from inside. But he had no words to let off steam. Anita had always found his muteness hard to take. She was about to let all restraints go and pour her heart out when Rick uttered a line which basically was a turndown. Not yet, he seemed to say. Anita knew that he didn't mean his words. Yet she understood well.

"I respect your father," mumbled Rick, sincere from the heart. "And the custom and traditions of your society. You may call me chicken-heart. But I am not making a bad example out of you to your people."

Anita could feel a blockage rising up her throat. She had decided to tell him that her father was not the old-school he made him to be.

Rick didn't let her. "Tell him we're just friends, that's all."

Anita knew it was better not to press on for now. She held Rick even in higher esteem for holding such regard for her father and their culture and traditions. But why should lovers be born in different societies, she lamented inwardly and got dammed up with barriers which are only but man-made? Why should social institutions always obstruct loving Romeos and Juliets? Is there a place where no customary dykes exist?

Rick read her mind. He took a step forward in a bid to articulate a word of comfort. But before his lips could form a meaningful sound—

Toot...tooooot!

The harsh call of the ferryboat awakened him from his flashback.

"Come on," he said, grabbing Anita's tender hand. "Let's board."

"I am taking the next launch," she declined, reluctantly disengaging her fingers.

"I'm sorry," said Rick, hesitantly loosening his hold, feeling her hand slide off till it came to the tip of her tapering fingers. His eyes threatened to cascade. His voice failed him at the time he needed it most.

Anita's cheeks were ripened apples dusted with the frosts of Kashmir valley. A crystal pool of tears swirled in her eyes. She clutched onto Rick's hands before it really slid off her fingers, the looming fountain beginning to spill. Holding them back was like fighting a tidal wave.

She never spoke. For her silence spoke louder. Unconsciously, drawn by the invisible force of attraction, they flung into each other's arms. And their lips met.

For a long time.

The merciless hooter blared again to bring the two lovebirds back to earth. Rick knew his boss wasn't a harsh type. But, coming to a close, close indeed that-two-hearts-beat-as-one kind of friendship with his doe-eyed daughter, it was another thing altogether. His transfer was untimely and extraordinary. He never wondered why.

Anita...

She responded with silence as though her entire energy had suddenly been spent. Her shoulders hung limp and frail, tears trickling down her sun-kissed cheeks.

Impatient passengers had started complaining from the decks, calling out to round up their daylight rendezvous. Not long before, the sea-borne craft began slashing the gulf between the lovers wider with every stroke of the paddlewheel.

Anita waved her little handkerchief to send kisses after him. She wanted to see the man who carried her heartbeat away till he merged with the horizon. But her eyes had broken free of her command and drew a thick curtain of salt to shield everything from view. Everything must come to an end. They seemed to say on seeing their mistress in distress. Traditions, she murmured to herself. But does God want them to stand in the way of his most precious gift to mankind—love?

Anita never went to Dibrugarh.

—This story was published in the North East Sun, April 15–30, 1999

Chapter 4

A LITTLE RUNAWAY

It was quite a few years now since my uncle quit the force. He was a very little-spoken person. Sometimes we wondered if he had some kind of speech impairment from childhood. Unless there's something very important to say or something that unduly jabs his mind, he would hardly articulate. Monosyllables which sounded more like grunts or snorts, would suffice for almost everything he wanted to communicate. It was that nature of his that made him very unpopular among us, his young nephews. Even among the grownup kith in general, I should say. So, when he gave up his service as a policeman, none of us dared to ask him why he had taken such a drastic decision.

My Uncle—his name was Mangpi, and I called him Uncle Mang—when he was in the force, was an inspector in the local constabulary. His reticent and uncommunicative disposition, coupled with dogged tenacity and steely perseverance, made him very well suited for stealth sleuthing. Unsurprisingly so, he had several cracked cases to his name. Proverbial feathers in his cap. However, his uptight nature also earned him quite a number of adversaries within and without the establishment. He never feared to speak his mind if he had one. He did not much care about the ramifications his few words would have. That made him an asset to somebody and a liability to another in the same weight.

As for me, I must give a brief introduction of myself for being the narrator of our tale. I am exactly the diametric opposite of my uncle. I could not stop talking. I am full of curiosity. I am inquisitive. However, one common thread runs in our blood. Like my uncle, I too, did not care what my words would mean as long as I thought I spoke the truth. And like him, again, I did not fear to speak my mind. Probably, it was this similarity of nature that endeared me to him. He liked me more than any of his nephews or other kinsfolk. Opposites attract. He even told me once that I was his favourite. That must be true. For, had it not been so, he would not have taken the trouble of spelling it out. Ridiculously though, none of my siblings envied me for that.

One fine day, having nothing of my own to do, I'd decided to pay my Uncle a visit. I met him in the front porch of their house. He was sawing a piece of log, sweat dripping from the tip of his nose. It was a hot day. And it seemed the handsaw was not at its sharpest best.

"A hard worker you are indeed, Uncle Mang!" I remarked halfway in the distance.

He grunted something like, "Hmph!" that I took as a "yes-I-always-am!"

As I walked up to him, he let down his work and offered me a latticed-bamboo stool with a rawhide top. "Sit, son," he said gruffly. "What brings you here?"

"As usual, a good for nothing nephew of yours," I replied, grabbing the latticed stool and slapping invisible dust out of habit before planting my butt on it. "Minding to waste time with you."

"Ha, ha!" he chuckled a little. Yes, Uncle Mang loved my jokes too. And that's a big laugh he'd just spared for his favourite young nephew. Moreover, he seemed to open up a little bit ever since he'd left his job. Perhaps, he was feeling a bit out of place and bored, having nothing to do or nowhere to go. Then, "Ching!" he cried out to his wife who was inside the house. "Muanpu is here. Bring us something to wet our parched throats, will you?"

In the meantime, I sidled up to him, picked up his tool and examined it as though I knew everything about handsaws. I pointed the far tip to my eyes and squinted down the rows of serrated teeth. "Sawing must be a harder job than policing, I guess," I remarked.

"And what makes you say so?" Uncle Mang took the bait.

We have not yet learnt the actual reason why he walked out of his service till date. I wanted to satisfy my curiosity. Whenever he sensed a hint of our probing, he would clam up like a snail or change the topic. But I was an obstinate fellow, much like him, so to say. And I know he wouldn't get upset with me. That's the benefit of being a favourite. I was trying to push my luck today, taking advantage of my 'most favoured' status.

"I never saw you come home sweating from the nose when you were a policeman," I went on, tossing the tool on the heap of logs he had cut.

Uncle Mang was not unaware of what I was driving at. Everyone in the family knew he did not want to talk about it. So, we had sort of given up enquiring. Not I, though. Even after all these years, I was still burning to know. As I mentioned, I am a nosy pest with an insatiable appetite for knowing the unknown. I was itching to uncover what people especially refuse to give up. And I was pestering Uncle Mang every now and then to tell me about his career and why he had decided to end it so abruptly.

"You have a very interesting way of putting yourself across," he chuckled. That was a pat on the back. He budged in his seat, readjusting his big arse, pulling himself a few inches away from me. "But I think some things are better left unsaid. Uncomfortable facts—"

The words he let off were the very ones that hooked me on. The grey matter inside the skull was tingling to know more.

"Why, please, Uncle Mang?" my ears perked, and my eyes popped with enthusiasm. "You mean you are manoeuvred and wronged?"

"You're perceptive," he remarked. "But I still think there's no point speaking about them. Especially telling to a youngster like you," he said matter-of-factly.

"Aha!" I exclaimed in mock exasperation. "So, you don't trust even your most favourite nephew, eh?"

"You're getting me wrong, son," he rejoined. Now, I was getting him into a conversation in which I'd hardly succeeded in my previous endeavours. At least, this is progress.

"I mean," he continued. "There's no use even if you could right the wrongs now. Yes, I was harassed and maltreated. But what can you do about it? You certainly cannot fight against an established system. If you nip one evil in the bud, well that's too harsh, (he corrected himself) I must say, a malpractice, in whatever form it is, another will spring up almost at the same instant. More insidious than before."

Uncle Mang must be really hard done by. The tone of his voice was defeated and deeply hurt.

"Why don't you talk to someone else?" I offered sympathy. "Like, someone who could really help?"

That was naïve. I know I was still wet behind the ears in matters of the world. But I wanted to egg him on. I was getting curiouser. He was serious and grim-faced now.

"It's dangerous to be right when the world is wrong," he said. "And even more dangerous to speak it out. You're dead meat, for sure."

Aunt Ching had brought us black tea, setting a cup each by our sides before returning to her chores. She did not bother to draw our attention seeing our deep engagement. Had it not been for the pleasant aroma of *Darjeeling,* we would never have been aware of the beverage being served. We even had no mind to thank her. We, or rather I, were too absorbed in our confabulation.

"But everyone is seeking the right thing," I chose to disagree. "How can you put it under your feet for so long?"

"The right thing to suit your interests," Uncle Mang retorted. "When it no more suits you, it becomes an inconvenient truth."

"But truth is truth. Everybody ought to uphold it."

"I did. It cost me my job."

"You could have reported it or appealed before a proper forum."

"That would be a threat to my life. The police have the power to take life and give it, too." It was sardonic, but I had no doubt he was stating a general fact. "You have to be on the 'right' side to survive," he went on. "It's not survival of the fittest any more, son. It's survival of the wittiest."

"Is there anything I could do to help?" I offered.

Uncle Mang gave a good belly laugh to it. He was thoroughly amused. I simply joined the merriment realising that my offer was well-intentioned but of no use. He quietened down as quickly as he started. "Well," he sighed, "I wish you could!"

"So, you mean I should stop searching for the truth?" I meant to provoke him into giving me some more. "What about justice?"

"Not at all! Do search for truth, by all means. Truth is power." He stated. "But truth is not necessarily justice. It is the winner that delivers justice."

"I mean the judiciary system, Uncle," I corrected myself. "Why not approach the courts for your reinstatement or at least seek justice for your mistreatment?"

"No system is uncorrupted!" he claimed. "No man is above corruption."

Uncle Mang was infused now. I seemed to have pressed the right button. But he still hadn't divulged the real reason behind his quitting. I could only guess he must've been absolutely wronged and aggrieved. Persecuted, even.

"At least there is divine justice," I said to lighten the distress. "God's justice is fair and—"

"God never dispenses justice," he cut me out in mid-sentence. "Humans dispense it for him."

"But Uncle Mang..." I budged uneasily in my seat on noticing his loss of trust even in the heavenly justice. In my agitation, I happened to upset the teacup sitting quietly by my side. Now gone cold due to lack of attention. In fact, none of us remembered to take sips of the fragrant black tea.

That little accident brought Uncle Mang back to his normal temperament. He relapsed into his reticent self and precipitously locked himself up in his cave again. I coaxed and cajoled him. But to no avail. I could not wheedle him out of his withdrawn nature any more. Instead, he picked up a bunch of lumber he had sawn. "I think I need a new saw," he said, adding the handsaw to the load and walking into the house.

That was a signal for me to call it a day and make myself scarce.

*

A few days later, I espied Uncle Mang in the distance, to the south side of the New Bazaar bus parking lot, walking into a certain hardware store. I thought I would catch up with him presently and give him company shopping. I was not in a hurry, though. I had the entire day to myself. I slowly ambled across the street, keeping an eye on him. I could soon see him running his eyes on some hand tools the shopkeeper had to offer over the counter.

I was at about hailing distance when I saw three tough-looking guys materialising from nowhere and hurrying into the shop. I recognised one of them. I didn't recall his name, though.

Uncle Mang had once told me, years ago, about a gang of ruffians rounded up by him and his team of detectives. It was his first assignment as skipper of a squad, he'd said. Despite his modesty, he did sometimes tell us stories about police achievements so that we may be inspired to render service to society and humanity. He was not a man to brag. That's how we know his stories were real and not figments of his imagination. He knew very well that policing is not heroing around like in the movies. As for the goons, he admitted, they had run into them in the act of extortion on his beat. Caught redhanded. "They were plain unlucky that day," he'd said. "There was no act of bravado on our part. We're just doing our duty. It was my men in civvies who held them up." Uncle Mang was always humble.

As the story goes, the extortionists turned out to be quite powerful in their own right. They were well-connected, operating under an invisible puppeteer. An authoritative shielding. The case was given him with the belief that he would botch up the investigation and end up a damp squib. But Uncle Mang was never a man to let go until he made it. The people in the higher echelons were yet to learn about his true character. There were many attempts to throw a spanner on the process of his inquisition. He did sometimes go slow but never let the flame blow out. He was a hardhead. And his bosses were to discover it in due course.

They were five of them, he'd said. When they were brought to the book, not all faces lit up. Even his superiors suggested he go easy behind bars. In course of the grillings, Uncle Mang unearthed many sordid secrets he could not share with anybody without putting his own existence in jeopardy.

"How did they start singing?" there goes me again, the curious kid. To which Uncle Mang recounted a little more in detail. Yet leaving out the gruesomer corners.

"They were indeed hard nuts to crack," he said. "They knew they were protected as long as they kept their traps shut."

"People shut their mouths till their deaths," I chipped in. "I saw in films."

"Reel life is far from real life. Torture may be the best but not the only way to pry a criminal's jaw."

"Such as?"

"One of my boys had done the first guy too hard he would never walk again," Uncle Mang continued. "And I did the second by accident."

"Accident?"

"Well, intentional, if you like." He winked at me, and we smiled at one another knowingly.

Let me continue the story for him. Garrulous me, I am itching to talk.

The first ruffian had gone limp on the chains when they brought in the second one. He tried to put up a defiant face. But he started to waver instantly, seeing his cohort being dragged out in a lifeless heap. They sat him on a chair and tied him up. A civvy, now in a mere vest, immediately applied the truncheon all over his torso. The man screamed but held back names and info which could incriminate him or his manipulators.

"Stop, stop," Uncle Mang yelled to his boy. "What are you doing? I didn't tell you to hit him that hard!"

The cop let up, grabbed the toughie by the locks and pulled his head back. "The sooner you sing, the better for you," he hissed on his face as he pushed the head away in a nasty jerk.

"Your friend has spilled enough beans before he lost his life." Uncle Mang began calmly. "It would've been much easier for him if he had not put up so hard."

"To hell with you," the felon leered. "I don't care if he speaks or not. I won't."

"Your friend started out the same way," Uncle Mang continued as though he did not hear the abuse. He could be cold if he needed to. "Until he let the cat out that two of you would be ending up on the row." The criminal's eyes flitted. Uncle Mang knew his bait had sunken. He kept on bluffing. "I cannot prevent you going to prison. But if you cooperate, I can ensure you'll walk again a free man. Your friend had taken the offer too late."

"Kill me if you must," grunted the detainee sarcastically. "I have better offers."

Uncle Mang's thumb flicked imperceptibly. His man beside the torture chair was well briefed. He swiftly pulled a handgun and cocked it at the goon's temple.

Uncle Mang yelled, "No, Jonathan, not yet."

"We still have three more to milk," Johnny playacted frustration. "Let's be done with this, too. He didn't have what we want. And he didn't mind to die. That's our best alibi."

"Give me the gun," the Inspector said. "I make the call for that."

It was clear that the felon was in two minds now. The private gave up his gun, which was presently examined by the Inspector. He spun the bullet chamber, and, seeing it fully loaded, flipped it shut and mock-trained the sights on the wall, squinting down the barrel. Then, he took out his handkerchief and dabbed the gun as though to wipe it clean. Suddenly, the gun barked.

The hooligan screamed in agony: "Oh! Oww! Shit, shit..."

A slug had just clipped him on the shin, slightly missing the centre of the tibial shaft.

"Oh, you got hit? I'm sorry!" Uncle Mang stated the obvious unperturbedly. "It was an accident. But shitting will not prevent another accident. Only I can." He sat back and never raised his voice.

Then, right away, he began to lean forward, grab his hankie and bring it over the barrel of the gun again. The ruffian got the message.

"Okay, okay," he rattled. "I take the offer."

Then, he not only sang but brayed loud and clear.

The villains ended up in prison, all right. But the forces at play were strong and formidable. They were indeed attached to strings pulled from somewhere high above. It was their greed that led them to that misadventure of extortion. Most probably, they had promised to be more careful and begged for a second chance. It didn't take long for them to bargain their liberation.

That's how one of the many nemeses of my Uncle was born.

He showed us a greyscale picture of the goons' leader and warned us to be wary of him. "If you catch sight of him, just inform me."

Back to the present.

Instantly, I realised that the men could definitely mean no good to my blood-kin. I knew it because it was not the first time an attempt was made on his life. An astute man that he was, it was not easy to pin him down, though. He was a bull, and an elusive eel rolled into one. And a smart one at that. But he was in service then. He always had his squad have his back, overtly and covertly. Now he was off-service. And alone. I must act quickly.

Just then, I saw the three hoodlums accosting Uncle Mang across the Thangzam Road-Tiddim Road-Apollo Veng junction. I slunk behind them at a safe distance, biding for an opportune moment. Uncle Mang had a new handsaw in his hand.

Suddenly, he bolted up a dark alley between two dingy shops across the New Bazaar plaza, taking the three men and me by surprise. I sprinted after them.

In the sudden dimness between the buildings, Uncle Mang lost his vision for a fraction of a second. His pupils took time to adjust. The goons were much younger and had better eyesight. Not a big distance later, they caught up with him and engaged him in a vicious scuffle. My Uncle might be strong. But three tough guys were one too much. They soon had him to the ground.

One of the assailants was about to club him with a wooden stump when I raised the alarm from the back. Astonished, he turned around to see who had dared to distract him. At that tiny loose moment, Uncle Mang freed his leg and connected it hard to his mandible.

I quickly jumped into action and lashed out at the man's face as he was reeling towards me with the impact of my Uncle's boot. At the same instant, Uncle Mang rolled over, shoved the muggers off, picked up his handsaw, and took to his heels. I know he was only intending to lead them away from me. For my own safety.

Now, we are man to man. Street fights are a common sight in the market area. They are free live-action flicks. A ring of spectators soon formed around us. We're equally matched, I guess, trading blow for blow. Admittedly though, I had to take more of the blows than I could deliver. I was a less fighter than my opponent was, actually. I was just a college boy a few months from graduation, still smelling of mother's milk in the ways of the cruel world. But I had the custom of keeping myself physically presentable since my early teens. Apparently, that stood me in good stead at the moment. The bad guy couldn't take me as easily as he would have liked to.

The ring of spectators moved along with us as if we were a drop of oil on the surface of soap water. We furiously boxed and kicked and warded and parried. And rolled and fell. The crowd hummed and booed in excitement. Somebody yelled encouragements from the midst, goading the both of us to go for the kill. Everybody loves a good fight. No wonder the ancient Romans got so fixated with their gladiatorial combats.

The fight went on for some time. Neither of us got the better of the other. Suddenly, the bad boy brought out a penknife from nowhere and flicked it around. Shifting it from his right hand to the left and back to the right again. The audience at once realised this was a fight to the finish. The timorous ones had begun to peel off. Yet, most of them got more exhilarated by the sight of blood and gore. They egged us on. More cheers rang out.

If someone cried out instructions, another would call for a defensive stance. "Go for it, man," somebody would cry out impatiently. "To the left! Attack!" There are more fighting experts in the crowd than you could imagine. It's not always easy to put their instructions into practice, though. The mob turned wilder.

In the ensuing contest, I gave my opponent a few bruises and batters. But I also received equal nicks and cuts from his stiletto. Mercifully though, the gashes were not deep and impactful enough to wear me down. I did bleed in several places.

Presently, we fought our way into the nearby town bus waiting shed. I grabbed the knife hand every now and again but could not hold it fast as it was too slippery. Probably with sweat and gore. My shirt was torn in several places on the front and back with not too deep scratches on the flesh.

Suddenly, my Uncle came to my mind. How would he fare? I was concerned. A moment of lose concentration. The attacker was quick to notice. He took a long jab as though to finish the battle once and for all. I feigned in time and managed to grasp the wrist in a tight grip. Then, I swiftly bent it up, threw my right arm behind the curve and grabbed the wrist, which I held in my left hand, forming a firm lock. The baddie wrestled with both hands trying to unlock the grip.

We ended up in a deadlock for a while, the grappling going

neither way. Then, with one strong heave, I twisted the hold with tremendous ferocity. The toughie squealed. Some bones snapped. It sounded like a bunch of celery being crushed near the ears. He won't be using that arm again.

I turned around, grabbed him by the neck and smashed his head against the metal pole of the waiting shed. I did not cease banging it until I saw a thick vital fluid spurt from the crown and heard the villain groan no more. Then, without bothering to see whether life-breath had abandoned him or not, I sprinted down the alley to Apollo Veng, past Suakhnun's kerosene wholesale depot, where I saw my Uncle lead away the two muggers.

Not far away, in a somewhat deserted open, I could espy my Uncle lying in the pool of his own blood. The scoundrels had had his own new handsaw to his throat. He was no match for them. I scrambled up and fumbled around. I could see that he was maliciously hammered even after he took the fall. The guys had been merciless and vindictive, probably taking turns in avenging themselves. Uncle Mang's face was badly bruised and battered. There was evidence of a violent struggle. My Uncle had not gone down easily.

I patted down the corpse for more indication and found it. I had suspected that he must have been somehow enfeebled. Otherwise, he would have taken at least one of his attackers with him. On the lower part of his thigh, about three inches above the kneecap, the material of his trousers ripped, showing a deep gash of yellowish-white fatty tissue. I flashed back to the chase and remembered that he once tripped in the alley as he was about to make it. An unseen protrusion must have clipped him down. It was not before his faltering that the goons caught up and brought him aground. The puzzle fell into place. There was nothing I could do, though.

I surveyed the surroundings for something to cover his mortal body and the ghastly sight in general. Several metres away, there was a dilapidated bamboo-slat-and-barbed-wire fencing running around an unkempt kitchen garden on which a few jute bags were hung to dry. I ran up, plucked the sacks off, and threw them on Uncle Mang, who was but a lifeless bundle now. That was unceremonious. He deserved much better. But there was nothing in my hands at the moment.

In a crime-infested town like Lamka, it may take some time to realise that a murder has just been committed. Especially in such a deserted place. But the baddie I had left behind at the town bus shed might not survive his wounds. That was in the middle of the marketplace. It won't go unnoticed for long. I could hear the police sirens inside my head already.

I was numb with confusion. Shall I rush to the police station and give myself up? Will the law-keepers find my statement believable? Will I be given justice and treated accordingly, I mean, with due clemency? Considering the men involved, I mean the two deceased as I doubted my sparring partner would ever breathe again. I strongly believe it would not be a case easy to sweep under the carpet. There would be staunch supporters for my Uncle, no doubt. But the puppeteers won't remain silent spectators either should the matter go out of their hands. The town would soon be up in protest. There would be mass uproar and political pressure. It was complicated. I was the killer and the victim at the same time. What shall I do? Sweat ran down my spine.

Even a strong-willed officer like my Uncle could not get justice. Could I, then? The chance was slimmer than a thread of hair. I had wasted almost half an hour in a dozen minds with no particular decision. Eventually, I decided to vanish for a while and wait for the fury to blow over.

So, I gathered myself together, took a deep breath, and stared down the shrouded corpse for a long moment before I made up my mind on what I thought would be the wisest decision for the moment. Then, I took to my heels. I didn't know where to go. But definitely not towards the heart of town. I fled south.

I ran, and ran. As fast as I could but slack enough to arouse no suspicion from watching eyes until I could get past the township. Before long, the area of human settlement gave way and the outlying fringes started to grow thicker with forest cover. I knew the cops would soon be on my tail. But, as for now, I did not hear any commotion that would give them away.

Now that I was out of human sight, I picked up speed and dashed as fast as my legs could carry me. The farther I get, the safer I thought I would be. A fugitive, I was in my own hometown. I still could not make out which way to go or where I would end up. I simply headed south without any particular destination in mind. The sun had travelled more than halfway to the western sky. I must make it as far as I can while the light still lingers. I kept running.

After what seemed like a long marathon, I arrived at a place where there was a dense grove of tall pine trees. Mists rose from the forest ground, sunrays piercing through the branches in long wispy arrows of bluish-white. The fragrance of pine nuts wafted pleasantly in the air. I was drowning myself in the pine-scented extravagance, considerably slowing down without being aware. I wished I could tarry here forever.

Ahead of me was a dirt trail. A pair of deep ruts cut by Shaktimans run down the middle. Shaktimans are sturdy logging lorries. Left-behind army trucks of the second world war. I was fortunate it wasn't a rainy season. Otherwise, the furrows would have been impossible to negotiate with small human legs. It would not be possible for police cars to tread the trail either. But there was a possibility of running into a bunch of loggers or some daring huntsman venturing out for a night game. So, I turned from the open track and bounded down the wild slope, following the spoors of beasts. Marks of tiny hooves, probably of boars, deer or wild goats, ran crisscrossed the underbrush. Sometimes I could see fresh pawprints of bears, I guess, or some larger quadrupeds. The day had advanced. It would soon be dusk. The night portended no comfort. I grimaced.

I pressed on.

For a moment, as the sun hovered above the hilltops before taking its final dive, I came to an open space where I could humour myself with the pleasure of a panoramic view. The mountains were lush and luxuriant. A thin haze of mist clung around the foothills. The sun glinted at an angle on their summits. Even under the auburn wash of the horizon, the peaks were still bluish-green, almost deep emerald. No wonder the ranges out here are called the 'Blue Hills'.

Shifting my gaze to the far right, I could see a tiny trail of burnt sienna snaking down the mountainsides. Bringing my eyes lower yet, I could see a meandering river with clear, sparkling waters bounding down into rapids. I had come to a tropical region that was much easier to navigate than the scrub I was struggling with until now. I hurtled down the hillside to get to the river as fast as I could. I must quench my thirst. It was almost killing me.

As I neared the river, a barrage of sombre thoughts bombarded my mind. Is it not better for me to jump into the river and end my misery once and for all? There are no mincing words. Not much hope lies for me in the hands of the authorities. But why should I die in the hands of Uncle Mang's antagonists, who have now become my enemies too? I heard a whisper in the wind. The sweat on the pate cooled a little. It must be Uncle Mang reproaching me for running such dastardly thoughts inside my head.

"A dawn would surely break when the abominable nexus between the authorities and the criminals is exposed and unlinked," I heard him say in the midst of the rustling leaves. "On that day, you must stand for me and make sure people hear the truth I have stood, and of course died, for."

"I'd surely do that, Uncle Mang." I murmured a promise to my imagination. In reality, I was simply self-pep-talking.

Galvanised for a moment, I picked up speed again and hurried towards the river. I could hear the rush of the waters getting much closer now.

By the time I reached the waterside and crouched down to take a sip from the crystal bubbles, the dusk had gone quite dark. Slaking my thirst, I scoured the riparian scene until I noticed a shallow fjord a little distance up ahead. The rapids were fierce. Mountain rivers are fickle. Even in the shallows, where they seemed mild and calm, the current could not be accurately gauged until you practically stepped into it. The tricky part is that even an easy surface can easily sweep you off your feet down below.

Besides, jungle airs in the hills are chilly. Especially at nights. It can easily bite off the tip of your ears. A fox howled somewhere up on the hillside. And I thought I heard a beast sniffing around in the bushes. Perhaps it was securing its nocturnal territory before curling up for the night.

I didn't have time to test the waters. I simply waded in, icing up instantly. My teeth chattered. Even before the crotch area touched the liquid hydrogen, the flexible pouch contracted, shrivelling up, forcing the balls into the warmth of the pelvic cavity. My manhood shrunk. It was painful. I must get to the other shore fast, lest my marbles harden up and shatter into pieces.

Once the night fell, it was fast. Within minutes you lose visibility, and the world is ink. It would take some time for the stars to come out and supply poor illumination. The waning moon would be a most welcomed guest. But I was not so lucky that night.

By the time I forded to the other side, my eyes had somewhat adjusted to the darkness. I could faintly make out the treelines and the boulders lying nearby. My feet hit the dry sand. I settled down for a while to gather my wits and strategise on my next course of action. And I needed rest. I had not rested for the whole day. I was dog beat. The warmth of the sand was comforting and absolutely soothing to the nerves.

I didn't know what happened next. The cooling sands and the frosty night winds woke me up. I had fallen off. I did not have a timepiece with me. So, I had no way of telling the time. It must be quite late in the night, almost to the little hours, in fact. The moon had risen and shone brightly in the sky. My dresses had already dried except in areas where the material is denser and less airy. My bones ached, and my muscles refused to respond with alacrity. But I could not spend the night in the open. I had to move. A night search party might have already been commissioned. And I was not keen to see myself squirming into the closing net.

The way ahead was up, uphill, literally. Under the faint moonlight, for the phoebe on yonder has been so graceful to make her ascendance by now, I could make out a hint of a trail overgrown with long and sharp-edged grasses. I snapped a branch of a tree nearly the size of my wrist—I am a lean man, and my arm is not humongous—to beat out my way and use as a weapon if the need should arise. The plan was to get to the nearest road, whether it be a highway or a dirt track, so that I could make out some sense of direction before I could move on farther.

My progress was slow not only because of the uphill ascent but for my feet and legs that had turned sore due to the day's exertions. I had never worked them so hard. They're pushed to their limits today. So, they're literally buckling under the strain. On a few occasions, my knees turned jelly, and I slumped on the pathway, forced to give them respite. The cover of darkness gave me but little insurance. It was cold, and the tight tissues took time to loosen up.

I was lucky that no part of my legs was injured or my hamstring got pulled. Not even a sprained ankle, for that matter. The light scrapes the penknife had inflicted on my chest and arms had hardened with scabs of blood and dry skin. Fortunately, they weren't deep enough to fester. I had collected some wild goatweed along the way, crushed them up and squeezed the greenish extract on the wounds. A traditional antiseptic. That helped a lot. The pain was generally gone, and the lacerations sort of healed in time.

Before long, my knees submitted again, forcing me to take yet another break. A little distance ahead, I saw the path levelling out and widening a little bit. And there was a huge oak tree a few metres to the path side. I took shelter under the umbrella of the tree, leaning on the massive trunk. And dozed off again.

I woke up in a fit. The east skies had already hinted at a pearly hue of light. I picked myself up again, my bones and tendons groaning under my weight. Then, stretching my arms and legs for a while, I hopped onto the trail and went on again with my self-banishment. The trail I joined was a derelict bridle path. It was overrun with leaves and grasses.

The sun had hardly broken from the jagged ridges when I came across a mountain spring trickling down between the mossy glens. I plucked a wide leaf from a thicket nearby, formed a cup and drank from it. The water was so cold I had to hold my jaws to relieve the ache that hit the molars without warning. I was practically tasting the cool springwaters my elders and ancestors had deeply longed for when they are away from their homeland. It was extremely delicious and satisfying. You really don't need a refrigerator to chill it. And you certainly don't need filtering devices and chemicals to sweeten it. It is naturally tasty and nourishing. The thirst and pain all over my body seemed to vanish in a trice. Surely, the springwater had a miraculous healing property.

Having had my fill of the alpine elixir, I stood there for a moment, holding my walking stick and facing east. Would my image have been captured at that moment, I think I would certainly look like an Arthurian druid, looking out long into the east skies with a jagged walking stick! The view was worth more than all human words put together. The horizon was bathed in bright colours of pink, cream and light purple. I couldn't stop admiring the beauty unfolding before my eyes. I had never seen such a splendid sunrise before. I was spellbound, to say the least. I had no words to describe it. It must be seen to be believed.

The jungle was soon filled with noises of all kinds of birds calling, cawing, squawking and chirping. I recalled our Sunday School teacher when we were small boys. She used to tell us that the birds were singing praises to God in the morning. And we, being made superior to mere fowls, should do the same. I was yet in no mood to lift my voice in adulation or kneel in prayer. Not that I was defying the Maker or unbelieving him. If I got down to my knees, it would take time to straighten up again. And I would be holding myself up for the onward journey, which I must presently make post haste. And on listening more intently to the voracious shrieks and squawks of the feathered congregations, I think, instead of singing hymns to heaven, they were more squabbling and quarrelling over breakfast and wrangling out who the earliest bird should be. For, it is said the early bird catches the worm. Everybody, even animals and birds, had to fight for justice and their share of rights. Ah, how coincidental.

The mesmerising dawn break and the ensuing beauty of nature had caused me great delay already. I reminded myself that I was not a recluse affording the luxury of pondering the magnificence of the Creator's creativity. I am an absconder on the run. And run, I must.

It took a great deal of time for my muscles to acclimatise. Not only with the super fresh atmosphere but with the trauma and tension too. My thighs were sore and taut. I could not hasten up as much as I liked to. However, with the sun intensifying its strength and brilliance, the tissue and tendons began to heat up and thaw. Slowly but surely, I was beginning to pick up speed. It was not before mid-morning that I could bring my pace to an easy canter again.

After about an hour's time trotting and galloping, the even path suddenly terminated. An impenetrable gridwork of twigs, branches, and undergrowth abruptly stood in the way. I turned away and took the up-gradient. It was in no way friendlier but the brushwood and the brambles were less dense. Before long, my arms and face began to burn from sweat that seeped into the scratches and abrasions. It was almost noon when I eventually emerged to a patch which thinned out considerably.

As I let out huge puffs to breathe easier, I suddenly heard a distant purr of a motorbike. I was not far from the highway, I realised. My heart skipped in fear. Was that the search party coming for me? What has given my position away? I had certainly not thrown breadcrumbs in my own wake. Is there something or someone following me all along? I was paranoid. But on second thoughts, I reasoned that it could be some well-off villager who was on his way to his farm. I could hail him to extract some news or at least ask for a lift. A lift to where I don't know yet. Or I could be unnecessarily exposing myself instead. You cannot trust anybody if you are, in my circumstance, running from the law. A prize might have already been announced on my head.

I was arguing with myself until I resolved to take a look whatsoever and decide what to do with the biker as I met him up. I scurried up the incline to catch sight of the highway and the motorcycle. It was much farther than I mentally extrapolated. I was completely exhausted by the time I got to an eyeshot range. I was a deer panting for the life-giving trickles of a watering hole.

I did not hear the bike any more. There was a deep curve in the distance between us at the moment. Perhaps he was negotiating the bend behind the hills. Or was he, on espying me somehow, turning back to pass on intelligence? And, of course, collect the head price.

There was a heavy thicket of broom shrub about seventy metres from an outcurve of the road. I scampered behind it to lie in wait. I was in no hurry. I had already made up my mind to take the risk, come what may. I slowed down my breath.

Before long, the distant drone resonated in the jungle air again. It was drawing nearer. I flattened myself on the dry leaves and found a tiny gap between the shrubbery to peek through. About two minutes later, the rider appeared in full view. My heart leapt in shock.

He was not at all a village farmer. He was an army man with

impeccable combat fatigue. But I could not make out what regiment he must have belonged to. He was in darkish blue with pale camouflaged patterns. He could be a pensioner, I thought. But the markings on the shoulders and a silver badge on the breast indicated active service.

Now, the sergeant was riding at a leisurely pace, looking left and right, squinting ahead and surveying the environment in general. He was definitely on a recce mission. I immediately ceased any sort of movement, not even a twitch of a muscle. My breath grew shallower. And I stilled myself as lifeless as possible.

The communication device strapped on his hip crackled. He then tooled his motorcycle to the roadside, kicked the side stand and walked over a few steps ahead, still looking side to side. Unclipping the walkie-talkie, he twisted something like a tuner on top and spat something to the mouthpiece. I could not make out the words as the voice did not come through distinctly. But I could easily see that an animated exchange was going on.

Had I been spotted somehow? But how? I thought I was travelling under the perfect cover of a jungle canopy. I never stepped out into a glade or a clearing that could give me away so quickly. I thought I was careful.

The cop seemed to take forever. I felt a tingle on my left flank. Red ants filing up my sides? That would be okay. But what if it was something more slithery than ants? I dared not move for fear of crunching a twig or creating a rustle. The leaves were dry on the ground.

Or shall I just pop up, confront the sergeant, of course from behind, and slam my rod on the back of his head? The chance of creeping up on the soldier was slender. Seventy metres is not a small distance to sprint. And the dry leaves on the ground would be a dead giveaway. Furthermore, it needs no elaboration that I stood no chance against the well-trained militaryman, even if I were to strike him from behind. He was meaty, and I was, well, bony at best. I better stay put and suffer whatever creature it was trying to dislodge me from my hiding place.

After what seemed an eternity, the army man came back to his bike, kicked it alive, turned around and sped off the way he came. In reality, it might be a little more than two minutes. Somebody said that time, for those who wait, is too long. How right he was! Or was it the queen of England who said it? Then it should be a she! I had no time to bother with the accuracy of my facts. As soon as the policeman was gone, I quickly sat up and dusted myself. There were no ants or vipers around. But the ticklish sensation I felt was absolutely real. Perhaps, it was my naughty instinct trying to prove Murphy's Law correct under the most inopportune circumstances. I heaved a sigh of relief.

With the immediate tension and anxiety waning away, I began to suddenly feel very hungry. I realised I had not eaten anything since yesterday. My stomach grumbled. The digestive juices began to churn the insides. A slight ache pinched me below the solar plexus.

The highway ran across the low mountains, with the summits only several hundred metres above. I analysed my location and deduced that there was no point in making a downhill advancement. That's where I came from. I looked up and saw the hilltops inviting. The sun was about crossing over to the third quadrant of the firmament. I was starving but not yet famished. I could hold on for a few more hours. However, I did not want to wait for more than necessary. I must find a way to replenish the strength before it really drains off. The large intestines began to complain vehemently.

Gingerly, I peered around, checking out the immediate vicinity at first. Then, I shifted my glance to the four cardinal horizons. I was coming out in the open. So, I must be doubly sure that my cover was not blown. Apprehensively, I stalked away from my protective shrub, furtively skimming all the sides every now and again like a fidgety squirrel.

Then, as fast as my legs could carry me, I sprinted, throwing all caution to the wind. A dash of hope. It could equally be a dash of death. In split seconds, I could lay my hands on the red-mud bulwark of the roadside. I thought I could easily clamber straight up. It was not Mt. Everest, after all. But it proved trickier than I guesstimated. I slipped even before I could gain a couple of feet up. I slid down and ended up with a few dry scratches on the knees and arms. I dared not try from a different angle. That would render me visible from even farther away. Without waiting for a proper pause, I filled my lungs with air and gunned for a second essay. Full throttle.

With the breakneck thrust, I could reach a bunch of dried roots jutting out from the mud wall about nine feet off the ground. I yanked myself up, grabbing another tree stump nearby for additional support. With the final heave, the desiccated root snapped and broke off. Lucky that the tree stub did not give way. I gained the safety of the young forest cover again.

Not long before, I scaled the mountain and emerged on the crown of a mighty range, stretching out as far as the eye could see. It felt like walking on top of the cape of good hope. If it really portends, any good or any hope remains to be seen, though. The view was breathtaking. But I had no time to admire the natural landscape.

I cupped my eyes as the sun rays began to slant at the eye line. Not at a great distance, I saw a hint of a *'loutul'*. For readers who don't speak my language, *'loutul'* is an abandoned field after all the harvests had been done and no more produce were left to extract. Yet, for the lucky ones, there could be some wilding fruits, nuts, legumes or roots that may serve enough for an emergency intake. As for the farmland, it was left fallow to naturally re-fertilise with the erosion of time. This is imperative because the topsoil was depleted by the traditional slash-and-burn cultivation. Such a style is ecologically destructive. But no alternative has yet been devised to sufficiently replace the antiquated model.

Taking deep breaths, I started again, heading towards the abandoned field with the hope to cull something that could fill the stomach for the approaching night. I was sort of dehydrated. I was breaking too much sweat. My muscles had started to cramp. And hunger was beginning to complicate things further, compelling me to consider meeting the intestinal demand double time.

The sun was kissing the jagged tips of the mountains when I made it to the old field. The grasses were extremely tall, serving well for the purpose of my concealment. But in contrast, they're also whelming the old edible crops and creepers, giving them no chance to flourish.

Looking around for a while, I found, not far away, upon a slightly raised knoll, a ramshackle lean-to. However, the walls had given way, dried and brittle, collapsing on their own weight. Half of the roof was blown away, probably by a storm some years ago. Even if I were to mend the hut, it would serve me no purpose. And the night was hanging imminently over the western skyline. I simply had no time to engage in revamping the tumbledown. Anyway, I rushed in and rummaged the premises, hoping to turn up something that could make me an implement.

Nothing.

I checked the horizon every now and again. Darkness was advancing ominously. My search operation yielded nothing despite my diligence and extra-thoroughness. It was disappointing. Perhaps, I better give it up and, instead, spare an effort to hunt tubers or edible leaves and stalks even as the light hung on. It was not before I lifted a rotten bamboo meshwork to clear my way out that I struck gold.

It was a blade, entirely rusted and broken in the middle. But it was complete with a handle. I picked it up and lovingly wiped away years of dirt from the surface of the metal. The owner must have discarded it as it evidently won't serve any domestic purpose. To me, it was the whole nine yards. My key to survival. Any sane man would have chosen it over a lump of gold or diamond in the given situation. My joy knew no bounds.

A few metres from the ancient shack, I saw a whetstone half buried in the mud. I excavated it, raised it to a convenient spot and started chafing away the layers of oxidization on the metal. The rust was tenacious. But I managed to hone it to some extent. Sufficing it for now, as the night was beginning to pounce on me, I hurried to the field and started looking around for something, anything, that looked good and appeared fit for consumption.

Twilight was about catching me up when I noticed a tantalising hint of a mound under a matting bush. Definitely, there must be something beneath it, I thought to myself. But there was no more time to waste on a wild goose chase. I had to find a place to rest my head. I had grown a day wiser. I could not simply spend the night on an open ground like I did the night before. I must lay a nest on the bough of a tree above terra firma. But the bulging soil was too inviting to not give at least a try. Quick seconds lapsed as I bound myself in momentary vacillation. The heavens were growing even deeper in the meanwhile. Eventually, I decided to take a chance.

Hewing out space from the tangled mess of creepers and wild grass, I started digging furiously with my newfound tool. Metal bit into mud. Lady Luck smiled at me. A few inches beneath the hardened soil, I hit the treasure. About the size of a fist. A sweet potato. Hoping for more, I made quick explorations around. Fruitless.

Enough for now, I decided and immediately started looking for a friendly tree to provide me with a good nesting place. As I was scouring for a more evenly stretched-out limb, I rubbed the sweet potato on my butt and took a slow bite from it. I didn't want to finish it in a hurry. The tuber was exceptionally delectable. I never liked sweet potatoes before. I was so wrong about them.

Before visibility was totally gone, I managed to pull together a rough aerie padded with green leaves and branches. Then, leaning on the trunk of the tree and stretching in its comforts, I took out my half-eaten sweet potato from my pant pocket and started nibbling onto it.

The night was calm, and the wind moaned gently. The animals seemed to sleep early in the deep woods. An owl hooted not far away from my roost. Sleepless birds chirped and cheeped around. Or were they saying their night prayers, I don't know. In no time, crickets and insects began to take over as the principal noise-makers of the jungle.

The night's going to be a long one. In the meantime, I popped the last chunk of my limited food supply and started gazing out into the black sky. The stars were clear and shimmering. The moon was yet to make its appearance. Even from this vantage point, I could not see any sign of human settlement near or far. I was anticipating a hamlet or something like that, at least at a far distance. There was not the slightest suggestion of a lamp glowing in the midst of the dense vegetation.

Much contrary to my belief, night in the deep woods was serene and tranquil. Even the phantoms seemed to have retired for a good night's sleep. Exhaustion took me over as my muscles began to relax. Gradually, I slid down on my back, turned to the side, and drew up my knees to reduce the surface area exposed to the elements. The digestive acids began to work. I farted. A birdling cheeped somewhere in the bush probably brought up in a start. I pinched my nose. Then, I think, I slept.

Soft rays of lunar brilliance filtered through the leaves. I sat up in a sudden. I'd never slept on a tree before. I am a town boy. Forget sleeping on it, I'd hardly climbed one in my life. Not even the peach tree in our backyard. Now, I was napping peacefully in a nest more than thirty-five feet above the ground. I shuddered. I could have rolled off easily.

I regained composure in an instant, though. Then, I rose to my feet, stretching my legs and easing my back and sides. They had started getting numb and sore from the stiff cushion of barks and twigs. Besides, I had never seen the moonlight so effulgent. I lifted my eyes, and lo, there it was. The moon, enormous and massive! Perhaps, it was pulling closer because I was at the edge of the horizon. Or is this what they called the supermoon? Perhaps not. But it appeared so near that I could make out the great banyan tree on it without straining the eyes. It was slightly reddish in colour. It was dazzling, indeed. In the town where there was constant supply of electricity, you hardly noticed even the brightest full moon. Now, I realized how marvellous and stunning a trivial moon could be!

In spite of the overpowering fatigue, I could not think of going back to sleep. The jungle was too fascinating to not observe and admire. The dark-green vegetation across the mountain ranges gleamed in silver. The world was awash in surreal radiance and bio-luminescence. I was silently celebrating the sovereign beauty of nature in the midst of inner turmoil and chaos.

After what seemed a mere minute, I began to hear a feeble complaint of a brood nearby. The hatchlings were hungry. Mama's got to flit away in a short while if she must win the first worm. More chirrups followed. Then, a low-pitched caw of a raven from somewhere in the lower ground. The moon above has started to lose its intensity, gradually washing out in a big watermark in the expanse of the blue firmament. A pale tinge of dawn had started outlining the contours of the eastern peaks. The morning would soon be bursting with the cacophony of birdsongs and murmurations.

With the first hint of daylight, I descended from my perch and set myself to work at once. Hunting tracks that I may pursue to lose myself in the tropical wilderness for yet another day. I was getting more experienced in tracking down paths now. Before the sun could fully come up, I found myself a trail winding down the mountainside. It was still slippery from the morning dew. I would not have spotted it if I had been an hour earlier. It was hidden under wild grasses and long sprigs. It was so slick that I slipped twice and slightly hurt my bums in the process.

A little more than two hours later, I came to a bubbling rivulet. The water was crystal clear and icy cold. I made a cup out of my palms and drank to my heart's content. It was truly rejuvenating. I quickly regained the strength to pull on.

I was tempted to follow the river downstream. Rivers always flow into bigger causeways that eventually lead you to a clearing or human settlement of some sort or another. However, I was not yet keen to make myself discoverable. So, I decided otherwise and proceeded upstream rather. Towards the headwaters.

Before long, my entrails began to whine and protest again. A less imaginative person would rush to the bamboo groves nearby and cut a stalk to shape into a javelin. And waste precious energy, of course. As for me, though, I remembered a story my father told me about fishing with machetes. Now, it's time to put the story to the test of truth.

I slowly waded into the crystal pool, about knee-deep, and stood in the middle of the shallow as still as I could be. I wished for a crane's nerve. It was not granted. I moved. A small fry was approaching me from a distance as if on the lookout. It flickered away, scared. I repositioned myself and willed my nerves to calm. In a moment, tiny schools began to flitter around my feet. They have gotten used to the alien object that has suddenly cropped up in the middle of their universe.

A quarter of an hour is a long time to stand still. But the effort paid off. A black indication wiggled towards my legs. Perhaps, he was coming to investigate the hairy twin towers the small sentry had reported. Then, another one followed not far behind.

Steadying, taking a deep breath... *Thwack!*

I brought down the blade in a flash on the backbone of the fish, instantaneously immobilizing it. It was almost cut in half. I scooped it up and threw it to the pebbly shore. I readied again for another strike. This time, the fishes turned up in bigger numbers, probably looking for their missing commanding officer. I hit out again. It was a mighty catch. About three to four pounds, to be precise. An experienced fisherman could have made an amazing haul with this method of fishing without posing an iota of hazard to the environment.

I had no mind of taking more than I needed. I was just happy that my father's tale turned out to be true and practicable. I got done with the fishing and started flipping the stones around, looking for a pair of quartzite rocks. When we were small kids, we would take these hard pearly river stones, throw a blanket over our heads, and in the total darkness, strike them together to produce sparks. Unknowingly, we had been playing with natural flints. That was one amusement we had before the advent of modern marvels like television or Youtube. Now, even without singular inspiration, I could randomly steal fire from the hearths of the gods.

The flintstones were not hard to find. I retrieved a huge pair from the pebbly shore and put them to good use. The rest is history. Even without salt or spice, the fish made me a scrumptious meal.

Inside an hour, I washed up, drank more water, and was begone on my way.

Having no particular destination in mind, my pace began to slow down of its own volition. Most of the time, I was occupied with plotting the future. I could not run forever. Surviving in the jungles was not an issue for a tribal-like me who has come out to embrace modernity for hardly a century. The natural instincts were still running thick in the veins. Even without a metal tool, I would be making out well enough, at least for a week without trouble. But reverting back to the early days was not a viable option for an extended period. I had to find myself a place to find peace and bide my time. First, I had to know where I was and what was happening in the world after my exile.

Days wore on. Nights passed. Sometimes I ended up in a glen of ferns. Sometimes I climbed steep upgrades. Yet, other times, I surfaced in a dale or meadow, which were invitingly open under the clear blue skies. Despite the strong urge to amuse myself once in a while with their openness, I had to avoid them scrupulously. So, I skirted them with a loser's complaint that the grapes were sour. I did not mind counting the sunups and sundowns anymore. I just made my survival and bathed in the glory of wild nature and its unsurpassed magnificence. I wished I had a medium to paint so that I might freeze the picturesque vistas splayed out in front of my eyes every moment of the day. The dawn, the sunrise, the daybreak, the noon, the eventide, the setting sun, the night sky, everything was matchless and superlative. It's unfortunate that there was only the canvas of my memory to capture the indescribable sights that I would never come back to see and experience again.

Presently, it was nightfall yet again. It must be a good number of days since I started living the apeman's life. It was not fancy, but not as bad either. I ceased hurrying around and worrying too much. In due course, my apparels began to fall apart for the excessive wear and tear. I must find myself a spare or a replacement. So, I was evidently excited when I saw something like a hutment in a far distance. I quickened my pace to make it before the night was too late. A scary surprise would not be lovely for the inmates. I must make myself look like an ordinary wayfarer who has lost his way.

Much to my chagrin, the distance was deceptive, and the darkness had terribly impeded my progress. So, when I made it to the hut, it was already very late. I tried to look around, but it was too dark to move around without making a noise. I was afraid to rouse the occupants as I did not know how they would react on seeing me. So, I decided to spend the night in the outskirts and wait for the first light of dawn.

A nasty jab between the ribs woke me up. I was not given time to stretch or yawn away the sleepiness that still hung thick on my eyelids. I was lifted off the ground from under my armpits without a touch of gentleness. As I decrusted my eyes, I saw two men in olive getups manhandling me towards the very hut I had seen earlier. I had landed myself in a military encampment.

I offered no resistance whatsoever. There was no point. I was disoriented and bewildered. So, I just dangled and kept my eyes and mind pried. As the two soldiers walked me between them, I did a mental reading with the hope that it would serve me well later. If I survived or managed to escape, that is, although it looked most unlikely, given the circumstance I was in right now. I could make out that the campsite was recently set up, consisting of just a few hutments, and probably manned by a small squad, perhaps a unit or a platoon.

The soldiers dumped me in the very hut I had decided to survey and knock in the morning. It was empty. No wonder I saw no streaks of light leaking through the holes of the bamboo-mat walling. Whether it was originally purposed for a detention facility, I don't know. But it served exactly that to me at present.

"Don't even think of breaking away," one of the soldiers warned me in accented Hindi before he walked away. His partner stood guard beside the door.

Lucky me, I was not bound or cuffed like a common criminal. But that wasn't promising anything either. Did the soldiers know who I was? Or had they merely picked me up on suspicion? Apparently, the presence of an unidentified person in such close proximity to a military campground would mean a security risk. It should be dealt with right away. But can I trust them to hear me out? Would it be wise to wait for them to pass their judgment? Too many questions. I simply leaned on the wall and tried to breathe easy. What more can I do? I decided to wait on my luck and see.

The soldiers paid me no more attention. Perhaps, they knew I was not intending to go anywhere. Perhaps, my innocent face took them in. Or was it my physical constitution that they found in no way suggestive of any violent aggression?

I could sense a shuffling of feet and a clipped exchange of words. It was indistinct, but the manner was crisped and neat. I groped the wall for an opening to view the outside world. I found none. The tiny gaps did let in daylight all right, but not a crack enough to let in visual images. The bamboo splats were still fresh and smelled of the forest. It would take at least half a year to shrink and give a chink to allow a peek. Till that time, I had to do without an observation port and rely on the aural sense alone. I cocked my ears. I could perceive that the watchmen were making a swap.

I did not hear anything anymore. The camp was unusually quiet. I did hear in the distance an order barked and responded in equal military promptness. Nothing more. I felt I could let my guard down. Being on the tip of my toes won't make any difference for a while. So, I took the far corner of the newly built prison cell, willing to snatch a catnap till the hour of judgment arrived.

I must have dozed off for real. It was already dusk when the flimsy door of my confinement flew open. Two soldiers came in to fetch me. I was not manhandled or shoved around this time. They must have fully realised by now that I was not posing any threat. Or maybe they thought I was too unassuming and harmless to even restrain with a rope. But they certainly kept me within their reach, careful not to let me off the hook. I surveyed the surroundings with the corners of my eyes.

The base was erected on the top of a hillock. The western border of the campus terminated at an abrupt edge. There may be a rocky ledge hanging down the steep, even a precipice. Probably a sheer drop. A few yards across the edge was a hedge of brambles and lantana, about five to six feet in height. From where the guards were presently walking me down, I could extrapolate we must not be more than fifty metres away from the rim. To my left was a barricade of military-grade barbed wire. The nearest thatch roof I could see was about a furlong away. A village below the campsite. The sentinel could keep a constant eye on the village from a vantage sentry post positioned at the outer periphery of the bastion.

My captors might not show any hostility for now. But there was no guarantee that they would not in the near future. Perhaps, they already knew who or what I was and were arranging to transport me to the higher authorities. That was a luxury I could not allow myself to have at the moment. I must stop acting docile.

I did a mental test run of what I had inside my mind for some time now. The only possible route to my flight plan was to the western fringe. My pulse raced, suffusing up the bloodstream with adrenaline.

I am a civilian. No surprise, I couldn't tell the pecking order of the officers who walked up to us in their elegant liveries. I had no doubts they're in the ranks of authority. Symbolic decorations glittered on their shoulders and jangled on their chests too. They conveyed nothing to me, though. Not that I disrespected them. All I could make out was that my near future depended on the humour and current condition of their minds. They were good paces away yet. But I could read the lines and expressions on their faces already. Worn and beaten. Undeniably from harsh duty. Being a soldier doesn't mean you should always be stern and stony. But the hope of clemency that titillated me in the morning has now vanished in a poof. Their countenances did not augur well. They seemed to be too eager to do away with me. It was foreboding. I could not play for time.

All of a sudden, I acted, taking the guards by utter surprise. Adrenaline provided all the speed and surge I needed. The guard on my left reeled to the ground with the first shove of my shoulder as I simultaneously elbowed the other to a stagger. I wheeled around and gunned for the bramble-lantana hedgerow. A shot rang out in the air right away.

I ducked as though I could dodge a bullet. Another shot. And yet another. Digging up dust around my feet. I did not turn back to see who fired the salvos. That was not necessary. They were spurts of a handgun, undoubtedly from the officers. The guards could only be regaining their feet and prepping their Self Loading Rifles even with their best reflexes. In an instant, I could hear the pins cocking into a lock.

I was still a pace too far to take a leap. But this was not a normal circumstance. A couple more steps and the automatic weapons could mow me down like a sitting duck. Even with a zigzaggy sprint, I was still an easy target for the trained shooters. My back tingled.

I vaulted into the air. The SLR's rattled. A volley of shots whizzed past harmlessly below me.

I felt like floating in the air. I didn't know from where came such strength and ability. Fear and flight could work together to make an average man pull off incredible feats, indeed. The velocity of the throw flipped me in midair. I coordinated it into a somersault. My fingers lightly brushed the tender shoots on top of the prickly fortification.

I wished I could replay the moment in slow motion. It would be fascinating to watch. But this was no time for digital fantasies. I could have fallen on the fence face-first like a dud rocket. I caught a fleeting glimpse of the guards lifting their guns to fire in the air. However, gravity played its part with textbook precision. It brought me down in a free fall which was too fast for the gunners to keep track. The slugs vanished into the empty skies with tiny concentric rings of vapour, reverberating with deafening reports.

Luck, too, played its part. I landed on my feet as though I had practiced the acrobatics a hundred times before. Newton's first law of motion almost undid everything, though. My feet touched down all right, but the body, having come to an abrupt rest, was still in motion. I went off-balance with a nasty force.

Willy-nilly, I rolled towards the edge of the border like a boulder chucked down a slope. Before I could reach for anything, I was already sliding down the face of the cliff. A cascade of gravel and dirt rained down after me. Large chunks of rocks are plummeting into the depths of the jungle below, which has now become a yawning shadow in the gathering dusk.

I was desperately grasping the air to arrest the slide when something caught me by the arm. The fall ended in an abrupt jerk. I dangled in the air for some time, swinging free like a piece of log. I was glad to be saved from a certain death drop. But I was already worried about who or what was that that saved me. Human?

Unhuman?

I looked up and saw a human face, all right, struggling to hold me tight. He was quite a burly man, extending his arms with roots hanging out from the cave-like hollow on the cliff wall. Just as he pulled me up, I could hear coarse yellings above the rock face. Obviously, the soldiers were checking out how I fared. Pieces of rocks and soil were still scattering down into the abyss. In no time, the voices drifted away. My captors would have surely thought I had fallen to my death.

In the safety of the space beneath a rocky ledge, I kept staring at my rescuer. I was afraid he would disappear in a whiff of smoke. I nearly regretted making such a silly escapade.

"Close your mouth and follow me," the man spoke up at last on seeing my mouth gape wide open. I was still in shock. Had I really fallen to my death and come to the House of the Dead? I am a strong believer in Heaven and its counterpart, the Hades. "We're not safe here anymore," he continued as he dissolved beyond a curve.

"Wh..who are you?" I stammered after him. "And what are you doing here?"

"You are the second criminal that escaped from the clutches of the authorities today," he said as he jumped off a huge rock.

"Second?" I echoed him.

"We must get to the fastness of the jungle before it's too dark."

He beckoned me to follow him suit. I jumped and landed on a grassy patch. I picked up, steadying myself with the solid hands the man offered. Without a word, we hurtled down the tiny mountain trail. My newfound friend seemed to know the thickets like the back of his hand. Despite his hefty built, he was nimble like a rabbit in the wild. I was still wondering if I was redeemed by a human, an angel or the Devil himself.

It was not before late into the night when we reached a brooklet gurgling cheerfully along. We drank as much as our stomachs could hold. Then, we strode across it. It was only about knee-deep. Then, the ascending gradient began. My friend sniffed around for a while and spotted yet another tiny trail.

Almost half an hour into the trail, my friend, at last, decided to take a break. He lay down on the ground, breathing heavily with a wheezy cough. He closed his eyes and murmured to himself. I sat down, too, and leaned on a small tree nearby, panting. We were both so hammered that none of us had the inclination to start a conversation.

Not long before, I could hear my burly man snoring gently away. Exhaustion has evidently taken over him. From the thirst, weakness, and now slumber, I was reassured that he's indeed a mortal. I, too, did not mind catching a few forty winks before we could move again. I brought my eyes together. They clasped tight without further encouragement.

I was shaken awake by my friend. It was still very dark. But considering the fact that we're on the run, we have overslept. It would soon be dawn, and we must get as far away as we could from the security forces. They would certainly be looking for a corpse to make sure that they had not let their captive slip away between their fingers. And they obviously won't find one. That's when they would be hot on our tails.

As we slowed down to an easier pace, I began collecting my sanity together to make a mental review of the recent turn of events. My head cleared up a bit, and my thoughts became a little more coherent. My machete was gone. I must have dropped it when the sentries picked me up near the cantonment. Then, I rewound the scene where the army officers approached us.

The two personal guards hemming them from each side looked somewhat familiar to me. Mani and Nongyai, two Manipuri classmates of mine. They were very good hockey players. They were our school's National Cadet Corps (NCC) commanders. They must have gotten into the regiment as soon as they passed out their high school. They didn't seem to recognise me. Or perhaps they did. But under the unexpected circumstances of the reunion, they had pretended not to. That was a much wiser thing to do, in fact. I think the shots that followed were certainly not taken by them. Or they had deliberately fired awry.

As for my new friend, he was rather reluctant to make a disclosure of his nature and identity. But I am a pestering bug. I could be a real pain in the ass when I chose to. And with nothing more to do than talk, I was at my peskiest best. Not before hours of badgering, he eventually condescended and spilled a few relevant beans. Indeed, he was as little-spoken as my Uncle Mang. A pang of reminiscence pinched me as he briefly came back to mind. I tucked the memory away for the moment. It was no time to succumb to emotional sensibilities.

My friend's name, as he told me, was Thawngpu. I guess he was fifty-ish. I did not mind asking his age. It was not important. I immediately addressed him as Uncle Thawng. He was a father to four daughters. A poor farmer with a wife of still poorer health. For that reason, they could not pay enough attention to their fields. So, their crops failed year after year until he was forced to steal to make ends meet. He thought he would one day make up everything he had pinched. But fate ruled otherwise. The other day, he was caught lifting some corn from the field barn of his neighbour. Out of fright and nervousness, he happened to fight back and hurt his neighbour's son, who was watching the corn store.

"I hope he survives..." Uncle Thawng broke down in a sob as he narrated his cruel fate. "It was while they tended the wounded boy that I made my escape," he continued. "What will happen to my family now, boo, hoo..."

I am not a good comforter. I did not know what to say. So, I just patted him on the back.

"God will take care of them," I said, really wishing it in my heart. "But why the grotto in the precipice?" I was still wondering how he ended up near the army camp.

"I have known of the cavern all along. I am a villager, you know," he replied. "And their own premises wouldn't be the first location they go over to find a criminal gone underground." He continued: "As for the armed forces, they are recently stationed here. Actually, they're the advance company. A battalion is supposed to arrive a week from today."

"But why?"

"Rumour has it that a faction of valley militants had broken into the hills," he went on. "And, in the absence of regular police, they are taking up post to stem the tide of this insurgency."

Ah, well, that adds up, I mused to myself. I now understand what the biker came for that day. "But what do you have to do with the army?" I asked aloud.

"The village authorities reported me to them," Uncle Thawng went on. "To my good fortune, the forces could not spare personnel at the moment due to pending arrangements in the campsite. They promised they would launch a small search party the following day, that is today. But that was not needed. You landed in their hands. They thought they had apprehended their culprit."

"But why didn't they hand me over to the authorities right away, then?"

"I don't know. Maybe they wanted to first find out whether you are a scout for the militants."

"But they did not torture me or grill me..."

"That too I don't know. Perhaps, they're waiting for the higher officials..." Uncle Thawng paused. "I really don't know. You must thank your stars," he simply ended. Then he asked about me. Fair enough. I recounted the portions that were immediately informative for the moment. Then, I called off the cross-examination session.

It was already high noon when we started foraging for the day's first meal.

We found some late monster figs hanging on the trees. Most of them had gone bad. But a few of them were still good to eat. We soon had our fill. As I had mentioned elsewhere, surviving in the wild for a few days is not an issue. Now that we are two of us, the ordeal was even less challenging. We could easily live off berries, tubers, wild yams, succulent stalks, peppery leaves, and occasionally, fruits. The only problem was that our onward progress was tremendously slackened by these necessary scavenging activities.

Days and nights were more or less the same. Eating, drinking, foraging, and taking flights in the times between. Then clambering up a nice tree or crawling into a safe recess for the night. We covered no big distances. But we did move nevertheless.

At nights, Uncle Thawng would read the stars, humming to himself and sometimes exclaiming aloud that we're indeed on the right track. Right track for what or to where he never bothered to tell me. And I did not bother to ask. As long as I had company, found something to sustain on, and did not re-land in the lap of our captors, I was feeling okay. I did not need to get anywhere. Just getting lost does me fine. I was in no hurry to make a reappearing act to humanity as yet.

I couldn't stop wondering whether the soldiers really came for us. So far, we ran into nobody. Be it a friend or a foe.

So, not to bore the reader with the monotony of our daily ordeals to get away as far as possible from humanity and the law, let me skip to the day we crossed the border. The only detail of interest may be that Uncle Thawng always kept the north star straight ahead when he had to make a choice between paths. Indisputably, we're heading north. That was exactly where I came from. I hope Uncle Thawng did not turn out to be the proverbial mole who was on his way to give me up.

It was not three days or perhaps more before we connected with a bridleway. The path was in a state of utter disrepair and overtaken by shrubs and brushes. It must have been jeepable in its prime. Presently, it was in a pathetic condition. In the median was a bare hint of wear, indicating occasional use. Ironically, that was absolutely fine. The more deserted the jungles and the paths, the better they are suited to us.

Quite a distance later, we heard crashing noises not far ahead. I was petrified. We stopped short in our tracks. "Take it easy," Uncle Thawng reassured me. "Just act normal. Nothing will happen."

My heart rapped against the chest bones. My hands trembled, and my legs weakened to a jelly.

In a moment, we came to a narrow section that was cut off by huge beams of timber crashing down from the top of the hill. Uncle Thawng called out for anybody who was responsible for the activity to cease and allow us to pass. Somewhere deep in the woods above, a voice rang out, to which Uncle Thawng responded immediately. They communicated in a language I was almost familiar with. Almost familiar is far from understanding it.

Presently some three men showed up from the woods and engaged the elder in a brief chat. What did they exchange? I completely did not know! The lumberjacks had strong south-east Asian features. Had we strayed into Burma? But that would be a distant east to our right. It can't be. I held my breath and looked the other way, pretending to admire the landscape while the men parleyed. They let us pass in a short while.

An hour later, I asked Uncle Thawng what the negotiation was about.

The tongue they spoke was Nagamese, he told me. And the men were sawyers camping at the foothills, logging for weeks now. They were extremely surprised to see us as nobody was known to pass this way for ages. Uncle Thawng told them I was his nephew, and we were on an urgent errand to the next village. I knew he was lying. But the men bought his bluff. He was good in the language.

"By the way, Uncle Thawng," I was curious. Yet again. "How do you get to speak it?"

"It was in the late sixties," he told me. "Or was it early seventies, I did not remember. We were taken to Kohima for training as fresh recruits of the Village Volunteer Force. About six months later we learnt that our unit was disbanded. Nobody told us why."

It was in those training months that he picked up a stammering of the language. A local girlfriend honed it to almost perfection, he admitted. Could it be that God was always preparing him for this situation? Food for religious thought, I guess. For the less religious, though, that was just a coincidence.

For the remaining day, we simply pressed forward without any more words. The sun was slipping fast. It would soon be dusk.

It was not quite dark when we reached a small village. Like it or not, we had to pass through it to catch the newer pathway that started off at the other end of the village. A little distance away from the path was a security picket. The wooden board nailed to a post announced: Border Security Force. What the hell was a BSF outpost doing at this end of the world? We crouched behind a bush. We had to wait for the night to clamp down.

The tapestry of darkness descended. But to our vexation, the corner house had a 100-watt electric bulb glowing on the porch, casting a wide orangey arc in the gathering nightfall. How did a fringe hamlet like this get a power supply while the town I came from suffered endless load sheddings? I was miffed more than angry.

Just then, a boy, probably in his early teens, was heading for the very house that spelled a setback to our onward progress. Uncle Thawng broke his cover and approached him. I could see him hand over a small black container to the lad. Was it a piece of intelligence? I almost got panicky. Can I still trust my partner? Should I just vanish and part ways right away? Before I could make up my mind, he was back at my side.

"Now, what did you say to the boy?" I queried with a hint of annoyance.

"I told him I am a nationalist lieutenant," he replied. "I had a very important person to transport. But that bulb was putting us at risk."

"What was that you gave him?"

"Ah, that was a gunpower vial I stole from the Chief's house on my way to escape," he sighed. "I anticipated it'll come in handy somehow. A bribe being the last thing in my mind though. There's nothing in my hand at the moment and—"

Before Uncle Thawng could state the obvious, the light on the veranda flicked off. He left his words there and grabbed me by the arm, tugging me abruptly along as we dashed for the village pathway. We hardly turned the corner when the light came on again. We have made it through.

A fresh bout of fear gripped my thoughts. We have come so close to human habitation. We could have been apprehended and brought to justice that in no way would be favourable to us. As though sensing my fear, Uncle Thawng reassured me that we need not worry for at least another sixty kilometres.

"What after sixty?" I couldn't keep my scepticism at bay. I was peeved for no valid reason.

"You're never going to make that far anyway," Uncle Thawng said matter-of-factly.

I shuddered. Had he really made up his mind to give me away? I kept mum. An idea was rapidly forming inside my head on how to elude his tutelage should we come to that eventuality. I just tagged along, not to arouse his suspicion that I had seen through his deception. When he slowed down to an easy pace, my feeling of distrust got further bolstered. We walked in silence for about another hour or so.

Suddenly Uncle Thawng bolted.

"Quick. Up the hill," he beckoned as he spurred up the hill where there was not even a proper trail.

What's going on? What's in his mind?

I was so taken aback that I could not find my feet at once. Uncle Thawng hissed under his breath, signalling me to make it fast. I darted up behind him. He was no match for me. He disappeared into the woods before I could even touch his tail. Instead of giving me up, it was he who rather departed from me. Suddenly, I felt I should not let him go. Perhaps, he was harbouring the same suspicion as I had of him. I snorted, revved up, and exerted all the remaining winds in the lungs to propel myself forward.

About a minute later, I caught up with him again. He was sitting nonchalantly on a rotting lumber, waiting for me.

"What is this?" I protested, huffing and puffing, holding my sides.

"Don't you see?" he said, almost surprised at my naïveté. "A patrol!"

"How do you know it's a patrol?"

"The lad told me that the army frequently patrols the area for obvious reasons and warned me to look out for them."

"You said we would never make the entire road, anyway?"

"I saw a tiny flicker already. I did not want to freak you out. Only when I was sure that the pin of light was a truck, I decided to dash."

Fair enough, I thought. We both gasped for air. In a few minutes, the trucks rumbled past beneath us. There must be around three to four of them. We waited for a few more minutes till the roar of the vehicles completely faded away. Then, Uncle Thawng took me on the same route—the north star straight ahead. We never returned to the dirt road again.

In the wee hours, when the night was at its darkest, my guardian angel—Uncle Thawng—decided that we must take a break. For the last few days, we have kept our day travel slow and intermittent for fear of running into some unexpected human strays. Besides, we had to hunt for food every now and again. That naturally slowed us down to a great extent.

"I think we can take things a lot easier now," my guardian angel said as he plopped on the grassy knoll.

I threw myself down on the back after him. Bubbles of spent energy gushed into my bloodstream. The veins and arteries tingled as the rush reached the tips of the nerve endings. "How can you say that?" I asked him casually.

"We've crossed the border some three miles ago," he stated.

I did not notice anything indicative of that sort. "How can you say that?" I repeated my question.

"I saw a worn-down sign," he replied. "But in our hurry, I managed to read only the bolder words that were equally weathered by time and elements. It says, 'Visit Again.'"

"It could be a normal parting gesture," I argued. "Like you commonly see at the ends of our own villages."

"It could be," he did not counter-argue. "But I doubt the hamlet we just passed would take the big trouble of putting up a sign as far as here. That too so long time ago."

"Makes sense," I agreed. "In which territory are we now, then?"

"My guess would be Nagaland," Uncle Thawng said.

"Aha!" I exclaimed. "That's where you're always taking us, eh?"

"Yes, I wanted to get to some old friends at Kohima to help me out," he admitted.

That explained it all.

With the muscular system fully rested and destressed, drowsiness began to fall upon me in one fell swoop. My guardian angel was already blowing wheezy breaths. The curse of smoking, he said. I sidled up against a rock nearby, propped myself up on the back and let down my guard for the night, praying the patrol party did not sniff up our bunghole in our sleep.

The morning dawned upon us. That's the best sleep I have ever had in recent times. I need not gloss over the grandeur of the sunrise and the accompanying scene again. I pulled a long yawn and stretched languorously, cracking bits of bones in the spinal column. I twisted my back, and the hip bones crunched as though with a chiropractor's touch. I wrung my knuckles to relieve them of the nitrogen fizz. Then, my fingers went down automatically to scratch—well, I couldn't help it, it's just natural—my balls. I was ready for the day.

"Good Mor—"

Where the hell was Uncle Thawng? I immediately panicked. Now that he has led me this far, I kind of relied on his guidance and, of course, longed for his company. He was nowhere to be seen. I just couldn't scream his name. The morning was rent with twittering din and racket from the undomesticated nationalities of the jungle. But a human voice would be totally out of place and easily detectable. I couldn't afford to take the risk. But where the bloody hell was he? How can he leave me here alone? Just like this!

My eyes began to brim with tears of anger and disappointment. I did not know where to look. And I did not know if I was really capable of proceeding without him. Am I still to take north? Should I turn east? Or west, in fact? I was bewildered even before I took the first step.

"Uncle Thawng, Uncle Thawng..." I called gingerly as I started fumbling around the glades. I dared not climb the trees for obvious reasons. I saw in my imaginary eyes a sentry man looking out with a pair of binoculars.

"Uncle Thawng! Uncle Thawng!" I squealed like a frightened mouse.

To no avail.

Coming to my wit's end, I reclined against a tree. Resigned. Then, I heard the dry leaves rustle and a twig snap from the hillside below. I turned around instantly, my heart sinking inside the ribcage. Am I finally rounded up? Has Uncle Thawng ultimately turned out to be what I had always feared him to be? I darted behind the boulder on which I leaned to sleep the night before.

My mind was dashed into smithereens. Luck may not always hold me up. I could not always fight off the security forces. Giving up is not an option either. I have come this far. I must make good my escape, at least till I voluntarily decided to resurface. What shall I do?

Then I heard the familiar wheezy cough. With that immediately appeared my guardian angel.

"Hah, you've woken up?" he called out as he noticed I was not where I lay the night before. "But Muanpu, where are you?"

You don't know how relieved I was to see the face of my guardian angel again. All my resentment evaporated in the blink of an eye. I wanted to run to him and give him a big bear hug. But real men don't hug. I stepped out from behind the rock as though I was simply waiting for him. Yet I couldn't keep my curiosity to myself. "Where the hell have you been?"

"Ta-da..." he singsonged as he dangled a dead bird in his hand with a mental fanfare in the background of his mind's picture.

I was filled yet again with fear. Ignorance is indeed a source of constant fear. "Where did you get that chicken? You have stolen from the village?"

"It's a jungle-fowl, you idiot," he snapped on hearing me charge him with thievery. "I don't steal at will. I am a good hunter."

I apologised and swore never to level the charge again. He was not angry. But I just felt obliged to say sorry. A burden seemed lifted off my heart. "But how do we prepare it? We could not build a fire right here."

"Certainly not," he agreed. "But we won't die of starvation at least for the next ten hours," he said, throwing the fowl over his shoulder. "Our next host will be giving us a dinner party."

Then, without more words, he took off. I could only hop after him like a small child running after his father.

Much to my chagrin, we did not come across any village, even after hours of trekking. Every now and then, I would whine and propose that we have our chicken roasted. Uncle Thawng adamantly refused. He insisted that we must have it with spice and pepper. Never before had I so deeply wished we had run into a village. The constant sight of ready poultry instigated my insides to rise in revolution. Thunders rumbled deep in the pit of the stomach. All my innards and entrails were up in arms, protesting Uncle Thawng's meanness. For the first time in all these days, I began to feel the real pangs of hunger.

By early afternoon, we came to a small streamlet, clear and crystal. In our haste, we had even forgotten our thirst. We slurped on the icy waters and relished it. It was invigorating.

"The village must not be far away now," remarked Uncle Thawng as we proceeded without tarrying for another moment.

Dusk was about setting in when we came to an easy bend on the dirt road. Right behind the curve, about fifty yards from the path, a teasing outline of the back of a farmhouse came into view. Uncle Thawng quickened his pace. I trotted after him like an obedient son. As we're about turning the corner, my guide suddenly stalled. I bumped into his back. Then, he scampered behind a nearby bush, where I followed him without question. He was making a mental assessment of the environment.

A long moment later, and undoubtedly feeling safer, we detached from the bushes and sauntered into the cottage.

There were no other huts around. The cottage was some kind of a seasonal lodge, surrounded by coffee shrubs. It was a plantation estate. Presently, I could see an elderly man lounging on an easy chair in the portico, a half-woven wicker basket lying nearby.

"Hallo, Sir, how do you do?" Uncle Thawng greeted the old man in Hindi.

The senior citizen had a struggling husky voice. He responded in English: "How do you do, gentlemen?" he was refined and cultured. "It's an honour to have guests out here."

He offered us a bench across the veranda, which we immediately occupied. Uncle Thawng picked up his previous bluff and added a little twist to it: "We're running an emergency errand and in our search for a shortcut, have lost our way until we ended up here."

The gentleman rapped his walking cane on the wooden post a few times. I was instantly agog. Was it a signal for the waylaying troopers in the bush? Was the old man a secret informer of the security forces? I nudged my partner and suggested we move on.

A little distance away, I could see the back of a woman bent to the ground. She was raking for something in the kitchen garden. From her movements and mannerisms, I could gauge that she was not alone. Yet I could not see her companion because he or she was beyond my line of sight.

In the meantime, Uncle Thawng seemed to throw all caution to the wind. He seemed completely laidback and unconcerned.

"We've never had uninvited visitors out here," the old man said. "This is a private estate. Nobody comes here even by accident."

That was foreboding. But my partner failed to read the hidden message. Or had he deliberately neglected it? He chuckled and chattered.

In a short while, the workers in the garden hung up their boots and appeared on the porch with their gleanings. An assortment of yams, tapioca, leafy vegetables, and of course, sweet potatoes. The old man spoke to them immediately. "Jennifer," he called out. "We're having guests today. Prepare a good dinner, will you?"

"Certainly, father," Jennifer, the elder woman, replied cheerfully.

"And the gentlemen brought us this nice fat chicken," the ageing host continued.

Uncle Thawng must have made his offer while I was busy investigating the vicinity with my mental faculty. Now, the lady came over and received the wildfowl with words of thanks. Behind her, the younger lady walked up, removing the stole that ran across half her face. She was stunning!

I had never seen such a beauty before. I was instantaneously smitten. I myself did not know that a romantic was holed up inside me. Needless to say, I was bowled head over heels. Something at the back of my head started inciting my willpower to refuse to leave. But the practical situation seemed to grant no permission whatsoever. Our eyes locked for a brief second. Cupid's arrows darted through my heart in quick succession. I almost felt the pain outwardly.

As she was about walking past us, the old gentleman indicated her and said, "This is my granddaughter. Her name is Pari." Pari smiled at us politely. "And there, her mother, you know her already."

Both ladies turned their beautiful heads and acknowledged the introduction. "Hi, nice to meet you, guys!" Pari said with a cute little giggle.

I was about to speak when Uncle Thawng overtook me. "Hallo, nice meeting you too." Then pulling me forward, he said, "This is my nephew, Muanpu. And I am Thawngpu."

Without looking back, the ladies departed into the cabin, which is the kitchen, in fact. Uncle Thawng turned to the elderly man and thanked him profusely for his hospitality. He communicated in passable Hindi while the senior citizen spoke immaculate English. They soon engaged in a friendly chat, chuckling and sharing light moments with one another. They're getting along well.

I felt left out.

A short while later, our host took us into the sitting room. The interior of the cottage was spacious and richly furnished. "Please, make yourselves at home," he bade us to the thick sofas. "The servants have gone to their homes. They'll not be back before Pari's vacation is over." Then, he cried out to the beauty personification and told her to provide us something to drink and bite. And to arrange fresh dresses for the both of us, of course.

I could see that they're rich but not ostentatious. There was no arrogance and pomposity in their personalities. I wanted to know more about this family.

In a moment, the gorgeous girl reappeared to serve us dark, aromatic cups of coffee and home-baked cookies. "Grandpa, I need to go to the stream to wash our work-clothes," she said as she walked back with her empty tray.

"By all means, darling," the elderly man gave his approval. "But be careful. The rocks are slippery."

At that moment, Uncle Thawng took me by complete surprise. He turned to the beautiful lady and made a suggestion. "Do you mind taking my nephew along? He stinks!"

That was extremely embarrassing. I didn't know whether I should smile or frown at the bad joke. I wanted to retort, "You stink too, old man." But I held my peace. I could avenge myself later.

Actually, I won't mind at all going to the pool with this paragon of beauty even if I stunk like a skunk. I was overjoyed inwardly. It may be embarrassing in one way, but on the other, I wanted to kiss Uncle Thawng for his presence of mind.

"Of course," the host agreed. "An escort is an excellent idea."

"Great!" The girl simply remarked with a wide smile as she walked into the kitchen yet again.

Now, am I supposed to go after her into the kitchen? Am I to wait for her to come out again with the laundry and collect me too? The gentleman came to my rescue. "Please, young man. The door is at the back of the kitchen itself."

I sprinted to the exit like a harried hare.

In no time, we were at the streamlet that I shall forever remember as Coffee Creek.

"Do you remember me, U Muan?" Pari called from the poolside as she rinsed the dirty linen.

I nearly slipped from the rock I was sitting on. Should I say yes? Or, no? What is the right answer? What is she driving at? I hesitated.

"No wonder you don't." She continued before I could come up with a reply. "But I still do."

I felt like snatching the soiled clothes from her tender hands and doing them myself. Her dainty little fingers were not made for such scrub work. But is this a good omen? Or is heaven going to crash on my head? She might be indescribably beautiful, but she was still a random girl. I've got lots of boyfriends and girlfriends back home. And she certainly was not one of them. How could I say I remembered her? I did not want to lie to her. She meant nothing to me at the moment. And she might never mean anything in the future. But something inside my heart told me not to be untruthful to her.

"I am really sorry," I confessed. "But I'll never forget you again in my life."

By the way, I nearly forgot to mention that she had shifted to my language, Paite, with the Dapzar variant. She had a heavy accent, though. Let me jump the gun. Pari told me a brief story about her family and, of course, about herself. Her mother was from Mimbung in Mizoram, from a respectable Paite family there. She was a rather old-school lady. And thanks to that, she conserved her mother tongue, although non-usage corrupted her with a slight accent.

Her father was a coffee magnate in Guwahati. He was an Assamese Brahmin. Her parents first met in Shillong, where they studied college together, fell in love and married secretly before they decided to go for further studies somewhere far away. Her father had thought that his father, that is, her grandfather, would disapprove of their relationship. That was why he took her to an undisclosed city under the guise of higher studies. Her father was a shy and innocent boy, Pari recounted and was scared of his father, who was a strict disciplinarian. But her grandfather was not a hard-hearted man. When he learned of his son's elopement, he hunted them down only to pardon and accept them. Her father never told her mother of their affluence till she was accepted by his family. He was not a man to vaunt somebody's opulence. "He is a very hard-working man himself," Pari lauded.

Then, they came back, of course, after completing their studies and settled in Shillong. That's where she, Pari, was born and brought up. As for the coffee estate, it was a private ancestral land since the time of the British Raj, long before the northeastern states were born. They hardly spoke her mother tongue at home, evidently. Her grandfather was a London-educated gentleman. No wonder he spoke English so well.

Her mother would often encourage her to speak her mother tongue too. "'Language is an asset,' she would often say," recalled Pari. "'It is your identity. No matter where you are or how high you climb the echelons of the society. Your language is still your identity. You should never forget it.'"

True to her principles, she would often insist Pari take part in their tribal institutions and organisations so that a constant connect with their roots is maintained. That was how she happened to get involved in the activities of Siamsinpawlpi, SSPP in short, the Paite Students' Welfare Association.

Now coming to me, I mean, how she came to know me.

It was about two or three years ago, she said. The Shillong Branch of Siamsinpawlpi was accorded the honour of being one of the special invitees for the SSPP HQ Flag Day at Lamka. She was selected to be one of the delegates. That was the first time she ever saw the famous Lamka town, which was then known as the 'Paradise of the East'.

Pari vividly remembered the feisty young boy who came on stage and carried the events along so effortlessly. She was of a very impressionable age. So, she immediately swooned for the dapper lad who appeared to be so accomplished and brilliant. There was no way to express her feelings to him as they were not on familiar terms. And she thought she was suffering from a transient sentiment. But the weak knee stayed with her for a long time. She locked the name and the memory deep inside her heart. Her first love was only a fleeting reminiscence. A stranger.

Then, out of nowhere, today, the Master of Ceremony reappeared, bringing all the memories back into sharp focus. Not that the memories have faded. But she had held no hope to behold her knight in shining armour in person ever again. The weak knee returned as in the old days.

It must be love! Oh, it must be love!

Pari suddenly became self-conscious. She lowered her eyes and stared at her own reflection on the limpid surface of the water. I edged up slowly, sat on the pebbles inside the silver eddy and lifted her chin.

"Hey, there's nothing to be ashamed of," I reassured her. "I too lost my heart the moment you removed your scarf."

"Do you?" Pari's eyes lit up.

"But things are not the same anymore," I interjected before we could go too far.

"Not with me, though," she averred.

"It's complicated," I said to her slowly and recounted the turn of events of the past few days for her general information. It was kind of lifting a load off my chest.

Not to dwell on the unnecessary specifics, let me right away admit that by the time we were ready to leave Coffee Creek, we had already declared our innermost feelings and were both over one another.

Dusk had descended upon us. I donned the dress Pari brought for me. It was a little sloppy on my wiry frame. I secretly creased and knotted every here and there and made it pass. I carried the laundry for her while she had the waterpot on her head.

The cottage was a good yards away. But my sensitive olfactory nerves had already picked up the powerful whiffs of spices lazily spiralling in the air. In our brief escapade into the world of quixotic dreams, I had forgotten that I was ravenous. Presently, my mouth started watering with the drifting aromas causing the gastric juices to overflow. Rats ran all over my tummy.

In the meanwhile, I could see that Uncle Thawng was also given a fresh set of attire. He was totally at home, laughing away and sharing jokes at the dining table. All sense of fear seemed to have disappeared from his head.

On the contrary, I was still mired in a mix. It could be a trap. I constantly reminded myself. Admittedly, a large part of me wanted to stay back to find out whether Pari's feelings for me were genuine. And, of course, to see if my feelings for Pari were genuine and true from the bottom of my heart. In the process of this inner tussle, I even forgot to properly savour the piquant curry of the wild chicken.

I was brought about with a jolt when Pari's mother asked, "Why, Muanpu, don't you like my cooking?"

I stammered and mumbled something unintelligible. The two gentlemen chuckled with their own gags, paying us no attention. They're getting along well, indeed.

Pari indulged me with a juicy piece of meat she had selectively picked from the bowl and dropped into my plate, seasoning the act with a cheeky smile. All that gesture added to my awkwardness and embarrassment. I could not even say thank you. I was burning. Despite my gnawing hunger, I wished the dinner session to end right away.

After what seemed forever, we finished dinner at last. Then, about half an hour later, as we gathered in the study, our hostess, Jennifer, brought us sparkling glasses of light lemon tea. How perfectly that complements the heavy meal!

After some time, she leaned over to grandfather and whispered something into his ears. The old man nodded. Then, excusing himself, he joined his daughter-in-law in the room adjacent to the study where Pari was already waiting. They pulled the drapes as though they were engaging in a war room consultation. Classified and confidential.

In the meantime, Uncle Thawng winked at me with a knowing smile.

"Stop that stupid grin of yours," I hissed between my teeth. "They could be plotting our handover..."

Uncle Thawng would not hear of it. "Young boy, I read your mind the moment the ladies came in," said he instead. "And we're not going from here."

"What if they're not what we think?" my voice shook with suspicion and irritation with Uncle Thawng's complacency.

"Yes, they're not what you make them to be," he gave me a mysterious reply. "You're not leaving. I am."

"What the hell are you talking about?"

"I mean, my boy," he patted my thighs as though to reassure me, "you're staying back, and I go ahead."

"Don't be funny," I was getting a bit upset with his jolly nature now. "You cannot leave me here."

"Why not? We never had the same destination in the first place."

That was true. I had nowhere in mind to go. I just wanted to disappear and find a refuge beyond the pale of my hometown and its authorities. But I also know that there is no place the tentacles of law cannot reach. Would I be safe here?

*

The night was clear and starry. Soft breezes blow from fragrant meadows, rustling through the coffee shrubs. The air was filled with the sweet scent of coffee berries and nightshades. It was like a dream. Pari took me to the garden, somewhere like a park.

There was a makeshift shelter, probably a shanty for plantation workers. It had no walling. And there was a bamboo seating on which the fair damsel bade me rest. She sat a few inches away from me, casually leaning on the bamboo backing.

Gently, the winds whispered sweet nothings among the leaves. The chill drew us closer until we had ourselves in each other's arms. Then, under the starlit night, snuggling up coyly into my bosom, Pari told me everything.

—*This story appeared in a specially adapted vernacular version in the 50th Zomi Nam Ni, Golden Jubilee Souvenir, 1948 – 1998: An Evening Post Publication*

Chapter 5

HER SECRET

Chingnu and I were childhood friends. We were close neighbours too. Our parents were on the pleasantest terms, especially our mothers. I am a begotten son. Chingnu's got an elder sister, Betsy. She didn't care to fraternise with us younger than her. No wonder, with not many siblings to give us company, we got drawn to each other ever since the day we first met. Well, um, I didn't remember when we actually first met. That's fine. That's not the point.

Needless to say, Chingnu was always nice to me, although I wasn't sure I was always to her. I was immature and rather conceited. I often took pride in my father's position in his office. I used to brag that he was the most popular man in the village. And I, being a juvenile fool, was extremely pompous when taking his name and social standing. It was not before I grew well into years that I realised the shamefulness of puffing one's chest with someone else's station. Not that it is wrong to be proud of one's father. But to build air on somebody's repute, even if he were your father, is a different thing altogether. It's despicable.

Well, despite my haughty bearings, Chingnu never snubbed me or disrespected me. Rather, she was kind and absolutely understanding. Even patronising, I should say. I think she was like already a grownup girl while I was still a puerile adolescent. And one thing: She would never fail to take my side should we pick a quarrel with any of our friends, which I did more often than not. Even when she knew I was to blame, in fact. She was as much attached to me as I was to her. Or so I thought.

We were living in an immediate neighbourhood, literally. The sprawling cottage-type government quarters in which we lived were adjacent to one another. Our elders would say, a spitting distance. Her father and my father were colleagues working in the same office. The Sub Divisional Office. My father was a senior to hers. I mean, rank-wise and probably age-wise, too. He must have married late. Without necessarily referencing to my own looks, my father would definitely not have created ripples as a handsome hunk even in his heydays. Now, as far as the immediacy of our habitation is concerned, if you need to draw attention for one reason or another, you don't have to holler as though the house was on fire. Just raise your voice a bit. Our ears were ever pricked in anticipation. And, we did buzz up more frequently than not to state the obvious.

Apparently, so, we never thought of having another friend as long as we were together. Never cared to strike up one in the first place. So engrossed with ourselves that we had to be dragged apart at dinnertimes. Or at any other time, for that matter. But then, we would soon meet up again on the dust dunes where we would build mud castles till the sun would be long gone. In the evenings, we would come together again and study alternately at each other's house. Our friendship was never objected even when we had grown into budding teenagers. We felt this round world existed solely for the two of us. We believed our friendship would strengthen with the passage of time.

Now, it was not until I was seventeen and she fifteen that fate began to play a nasty game with our lives.

One day, which turned out to be not so fine, back from school, I saw Chingnu walk rather sullenly in the midst of her friends. Her eyes lifted every now and then as though looking for somebody. Perhaps, me, I guessed. But I couldn't simply walk over to her with all her pals fluttering around like butterflies. In small villages like ours, every love affair was considered reprehensible and not well countenanced. Especially those between budding fledglings. Rumourmongers were always on the lookout for juicy titbits to spread like a pandemic virus. Now that we are yet to be proper grownups, we had to be extra circumspect so that gossip hunters don't get the wrong whiff and sully our wholesome relationship. They won't spare us even for the fact that we have been friends ever since our childhood. Our society was still in the vice grip of Victorian morality. The scandalmongers were ruthless. And for that very consideration, we had significantly curtailed our exchanges and interactions, minding distance and getting in touch only when requirement calls for it. We may not be full-fledged adults yet, but we're no more small kids that could chum up anytime we liked. And we had to be responsible youths, maintaining social decency and decorum, as customarily expected of us. And boy, just for trivia, teenagers were treated more or less as grownups in those days.

Presently, our eyes clashed for a brief moment. That was more than enough to perceive the sentiment running high in our hearts that share a beat. It was a blink. Almost imperceptible. But the fleeting pattern was unmistakable. A visual morse code. That was not a mystery to me. I got the message.

In a short while, her pals began to drift away one by one at the cross paths, saying their see-you-agains. As they were turning the last curve on the dirt road, Chingnu eyed me again. She was seeing off her last bevy. I hastened my stride and caught up with her in a moment.

Now, on our own, we sauntered leisurely under the patchy rows of wild trees that lined the village paths. It was the first time Chingnu faltered speaking to me as she called out my name. Her voice was breaking.

"What's the matter, Ching?" I enquired concernedly.

"I...I..." she stammered and took a pause to compose herself. Then she continued: "I think it's time for us to say our last byes too."

That was a real bolt from the blue.

"Why?" I shot back, flabbergasted. "What's getting into you?"

She didn't say a word. We ambled in silence for a long time. By the time she picked up again, we were already at the outskirts of the village. The woods were damp with early dew. The shades were deep and quiet. A perfect contrast to the tempest raging inside our hearts. The sun was hovering low above the ridges of the western mountains. Misty rays were stealing through the tropical trees, piercing the dense foliage with golden streaks. We sat ourselves down on the roadside, looking towards the village. A panoramic view. Then, leaning gently on my shoulder, Chingnu spoke again.

"My mother has been transferred," she blurted, eyes glistening with tears. Her cheeks turned pale with an unspoken sense of melancholy.

"Transferred?" I echoed, nonplussed. I started so hard that she had to pull her face away to avoid my shoulder bone bumping up on her jowl.

Chingnu's father had passed away about six years ago. We, as children, did not know much of his ailment. Chingnu, of course, got a hint from elders' talk that it was cancer. Shortly later, in her father's place, her mother, a well-educated lady, was inducted as a clerk under the government's die in harness scheme.

If lightning were to strike me on the forehead, that would be an understatement of my astonishment when Chingnu broke the news. The unhappy news. The big round world was not meant for the two of us alone after all. Despite the balmy breeze sweeping every now and then down the northern hills, drops of perspiration collected on my back and began to roll down the spinal column.

Chingnu was fighting her own ghosts. There was nothing we could do but silently accept our fate. She snuggled up on me again and sighed shakily. This time closer to my heart as though trying to listen to its rushing rhythm. I rubbed my cheek on her crown, stroking her hair gently as though that would give her any comfort. I could hear her sob gently as she threw her arms around me. I batted my eyelids swiftly together to drive away the menacing tears. Every passing second makes it harder to behave like a real man. I am afraid a few drops of tears had escaped without my knowledge. And I sniffled.

We wished the world would end right then and there, freezing us in that frame forever. But wishes are not horses you ride so easily. We had to wake up to the harshness of reality at some point in time. And that some point in time is always now.

The sun had already gone home. A nondescript night bird squawked loudly nearby as though disapproving of our lovey-dovey cuddle. We stirred. The twilight had set in. Lots more to say but no more words we found. So, we rose and walked back home in deafening silence. As far as the village fringe permits, we walked hand in hand, arms locked and entwined as though frightened that somebody would walk into us and tear us apart. Chingnu leaned on my shoulder and snivelled all the way. Neither of us had words to console the other and raise the spirits. We simply promenaded like two dumb lovers. I was missing her already, and they had not even left.

As lovers naturally do when a dark prospect of separation looms over them, Chingnu and I, too, became despondent by the day. We could not just break the news to our families that we're in love. In truth, neither of us had ever uttered the four-letter word despite our firm belief we were in it. Perhaps, we had taken it for granted and considered it frivolous to make the formal declaration. Perhaps we're thinking it's just a matter of time. It's true that we're not ready for a serious relationship. Certainly not because we're not in love. It's just the age bracket that did not suit us right for the moment. And we seemed to have a tacit agreement on that.

We did meet up whenever we could make time. But we could not linger as long as we would love to, like the days when we were mere kids. We had to sneak away from the prying eyes of the gossipmongers and our families alike. We did hang out even more often than we'd used to prior to the breaking news. But, all of a sudden, the zing and passion that filled our moments seemed to have been sucked high and dry. All zest and vigour faded, withering our very lives in the process. Words failed us every time we met. The little niceties we could mock up would fall miserably short of conveying what we truly meant inside our hearts.

Yet, time and tide waited for no man. Only a week more!

We're squandering precious time in useless despair and self-pity. But what could we do? Days were fleeting too fast. We were yet to regain our bearings. The recent events were too hot for us to handle. We were mentally and physically tortured. Sleepless nights became the new norm. And the days seemed to be as hollow as the ones before. Much to our disenchantment, despite our inner sufferings, words would still not come to our aid when we could rip a shred of time to spend together. Are we to fritter away our remaining days in hapless misery?

Chingnu and her family were leaving the following Monday. Only Sunday stood in the way now. As usual, we made time by the afternoon. After church service, we headed straight for our customary haunt. The countryside.

We both wanted to cheer up one another. But reality staring at our faces was too grim. Neither of us could launch a proper conversation. More of our time would pass in keeping our silences. Needless to say, we were busy with our own thoughts. Thoughts worth nothing to the world of the grownups but pregnant with stress and anxiety, meaning the world to us. After some prosaic tête-à-tête, Chingnu eventually managed to say something that made sense.

"Whatever be case, there's nothing we can do. We're mere children," she said. "We can only hope God will let us meet again someday."

"Of course," I simply agreed, having nothing more to add.

We went quiet again for a long moment. Then, she started again: "I hope you'll come to see us off at the bus-stand tomorrow?"

"No doubt about that!" I took her hands and stroked them lovingly as though to reassure her. "I am but afraid I would lose myself and make a fool of myself in front of everyone."

Before we could say many more things, the sun slipped behind the hills, and we had to call it a day.

Sleep had not entered my chamber ever since. Yet, that night was worse. Even a wink did not pass by. Cold sweat broke all over my face. Before I could realise, brackish streams of tears escaped from the corners of my eyes, drenching the pillows in a salty bath. With slumber nowhere in sight, I went adrift into the ocean of retrospection.

I didn't understand why I cried so hard. Had I really fallen in love with Chingnu? Call it pubertal infatuation. Call it puppy love. But I know it's down there, deep and hurting all the same. Yes, I was not a good judge even of myself yet. And neither I nor she had ever spelled the magic word loud. But does that mean she's not in love with me? No. It can't be. Every comport and conduct of her suggested that she was all over me. And she was fair, kind, perfect and flawless to my beholding. She's a seraph. My guardian angel. My love. And there's no reason why she should not love me too. Just suppose that she didn't love me. Then, why did she struggle so hard when she broke that obnoxious news to me? Why did she cry on my shoulder?

I found no reason to suspect that Chingnu did not love me too. I sighed. I tossed and turned. Only to drive sleep away farther. All through the night, more profound quests and salvos bombarded my waking brain. The oval clock on the wall chimed the small hours of the morning. A dull two ante-meridian. Sleep was still a far cry. Wriggling and writhing for an hour more. I at last tried to steal a wink so that the redness in the eyes did not betray me in the packed marketplace in the morning.

When I opened my eyes again, the sun was already dancing high on the eastern skies, flooding my tiny bedroom with a blazing splendour. My eyes felt sore. Lack of sleep had deadened my skull. I was a bit dizzy too. I strained my eyes to shut the pain and the blinding lights out. I gently tossed over, turning the glare on my back, grabbing an extra pillow and tucking it between my bended knees. The bouncy mattress and the cosy warmth of the morning sunshine instantly lulled me back to sleep.

Realisation dawned. I sprang out of bed as though a farm of needles had suddenly spurted out of the sheets. Whatever followed was a blur. I slipped into my pyjamas and, without bothering to brush my teeth or wash my face, raced towards the village bus stand as fast as my legs could carry me.

Alas, the morning hubbub had already died in the marketplace. Except for a few frequenters to the village tea stall wrangling out rustic philosophy and street politics, there were not many people to be seen loitering around. The morning activities had been done. And the villagers had already gone back to their homes, having hawked their wares and seen off whoever they had to travelling to town. The bus had long gone. I could see in the distance some villagers beginning to head for their fields. They were early starters. The day's work had begun.

Leaning on a wooden signpost, I simply watched the direction where the bus had taken off. Tears started brimming in my eyes. But what am I crying for? Everything's my fault. I had overslept. I've missed the bus. Chingnu must have craned her neck to see me run to her in the distance. Like in the movies, I guess. The problem is, we're not in the movies. And the bus didn't tarry till I appeared at the eleventh hour, waving desperately and calling out to wait. I wanted to break down on the spot itself. But what is the point of creating a scene now? No bus, no girl, not even a crowd to observe the melodrama!

I snivelled and straightened up, encouraging myself to be a man. My steps back home were exceedingly heavy. The pain in the chest was unspeakable. The tears seemed to come from a source that had no end. I was fully exhausted and crucified. How can fate be so cruel to me? I blamed God. I blamed destiny. I blamed everything and everyone but me. Yet inwardly, I knew it was I that should exclusively carry the cross.

I knew it was useless to cry over spilt milk. But the urge was too strong to resist. So, I freshened up, pulled over a random dress I could readily grab, and hurried to the end of the village where the bus had taken my beloved away.

At a certain vantage point, I sat the whole day watching the black meandering road, undulating and shimmering under the scorching sun. Sometimes I saw the bus returning back. Sometimes I saw it departing until it vanished into the bend behind a foothill. Every now and then, I got up on my feet and waved to the empty horizon wishing my love would look back and catch sight of me somehow. I could even see her smile at me as the bus turned a corner. But everything was a daydream. To be washed away by a profuse stream of tears and bring me back to reality. I was standing alone on a hilltop, watching the empty highway and waving stupidly at the open space.

With a very heavy heart, I waved yet again before I turned around and decided to leave the place.

As I came home, I learned that the departing family had left behind many household items. That gave me a glimmer of hope. I might see Chingnu once again, not in the distant future. However, fate chose to play hostile with me. The flickering light blew away when an elderly relative of theirs came to collect their remains. And decamped before I could approach him for a lifeline—their address.

I still held on to my optimism. They say positivity could work wonders. I was hopeful and, of course, praying that Chingnu would write me, telling me everything and how she does in her new surroundings. We have never exchanged missives before. The need simply didn't arise. Now, we're living great distances apart. There's no way of getting in touch except through the medium of squiggles. Only one thing bothered me. Would Chingnu care to drop me a note?

Till that all-important first letter makes its way, I couldn't help but dabble in the mire of wistfulness and perpetual yearning.

To state the obvious, I shall never be able to efface the moments we spent together with my dear Chingnu. They were golden memories etched deep on the granite slab of my heart. The paths we trod every morning to school and back in the afternoon. The sombre shades beneath which we played the entire Sundays and holidays.

Until eventide and the slanting rays of the sun would drive us home. How can I forget the orange aura that bathed the western skies when we tried to comfort one another without uttering a word? The sand-filled courtyard and the fragrance of citrus trees that filled the night air as we shuttled back and forth between our homes. The trumpets of morning glory in the midst of wild creepers along the dirt tracks, blossoming at their best as though to draw our admiration—but faded now! Chingnu's laughter at my stupid jokes and naughty disses that still hung in the air. It seemed just the other day. But they were mere memories now. Gone. Never to return.

They say time is a great healer. Ironically though, it was its very passage that made the memories sharper and the heart grow fonder. To me, time is a great killer. The pang of separation was as painful as the day it happened. The sweet reminiscences only added fuel to the agony, reliving every detail with the change of seasons. And I still wondered whether I really loved her or she me.

The earth seemed to stand still ever since. Yet, the sun had not stopped following the natural laws, rising in the morning and setting in the evening. My sense of judgment and awareness might be clouded and erratic, but time and tide operated as they logically should. Time had decided to pull on somehow without me or my concern.

Now, things have come to such a pass that when everything seems to have been lost, nature does have more surprises to spring. My joy knew no bounds when, one late evening, my father came home bearing the news that he was transferred, too. Actually, he had been petitioning for the last few years. He has hungered for a change of environment. He had longed to spend time with his near and dear ones in the town before the sun set on his service. And now, after long overdue, here he is. Transferred to Lamka! Can you believe it? I wanted to dance and prance. My face lit up literally, smiles cutting from ear to ear. And mothers, they never missed the change in their children's behaviours.

"Thank God, you're coming alive again," my mother said, noticing my ill-concealed joy.

"Yes, mother," I answered. "I had long wanted to experience life in Lamka."

I need not mention that Chingnu would be waiting there for me. She knew it. But did she know the true colour of my feelings? If she had known, would she approve of it? That's even vaguer. However, I think she was happy to see me happy again. And that's all that matters for now.

"Town life can be treacherous," she said. Obviously, she was not as eager as us to leave the village behind. But my ears were too thrilled to listen to her at that moment. My heart was blazing with the prospect of seeing my—shall I say—beloved once again.

*

Some people may call it a coincidence. I was tempted to take it that way too. But on pondering with a clearer mind, I thought even God had regretted the way he had wronged us all this while. Perhaps he wanted to make amends so that we don't gripe at him forever. And what was that wonder that inspired me to thank God so profusely?

As luck would have it—I couldn't avoid the figure of speech, although I believe it was more a godsent than just a passing luck—we happened to live in close vicinity of Chingnu's family again! Of course not, we are in spitting distance any more. 'At a stone's throw' would probably be a more accurate description now. But ours was not a huge locality. I could trace out Chingnu's abode without much effort. Is it any wonder that a powerful magnet should naturally attract another oppositely charged magnet, and they would eventually stick together?

I'd thought Chingnu would be mad at me and refuse to talk to me for my not seeing her off several years ago. I didn't even have an alibi. It was embarrassing. But Chingnu had not changed a bit. She was as caring and understanding as she always was. She was equally shocked with joy and surprise to see me and to learn the fact that we were settling in close proximity. Her eyes misted when I recalled the anguish and torment I had undergone since she left the village.

We're on track again.

Now that we're attaining early adulthood, our meetings have become courtships. And when a man pays a visit to a woman, it is called wooing. But to us, all these social mores and implications seemed to carry no weight. Whenever we got together, the clock would turn back on its own, and we would relapse back into bouts of bickering, cackling, and taunting like the little children we had been. The difference being we took no interest in dirt and mud castles anymore. In their place, we would indulge in buying one another trinkets and sweetmeats, treating one another to lunches and dinners, and all those grownup stuff. And, of course, we refrained from holding hands as we used to as tiny tots. That was unnecessary, and we also became a tad conscious about the very act.

Knowing that we're back to the good old days, my presumption that Chingnu feels the same for me as I did for her resurfaced. So, I had no intention of verbally enunciating the old news. It would blush her unnecessarily and render the situation awkward. It's sheerly superfluous, I guessed.

Days passed.

Weeks turned into months. And months into years.

For me, happy days were back. And I wished life stayed that way forever. All those years of pain and torture were now being healed and soothed. Rosy sunrises took their place every morning. The pattering rains became a harmonious rhythm matching well with the beat of my heart. Thunders clapping in the distance sounded as periodic percussions for the elemental melodies. Lingering fogs and monsoon drizzles were but reminders of our small village where we spent whole days indoors singing nursery rhymes like *Rain, rain, go away...* and wishing for the sun to break through the clouds.

Then, come a certain December. Yuletide was approaching. And the excitement inside me was threatening to blow the roof away.

On the other side, Chingnu seemed to lately develop a strange tendency. She had started throwing tantrums, behaving rather childishly and easily lost herself. She had never done those things before. She must be up to something, I speculated. And she was, in fact, treated like a child in her family. Apparently, for being the younger of the two siblings. That makes all her conduct understandable in a way, straight or aberrant. She was making the most of it probably for some reason. She even started avoiding me, playing truant on occasions more than one. But when we could make up again, her ready giggles and disarming smiles would put all my budding doubts and suspicions to rest. Most probably, she was planning a surprise for me, and she did not want me to get wind of it.

I began to visit her more frequently, though. It was holiday season, and we had plenty of time in our hands. There was no hurry. No pressure. Oftentimes, Chingnu would leave me behind to run her personal errands. "I had to go alone!" she would always say, refusing the company which I never failed to offer. And when I asked where she was going, she would simply reply, "I cannot tell you now but will sooner or later."

"Better be sooner," I thought to myself with a self-satisfied grin. That was what convinced and reassured me that she was brewing a surprise. Solely for my pleasure, of course. I could not wait for it. I was tickling all over to think what she would get for me. I was all smiles all the way every day.

To heighten the excitement, I decided to play my little part. I pulled together my savings and proposed a midnight party at Chingnu's on the Christmas Eve. Chingnu was as excited as any of us.

We extended our invitations to everyone—my friends, her friends and even her sister's friends.

Days seemed to suddenly crawl at a snail's pace. I was on needles and pins, unable to keep my calm, too eager for the auspicious day to come. Chingnu seemed to drift farther apart lately. She often seemed unfocussed and avoiding my company.

"It's only a surprise. Not a wedding," I wanted to think when frustration threatened to have the better of me. She was no doubt affable. Cheery up to the neck when we did manage to catch up. But she ceased sparing as much time as I would like her to. She seemed busy and occupied all the time. What is she really up to?

The awaited day ultimately dawned. Chingnu was at home, all right. We spent the day shopping and preparing for the night's party. Her preparations seemed to have all been set. She was calm and composed. She giggled and guffawed at my jokes again. What could be the surprise? I couldn't stop surmising. Much less wait!

Night fell. All friends and invitees descended upon Chingnu's abode. Winter nights mature very soon in the hills. But it was only eight yet. The party has to wait for some more time.

Hustles, murmurs and asides rose. Just then, a certain guy who was unable to keep his excitement to himself happened to hit the music. The gathering at once started to groove. Drinks began to do the rounds. I mean soft drinks. You cannot splurge on hard drinks in your girlfriend's house. And the good news is that no one in the crowd insisted on having one. Not that they had not taken to the habit, but out of propriety and decorum given the situation.

In eastern regions like ours, dinners are early. And by half past nine, our tummies are grumbling again already. Fritters, crackers, fizzes and light delicacies passed around liberally. We talked, we joked, we flirted and coquetted. The environment is building up all right. It would soon be midnight.

Chingnu's sister and I were playing hosts while Chingnu was conspicuous by her absence. I did not consider it an anomaly. Instead, I was secretly anticipating she would turn up at the right moment with all that in her mind. I would stand in for her whenever friends threw inquisitive queries, bearing her absence with a grin.

However, I began to feel ill at ease when the clock was about pushing midnight. I started making secretive enquiries of my own. Her sister told me that an immediate friend of hers had arrived late yesterday. And she has probably gone to fetch that friend.

"Don't you worry," she reassured me. "She'll turn up on the dot.

It's hardly eleven."

We're hitting midnight, I reminded her inwardly. Aloud I said nothing but rested assured. I lifted a glass of mocktail and drank to the upcoming surprise.

Minutes ticked on. Winter nights are long and hard to wait. But nobody seemed to mind. And there was still no trace of the hostess. Nobody seemed to mind that too. Just then, the clink of a spoon against a glass tumbler drew everybody's attention. Hush fell like a drape of satin.

It was Betsy, Chingnu's sister, playing the hostess. Now, in the absence of her little sister in whose name the party was thrown, she proposed an impromptu amusement item. "Listen up, guys!" she cried with a wide smile. "As we're approaching the turn of midnight, why not crank up the excitement even more...."

And to kick off the extempore exercise, she uncorked a bottle of imitation champagne and raised a toast. Cheers and whoops ensued. Then, complying with the proposition, boys and girls would be forced to couple up in random pairs before they were shoved to the dance floor to gyrate to a blind track. Some pairs would sync up so well, like they had been practicing for this moment a long time. Yet, most of them couldn't match their steps and goofed up so badly that they made us hold our sides and double up on the ground with merriment. And that was exactly what Betsy had in mind. The night was rolling on well!

Slowly yet surely, time had inched to the other side of the night. And I began to get more restive. The first roosters would soon be crowing. True to the yuletide fervour, loudspeakers from somewhere afar would soon be blaring traditional Christmas solos and carols in the foggy dawn that was yet to break. And some folks, sleepless in their burning enthusiasm, would roam the hazy twilight streets and call out 'Merry Christmas! A Saviour is born unto us!'

Inside me, a deep sense of resentment and humiliation was beginning to take shape. I was confused and hot. The partiers would soon be rounding up and wending their ways. Most of them in pairs. Am I to leave now as no mate would be giving me company anyway? Am I to stay behind and help clean up the party mess? Had Chingnu fallen sick somehow and locked herself up in her room without letting me know lest the entire mood of the night be spoiled? Something is not going right at all. Very wrong, in fact. Everything amiss indeed from the very start of the revelry.

The revellers started crashing on the sofa sets one after another, done and beat for the whole night's jazz. But the mirth and gaiety were still hanging in the air. They laughed, drank, ate, and partied a little more.

At that juncture, a strong urge of nature's call came over me. As I stole away to take a leak outside—our houses are traditionally not attached to restrooms—I had to pass by Chingnu's boudoir. I am not a habitual voyeur. But I couldn't stop myself that day from taking a peek into her casement. All I wanted was to make sure Chingnu was not lying on the bed sick and indisposed.

The window pane was frosted with the morning vapour. The glass creaked as I wiped it clean. Then cupping my face with both palms, I scanned the dimly lit room to see if Chingnu was slumbering on the bed. Or, in a worst-case scenario, sprawling on the floor, out cold and unconscious. Nothing of such sort encountered my sight, though.

I panned slowly to make sure I did not miss any crucial evidence. The vision was poor. But something beneath the *Kurl-on* pillow caught my eyes. The room was washed in a subdued gleam under the dim zero-watt lightbulb. I strained my eyes, pulling the focus. It was a neatly folded paper protruding from under the edge of the padding. What was that? It is not my nature to spy on anybody, much less my friends, especially my girl-friend. Lady-friend might be a more appropriate term now, I guess. But the curiosity was too strong to fight. A sort of sixth sense instigated me to go ahead and make a more thorough investigation. I succumbed.

I tiptoed back into the house and snuck between the bedroom door as unobtrusively as possible. With a gentle prod of the foot, the door gave way. There was no ghostly creak that doors are notoriously known to do in horror movies. The hinges were well-oiled. Nudging it ajar, I skipped into the room and closed the door behind me.

In two big strides, I made it to the bedside and dislodged the chit from under the pillow. A pang of hesitation shot me somewhere on the left chest. I vacillated. What am I doing? Spying on my girlfriend? I was ashamed of myself. But I was already deep in the probing shit. I took a long breath and made up my mind.

Slowly, I unfurled the leaf, brought it closer to the low-wattage bulb, and read. A terrible ache hit me on the head. My heart was pummelling furiously against the ribcage. Sweat seeped through the pores of every single hair, percolating the flimsy vest under my thick fur coat.

...*and a diamond for my dearest love*...

My hands began to tremble. I could not dispute the fact that diamonds are woman's best friend. I could read no further. The words began to dance bizarrely until they became unreadable. And the lines began to blur until they ran out of sight altogether. Tears covered up my eyes, preventing me from taking another blow from the merciless despatch.

I returned the letter exactly as I found it. Then, I slipped out of the room. Not as carefully as I slipped in, though. I did not mind if I was caught in the act anymore. So shocked was I that a milder emotional expression like anger did not have a place.

How adroitly had Chingnu kept her true self from me! She deserved at least Bollywood's Black Lady, if not the Oscar. I was now at my wit's end. What was all that bond and companionship I thought we had shared? Was she pulling the wool over my face for all these years? Did she ever love me? Was I too presumptuous in the first place? How did she manage to pull the feat so well? What about the puddle in her eyes when she told me that her mother had been transferred? Was she avenging herself for the pain and mortification I'd caused her by oversleeping many years ago? Why, why, why? I was staring blankly into the empty space. Yet again.

My mother's voice returned to my ears. I think I now learnt the true import of the wisdom in her words. Town life is indeed treacherous.

The night was almost over. Partiers began to fly away in pairs to take in the crisp morning air. But I just couldn't excuse myself at that ungodly hour. I simply slumped on the springy settee, throwing my arms behind the back of my head, leaving one leg on the ground, and pretending to steal a couple of forty winks.

Seeing me so unbecomingly splayed, Betsy came over, picked up my leg and set it straight on the upholstery. She must be thinking I was asleep. I didn't bother to stir.

She gently whispered: "Sleep! You must be tired!"

—Published in the fortnightly North East Sun, 1995

Chapter 6

THE UNSIGNED LETTER

Several weeks have flown since our school reopened after the summer break. But we were still without a science teacher. The old teacher, who'd taught for hardly a year, had refused to turn up after the vacation for reasons best known to him. He had not had a good relationship with us anyway. No wonder.

Two more weeks later, the face of our new teacher appeared. We had expected a dapper, classy young guy because he was to be our homeroom teacher. We called it class-master. His face was roundish and dark, like a cloud pocket on a dreary day. However, he had a constant smile playing on his lips as though trying to win us over. That doesn't make him any handsomer though. His nose seemed a little too peculiar, no much of a curve, and terminating abruptly in a bulbous end from where it flared out like a brass horn. His eyes were deep-set, sharp and penetrating like an eagle's. Not to overstate, a mere glance from them could send tremors down the spine. His lips were thick purple meat. Perhaps, he has turned up after receiving a few rounds of punches from a roadside boxer. Despite his disagreeable features, he did radiate a perpetual smile and warmth that was disarming and intriguing at the same time. A saying I heard somewhere rang in my ears: "A man may smile, and smile, and still be a villain." Years later, somebody told me that was Hamlet, and I was quoting him my own way.

To say the least, we, the entire class, were dismayed.

It didn't take long for him to make an impression, though. He's no doubt at home and supremely well-versed in his subject. He could've been a Newton or an Einstein in the right place at the right time. Besides, he spoke an imitation American accent, imperfect though it might be. Where he learnt to speak like that nobody knows. But that was our consolation, at least. Being the 'brightest' student of the class, I at once took it upon myself and gave him a name: Hippolips, borrowed from the hippopotamus.

I couldn't get enough of describing his appearance: He was short-statured. The lack of height being gravely accentuated by a grotesquely protruding paunch. On top of that, he was tanned. Blacker than the blackest nigger, as I put to my class's delight.

Usually, we—the top standard gangs—counted on the person's looks and physical refinements for obeisance. This Hippolips could never court such obligations. He was too far from pleasing.

Regardless of our disappointment with his outward appearance, the classes had to roll on.

We would indulge in asides and snickers more to distract him than to amuse ourselves. Hippolips would kindly plead for our attention and cooperation. We paid him back with more trolls and abuses. I, being the ringleader, would often whisper nonsense into my benchmates' ears, sending them down with shivers of laughter. That's how we passed the initial few days.

About a week later, Hippolips decided to get down to business. He asked me to my feet and told me to call out my name for all to hear. Of course, with that repulsive grin cutting his face from ear to ear. It was insulting.

"What good's my name gonna do you?" I aped his drawl. The whole class burst into a peal of laughter.

"Awright," Hippolips reconsidered, still smiling though, "if you minded so much." He allowed me to reclaim my seat.

The ladies were not to be outdone.

One day, he happened to spare them a mild reproach for using the mother tongue in communicating among themselves: "Girls, you're supposed to speak only English in the school."

"Hah! We're just supposed to," Gracie, the school's beauty queen, retorted with candid scorn. "We don't speak English like you, Sir!"

Hippolips could only gape in amazement at such blatant audacity. He seemed to lose it for a moment. But in seconds, he recovered, and the familiar beam broke through again like sunshine between two black clouds. "You must learn, girls."

Then, he slowly walked away from them, arms locked behind the back.

Hippolips dealt with us severely alright if we didn't perform in his subject or neglected his class. But he would never take offense with our jeers and sneers, even those that grazed upon his person and character. Rather, he would laugh equally heartily as though the cruel jokes were never shot at him. He never returned the mockeries or took anybody as objects of his reprisal.

Perhaps blinded by hero worship and youthful lust for good looks, we never cared to notice the humanity hidden within this new teacher. We would be brutally critical of him, prising the tiniest cracks for faults and throwing him the most unreasonable jests. Even when we couldn't find one, we would still complain that his way of speaking English was too flamboyant. "Over-pompous for a simple school like ours," as we would sarcastically put.

Surprisingly though, despite our disregard for him, we did pretty well in his subject. Umm, well, the pronoun 'we' might be a little overextended here. For to admit, it doesn't always include me. Actually, I wasn't the brightest student as you'll see down the line. Yet, I do brag that even I, too, did improve considerably in his subject.

And it came to such a pass that, over time, some students began to warm up to his easy way of putting his points across. Some girls even started singing his praise. That was certainly not to my fancy. I admit he's had a way with girls. But that way should never cross paths with Gracie's. I had secretly kept that on my preserve.

I began to sense dislike welling up from the pit of my stomach. Try as I might, I couldn't curry favour or any rapport with him. He did award me two canes. I didn't mind them. They were for my own poor conduct and performance in the tests. But some indescribable detestation fermented inside me, instigating me to have him out of the school. Was it his ugliness? Was it his fluency? Was it his indifferent poise? Was it his mesmerising skills for winning hearts, especially those of the female species of the class? Or, boy, was I jealous?

I couldn't afford to be jealous. He was simply above my station and envy. I did resent his winning ways with girls, especially that secret interest of mine. But I think that was not the only reason. Or was it?

One day, Hippolips was talking about resistance in the class. What resistance? I didn't care. I just got up and called out of context: "Sir, what's the difference between electrical resistance and political resistance?"

I just wanted him empurpled and shout at me. That would give me the pretext to kick him out of the school and of course, my life. He stared at me in silence. I thought I had struck the bull's eye. Then, the pouty lips slowly contorted into that repugnant smirk.

"You'll make a famous critic," he said nonchalantly.

What he meant by that I couldn't make out till this day. Was it meant to be a sarcasm? Was it a harmless remark just to avert a confrontation? Or did he mean I could really become one?

The whole class tittered. They knew my temper and the length I could go to vent it. That prevented them from having a proper laugh.

But my plan had backfired. I ended up at the receiving end of the joke. My face turned red, burning with embarrassment.

"Critter," I swore under my breath. "You'll pay for this!"

If Hippolips had loathe for me or anybody else, for that matter, he never let it show. Rather, he would treat us equally well, without any partiality, I must admit. But when my mates started striking up conversations with him, I would keep my distance in silent protest against their drawing too near to him. I believe he was fully aware of my disdain for him. But his expression or tone would never betray a negative sentiment. He was calm and composed, elegant even, as I couldn't help but admit in hindsight. Instead, he would carry himself assuredly unaware of the antipathies running wild inside my head. He would never treat me differently. Rather, in spite of my not-so-well concealed cold-shoulderings he would make sure I was never left out in the chat sessions we often had in the classrooms or on the school lawns.

A priggish snob that I was, I took all that indifference as an insult heaped upon my face. Truth be told. He did birch me the third time a few days ago. I'd got red marks all over my papers in the last term.

I had purposefully flunked it. Not that I would make it with excellence even had I wanted to. I might be known as the 'brightest' student of the class. But that doesn't mean I was indeed. There were ways more than one to bag the status. Bullying, for example, which I found quite easy and self-fulfilling. It always elicited the desired results. I know I could never be that guy in the proper sense of the term, no matter how hard I try.

One fine day, as everybody seemed to be in a light mood, I decided to take another chance.

I rose to my feet and cried: "Sir, almost a few months have gone since you've joined. But we still don't know your proper name other than Hippolips?"

A few laughed.

"Oh, aw—it's Simon," he said with his typical nasal drawl.

"Simon," I repeated in a contemptuous repartee. "Simon, the Fisher?"

My sardonic pranks seemed to wear off in time. Only a few more laughed. Anyway, I was pleased enough to see him uncomfortable under his shirt. I grinned naughtily in satisfaction.

Just then, the Principal happened to pass by on his routine round. As was his custom, he would take a peek into every classroom. Ours was not an exception. He turned his head and caught me with my wide elfish grin. I was caught red-handed. Inside a minute, we're in his chamber for a cup of tea.

The Principal was obviously restraining himself, afraid to lose it. Good for me, he happened to be no strict disciplinarian. However, the pitch in his voice and his body language told me that I was long on the list marked for 'disciplining.'

I was not unaware of the scarlet letter pinned on my character and the overdue chastisement. But I chose to play it down since there was nothing I could do to help it. Between gritted teeth, the Principal presently gave me a large dose of his mind and a crash course on how to carry myself in the class, with elders and teachers, and everywhere in general. A full half hour later, I was let off with a strong advice and caution.

Whew! Escaped corporal punishment which I fully expected. I blew a sigh of relief. For now, at least.

Then, aha, a realisation suddenly dawned. So Hippolips had been taking things to the authorities all this while, eh? That's why he could laugh all the jokes off as though they had never meant shit to him? I nodded to myself. My mind instantly went overdrive, mentally putting together ways and means to square the score.

*

Monsoon had long arrived. Days were endless drizzles. It was late in August.

One overcast night, as was usual with the rainy season, the heavens opened and poured cats and dogs. The invitation of a cosy bed was very hard to fight back. But I had set up a meeting with an obscure local gang at some undisclosed downtown location.

Presently, I was waiting in a certain back alley under the dripping rain, parasol in hand. Let alone the backstreets, the entire town had gone out of lighting. It is a normal in this sleepy town for the power supply to go bust at the slightest hint of rain or foul weather. Silent bursts of lightning with occasional thunderclaps made for the only sources of illumination.

Right at the appointed hour, a dark figure detached itself from the shadows at the other end of the alley. It was unmistakable. About three or four shadowy figures followed close behind him. They had no umbrellas. They just walked towards me as though the monsoon was not in spate. I had doubted they would turn up at all. I kept my side of the word simply because I did not want to be the defaulting party. Otherwise, the call of my snugly bed was extremely seductive.

It's good that they kept their part of the appointment, too.

Not to keep the reader in the dark, let me tell right away what's really going on down here.

I had contracted these local thugs to set upon Hippolips. To teach him a little lesson so that he would take to his heels of his own volition. I had thought they were just plain muggers, ready to pounce on everything with the lure of money. Ironically though, they seemed to act only with a motive. Is there really what Jeffery Archer, the English pulp fiction writer, called 'Honour Among Thieves'?

The dark figure walked up in silence. His oversized hoody made him appear more ominous than he really was. He thrust his hand out and grunted two monosyllables: "Who? Why?"

Slapping the cash wrapped in a manila envelope which, I could feel, was soaked already on his outstretched palm, I described the target. As for the second question, I hesitated.

"No reason," I just mumbled.

"We may be goondas alright, but we're no sons of bitches." The gangster's voice was gruffy. "We don't tick off at will."

They might be little-known, but they seemed to mean business. That's promising, I thought to myself.

My three canings did not warrant avengement. I did really deserve them. But I needed an excuse. It was lame. Yet, I must exploit it to serve my purpose to the hilt. The goons bit it and asked no further questions.

"But his life must be spared," I cried after them as they turned their backs to me. "I only want him pissed off."

*

For a good number of days that followed, things returned to normalcy. My friends were back around me like moths to the flame. My jokes began to get funny again. I felt a lump lifted from my chest. I was lightheaded from the sparkling wine of joy.

However, as though to prove the saying 'every good thing has to come to an end' true, my relief soon turned into dismay. That was about a month later.

As we're at our naughty selves, pulling and pushing around in the corridor on the second floor, waiting for the first bell to go, a commotion at the northern end of the campus suddenly drew our attention. Hippolips was laming through the school gates in crutches and concealed bandages. Teachers and students were already forming a crowd around him.

We galloped down the stairs. In truth, I was tagging along only because the school's beauty queen was the first to hurry away. Being the big boys and girls of the school, we found no difficulty in getting into the inner circle.

"Awmigawd," exclaimed Gracie on seeing the teacher's plight. Hippolips's charm seemed to rub off on her for real. "What's hap'nin', Sir?" She even started emulating his style of speaking. I revolted inwardly.

"Heh, heh, it's nuthin'," Hippolips chuckled. "Just a mild mishap. C'mon…"

*

"John, you've forgotten to respond to your roll number."

I was brought up in a start when that son-of-a-gun-who-refused-to-go-away-from-my-life called aloud.

In my bewilderment, I had lost all my consciousness: not knowing when we went away from the entrance gate and back to the classroom, not remembering the bell go, not aware of having attended the morning assembly nor when it ended. I didn't even know when the class had started. I was in sheer automaton mode.

I was anticipating a furious blow from the silver crutches leaning on the side of his chair. Yet, a gentle voice still rang out from his mouth. That seemed to strike something inside my heart. I thought I saw a pool of tears hiding beneath those sockets, now staring at me knowingly. Accusingly, as I rather felt. That was kind of disconcerting. Were they tears of suppressed rage? Was that fury waiting for payback time? How could he still check his temper after such agony?

The class had not proceeded beyond the roll call when the Principal knocked on the classroom door and whisked Hippolips away. I shadowed them with the intention of eavesdropping upon their discussion. They were already done with the pleasantries when I managed to tiptoe up to the office's oaken door.

"It's really appreciable you turned up after all this," the Principal lauded. "But I think you better recover fully…"

"It's just a matter of time, Princy Sir," Hippolips replied. "I'm never fitter, you see."

I could see in my mind's eyes Hippolips flexing his arms and stretching his legs to prove his point.

"Yet, you still need to rest," the boss insisted. "If you're feeling embarrassed to ask for leave, don't. I stand your guarantee."

"I'm really okay, Sir," Hippolips maintained. "I cannot allow my classes to run behind. Moreover, the selection exams will soon be round the corner."

The conversation went on that way for a while, the same points going back and forth. One insisting on more breather to sufficiently recoup and the other persisting to be in fine fettle, fit enough to work and stressing the paramountcy of covering the syllabus. I think the school was insisting on longer respite because it did not want to bear responsibility would there be any relapse in Hippolips's condition.

I was about letting my guard down and walk off when I suddenly sensed a shift in the topic.

"By the way," said the Principal in a casual note, "what do you think of that boy—uh, what was his name—John?"

Ceramic cup grating against ceramic saucer nearly drowned the response. The Principal was draining his cup of tea. Audio signals are not great through partitions. I pressed my ear harder to the wooden block. It may be a routine query on the part of the headmaster. But to me, it was Fat Man on Nagasaki. My heart leapt a foot. I had snooped on them, anticipating that their chat would somehow veer around me in due course. Now that my name was taken, it shook me up no less as though I had never expected it.

Had they discovered my conspiracy? Had they got wind to hold me suspect? Had Hippolips somehow found out who sent the hounds after him? Thoughts began to run berserk inside my little head. I always thought it was a foolproof plan. Was the case cracked somehow? Were there traitors among the gangsters?

My fingers began to tremble. My skull felt like the size of a chicken coop and still growing.

"Well," Simon drawled, "he, um...he's not a bad boy, I must say—"

His deliberative speech mannerism drove the stake of terror deep into my core. Was he a wolf in sheep's clothing? Was he really a saint incapable of evil thoughts? Was he a cold calculator? Was he goodness personified? My chain of thoughts was shattered, losing coherence by the second.

Simon continued. "Despite his ill manners, I think he's got no bad heart. He could do very well if we could instil in him the right will and determination."

Before I could make anything out of Simon's reply, hot streams began to roll down my cheeks. *Sir,* I prayed silently, *why don't you hate me too, as I hated you so much?*

I stopped bugging at once and rushed back to the classroom. Could that hideous creature be anything but evil? Was he taking the authorities for a ride so that no eyebrows would be raised when he executed his cold scheme? Could you really trust him? *A man may smile, and smile...* Hamlet re-rang in my ears.

Years later, an old classmate reminded me that I was cringing in the corner of the bench like a threatened mouse for the whole day, lost in thought, eyes fixed on empty space. "We thought you had gone mad," he taunted. My old self was well past by then. So, I took the teaser in a good stride.

*

Not a day passed that I did not fight with the devils inside my head. For some reason, I started addressing Hippolips with more respect. I even called him 'Sir' to astound my circle of chaps. I hardly addressed him so. For the seldom occasions that I did, they were compulsions of the situations. Some teachers even started praising me for the improvement in my behaviour although I never consciously tried so. Before I could make out what's really gone into me, I, began to feel that this guy was going to do me some good turn which I could never repay in my life.

My readers would not be incorrect to guess that my marks and grades were consistently poor. I believed I wasn't much of a bad boy. I never held myself poor in studies either, despite having never excelled in them. Above average, as I would always score myself. But the school thought otherwise.

Now, as luck—or bad luck rather—would have it, I was suddenly taken ill by a nasty bout of flu. My body ached all over as though thoroughly pounded with a heavy piece of log. A slight toss, even on a six-inch mattress, was a pain. My head thumped continually as though it would soon split into smithereens. There was an almost solid blockage in the nasal cavity. Full breaths come only with huge efforts. My eyes burned intensely, getting bloodshot due to lack of sleep. My mouth was bone-dry and bitter. Not a scrap of food nor a sip of water went down without being forced. With complete loss of appetite, I began to lose weight fast. In no time, 1 could feel skeletal lines beginning to hint across the ribcage.

The doctor had diagnosed complications. But he would confide only with my parents. From the hushed tones, though, I could somehow make that my sickness was more than a mere flu.

In such a circumstance, I spent several weeks in torture and agony. To make things worse, selection tests for the board exams were beginning to peep round the corner. As for me, who couldn't even prop himself up to read, taking the tests became a question out of tune.

My worried parents went to the Principal to plead my case, armed with full medical reports. But he wouldn't hear of them one bit. I understand. He had never been my admirer, to say the least. It was only my longstanding studentship that retained me in the school. I often boasted that I was the oldest student in the school—from nursery to class ten! No breaks. No school hopping. Regardless of repeating some classes, I must add with a pinch of embarrassment.

To wash his hands, the Principal referred my parents to the managing board. But no board member would take a different stand to show solidarity and integrity. They said they trusted the Principal's sense of justice and fair play when it comes to matters academic and daily administration. In short, I was not allowed to take the exams under any circumstances.

I never saw my father lose a tear. My mother, ah, what should I say? She's a woman, after all. Tears are women's readiest weapon. When they came home that day, I noticed a crack in my father's voice, punctuated with soft sniffles that he somehow tried to keep under wraps.

"I've never felt so helpless—" he muttered, taking deep, jagged inhalations.

My mother had no words. She could only give him a hug if that should be of any comfort. I could hear them both sinking into gentle sobs. "Things might have been different," wished my father with a sigh, "had our son been a little better in his studies!"

It suddenly came to dawn upon me that I had badly disappointed my parents. In fact, such a thought had never occurred to me before. I made a quick reflection of my life and found no moment to make me a son to be proud of. How many times had my mother tried to lift me up with wings of towering hopes and dreams for me? I have failed her utterly. A searing pain tore through my heart, shooting guilty holes into it. I wanted to scream. But everything was gone and done. I could not take back time. I could see my future only in shambles. Not a drop of tear came to relieve my agony. I cursed myself.

As I was desperately contemplating on what to do with this useless life, a soft knock on the door came to distract me. My parents quickly turned around like shy lovers caught in an emotional tangle. My mother, still snivelling, dried her eyes on her sleeves as she walked across to get the door.

"Hallo, Madam!"

I couldn't see the visitor, but his voice was unmistakable. It was Hippolips. I mean, Sir Simon.

"Hi, Simon Sir..." My mother stammered. "What brings you here? Please come in."

Seeing moisture in my mother's eyes, Simon seemed to be a little apprehensive. "Is everything okay, Madam?" he said, still in the doorway. "I hope I'm not making the wrong time."

"No, not at all," my mother solicited him in. "Please!"

Nobody called me up except for one or two that I termed friends. Not one teacher enquired after my health or welfare, in fact. I wasn't surprised, though. But now, somebody I never cared to like had the heart to drop along.

In a moment, my parents and their guest made themselves comfortable. My mother presently vanished into the kitchen, rattled around for a while and reappeared with her best serving tray and glassware. It was *Manifru Squash*, the exquisitely sweet pineapple juice, the only product ever exported from our home state, Manipur, they say. And, for trivia, who was the importer? Russia! Urban legends had it that the Russkies loved the juice a lot until they felt it a little too sweetish. Upon lab-testing, it was said, they found an excessive dosage of sugar in it. And the export stopped. Whether there was any truth in that buzz, I never heard of it. I didn't care. I am simply digressing to lighten the air.

The engagement in the sitting room had seemed to normalise after the little awkward preliminaries. I drew closer to the partition that separated my room. The barrier was a thin plywood panel. So, I could hear them talk as though I was sitting in the study itself. A tad lower in volume, that's all.

"So," Simon said, clearing his throat. "How's John doing?"

"The doctor said he'll take another week to start recovering," my father informed, "I don't think he'll make it for the tests."

"That's exactly what I am here for," Simon leaned forward to return his glass. He seemed to like his drink. "I heard you met the Principal and the Board members?"

He smacked his lips in non-verbal appreciation of the sweet pineapple juice.

"They're right," my father said, sighing in resignation. "It's all our fault. We've failed to make a good son."

"Please, don't say that," Simon consoled. "I won't hear of my students left behind in that manner."

My heart suddenly raced. Was that really Simon, Sir? Perhaps, after all, he was not a potential cold=blooded murderer as I imagined him to be. I am not a good judge of character. But I can tell when a man speaks from the heart. Shame, guilt and hope rushed into my veins all at once, pumping extra blood into the heart, causing my face to flush. I could hear a furious throb from the pit of my stomach.

"It's still a couple of weeks more," Simon continued. "Let him get well and start preparing. I will talk to the Principal and the members."

My parents looked at each other. They did not believe their ears as much as I didn't mine.

"You're not giving us false hope, Sir Simon?" My father mumbled. "At least your words are balms to the ears."

"I'll not give up on my students," said Simon firmly. "I may not be able to change opinions. But is there any harm in trying?"

I could hear my father take deep, raspy breaths. My mother was unusually quiet. Simon Sir continued his soliloquy: "Let the young man give his best fight. And I will mine. The rest is in the hands of God. What's in despairing? Look at the brighter side and never give up. Whether I succeed in persuading the Principal or not is not important. What's important is that John should always be ready. Who knows the Principal is relenting as we speak! It is better to be prepared and not run than to run and be not prepared."

A teeny smile played on my lips. I know my parents didn't get the last sentence at all. The well-read teacher was merely rephrasing Whitney M. Young. I realised that Simon was reading not only his textbooks. I bit my lips to stifle the smile from breaking out into a silly chortle. I shook on my bed like a silly boy going sillier. My heart thumped with hope and exhilaration.

Such was the effect Simon Sir had on me that day.

Losing myself in the whirlpool of a newfound zest for life, I forgot to follow the conversation in the study. Only when the guest rose to take his leave I realised I was beyond myself. I pressed against the wood. One mysterious thing about this Simon was that he never asked to see me.

As if reading my mind, "My seeing him won't do him any good," he said as he was on his feet, "Let him just get well and get set for the race. It's gonna be tough ahead."

Fresh tears flowed down my temples as I cocked my ears on my sickbed. I could hear my parents thanking him profusely. His voice trailed off. The quiet thud of the door jolted me as though I was all the while in a reverie building castles in the air. Was I indeed dreaming? I don't care. Let the dream go on. I seldom had a dream so filled with hope and delight. I don't want to wake up.

All of a sudden, a feeling of deep respect for Sir Simon began to creep into my being. The ugly face suddenly turned into a promising ray of sunlight after a gloomy day. And his ever-present smile seemed to be a resplendent silver lining around the dark clouds of my purposeless life. I began to find hope in somebody I had considered a pest.

To cut the unnecessary details of the story, Simon Sir had indeed changed the opinion of the Principal and the board members. My faith in him, and of course, a deeply grateful heart, made my recovery a breeze. The doctor couldn't believe what happened. I got well soon enough to catch the exams in time. And I did well by the grace of everybody, unquestionably including God.

*

Along with the selection exams, the school's final semester also rounded up. Before long, we're staring at the end of the year. The winds had already grown nippy. The roadside stalls began to see a comeback of secondhand clothes.

In no time, the year drew up for the extravagant annual farewell programme: The event every student looked forward to, the event that's always celebrated with great pomp and fanfare.

Numbers—speeches, prizes, presentations, songs and dances—fleeted one after another in a blur. I used to be an attraction for years for reaso,ns good and bad. But this year, everything was different. Nothing was as exciting as before. I used to be an over-enthusiastic participant in everything, from planning to execution. There was no area my presence was not felt. Not that they were always helpful and appreciable. Yet this year, very uncharacteristic of me, I was a quiet spectator in one corner at the back of the makeshift hall. My friends thought I had not properly recovered from my sickness. And I believe the teachers would feel a sense of relief. They used to have more than they could handle of me and my mischievous antics. What I mean is, nobody paid me attention. Nobody cared.

I was invisible.

The itinerary wound up speedily till the much-awaited time for the presentation of the Student of the Year Award arrived. That was the main event. But it didn't excite me any better. All I wanted was for the items to round up fast and for I to steal away from everybody, if possible, without partaking in the refreshments that usually followed the gala.

I had suddenly become a stranger, even inside my friends circle. I felt every eye probing, seeking uncomfortable answers.

Answers only I knew.

The burden was weighing like lead inside my breast. I tried my best to put it behind me and pretend it never happened. But I am not a good pretender. The night always haunted me back. I had only wanted him thrashed, not killed or maimed. But the ruffians seemed to have had a handful of him. When we squared up the balance payment, Al Capone rued that the quarry was quite a hard target. He was strong and fought well, he admitted. Well, even a cornered rat would give his life to fight back. I had no words for that. And the safest way for them to get away uncaught was to break his leg and slow him down. They never thought the damage would be a major one.

Even with eyes wide open, I never saw the Principal take the stage. My mental rerun of where things went wrong had blinded me until I heard the familiar drone.

"This year's Award is extremely special," declared the Principal, sonority and resonance added to his voice by the sound system's bass boost and reverb. "Because, the winner is not decided by the Board as usually done." He paused for effect. "This year, the Board has decided to allow Sir Simon to choose his favourite as a mark of admiration and respect for his dedication and sincerity...."

The voice droned on with a 'little' speech. Little speeches are always too long on such occasions. I was fidgeting. I had wanted the event to get over and me to vanish into thin air or whatever. I did not want to leave in the middle and draw unnecessary attention. So, I just stayed put in my place, not squeaking once, not clapping once. Not that I did not want to. I simply seemed to forget to do so. By the way, to kill the boredom which only I felt, let me let the cat out of the bag: The Award normally goes to the tenth-standard students, which was us!

The audience applauded excessively as the Principal ended his long little speech and invited Sir Simon on stage.

Sir Simon walked up, awkward in his crutches. He was yet to get used to the props. It will take time. He hobbled to the centre of the stage. The Principal yodelled like Bruce Buffer, introducing the fighter from the red corner. "Siiiiiir...Simonnnnnnn....." He does deserve such an introduction, I guess.

The trophy dangling in one hand and a scroll in the other, Simon took the microphone as the headmaster made his exit. He tried to speak but swallowed hard. I felt a lump rise in my throat to see the metal struts which would probably stay with him forever.

Despite being smooth and persuasive with his subjects, he was certainly not a public speaker. He tried a few more opening words but only drew chuckles from parents and the more senior members of the audience. The few sentences he managed were poor and humble. He was erratic. Was he emotional? Was he trying to spill the beans but fumbling for milder, less destructive expressions? Or was it just the opposite? A fresh charge of fear sent shivers down my spine. *Don't speak, don't speak*, I incanted in my seat like a voodoo practitioner.

My prayers worked.

Without any further ado, and without any melodrama, he pronounced: "This year the award goes to…" The audience gasped in unison. Graveyard suspense.

"To—Mr. John of Class X."

Complete silence. I think a gentle gust of wind was sweeping across the silence like a visitation from the Holy Spirit.

Everybody looked at one another and exclaimed a silent 'huh?'

I think never before had an audience been so stunned with such precise simultaneousness and at the same degree. The silence didn't last though. Murmurs and whispers began to rustle among the crowd, building up, rising steadily in pitch and fever. Then, in a split second, a thunderous applause broke out. It was as though Niagara Falls had crashed into the hall with its full impact. Deafening cheers and whistles blew the roof away.

I couldn't believe my ears. God, I couldn't accept the award. I felt like floating in the air. I hated him until I loved him. No. But my bench mates had already pushed me off my seat. Much like a zombie, or rather like Dracula's vamps, I felt like gliding in the air towards the dais. *Lord*, I prayed audible to myself alone, *please forgive me*. I know I am incoherent. I was delirious.

My teardrops fell like rain that day, if I should borrow from Conway Twitty and Joni Lee's duet *Joni Don't Cry.*

I didn't know when I climbed the stage. I just mindlessly walked over to Sir Simon. Did I wave to the crowd? Did I smile? Did I bow to show my respect? All forms of etiquette escaped my senses at that moment in time. As Simon Sir handed me the trophy and shook my hands, I thought I saw a stringent line of tears stealing down behind his rimmed glasses.

"Sir, you don't know—" I tried a weak confession.

"I know," he interjected. "You remind me of my own days."

I let the mingled tears of joy and sorrow bleed freely as I said I love you to the ugliest yet most beautiful man in my life.

—*The Award goes to...*—

*

Several months later, the results of our High School Leaving Certificate Examinations were declared.

In those days, when technological marvels like the internet were yet to make penetration, we had to wait for the morning papers to see the results. The more impatient ones would wait for the newsboy in their porches. Those who could not afford to subscribe to one—most of us couldn't—we would throng the local tea stalls as early in the morning as possible to have a glimpse of the digital matrix printed across the pages. Some enterprising guys would sell cyclostyled copies for a rupee or two on the roadside or in local stationery stores.

As for me, I was not so keen to know how I fared. I could ill afford to be romantic. I was in no hurry. On my way to the tea shop, I came across boys in tears, some grumbling and complaining that they must have scored better. I did not know what to expect.

Since I could not get to see the result sheet myself, I passed a chit on which my number was scribbled to the nearest man. He was somewhat of an old-fashioned type, with his weakening eyesight, peering as close as possible and getting irritated when someone asked to share space. Fathers, as they're mostly jostled like school kids to steal a glance into the paper. My heart did not miss a beat. I was deadpan. Almost a minute later, the old man looked up, returned my chit, and mumbled: "Third Class!"

"What!"

We don't say 'class' anymore, you archaic relic! But aloud, I said 'thank you,' and took my leave.

By the way, am I to skip around in joy? Am I to break down in disappointment? I just walked back the way I came. No reaction. No sentiment. Only preoccupied with my own thoughts. Just then, something hit me in the head. "You've made it, man! You've made it!"

Yes, I have made it, although in the Gandhian division. I have come out with flying colours, nevertheless. I should be proud of myself. I have beaten the Board exams, which many people didn't. I have made it despite all odds! Nobody believed I would make it. Despite being bedridden, I got well just in time to take the test. All because of Simon Sir!

Simon Sir?

My God, I nearly forgot him in the outpouring of sentiments. I must go tell him. Of course, he deserved to know even before my parents. I turned back and headed straight for his house.

Passion rekindled inside my being. I suddenly realised the joy of success in the face of certain failures. Zeal and enthusiasm refilled my heart. The spring returned in my footsteps. I quickened them for a while until I broke into a sprint. By the time I reached the residence, I was out of breath, panting and sweating despite the cold morning air. I slowed down into a fast-paced walk.

"Sir! Sir!" I called out, hopping over a puddle on the dirt track across the fencing.

There was a small kitchen garden in the front yard. The landlord's wife was pinching some herbs. She stood up as she heard me rave and rant. A picture of a meerkat looking out for danger appeared in my mind's eye. I couldn't help but spare myself a little naughty smile.

"He's gone, boy!" she cried aloud to me.

I stopped in my tracks. "Wh..what do you mean, aunty?"

"It's more than a month since," the landlady called from where she was. "He's left lock stock and barrel."

"Did he leave any address?"

"I am afraid not," said she.

I was devastated. My spirit sank as quickly as it rose. Crestfallen, my hands started trembling slightly, and tears began to well up in my eyes. The landlady eyed me curiously. She seemed to get concerned, "But who are you, my young lad?" she inquired.

I told her who I was and why I was looking for him. Perhaps I was appealing to her pity enough that she recalled, "Ah, he did write us a thank you note a week after he left. Who cares to write thank you notes nowadays? A fine gentleman! That Simon." She put her task on hold. "Just wait here!" She said, disappearing into the house only to reappear not seconds later with a slip of paper in her hand. "I hope this is it and he still lives there."

I almost snatched it from her hands, and having nothing more than words to thank her, I expressed myself as effusively as possible until she had enough of me and sent me on my way.

Reaching home, I wrote my teacher my success, unable to string enough words to thank him and tell him that I owed him everything. And, of course, adding an oblique hint of confession that cumbered my heart for so long. It was rather a cheeky line expressing sympathy. All my guts taken together could not give me enough courage to make a clean breast of it. Once a coward, always a coward. That's me.

*

Months later, I received an unexpected letter in which the writer said he had obtained an esteemed job in the public sector under a handicapped category. He extended his heartfelt thanks to those who crippled him.

The letter was unsigned!

—*This story appeared in the North East Sun, a fortnightly magazine from New Delhi, in its Oct. 1-14, 1997 issue.*

You Write. We Publish.

To publish your own book, contact us.

We publish poetry collections, short story collections, novellas and novels.

contact@thewriteorder.com
Instagram- thewriteorder
www.facebook.com/thewriteorder

www.ingramcontent.com/pod-product-compliance
Lightning Source LLC
LaVergne TN
LVHW091619070526
838199LV00044B/850